PROSE
MODELS

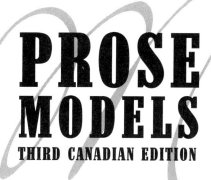

PROSE MODELS

THIRD CANADIAN EDITION

Gerald Levin
UNIVERSITY OF AKRON

David Rampton
UNIVERSITY OF OTTAWA

Gerald Lynch
UNIVERSITY OF OTTAWA

HARCOURT
BRACE
CANADA

Harcourt Brace & Company, Canada

Toronto Montreal Fort Worth New York Orlando
Philadelphia San Diego London Sydney Tokyo

Requests for permission to make copies of any part of the work should be mailed to: Permissions, College Division, Harcourt Brace & Company, Canada, 55 Horner Avenue, Toronto, Ontario M8Z 4X6.

Every reasonable effort has been made to acquire permission for copyright material used in this text, and to acknowledge all such indebtedness accurately. Any errors and omissions called to the publisher's attention will be corrected in future printings.

Canadian Cataloguing in Publication Data

Levin, Gerald, 1929–
  Prose models

3rd Canadian ed.
Includes bibliographical references and index.
ISBN 0-7747-3512-0

1. College readers.   2. English language—Rhetoric.
I. Rampton, David, 1950–   . II. Lynch, Gerald,
1953–   . III. Title

PE1417.L48   1997   808'.0427   C95-932933-1

Director of Product Development: Heather McWhinney
Acquisitions Editor: Kelly V. Cochrane
Projects Manager: Liz Radojkovic
Developmental Editor: Su Mei Ku
Editorial Assistant: Martina van de Velde
Director of Publishing Services: Jean Davies
Editorial Manager: Marcel Chiera
Supervising Editor: Semareh Al-Hillal
Production Editor: Laurel Parsons
Production Manager: Sue-Ann Becker
Production Co-ordinator: Sheila Barry
Copy Editor: Beverley Endersby
Cover Design: Sonya V. Thursby/Opus House
Typesetting and Assembly: Sharon Moroney
Printing and Binding: Kromar Printing Ltd.

Cover Art: Kathy Ruttenberg, *Off to Upstate on August Fifth at Five* (1992). Oil on linen, 80" x 30". Photo courtesy of Gallery Henoch, New York. Reproduced with permission of the artist.

This book was printed in Canada.

1 2 3 4 5   01 00 99 98 97

PREFACE

The American edition of *Prose Models*, which first appeared in 1964 and is now in its ninth edition, was edited by Gerald Levin. The first Canadian edition, published in 1989, was based on it. In our selection of new material for the third Canadian edition, we have again followed the original editor's practice regarding sampling of writers and disciplines, variety of models, and introductions to each section. The third edition, like the second, offers examples of writing from literature, science, history, autobiography, and journalism. We have also streamlined this edition of the book and made it more user-friendly.

Prose Models contains a preface addressed to the student that discusses the relationship between reading and writing and the general uses of the book, and an introduction to each part that relates the topics to the student's own writing. Part 1, "Methods of Organization," is structured so that attention is focussed immediately on the coherence of the whole essay. Part 2, "Methods of Development," presents the traditional rhetorical modes. Part 3, "Matters of Style," deals with tone and figurative language. Seven essays in which writers discuss their vocation, followed by a discussion of diction and writing effective sentences, conclude this part.

Each selection contains a headnote that provides biographical details about the author and information about the essay or the context of an excerpt. Questions and suggested writing assignments follow all selections except the supplementary essays on the craft and business of writing.

In an essay on composition, Mark Twain refers to the "model-chamber" in the head of the writer—a store of effective sentences gathered from many kinds of reading. As important as such models are, the student writer should also be reminded of Stephen Leacock's dictum: "Writing is thinking." These statements express the philosophy of this book. Student writers need to understand the methods of prose composition and must learn to think clearly. But this approach alone cannot teach the skills developed in the composition course.

Students must have practice in applying these models. Although discussion of the writing process and exercises in invention enhance writing skills, analysis and exploration of a wide selection of readings are essential.

The following writers are new to *Prose Models* or are represented by new essays: Arthur Black, Joseph Brodsky, Meredith Chilton, Daniel C. Dennett, Allan Fotheringham, Charles Gordon, Wayne Grady, Hugh Graham, Michael Ignatieff, Pico Iyer, Marni Jackson, Dany Laferrière, Thomas Lynch, David Macfarlane, Ian McEwan, William J. Mitchell, Alice Munro, David Warren, John Postgate, Stephen J. Pyne, Jonathan Rauch, Carol Shields, Jane Smiley, Jeff Taylor, Bronwen Wallace, and Howard White.

To the Student: How to Use This Book

The readings in this book are examples of effective writing by Canadian, American, and British authors. They show how various writers have chosen to organize and build their sentences, paragraphs, and essays. They do not, however, represent every kind of effective writing, nor are they "models" in the sense that they represent the best and only ways to write essays. Rather, they constitute a repertory of choices available to you in practising and refining your own writing skills.

Although the reading, study, and discussion of paragraphs and essays are not the whole process of developing writing skills, they are indispensable, for you learn to write as you learn to speak—by reading and listening to the words of others. Thus, in drafting and revising your own essays, you should take the opportunity to return to your reading and discover new ways to build and develop your ideas.

The vocabulary list that follows each selection contains unfamiliar words as well as many that you use every day. These familiar words are singled out because the author of the reading uses them in a special or unusual way. Often you will recognize the general meaning of a word, but you will need your dictionary to discover a subtler meaning that the author has in mind. In preparing for class discussion of these essays, you will gain the most from your reading if you keep a dictionary at hand and check the meanings of these words and any others about which you are doubtful.

The readings in this book have been selected to help you draw on your personal experiences and observations in writing your own essays. You will discover that many of the selections connect in theme or point of view. The expository and argumentative essays—many dealing with important issues in our time—offer an opportunity for you to work out your own ideas and to bring your experiences to bear on the issue.

In your reading, you probably have noticed that a particular writer often uses similar types of sentences, favours certain expressions or ways of phrasing ideas, or builds paragraphs and essays in the same way. The word *style* describes this recurrent quality in a writer. Though still connected for many people with what is "correct" or proper in writing (style for the eighteenth-century writer Jonathan Swift was "proper words in proper places"), style refers commonly to the individual choices in diction and sentence construction as well as in organization. It is in this sense that people refer to a "Hemingway style" in fiction or a "Woody Allen style" in the movies.

However, probably much of what we describe as style in speaking and writing is not a matter of choice at all. One writer may favour long, heavily co-ordinated sentences, as in the speech of a non-stop talker. Another person, used to speaking in a clipped manner, may write in very short sentences or very short paragraphs. Your writing is governed by habits that develop as you grow up. Habits of speech strongly influence how you write, though written communication requires more attention to such matters as sentence structure, punctuation, and the organization of material.

You do have control, then, over your writing. Though you will continue to speak and write in ways natural to you, you can make your writing more expressive and effective. The more writing you do, the more aware you will become of your own habitual choices. As your awareness increases, you will be able to experiment with new ways of writing — as college and university give you the opportunity to think about new ideas in new ways. The discovery and mastery of your own style of writing and thinking is one important purpose of this book.

Acknowledgements

We would like to thank Heather McWhinney and Su Mei Ku of Harcourt Brace & Company Canada for their support and guidance. We are also grateful to the readers and reviewers of the second Canadian edition for their many helpful suggestions: John Adames (University of British Columbia), Jill Andrews (Mount Royal College), Joanne Buckley (University of Western Ontario), James Eadie (Grant MacEwan Community College), Robert Einarsson (Grant MacEwan Community College), Don Fisher (Grant MacEwan Community College), Wendy Katz (Saint Mary's University), Mary Keating (University College of Cape Breton), Sandra Mallett (Grant MacEwan Community College), David Matthias (Mount Saint Vincent University), Ross McKay (Malaspina University College), and Theresa Moritz (University of Toronto).

A NOTE FROM THE PUBLISHER

Thank you for selecting *Prose Models*, Third Canadian Edition, by Gerald Levin, David Rampton, and Gerald Lynch. The authors and publisher have devoted considerable time to the careful development of this book. We appreciate your recognition of this effort and accomplishment.

We want to hear what you think about *Prose Models*. Please take a few minutes to fill in the stamped reader reply card at the back of the book. Your comments and suggestions will be valuable to us as we prepare new editions and other books.

CONTENTS

Part 3: Matters of Style   287

CONTENTS

By Theme

SOCIETY AND VALUES

WOMEN'S ISSUES

READING AND WRITING

1

Methods of Organization

Introduction

An essay can be defined as the explication of a thesis. Whether it argues in support of or against some proposition, explains the steps of some difficult process, or simply displays the humour of the writer on some whimsical subject, every essay contains a thesis; that thesis is the essay's *raison d'être*, its purpose, its justification—which is to say, the justification for the writer's decision to write, and consequently to make his or her demands upon the reader's time. The thesis of an essay may be stated forthrightly in its opening sentence, deployed as the concluding statement of the introductory paragraph, concealed until the end of the essay, or left implied. Student writers may do a great deal of thinking and planning before they begin to write and so be able to summarize their essay's central concerns in a thesis statement, or they may not discover the thesis of their essay until they have begun to write or until they finish the first draft of their essay. Different writers employ different methods. What is of prime importance is that the writer have something to say—an idea—and that the essay have a thesis that the reader can point to or infer and paraphrase. When the writer has a thesis and a first draft, then begins the next important task: revising and organizing the material to display the thesis to greatest advantage.

"Organization" refers both to the way in which the writer arranges ideas and arguments in support of the thesis and to the way in which the essay's structure facilitates the retention of those ideas and arguments. In this first part of the book, "Thesis and Unity" comes first because having a subject to explain or an argument to make, and developing it in paragraphs that cohere around a central idea, is the *sine qua non* of good writing. In "Order of Ideas," we explore the different ways in which such ideas and paragraphs can be organized within the essay itself. Devices used to create effective introductions, conclusions, and smooth transitions are dealt with in the third section, "Beginnings, Middles, and Endings."

Thesis and Unity

The thesis of an essay is its central or controlling idea, the proposition or chief argument—the point of the essay. The topic sentence of a paragraph may be either a full or a partial statement of the controlling idea: the thesis is always a full statement of it.

Where the thesis appears in an essay depends largely on the audience. If we believe that the audience requires no introduction to the thesis—no background or explanation of the issue or important terms—we may state it in the first sentence. Many newspaper editorials begin with a statement of the thesis—a practice consistent with that of putting the important information in the opening sentences of a news story. Most essayists, by contrast, prefer to build to the thesis—stating it partially or fully in the introductory paragraphs, in company with an explanation of important terms and the issues to be discussed. William Zinsser gives such an explanation in the opening paragraph of "Simplicity":

> Clutter is the disease of American writing. We are a society strangling in unnecessary words, circular constructions, pompous frills and meaningless jargon.

In the opening sentence of his second paragraph, Zinsser expands this statement to cover the specific concern of the essay—the importance of simplicity in writing:

> Who can understand the viscous language of everyday American commerce and enterprise . . .?

In later paragraphs he restates his thesis as he presents various evidence in support of it:

> But the secret of good writing is to strip every sentence to its cleanest components.

> Thinking clearly is a conscious act that writers must force upon themselves. . . .

Zinsser introduces his thesis early in his essay and restates it throughout. If the thesis needs extensive background and discussion to be understood—or perhaps is so controversial that we will win our audience only by building to it slowly—we could put it at the end of the essay. In some essays we might not want to state the thesis at all, but rather let the reader draw conclusions from the details or facts we provide. In this case the thesis is said to be *implied*.

In reading an essay, we depend on the opening sentence of each paragraph to direct us from one idea to the next. As in the following paragraph from Margaret Atwood's essay "True North," the opening sentence (italicized here) sometimes directs us through a topic sentence or statement of the central idea:

> *Where is the north, exactly?* It's not only a place but a direction, and as such its location is relative: to the Mexicans, the United States is the north, to Americans Toronto is, even though it's on roughly the same latitude as Boston. . . .

Not all opening sentences state the central idea fully. Some feature only the subject or topic of the paragraph, as in this example by Daniel C. Dennett from "Darwin's Dangerous Idea":

> To appreciate how deeply Darwin's universal acid has etched its way into the intellectual landscape, it may help to see how the world looked before Darwin inverted it.

The subject or topic might also be introduced through a question that the remainder of the paragraph answers:

> What is the difference between order and design? As a first stab, I would say that order is mere regularity, mere pattern; design reflects Aristotle's *telos*, an exploitation of order for a purpose, as a cleverly designed artifact. The solar system exhibits stupendous order, but (apparently) it has no purpose—it is not *for* anything. An eye, in contrast, is for seeing. . . . (Dennett, "Darwin's Dangerous Idea")

In paragraphs that open with a statement of the subject or topic, discussion of the central or topic idea may follow immediately, as in the paragraph just cited. In other paragraphs, details and explanatory statements may build to the central idea. Paragraphs of this latter sort sometimes generate suspense or a sense of climax, for the reader must wait for the central statement to gain the full impact of the paragraph. The paragraph is said to have an implied topic sentence when the details alone make the point; the central idea or generalization remains unstated.

The topic sentence is important in unifying the paragraph. A unified paragraph not only develops one idea at a time but also makes each idea and detail relevant to the topic idea. In a unified paragraph, the reader immediately sees the relation of ideas and details. A disunified paragraph, by contrast, seems disconnected, its ideas and details introduced without transition or apparent reason.

Most paragraphs develop one impression or idea fully, as a unit; the paragraphs presented and discussed in this section are of this type. Other paragraphs are transitional, as is this linking paragraph that asks questions to be answered in the remainder of the essay:

> After twenty years of feminism, you may ask, why don't little boys play with Barbies? What is it about girls and dolls, anyway? (Marni Jackson, "Gals and Dolls")

Many paragraphs also serve as summaries, sometimes pinpointing the central impression, idea, or thesis of the essay:

> It came about that all the varieties of female desirability conceived by the twentieth century seemed ideally housed in a thin, resilient, and bony body. Healthy innocence, sexual restlessness, creative zest, practical competence, even morbid but poetic obsessiveness and intelligence — all seemed appropriate in size ten. During the six decades following the First World War, styles in gesture, posture, and erotic emphasis have undergone many changes, but the basically slim female ideal has been maintained. Throughout all the shifting levels of bust and waist and the fluctuating taste in gluteal and mammary thrust, the bodies of women have been conceived as ideally slender, and clearly supported by bones. (Anne Hollander, "Fashion and the Female Body")

The following examples illustrate ways in which well-developed paragraphs and essays can be organized.

STEPHEN J. PYNE

Stephen J. Pyne is a professor of American Studies at Arizona State University West and the author of seven books, including *Burning Bush* and *Fire in America*. The following excerpt is from *World Fire: The Culture of Fire on Earth*. Pyne begins by claiming that the discovery of fire makes human history intelligible, and notes that "among human societies the belief in a world-creating and world-ending fire is nearly universal." He goes on to explore how this belief manifests itself in our own time.

Let It Burn

STEPHEN J. PYNE

I ncreasingly, as humans have urbanized and industrialized, the vision of a world-ending fire has endured, whereas the image of a world-creating one has vanished. [2]Over the past decade this ancient mythology has found a new avatar—the environmental catastrophe in its multiple incarnations. [3]Nuclear winter, in which fire-spawned smoke would plunge Earth into the cold and dark of a new ice age. [4]Greenhouse summer, its complement, whose heat-trapping gases—released by fire—promise to convert Earth into an oven. [5]Uncontrolled slash-and-burn clearances in Amazonia, Indonesia, India—all threatening biodiversity, all belching greenhouse gases. [6]Smoke plumes that fill the Amazon Basin, and pastoral burns that pull the Sahara southward. [7]The Great Black Dragon fire that incinerated China's Hinggan forest. [8]The East Kalimantan fires that leveled nine million acres of Borneo rain forest. [9]Australia's Ash Wednesday fires that, within hours, brought an industrialized nation to its knees. [10]Conflagrations through Yellowstone National Park, a fiery black hole that in 1988 sucked in more than $130 million worth of fire-fighting resources without effect. [11]Forest-powered holocausts in Oakland and Malibu, California. [12]Oil fires in Kuwait that replaced the traditional imagery of a scorched earth with that of a scorched sky. [13]Fire has given environmentalism a graphic iconography of great power. [14]Whatever their message of destruction, activists have sought to dramatize it for the media with images of fire. [15]The result is that by associating fire with various images of devastation, fire itself has become identified as merely an agent of devastation.

Vocabulary

avatar, biodiversity, iconography

Questions

1. How do sentences 3 through 12 illustrate the topic sentence of the paragraph?
2. How does Pyne remind us of the topic idea in later sentences?
3. Are the examples arranged in any particular order?

Writing Assignments

1. Organize a paragraph around a series of examples (leisure activities, television shows, rock musicians, etc.), and draw a conclusion about these examples.
2. Use one of the following statements, or a similar statement of your own, as the topic sentence of a paragraph, and develop it through a series of illustrations:
   a. Winter or summer sports make special demands on participants or spectators.
   b. Riding the bus [or a similar activity] requires special skills.
   c. People have different driving habits.

JOSEPH EPSTEIN

Joseph Epstein was born and educated in Chicago. He teaches literature and writing at Northwestern University and edits *The American Scholar*. His books of essays, which have established him as one of America's most thoughtful and accomplished practitioners of the genre, include *Familiar Territory, The Middle of My Tether, Plausible Prejudices, Once More Around the Block, Partial Payments,* and *Pertinent Players.* The following paragraph introduces an essay in which he takes a new look at an old vice.

Outgrowing Envy

JOSEPH EPSTEIN

You may as well know the worst about me, Doctor: I have not coveted my neighbor's wife in years, and I certainly do not want his Rolls-Royce, his duplex, or his shiny new fax machine. The young walk by, with their lithe limbs and clear minds, the years and years stretching out leisurely before them, and I feel no longing to change places with them. Neither do I desire to be a United States senator, a university president, the benevolent dictator of a small, mineral-rich country nestled in a lush setting in a lovely mild climate. I have no longing to enjoy the emoluments of the editor of the *New York Times*, the president of L'Académie Française, or Magic Johnson. Please do not understand me too quickly here, Doctor. I am not, I assure you, expressing complacency, smug (isn't "smug" the inevitable adjective here?) self-satisfaction with my own lot in life. No, something deeper, more mysterious, is going on. I am, not to put too fine a point on it, losing my capacity for envy, and I wonder, Doc, what can it mean?

```

```

Vocabulary

coveted, lithe, benevolent, emoluments, complacency

Questions

1. Epstein builds to his central idea instead of starting the paragraph with it. How does the opening sentence introduce the subject and prepare the reader for the details that follow?
2. How do the details develop the central idea, stated in the final sentence?
3. Did Epstein need to state the central idea, or could he have depended on the details to convey it implicitly?
4. How is the paragraph organized around the figure of the doctor?

Writing Assignments

1. Use Epstein's paragraph as a model for your own confession regarding one other of the seven deadly sins (gluttony, lust, sloth, pride, envy, anger, and greed), building through a series of details to the central idea as Epstein does.
2. Write a paragraph in which a series of details builds toward a general impression. You might consider describing a room, a landscape, or a friend. Let your details develop the idea; do not state it explicitly. Your details should be so vivid and well organized that the idea is clear to your reader.

```

```

BARBARA EHRENREICH

Barbara Ehrenreich is a social commentator who believes that "there is something grievously wrong with a culture that values Wall Street sharks above social workers, armaments manufacturers above artists, or, for that matter, corporate lawyers above homemakers." In *The Worst Years of Our Lives: Irreverent Notes from a Decade of Greed,* from which the following essay is taken, she makes a witty and persuasive case for the mix of socialism, feminism, and environmentalism that she recommends for America.

The Cult of Busyness

BARBARA EHRENREICH

Not too long ago a former friend and soon-to-be acquaintance called me up to tell me how busy she was. A major report, upon which her professional future depended, was due in three days; her secretary was on strike; her housekeeper had fallen into the hands of the Immigration Department; she had two hours to prepare a dinner party for eight; and she was late for her time-management class. Stress was taking its toll, she told me: her children resented the fact that she sometimes got their names mixed up, and she had taken to abusing white wine.

All this put me at a distinct disadvantage, since the only thing I was doing at the time was holding the phone with one hand and attempting to touch the opposite toe with the other hand, a pastime that I had perfected during previous telephone monologues. Not that I'm not busy too: as I listened to her, I was on the alert for the moment the dryer would shut itself off and I would have to rush to fold the clothes before they settled into a mass of incorrigible wrinkles. But if I mentioned this little deadline of mine, she might think I wasn't busy enough to need a housekeeper, so I just kept on patiently saying "Hmm" until she got to her parting line: "Look, this isn't a good time for me to talk, I've got to go now."

I don't know when the cult of conspicuous busyness began, but it has swept up almost all the upwardly mobile, professional women I know. Already, it is getting hard to recall the days when, for example, "Let's have lunch" meant something other than "I've got more important things to do than talk to you right now." There was even a time when people used to get together without the excuse of needing something to eat—when, in fact, it was considered rude to talk with your mouth full. In the old days, hardly anybody had an appointment book, and when people wanted to know what the day held in store for them, they consulted a horoscope.

It's not only women, of course; for both sexes, busyness has become an important insignia of upper-middle-class status. Nobody, these days, admits to having a hobby, although two or more careers—say, neurosurgery and an art dealership—is not uncommon, and I am sure we will soon be hearing more about the tribulations of the four-paycheck couple. Even those who can manage only one occupation at a time would be embarrassed to be caught doing only one *thing* at a time. Those young men who jog with their headsets on are not, as you might innocently guess, rocking out, but are absorbing the principles of international finance law or a lecture on one-minute management. Even eating, I read recently, is giving way to "grazing"—the conscious ingestion of unidentified foods while drafting a legal brief, cajoling a client on the phone, and, in ambitious cases, doing calf-toning exercises under the desk.

5   But for women, there's more at stake than conforming to another upscale standard. If you want to attract men, for example, it no longer helps to be a bimbo with time on your hands. Upscale young men seem to go for the kind of woman who plays with a full deck of credit cards, who won't cry when she's knocked to the ground while trying to board the six o'clock Eastern shuttle, and whose schedule doesn't allow for a sexual encounter lasting more than twelve minutes. Then there is the economic reality: any woman who doesn't want to wind up a case study in the feminization of poverty has to be successful at something more demanding than fingernail maintenance or come-hither looks. Hence all the bustle, my busy friends would explain—they want to succeed.

6   But if success is the goal, it seems clear to me that the fast track is headed the wrong way. Think of the people who are genuinely successful—path-breaking scientists, best-selling novelists, and designers of major new software. They are not, on the whole, the kind of people who keep glancing shiftily at their watches or making small lists entitled "To Do." On the contrary, many of these people appear to be in a daze, like the distinguished professor I once had who, in the middle of a lecture on electron spin, became so fascinated by the dispersion properties of chalk dust that he could not go on. These truly successful people are childlike, easily distractable, fey sorts, whose usual demeanor resembles that of a recently fed hobo on a warm summer evening.

7   The secret of the truly successful, I believe, is that they learned very early in life how *not* to be busy. They saw through that adage, repeated to me so often in childhood, that anything worth doing is worth doing well. The truth is, many things are worth doing only in the most slovenly, halfhearted fashion possible, and many other things are not worth doing at all. Balancing a checkbook, for example. For some reason, in our culture, this dreary exercise is regarded as the supreme test of personal maturity, business acumen, and the ability to cope with math anxiety. Yet it is a form of busyness which is exceeded in futility only by going to the additional trouble of computerizing one's checking account—and that, in turn, is only slightly less silly than taking the time to discuss, with anyone, what brand of personal computer one owns, or is thinking of buying, or has heard of others using.

If the truly successful manage never to be busy, it is also true that   8
many of the busiest people will never be successful. I know this
firsthand from my experience, many years ago, as a waitress. Any
executive who thinks the ultimate in busyness consists of having
two important phone calls on hold and a major deadline in twenty
minutes should try facing six tablefuls of clients simultaneously
demanding that you give them their checks, fresh coffee, a baby
seat, and a warm, spontaneous smile. Even when she's not busy, a
waitress has to look busy—refilling the salt shakers and polishing
all the chrome in sight—but the only reward is the minimum wage
and any change that gets left on the tables. Much the same is true of
other high-stress jobs, like working as a telephone operator, or
doing data entry on one of the new machines that monitors your
speed as you work: "success" means surviving the shift.

Although busyness does not lead to success, I am willing to   9
believe that success—especially when visited on the unprepared—
can cause busyness. Anyone who has invented a better mousetrap,
or the contemporary equivalent, can expect to be harassed by
strangers demanding that you read their unpublished manuscripts
or undergo the humiliation of public speaking, usually on remote
Midwestern campuses. But if it is true that success leads to more
busyness and less time for worthwhile activities—like talking (and
listening) to friends, reading novels, or putting in some volunteer
time for a good cause—then who needs it? It would be sad to have
come so far—or at least to have run so hard—only to lose each
other.

```
┌─────────────────────────┐
│                         │
│                         │
└─────────────────────────┘
```

Vocabulary

   a. *paragraph 2:* incorrigible
   b. *paragraph 3:* conspicuous
   c. *paragraph 4:* insignia, tribulations, ingestion, cajoling
   d. *paragraph 6:* dispersion, fey, demeanor
   e. *paragraph 7:* adage, slovenly, acumen

Questions

1. Ehrenreich uses examples throughout the essay. What do these contribute to the development of her thesis?
2. Find a topic sentence for each paragraph and determine whether or not they constitute a unified argument.
3. Discuss the use of specific examples. How do they help Ehrenreich prove her contentions?
4. How are transitions made through the nine paragraphs?

Writing Assignments

1. Think of another aspect of contemporary culture and write a short essay analyzing its contradictions.
2. Consult a similar essay in magazines such as *Saturday Night* and *Harper's*. Write a short summary of its thesis and show how the author uses evidence to support his or her claims.

JOYCE MAYNARD

Joyce Maynard was brought up in New Hampshire and educated at Yale. She has written *Growing Up Old in the Sixties* and the novels *Baby Love, To Die For,* and *Where Love Goes.* At eighteen she wrote, in an essay published in *The New York Times*, "I feel immortal while all the signs around me proclaim that I'm not." In the following essay on the death of her grandmother, she is led to think again about death and continuity.

Four Generations

JOYCE MAYNARD

1   My mother called last week to tell me that my grandmother is dying. She has refused an operation that would postpone, but not prevent, her death from pancreatic cancer. She can't eat, she has been hemorrhaging, and she has severe jaundice. "I always prided myself on being different," she told my mother. "Now I *am* different. I'm yellow."

2   My mother, telling me this news, began to cry. So I became the mother for a moment, reminding her, reasonably, that my grandmother is eighty-seven, she's had a full life, she has all her faculties, and no one who knows her could wish that she live long enough to lose them. Lately my mother has been finding notes in my grandmother's drawers at the nursing home, reminding her, "Joyce's husband's name is Steve. Their daughter is Audrey." In the last few years she hasn't had the strength to cook or garden, and she's begun to say she's had enough of living.

3   My grandmother was born in Russia, in 1892—the oldest daughter in a large and prosperous Jewish family. But the prosperity didn't last. She tells stories of the pogroms and the cossacks who raped her

when she was twelve. Soon after that, her family emigrated to Canada, where she met my grandfather.

Their children were the center of their life. The story I loved best, as 4 a child, was of my grandfather opening every box of Cracker Jack in the general store he ran, in search of the particular tin toy my mother coveted. Though they never had much money, my grandmother saw to it that her daughter had elocution lessons and piano lessons, and assured her that she would go to college.

But while she was at college, my mother met my father, who was 5 blue-eyed and blond-haired and not Jewish. When my father sent love letters to my mother, my grandmother would open and hide them, and when my mother told her parents she was going to marry this man, my grandmother said if that happened, it would kill her.

Not likely, of course. My grandmother is a woman who used to 6 crack Brazil nuts open with her teeth, a woman who once lifted a car off the ground, when there was an accident and it had to be moved. She has been representing her death as imminent ever since I've known her—twenty-five years—and has discussed, at length, the distribution of her possessions and her lamb coat. Every time we said goodbye, after our annual visit to Winnipeg, she'd weep and say she'd never see us again. But in the meantime, while every other relative of her generation, and a good many of the younger ones, has died (nursed usually by her), she has kept making knishes, shopping for bargains, tending the healthiest plants I've ever seen.

After my grandfather died, my grandmother lived, more than 7 ever, through her children. When she came to visit, I would hide my diary. She couldn't understand any desire for privacy. She couldn't bear it if my mother left the house without her.

This possessiveness is what made my mother furious (and then 8 guilt-ridden that she felt that way, when of course she owed so much to her mother). So I harbored the resentment that my mother —the dutiful daughter—would not allow herself. I—who had always performed specially well for my grandmother, danced and sung for her, presented her with kisses and good report cards— stopped writing to her, ceased to visit.

But when I heard that she was dying, I realized I wanted to go 9 to Winnipeg to see her one more time. Mostly to make my mother happy, I told myself (certain patterns being hard to break). But also, I was offering up one more particularly fine accomplishment: my own dark-eyed, dark-skinned, dark-haired daughter, whom my grandmother had never met.

I put on my daughter's best dress for our visit to Winnipeg, the 10 way the best dresses were always put on me, and I filled my pockets with animal crackers, in case Audrey started to cry. I scrubbed her face mercilessly. On the elevator going up to her room, I realized how much I was sweating.

11   Grandma was lying flat with an IV tube in her arm and her eyes shut, but she opened them when I leaned over to kiss her. "It's Fredelle's daughter, Joyce," I yelled, because she doesn't hear well anymore, but I could see that no explanation was necessary. "You came," she said. "You brought the baby."

12   Audrey is just one, but she has seen enough of the world to know that people in beds are not meant to be so still and yellow, and she looked frightened. I had never wanted, more, for her to smile.

13   Then Grandma waved at her—the same kind of slow, finger-flexing wave a baby makes—and Audrey waved back. I spread her toys out on my grandmother's bed and sat her down. There she stayed, most of the afternoon, playing and humming and sipping on her bottle, taking a nap at one point, leaning against my grandmother's leg. When I cranked her Snoopy guitar, Audrey stood up on the bed and danced. Grandma wouldn't talk much anymore, though every once in a while she would say how sorry she was that she wasn't having a better day. "I'm not always like this," she said.

14   Mostly she just watched Audrey. Sometimes Audrey would get off the bed, inspect the get-well cards, totter down the hall. "Where is she?" Grandma kept asking. "Who's looking after her?" I had the feeling, even then, that if I'd said, "Audrey's lighting matches," Grandma would have shot up to rescue her.

15   We were flying home that night, and I had dreaded telling her, remembering all those other tearful partings. But in the end, I was the one who cried. She had said she was ready to die. But as I leaned over to stroke her forehead, what she said was, "I wish I had your hair" and "I wish I was well."

16   On the plane flying home, with Audrey in my arms, I thought about mothers and daughters, and the four generations of the family that I know most intimately. Every one of those mothers loves and needs her daughter more than her daughter will love or need her some day, and we are, each of us, the only person on earth who is quite so consumingly interested in our child.

17   Sometimes I kiss and hug Audrey so much she starts crying— which is, in effect, what my grandmother was doing to my mother, all her life. And what makes my mother grieve right now, I think, is not simply that her mother will die in a day or two, but that, once her mother dies, there will never again be someone to love her in

quite such an unreserved, unquestioning way. No one else who believes that, fifty years ago, she could have put Shirley Temple out of a job, no one else who remembers the moment of her birth. She will only be a mother, then, not a daughter anymore.

Audrey and I have stopped over for a night in Toronto, where my mother lives. Tomorrow she will go to a safe-deposit box at the bank and take out the receipt for my grandmother's burial plot. Then she will fly back to Winnipeg, where, for the first time in anybody's memory, there was waist-high snow on April Fool's Day. But tonight she is feeding me, as she always does when I come, and I am eating more than I do anywhere else. I admire the wedding china (once my grandmother's) that my mother has set on the table. She says (the way Grandma used to say to her, of the lamb coat), "Some day it will be yours." 18

Vocabulary

a. *paragraph 1:* pancreatic, jaundice
b. *paragraph 3:* pogroms, cossacks
c. *paragraph 4:* coveted, elocution
d. *paragraph 6:* imminent, knishes

Questions

1. Why does Maynard divide her essay into three parts? What does this structure contribute to its unity?
2. What does Maynard achieve by the use of reported dialogue at various points in the essay?
3. Maynard is dealing with a highly emotional subject. Does she manage to avoid sentimentality?
4. How does Maynard's use of narrative prepare for the statement of her thesis in paragraph 17?

Writing Assignment

Write an essay dealing with the death of someone close to you. Avoid any direct statement of personal feeling. Use specific examples and allow your tone to convey your attitude.

CHARLES GORDON

Charles Gordon belongs to one of Canada's distinguished literary families. He is the grandson of Charles Gordon, who wrote under the pen name

Ralph Connor, and the brother of popular mystery writer Alison Gordon. He is the book-section editor of *The Ottawa Citizen* and a regular columnist for *Maclean's* magazine. As well, Gordon has published a number of highly praised and popular works of social commentary and literary humour, including *The Governor General's Bunny Hop,* which was short-listed for the Stephen Leacock Medal for humour, and *At the Cottage.* In the following *Maclean's* essay, he rails good-humouredly against the materialism of the age, a time which, to borrow from Oscar Wilde, risks knowing the price of everything and the value of nothing.

A Destructive Love Affair with Money

CHARLES GORDON

1   Needing something to believe in, people have begun believing very strongly in their money. This is happening all over the world, not just here. Loyalty to money is making it difficult, perhaps impossible, for governments to act, for countries to exist.

2   But that seems to be the way people want it. Particularly people with money. Their love and respect for money transcends all boundaries. Our job now, if we want to save the nation and keep it from being something other than just a place where banks are located, is to make people realize how flawed money is, in terms of the overall meaning of life.

3   Money can't buy you love, as the philosopher once sang. Except for the love of money. It can't make the sun shine or your kids appreciate you. Thinking about money too much can give you ulcers, cause people to hate you, and make you forget to vote.

4   It can make you grouchy. Just the other day, a guy from Alberta was on the CBC complaining about one of those nice international surveys that showed Canada being the best place in the world to live. No it wasn't, the guy from Alberta said. Canada had a terrible deficit and taxes were too high, and people should stop feeling it was a good country if they knew what was good for them.

5   Money can do that to you. These tax-revolt people are distinctly unhappy in Canada. So are the people who keep forcing the dollar down and the interest rates up because they get rid of Canadian dollars every time they are feeling a bit out of sorts. Then, they blame the government and say the government better balance the budget (without taxing them) or else they will make matters worse.

You don't see people without money making such nuisances of themselves. But when you give all your love to your money, it makes you fretful. If you loved your country more, you would be comforted by the return of hockey and how pretty the Rockies are at this time of year.

A few weeks ago, *The Wall Street Journal*, an American financial newspaper with a once-respected editorial page, ran an editorial that slapped us around a bit, notably with the now familiar suggestion that Canada "has now become an honorary member of the Third World in the unmanageability of its debt problem." The editorial then went on to tell the Canadian government what it had to do, mentioning some of the recommendations of the Fraser Institute, a right-wing think-tank on Canada's West Coast. 6

In countries that valued such concepts as sovereignty, there would have been a mighty hullabaloo, with politicians, economists, business people and laborites rising up to tell *The Wall Street Journal* that we are quite capable of making our own decisions on these matters, thank you. Instead, members of the international money fan club began sending love letters to themselves. The flower of Canadian neoconservative thought raced to the nearest microphones to tell *The Wall Street Journal* how right it was. Canadian newspapers put up a mighty wail about the great crisis the country faced, all because somebody to the south of us wrote an editorial. Then the Fraser Institute's executive director himself paid *The Wall Street Journal* the distinct compliment of venturing onto its own pages to say that *The Wall Street Journal* editorial might just be on to something. 7

We were seeing an example of the love that crosses borders, that makes, perhaps, borders obsolete. At almost the same time, the very magazine you hold in your hands was running an advertisement from Friedberg Capital Markets, a member of the Toronto Stock Exchange, urging Canadian investors to "get the strength of foreign countries working for you." The ad said that "over the last 12 months, almost every major currency in the world outperformed the Canadian dollar, handsomely rewarding Canadian investors who had the foresight to diversify their financial portfolios." 8

Once upon a time, we were told that investing in Canadian dollars was good for the Canadian dollar. And a good Canadian dollar was good for the country. It meant lower interest rates, economic expansion, jobs. Conversely, selling Canadian dollars was bad for the country. Was that not right? 9

Irrelevant, is what it was, and is. We are in the midst of what the late Christopher Lasch called the "the revolt of the elites." In *The Revolt of the Elites and the Betrayal of Democracy*, completed just before his death and published last month [in January 1995], the 10

American social historian says that "local and regional loyalties are sadly attenuated today. The mobility of capital and the emergence of a global market contribute to the same effect."

11   Is it sadly ironic that an opinion piece in a Canadian magazine would rest heavily on the work of an American intellectual? Of course. But, hey, it's a global world out there. Of today's elites, Lasch observes that "their fortunes are tied to enterprises that operate across national boundaries. They are more concerned with the smooth functioning of the system as a whole than with any of its parts. Their loyalties—if the term is not itself anachronistic in this context—are international rather than regional, national or local."

12   Lasch points out that opposition to such new loyalties is undermined by the weakening of the nation state. It should be added that nationalism is out of favour, dismissed as obsolete—thanks in part to the efforts of such intellectuals as our own Pierre Trudeau—and discredited daily by the activities of breakaway nationalists on all the continents of the globe. Internationalism is the thing, especially where earning money is concerned, although the notion somehow does not extend to helping poor nations with unbalanced budgets.

13   When the new elites warn us that world money markets will be displeased with Canada if Canada does not obey market dictates, the notion of diminished sovereignty does not concern the new elites at all. The question, "Is it possible to have a country any more?" is not one the new elites ask. The answer is not one that worries them. Does this government—does any government—have the courage to oppose such forces? Or will the government let the international money fan club continue its love affair with itself?

Vocabulary

a. *paragraph 7:* sovereignty, hullabaloo
b. *paragraph 8:* obsolete, diversify, portfolios
c. *paragraph 10:* attenuated
d. *paragraph 11:* anachronistic

Questions

1. Where does Gordon indicate his attitude toward materialism? What is his thesis?
2. How does the selection of detail in the essay support the dominating impression Gordon creates of the destructive influence of our obsession with money?
3. What does Gordon mean when he quotes Christopher Lasch's observation that the fortunes of today's elites "are tied to enterprises that operate across national boundaries" (paragraph 11)?

4. According to Gordon, how does the preoccupation with purely economic considerations threaten Canada's autonomy?

Writing Assignments

1. Describe the economic changes that have occurred in the community where you grew up and discuss the reasons for these.
2. Select a segment of the entertainment industry—movies, music, books—and discuss how it has been influenced by economic considerations.

STEPHEN JAY GOULD

Stephen Jay Gould was born in New York City in 1941 and educated at Antioch University and Columbia University. He is a professor of geology and history of science at Harvard. He is also one of the great popularizers of twentieth-century science: he writes a monthly column for *Natural History*, serves as an adviser to the television program *Nova*, and has won innumerable awards and honorary degrees. His books include *Ever Since Darwin, The Panda's Thumb, Hen's Teeth and Horse's Toes,* and *The Flamingo's Smile,* from which the following essay is taken. He has also written a book attacking IQ testing, *The Mismeasure of Man;* a fascinating account of the history of the Burgess Shale, *Wonderful Life;* and, most recently, an exploration of natural history, *Dinosaur in a Haystack.*

Sex, Drugs, Disasters, and the Extinction of Dinosaurs

STEPHEN JAY GOULD

S cience, in its most fundamental defini- 1
tion, is a fruitful mode of inquiry, not a list of enticing conclusions. The conclusions are the consequence, not the essence.

My greatest unhappiness with most popular presentations of 2
science concerns their failure to separate fascinating claims from the methods that scientists use to establish the facts of nature. Journalists, and the public, thrive on controversial and stunning statements. But science is, basically, a way of knowing—in P.B. Medawar's apt words, "the art of the soluble." If the growing corps of popular science writers would focus on *how* scientists develop and defend

those fascinating claims, they would make their greatest possible contribution to public understanding.

3   Consider three ideas, proposed in perfect seriousness to explain that greatest of all titillating puzzles—the extinction of dinosaurs. Since these three notions invoke the primally fascinating themes of our culture—sex, drugs, and violence—they surely reside in the category of fascinating claims. I want to show why two of them rank as silly speculation, while the other represents science at its grandest and most useful.

4   Science works with testable proposals. If, after much compilation and scrutiny of data, new information continues to affirm a hypothesis, we may accept it provisionally and gain confidence as further evidence mounts. We can never be completely sure that a hypothesis is right, though we may be able to show with confidence that it is wrong. The best scientific hypotheses are also generous and expansive: they suggest extensions and implications that enlighten related, and even far distant, subjects. Simply consider how the idea of evolution has influenced virtually every intellectual field.

5   Useless speculation, on the other hand, is restrictive. It generates no testable hypothesis, and offers no way to obtain potentially refuting evidence. Please note that I am not speaking of truth or falsity. The speculation may well be true; still, if it provides, in principle, no material for affirmation or rejection, we can make nothing of it. It must simply stand forever as an intriguing idea. Useless speculation turns in on itself and leads nowhere; good science, containing both seeds for its potential refutation and implications for more and different testable knowledge, reaches out. But, enough preaching. Let's move on to dinosaurs, and the three proposals for their extinction.

1. Sex: Testes function only in a narrow range of temperature (those of mammals hang externally in a scrotal sac because internal body temperatures are too high for their proper function). A worldwide rise in temperature at the close of the Cretaceous period caused the testes of dinosaurs to stop functioning and led to their extinction by sterilization of males.
2. Drugs: Angiosperms (flowering plants) first evolved toward the end of the dinosaurs' reign. Many of these plants contain psychoactive agents, avoided by mammals today as a result of their bitter taste. Dinosaurs had neither means to taste the bitterness nor livers effective enough to detoxify the substances. They died of massive overdoses.
3. Disasters: A large comet or asteroid struck the earth some 65 million years ago, lofting a cloud of dust into the sky and blocking sunlight, thereby suppressing photosynthesis and so drastically

lowering world temperatures that dinosaurs and hosts of other creatures became extinct.

Before analyzing these three tantalizing statements, we must establish a basic ground rule often violated in proposals for the dinosaurs' demise. *There is no separate problem of the extinction of dinosaurs.* Too often we divorce specific events from their wider contexts and systems of cause and effect. The fundamental fact of dinosaur extinction is its synchrony with the demise of so many other groups across a wide range of habitats, from terrestrial to marine.

The history of life has been punctuated by brief episodes of mass extinction. A recent analysis by University of Chicago paleontologists Jack Sepkoski and Dave Raup, based on the best and most exhaustive tabulation of data ever assembled, shows clearly that five episodes of mass dying stand well above the "background" extinctions of normal times (when we consider all mass extinctions, large and small, they seem to fall in a regular 26-million-year cycle). The Cretaceous debacle, occurring 65 million years ago and separating the Mesozoic and Cenozoic eras of our geological time scale, ranks prominently among the five. Nearly all the marine plankton (single-celled floating creatures) died with geological suddenness; among marine invertebrates, nearly 15 percent of all families perished, including many previously dominant groups, especially the ammonites (relatives of squids in coiled shells). On land, the dinosaurs disappeared after more than 100 million years of unchallenged domination.

In this context, speculations limited to dinosaurs alone ignore the larger phenomenon. We need a coordinated explanation for a system of events that includes the extinction of dinosaurs as one component. Thus it makes little sense, though it may fuel our desire to view mammals as inevitable inheritors of the earth, to guess that dinosaurs died because small mammals ate their eggs (a perennial favorite among untestable speculations). It seems most unlikely that some disaster peculiar to dinosaurs befell these massive beasts—and that the debacle happened to strike just when one of history's five great dyings had enveloped the earth for completely different reasons.

The testicular theory, an old favorite from the 1940s, had its root in an interesting and thoroughly respectable study of temperature tolerances in the American alligator, published in the staid *Bulletin of the American Museum of Natural History* in 1946 by three experts on living and fossil reptiles—E.H. Colbert, my own first teacher in paleontology; R.B. Cowles; and C.M. Bogert.

The first sentence of their summary reveals a purpose beyond alligators: "This report describes an attempt to infer the reactions of extinct reptiles, especially the dinosaurs, to high temperatures as based upon reactions observed in the modern alligator." They studied, by rectal thermometry, the body temperatures of alligators under changing conditions of heating and cooling. (Well, let's face it, you wouldn't want to try sticking a thermometer under a 'gator's tongue.) The predictions under test go way back to an old theory first stated by Galileo in the 1630s—the unequal scaling of surfaces and volumes. As an animal, or any object, grows (provided its shape doesn't change), surface areas must increase more slowly than volumes—since surfaces get larger as length squared, while volumes increase much more rapidly, as length cubed. Therefore, small animals have high ratios of surface to volume, while large animals cover themselves with relatively little surface.

10   Among cold-blooded animals lacking any physiological mechanism for keeping their temperatures constant, small creatures have a hell of a time keeping warm—because they lose so much heat through their relatively large surfaces. On the other hand, large animals, with their relatively small surfaces, may lose heat so slowly that, once warm, they may maintain effectively constant temperatures against ordinary fluctuations of climate. (In fact, the resolution of the "hot-blooded dinosaur" controversy that burned so brightly a few years back may simply be that, while large dinosaurs possessed no physiological mechanism for constant temperature, and were not therefore warm-blooded in the technical sense, their large size and relatively small surface area kept them warm.)

11   Colbert, Cowles, and Bogert compared the warming rates of small and large alligators. As predicted, the small fellows heated up (and cooled down) more quickly. When exposed to a warm sun, a tiny 50-gram (1.76-ounce) alligator heated up one degree Celsius every minute and a half, while a large alligator, 260 times bigger at 13,000 grams (28.7 pounds), took seven and a half minutes to gain a degree. Extrapolating up to an adult 10-ton dinosaur, they concluded that a one-degree rise in body temperature would take eighty-six hours. If large animals absorb heat so slowly (through their relatively small surfaces), they will also be unable to shed any excess heat gained when temperatures rise above a favorable level.

12   The authors then guessed that large dinosaurs lived at or near their optimum temperatures; Cowles suggested that a rise in global temperatures just before the Cretaceous extinction caused the dinosaurs to heat up beyond their optimal tolerance—and, being so large, they couldn't shed the unwanted heat. (In a most unusual statement within a scientific paper, Colbert and Bogert then explicitly disavowed this speculative extension of their empirical work on alligators.) Cowles conceded that this excess heat probably wasn't enough to kill or even to enervate the great beasts, but since testes

often function only within a narrow range of temperature, he proposed that this global rise might have sterilized all the males, causing extinction by natural contraception.

The overdose theory has recently been supported by UCLA   13
psychiatrist Ronald K. Siegel. Siegel has gathered, he claims, more than 2,000 records of animals who, when given access, administer various drugs to themselves—from a mere swig of alcohol to massive doses of the big H. Elephants will swill the equivalent of twenty beers at a time, but do not like alcohol in concentrations greater than 7 percent. In a silly bit of anthropocentric speculation, Siegel states that "elephants drink, perhaps, to forget . . . the anxiety produced by shrinking rangeland and the competition for food."

Since fertile imaginations can apply almost any hot idea to the   14
extinction of dinosaurs, Siegel found a way. Flowering plants did not evolve until late in the dinosaurs' reign. These plants also produced an array of aromatic, amino-acid–based alkaloids—the major group of psychoactive agents. Most mammals are "smart" enough to avoid these potential poisons. The alkaloids simply don't taste good (they are bitter); in any case, we mammals have livers happily supplied with the capacity to detoxify them. But, Siegel speculates, perhaps dinosaurs could neither taste the bitterness nor detoxify the substances once ingested. He recently told members of the American Psychological Association: "I'm not suggesting that all dinosaurs OD'd on plant drugs, but it certainly was a factor." He also argued that death by overdose may help explain why so many dinosaur fossils are found in contorted positions. (Do not go gentle into that good night.)

Extraterrestrial catastrophes have long pedigrees in the popular   15
literature of extinction, but the subject exploded again in 1979, after a long lull, when the father–son, physicist–geologist team of Luis and Walter Alvarez proposed that an asteroid, some 10 kilometers in diameter, struck the earth 65 million years ago (comets, rather than asteroids, have since gained favor. Good science is self-corrective).

The force of such a collision would be immense, greater by far   16
than the megatonnage of all the world's nuclear weapons. In trying to reconstruct a scenario that would explain the simultaneous dying of dinosaurs on land and so many creatures in the sea, the Alvarezes proposed that a gigantic dust cloud, generated by particles blown aloft in the impact, would so darken the earth that photosynthesis would cease and temperatures drop precipitously. (Rage, rage against the dying of the light.) The single-celled photosynthetic oceanic plankton, with life cycles measured in weeks, would perish outright, but land plants might survive through the dormancy of their seeds (land plants were not much affected by the Cretaceous extinction, and any adequate theory must account for

the curious pattern of differential survival). Dinosaurs would die by starvation and freezing; small, warm-blooded mammals, with more modest requirements for food and better regulation of body temperature, would squeak through. "Let the bastards freeze in the dark," as bumper stickers of our chauvinistic neighbors in sunbelt states proclaimed several years ago during the Northeast's winter oil crisis.

17   All three theories, testicular malfunction, psychoactive overdosing, and asteroidal zapping, grab our attention mightily. As pure phenomenology, they rank about equally high on any hit parade of primal fascination. Yet one represents expansive science, the others restrictive and untestable speculation. The proper criterion lies in evidence and methodology; we must probe behind the superficial fascination of particular claims.

18   How could we possibly decide whether the hypothesis of testicular frying is right or wrong? We would have to know things that the fossil record cannot provide. What temperatures were optimal for dinosaurs? Could they avoid the absorption of excess heat by staying in the shade, or in caves? At what temperatures did their testicles cease to function? Were late Cretaceous climates ever warm enough to drive the internal temperatures of dinosaurs close to this ceiling? Testicles simply don't fossilize, and how could we infer their temperature tolerances even if they did? In short, Cowles's hypothesis is only an intriguing speculation leading nowhere. The most damning statement against it appeared right in the conclusion of Colbert, Cowles, and Bogert's paper, when they admitted: "It is difficult to advance any definite arguments against this hypothesis." My statement may seem paradoxical—isn't a hypothesis really good if you can't devise any arguments against it? Quite the contrary. It is simply untestable and unusable.

19   Siegel's overdosing has even less going for it. At least Cowles extrapolated his conclusion from some good data on alligators. And he didn't completely violate the primary guideline of siting dinosaur extinction in the context of a general mass dying—for rise in temperature could be the root cause of a general catastrophe, zapping dinosaurs by testicular malfunction and different groups for other reasons. But Siegel's speculation cannot touch the extinction of ammonites or oceanic plankton (diatoms make their own food with good sweet sunlight; they don't OD on the chemicals of terrestrial plants). It is simply a gratuitous, attention-grabbing guess. It cannot be tested, for how can we know what dinosaurs tasted and what their livers could do? Livers don't fossilize any better than testicles.

20   The hypothesis doesn't even make any sense in its own context. Angiosperms were in full flower ten million years before dinosaurs

went the way of all flesh. Why did it take so long? As for the pains of a chemical death recorded in contortions of fossils, I regret to say (or rather I'm pleased to note for the dinosaurs' sake) that Siegel's knowledge of geology must be a bit deficient: muscles contract after death and geological strata rise and fall with motions of the earth's crust after burial—more than enough reason to distort a fossil's pristine appearance.

The impact story, on the other hand, has a sound basis in evidence. It can be tested, extended, refined, and, if wrong, disproved. The Alvarezes did not just construct an arresting guess for public consumption. They proposed their hypothesis after laborious geochemical studies with Frank Asaro and Helen Michael had revealed a massive increase of iridium in rocks deposited right at the time of extinction. Iridium, a rare metal of the platinum group, is virtually absent from indigenous rocks of the earth's crust; most of our iridium arrives on extraterrestrial objects that strike the earth. 21

The Alvarez hypothesis bore immediate fruit. Based originally on evidence from two European localities, it led geochemists throughout the world to examine other sediments of the same age. They found abnormally high amounts of iridium everywhere—from continental rocks of the western United States to deep sea cores from the South Atlantic. 22

Cowles proposed his testicular hypothesis in the mid-1940s. Where has it gone since then? Absolutely nowhere, because scientists can do nothing with it. The hypothesis must stand as a curious appendage to a solid study of alligators. Siegel's overdose scenario will also win a few press notices and fade into oblivion. The Alvarezes' asteroid falls into a different category altogether, and much of the popular commentary has missed this essential distinction by focusing on the impact and its attendant results, and forgetting what really matters to a scientist—the iridium. If you talk just about asteroids, dust, and darkness, you tell stories no better and no more entertaining than fried testicles or terminal trips. It is the iridium—the source of testable evidence—that counts and forges the crucial distinction between speculation and science. 23

The proof, to twist a phrase, lies in the doing. Cowles's hypothesis has generated nothing in thirty-five years. Since its proposal in 1979, the Alvarez hypothesis has spawned hundreds of studies, a major conference, and attendant publications. Geologists are fired up. They are looking for iridium at all other extinction boundaries. Every week exposes a new wrinkle in the scientific press. Further evidence that the Cretaceous iridium represents extraterrestrial impact and not indigenous volcanism continues to accumulate. As I revise this essay in November 1984 (this paragraph will be out of date when the book is published), new data 24 include chemical "signatures" of other isotopes indicating unearthly provenance, glass spherules of a size and sort produced by impact and not by volcanic eruptions, and high-pressure varieties of silica formed (so far as we know) only under the tremendous shock of impact.

25   My point is simply this: Whatever the eventual outcome (I suspect it will be positive), the Alvarez hypothesis is exciting, fruitful science because it generates tests, provides us with things to do, and expands outward. We are having fun, battling back and forth, moving toward a resolution, and extending the hypothesis beyond its original scope.

26   As just one example of the unexpected, distant cross-fertilization that good science engenders, the Alvarez hypothesis made a major contribution to a theme that has riveted public attention in the past few months—so-called nuclear winter. In a speech delivered in April 1982, Luis Alvarez calculated the energy that a 10-kilometer asteroid would release on impact. He compared such an explosion with a full nuclear exchange and implied that all-out atomic war might unleash similar consequences.

27   This theme of impact leading to massive dust clouds and falling temperatures formed an important input to the decision of Carl Sagan and a group of colleagues to model the climatic consequences of nuclear holocaust. Full nuclear exchange would probably generate the same kind of dust cloud and darkening that may have wiped out the dinosaurs. Temperatures would drop precipitously and agriculture might become impossible. Avoidance of nuclear war is fundamentally an ethical and political imperative, but we must know the factual consequences to make firm judgments. I am heartened by a final link across disciplines and deep concerns—another criterion, by the way, of science at its best: A recognition of the very phenomenon that made our evolution possible by exterminating the previously dominant dinosaurs and clearing a way for the evolution of large mammals, including us, might actually help to save us from joining those magnificent beasts in contorted poses among the strata of the earth.

Vocabulary

a. *paragraph 3:* titillating
b. *paragraph 4:* hypothesis, provisionally
c. *paragraph 5:* Cretaceous, psychoactive, detoxify, photosynthesis, synchrony
d. *paragraph 9:* thermometry

e. *paragraph 11:* extrapolating
f. *paragraph 12:* optimum, empirical, enervate
g. *paragraph 13:* anthropocentric
h. *paragraph 14:* ingested
i. *paragraph 16:* megatonnage, scenario, dormancy, differential
j. *paragraph 18:* paradoxical
k. *paragraph 19:* siting, ammonites, diatoms, gratuitous
l. *paragraph 20:* strata, pristine
m. *paragraph 21:* indigenous
n. *paragraph 23:* appendage
o. *paragraph 24:* volcanism, isotopes, provenance, spherules, silica
p. *paragraph 27:* precipitously

Questions

1. Why does Gould delay citing the three theories of dinosaur extinction until paragraph 5? Why does he begin with a general discussion of scientific method?
2. How does Gould organize his material? Make an outline that shows how the essay is divided.
3. Summarize in a sentence the main idea of each paragraph. Do the sentences, when put together, make a coherent argument?
4. Gould argues that researchers should generalize carefully from clearly identified evidence. How does Gould suggest to the reader the relative importance of the various kinds of evidence presented?
5. For whom is this essay written? How much scientific knowledge is the reader assumed to have?

Writing Assignments

1. Choose a subject in which scientists are working for a breakthrough—cancer, AIDS, Alzheimer's disease—and summarize the current state of the research.
2. Discuss ways in which your prospective field of study might benefit from interaction with other disciplines.

Order of Ideas

An author may develop the main or central idea of a paragraph through a series of subordinate ideas. Consider the opening sentences of Stephen J. Pyne's paragraph on fire. The first two sentences contain the main idea; the third sentence is the subordinate idea that develops it through illustration:

> Increasingly, as humans have urbanized and industrialized, the vision of a world-ending fire has endured, whereas the image of a world-creating one has vanished.

> Over the past decade this ancient mythology has found a new avatar—the environmental catastrophe in its multiple incarnations.

> Nuclear winter, in which fire-spawned smoke would plunge Earth into the cold and dark of a new ice age. (Stephen J. Pyne, "Let It Burn")

Notice that the fourth sentence has the same importance as the third in developing the main idea:

> Greenhouse summer, its complement, whose heat-trapping gases—released by fire—promise to convert Earth into an oven.

In subsequent sentences, Pyne uses parallel structure to show that ideas have the same importance:

> Smoke plumes that fill . . .

> The Great Black Dragon fire that incinerated . . .

> The East Kalimantan fires that leveled . . .

> Australia's Ash Wednesday fires that . . .

In writing paragraphs you need ways of showing the relative importance of your ideas: the break for a new paragraph—through an indentation—tells the reader that you are introducing a new idea or topic. Later we will consider other devices that show the relative importance of ideas—among them transitional words and phrases (for example, *Even more striking . . .*, *Similarly . . .* , and *Here, then . . .* in Dennett's essay on Darwin).

In longer paragraphs, the main idea may be distinguished by repeating or restating it at the end. We will see in the last section, "Writing Effective Sentences," that the beginning and ending are usually the most emphatic parts of sentences because of their prominence. The same is true of paragraphs and essays.

A unified paragraph develops one idea at a time and makes each idea relevant to the topic idea. You will keep a paragraph unified if, as you write, you consider the order in which you want to present your ideas and details. This order is sometimes determined by the subject of the paragraph and sometimes by the audience you have in mind—and sometimes by both. For example, in describing parallel parking to people learning to drive, you usually will present each step as it occurs. But in describing the same process to driving instructors, you might present these steps in the order of their difficulty, to single out those steps needing most practice.

An account of a process, or a narrative, is usually chronological. A description of a scene is generally spatial in organization—the details are presented as the eye sees them, moving from one part of what is seen to another. The details or ideas can also be ordered in other ways. For example, you can write them

- from the easy to the difficult, as in the paragraph written for driving instructors;
- from the less to the more important;
- from the less to the more interesting or exciting;
- from the general to the specific—for example, from the theory of combustion to the details of the process; or
- from the specific to the general—for example, from simple effects of gravity, like falling off a bike, to a definition or a comment on these effects.

A paragraph may combine two or more orders of ideas. For instance, a paragraph written for driving instructors may move from the easy to the difficult steps of parallel parking, and at the same time from the less to the more important, or even interesting.

The same is true of the order of ideas in an essay. Both the nature of the essay and the nature of the audience influence the choices you make. An essay describing a process requires the usual step-by-step presentation. If the audience is already familiar with the general process, you may refer briefly to the familiar steps and then focus on the more difficult ones. In a persuasive essay, you may introduce your thesis at the beginning if your audience will understand it without explanation; if the thesis requires explanation or is controversial, you may decide to build to it through explanatory details and ideas.

The essay of personal experience can follow a freer course than a formal essay of ideas. In her book *Pilgrim at Tinker Creek*, Annie Dillard divides an essay on winter into sections, each dealing with experiences and reflections suggested by the subject. Here are sentences that introduce the opening sections:

> It is the first of February, and everyone is talking about starlings.

> It is winter proper; the cold weather, such as it is, has come to stay.

> Some weather's coming; you can taste on the sides of your tongue a quince tang in the air.

> This is the sort of stuff I read all winter.

An expository essay, one that explains, analyzes, or clarifies, will show the logical relationship of ideas, as these sentences from Arthur Schafer's essay "Morals in the Rat Race" illustrate:

> The most profoundly important innovation of Western liberal society has been to put the marketplace at the centre of all social transactions.

> Or so the theory would have it.

> Neo-conservatives such as U.S. President Ronald Reagan and British Prime Minister Margaret Thatcher lament the collapse of traditional social values: family, work, patriotism, restraint.

> Ironically, it is the very marketplace morality at whose shrine the neo-conservatives worship that produces the social disintegration they lament.

> As long as only a minority is motivated by ruthless self-interest, social bonds can remain largely intact.

The ordering of ideas can reveal a characteristic way of thinking—one that we find in other essays by the same writer. Even expository and argumentative essays may reveal a method of organizing ideas that is characteristic of the writer's style—perhaps a tendency to build to the thesis instead of introducing it early in the essay.

We can sense this relative importance of ideas in the topic sentences, as in these sentences that open the first six paragraphs of Pico Iyer's essay on the global village, "Strangers in a Small World." The different indentations show the relative weight of each idea:

> The global village is one of those ideas to which almost everyone can give assent . . .

>> We accept, of course, that with proximity come problems . . .

> Yet it is precisely the blessings of this order — evident and indisputable as they are — that can blind us to its dangers . . .

>> The dangers of the global village begin, not surprisingly, with the problems of mobility . . .

>> Even capital is not immune to the novel challenges of the "borderless economy" . . .

> Technology has, to be sure, eliminated some of our old divisions and corruptions; but it has also given us new ways of refining and compounding them.

Iyer develops his thesis through a series of equally broad generalizations. Here are the topic sentences of the next five paragraphs:

> Deeper than the problems of sudden connectedness, however, are the fundamental disconnections that the new globalism obscures.

> That is one of the great shadows of the illusory smallness our new world offers.

> The problem is not one of complete misunderstanding but rather — and more dangerously — of a partial understanding, or the illusion of understanding.

> It is disguised heterogeneity that is the threat, a world of differences that is veiled by surface similarities.

> None of this, of course, is an argument for hardening our differences, or for living alone, or for denying the richness and opportunities that polyculturalism makes available.

Iyer's sentences show the skill with which he develops his argument by considering various alternatives, providing clear transitions, and avoiding unfounded conclusions.

SUSAN SONTAG

Susan Sontag was born in New York City and raised by aunts because her parents spent most of their time in China. Her essays on popular culture, which appeared in various East Coast magazines, gained her a considerable reputation, as did her anti-establishment stance in her book on literary criticism, *Against Interpretation*. Her books include novels (*The Benefactor, Death Kit, The Volcano Lover*) and non-fiction (*Styles of Radical Will, On Photography, Illness as Metaphor, Under the Sign of Saturn,* and *AIDS and Its Metaphors*). She has also written and directed a number of films. Sontag has been in the middle of all the battles fought by the American left in the last 25 years. The following definition of female beauty is a feminist's trenchant argument against ideas imposed on women by patriarchal culture.

A Woman's Beauty: Put-Down or Power Source?

SUSAN SONTAG

1   For the Greeks, beauty was a virtue: a kind of excellence. Persons then were assumed to be what we now have to call—lamely, enviously—*whole* persons. If it did occur to the Greeks to distinguish between a person's "inside" and "outside," they still expected that inner beauty would be matched by beauty of the other kind. The well-born young Athenians who gathered around Socrates found it quite paradoxical that their hero was so intelligent, so brave, so honorable, so seductive—and so ugly. One of Socrates' main pedagogical acts was to be ugly—and teach those innocent, no doubt splendid-looking disciples of his how full of paradoxes life really was.

2   They may have resisted Socrates' lesson. We do not. Several thousand years later, we are more wary of the enchantments of beauty. We not only split off—with the greatest facility—the "inside" (character, intellect) from the "outside" (looks); but we are actually surprised when someone who is beautiful is also intelligent, talented, good.

It was principally the influence of Christianity that deprived   3
beauty of the central place it had in classical ideals of human excellence. By limiting excellence (*virtus* in Latin) to *moral* virtue only,
Christianity set beauty adrift—as an alienated, arbitrary, superficial
enchantment. And beauty has continued to lose prestige. For close
to two centuries it has become a convention to attribute beauty to
only one of the two sexes: the sex which, however Fair, is always
Second. Associating beauty with women has put beauty even further on the defensive, morally.

A beautiful woman, we say in English. But a handsome man.   4
"Handsome" is the masculine equivalent of—and refusal of—a
compliment which has accumulated certain demeaning overtones,
by being reserved for women only. That one can call a man "beautiful" in French and in Italian suggests that Catholic countries—
unlike those countries shaped by the Protestant version of Christianity—still retain some vestiges of the pagan admiration for
beauty. But the difference, if one exists, is of degree only. In every
modern country that is Christian or post-Christian, women *are* the
beautiful sex—to the detriment of the notion of beauty as well as of
women.

To be called beautiful is thought to name something essential   5
to women's character and concerns. (In contrast to men—whose
essence is to be strong, or effective, or competent.) It does not take
someone in the throes of advanced feminist awareness to perceive
that the way women are taught to be involved with beauty encourages narcissism, reinforces dependence and immaturity. Everybody
(women and men) knows that. For it is "everybody," a whole society, that has identified being feminine with caring about how one
looks. (In contrast to being masculine—which is identified with caring about what one *is* and *does* and only secondarily, if at all, about
how one looks.) Given these stereotypes, it is no wonder that
beauty enjoys, at best, a rather mixed reputation.

It is not, of course, the desire to be beautiful that is wrong but   6
the obligation to be—or to try. What is accepted by most women
as a flattering idealization of their sex is a way of making women
feel inferior to what they actually are—or normally grow to be.
For the ideal of beauty is administered as a form of self-oppres-
sion. Women are taught to see their bodies in *parts*, and to evaluate
each part separately. Breasts, feet, hips, waistline, neck, eyes, nose,
complexion, hair, and so on—each in turn is submitted to an anxious, fretful, often despairing scrutiny. Even if some pass muster,
some will always be found wanting. Nothing less than perfection
will do.

In men, good looks is a whole, something taken in at a glance. It   7
does not need to be confirmed by giving measurements of different

regions of the body, nobody encourages a man to dissect his appearance, feature by feature. As for perfection, that is considered trivial—almost unmanly. Indeed, in the ideally good-looking man a small imperfection or blemish is considered positively desirable. According to one movie critic (a woman) who is a declared Robert Redford fan, it is having that cluster of skin-colored moles on one cheek that saves Redford from being merely a "pretty face." Think of the depreciation of women—as well as of beauty—that is implied in that judgment.

8   "The privileges of beauty are immense," said Cocteau. To be sure, beauty is a form of power. And deservedly so. What is lamentable is that it is the only form of power that most women are encouraged to seek. This power is always conceived in relation to men; it is not the power to do but the power to attract. It is a power that negates itself. For this power is not one that can be chosen freely —at least, not by women—or renounced without social censure.

9   To preen, for a woman, can never be just a pleasure. It is also a duty. It is her work. If a woman does real work—and even if she has clambered up to a leading position in politics, law, medicine, business, or whatever—she is always under pressure to confess that she still works at being attractive. But in so far as she is keeping up as one of the Fair Sex, she brings under suspicion her very capacity to be objective, professional, authoritative, thoughtful. Damned if they do—women are. And damned if they don't.

10   One could hardly ask for more important evidence of the dangers of considering persons as split between what is "inside" and what is "outside" than that interminable half-comic half-tragic tale, the oppression of women. How easy it is to start off by defining women as caretakers of their surfaces, and then to disparage them (or find them adorable) for being "superficial." It is a crude trap, and it has worked for too long. But to get out of the trap requires that women get some critical distance from that excellence and privilege which is beauty, enough distance to see how much beauty itself has been abridged in order to prop up the mythology of the "feminine." There should be a way of saving beauty *from* women—and *for* them.

Vocabulary

a. *paragraph 1:* paradoxical, pedagogical
b. *paragraph 3:* arbitrary
c. *paragraph 4:* vestiges, detriment
d. *paragraph 5:* narcissism
e. *paragraph 6:* idealization
f. *paragraph 7:* depreciation

g. *paragraph 8:* lamentable, censure
h. *paragraph 9:* preen
i. *paragraph 10:* disparage

Questions

1. Sontag orders her examples chronologically. Where does she begin, what period does she cover, and where does she end?
2. What is the main idea of paragraph 1? How are subordinate ideas distinguished from the main idea?
3. What overall definition of beauty does Sontag create? Does she state it directly, or does she let it emerge from the argument?
4. How does the development of the essay prepare the reader for Sontag's conclusions about gender bias and notions of beauty?

Writing Assignments

1. Using Sontag's method of development, discuss traditional ideas of male attractiveness and the cultural biases that result from them.
2. Describe a neighbourhood you remember from childhood. Decide on a dominant impression and choose details that develop it. Then decide on an order of details appropriate to your purpose. Remember that, although your reader has not seen the neighbourhood, you need not give all of its details to develop the impression.

KATHERINE GOVIER

Katherine Govier was born in Edmonton and educated at the University of Alberta and York University. A winner of numerous awards for her work as a free-lance journalist, she is also a writer of short stories and novels, including *Fables of Brunswick Avenue* and *Hearts of Flame.* The following essay displays her ability to typify remembered experiences and to build toward meaning that is both personal and universal.

Rethinking the Nature of Charity

KATHERINE GOVIER

When I was a child in Edmonton, the thrill of Christmas was performing in "hospital shows" organized by my

intrepid ballet teacher, Miss Heavener. Beginning just after Halloween, Miss Heavener, by sheer creative necessity and with the aid
of intimidation and a sharp cane, transformed an ill-assorted bunch
of kids into a traveling entertainment that would have graced a
West End stage—or so we thought.

2   Weekend after weekend, we rehearsed our jazz, tap and ballet
routines to the music of *Frosty the Snowman* and *Silver Bells*. One girl
even sang *On the Good Ship Lollipop* like Shirley Temple. Our mothers made white net tutus with sparkles, hula hoops circled with
crepe paper, tiaras out of tinsel, and red flannelette pajamas with
Wee Willie Winkie candlesticks for the lights-out finale.

3   Anticipation mounted: who would lead the line? Who had the
12-bar solo in the middle of the military tap? When Christmas season came, we loaded our hatboxes stuffed with tutus, our clutch of
wands, baubles and shoes onto buses. Singing carols all the way,
we rode off to the local old-age home or children's ward lucky
enough to witness the product of our labor as the patients' Christmas entertainment.

4   It was all great fun—the jolting bus rides, with our stern doyenne hiding her smile as she gripped the overhead rail and rode the
centre aisle; the gentle fluster of the long-suffering pianist; the
whispering nurses who herded us in lines through pale green hall-
ways to some room—the staff lunchroom perhaps, or the laundry—
to dress. There were always difficult professional considerations;
each "stage" had its peculiarities—oblong, or a slippery floor, too
many steps up, or no room for the piano. We had to size it up from
the "wings," and the leader had to decide how to place herself, the
rest of the line how to space itself. We were likely to be seized by
desperate last-minute giggles while pawing through the hatbox for
hairpins and a net for that neat, little balletic bun.

5   We did many hospital shows, but I remember the one at
Charles Camsell Hospital best. Once a Jesuit college, it now housed
Inuit and Indian kids who had tuberculosis. They'd been taken
from their homes to live here until they recovered, which sometimes took years and sometimes did not happen at all. We danced
out a side door and made a circle in the ballroom to start *Waltz of
the Flowers*. There, heads lolling back on pads made of white sheet-
ing, legs shrouded in blankets, with flat bewildered faces, were the
first native children I had ever seen.

6   The best part of hospital shows was not the costumes and dancing, but the cozy feeling that we were doing good, that we brought
a gift to make our audience happy. Usually, we did. Old people
dimpled and exclaimed, they clapped and blew kisses, sometimes
they cried, the good kind of tears. Children gazed at us as if we
were not real, but, like Santa, another order of being.

But at Camsell the children were still, trapped, it seemed, in a lethargy that was greater than illness. Dislocation, loneliness—they had been pulled from their families at who knew what latitude, in who knew what kind of house. They did not understand much English, and *Frosty the Snowman* must have seemed like a sick joke. I saw the distance between them and me, a distance that no song and dance could bridge. It filled me with guilt, I felt sad, and I never forgot. The image of those children watching open-mouthed stayed with me, unresolved, puzzling me, for 30 years.

Then, last year, I took a job as writer-in-residence in the public library in Parry Sound, Ont. A woman came to see me who wrote about her experience growing up in the north. As we talked, she happened to mention that she had a sister who had been a nurse at Charles Camsell Hospital in Edmonton, in the '50s. And we talked about those children who were taken away from their families to live in the hospital. It was one of her sister's jobs to deliver the children who recovered back to their northern homes. This nurse, who had come to love the children and think of them as her own, who had spoken to them in English and fed them cream-of-chicken soup, flew up north, landed on the ice and gave the children back to fur-clad Inuit driving dogsleds to far-flung villages. She sent them off in terror to rejoin parents and a life that was now as strange to them as the sterile sheets of the hospital had been months or years before. And her face twisted as she told the story.

"What terrible things we did to those people," she said.

"And in the name of kindness."

The conversation that day was a gift, one of the little miracles life throws at us. I was grateful to try once more to understand that troubling haunting memory, to have at least one more image—the children setting out across the northern ice on that sled with their parents beside them—to add to my mental photographs. It made me feel more complete to find this point of commonality with her and my past.

But it raised more questions too. Was it true, then, what I suspected, that in our satin shorts and tap shoes, our little sailor caps, singing about candy shops, we were like creatures from outer space to these children? Was our well-intentioned show sadly misaimed, ineffectual, at bringing happiness to sick kids at Christmas? If I went to their village, would they have donned costumes and danced for me?

Christmas is the time for indulging in ritual, costume, and gift-giving. I love it. But as I load up the bags with tinned goods for the kids' school hampers, as I pack the old clothes in cartons to deliver to a storefront for refugees, I ask myself about giving. If the real gift is understanding and the happiness this brings, are our prescribed ways the best we can manage? Is the receiver being heard as well as the giver? Society learns and changes, thank God, and rituals carry on from century to century. Yesterday's good deed to the "have-nots" can be seen today as harmful. Our Christmas traditions and our self-pleasing notions of charity must be open for negotiation.

14   I'll never outgrow my love for costumes, carols and decorations. As I unpack the wreath from the basement, I think about the old electric lights for our Christmas tree we had at my parents' house. The bulbs were thin and pointed, the glass ridged. They gave a soft fine light. The trick about these strings of lights was that if one bulb burned out, the whole string went off. And you couldn't tell by looking which bulb needed to be replaced.

15   By the curious means in which roles are assigned in families, I became the lighting technician. The lights drove the rest of us mad, but I loved the puzzle of these faulty strings, laying them out, tightening the loose bulbs and replacing any suspicious-looking ones until I got at least one string to light when I plugged it in.

16   Then, I could test the others. I would go down a string, taking out each bulb in turn and screwing it into one of the sockets on the working string to test it. When, after hours of this, I had all the strings lit, and we tucked them in branches on the Christmas tree, I shone myself, with satisfaction.

17   Of course, every day or so, a string went out, and the testing had to start all over again. But I knew I could make it all work and have the celebratory glow of red and yellow and green in the branches of the pine tree. At Christmastime, I think about wholeness; the chain only gives light when all the parts are working.

Vocabulary

a. *paragraph 1:* intrepid
b. *paragraph 2:* tiaras
c. *paragraph 4:* doyenne
d. *paragraph 5:* tuberculosis
e. *paragraph 7:* lethargy
f. *paragraph 11:* commonality
g. *paragraph 12:* ineffectual

Questions

1. What is Govier's unifying idea? What makes the essay more than a collection of reminiscences?
2. How do paragraphs 1 through 4 create a sense of the recurrent and the unique?

3. How does Govier manage the transitions between paragraphs 4 and 5, 10 and 11, and 13 and 14?

Writing Assignment

Write two or more paragraphs of your own that open with a dominant impression of a remembered event, and then develop this impression through details.

KEN DRYDEN

Ken Dryden was arguably the best National Hockey League goalie of the 1970s, leading the Montreal Canadiens to a string of Stanley Cups, and Team Canada to its dramatic seventh-game win over the Soviet all-stars in the famous "Summit Series" of 1972. He is also a graduate of Cornell University and a lawyer. After his retirement from hockey while at the top of his game, Dryden was appointed to a term as Ontario Youth Commissioner in 1984. *The Game*, from which the following reminiscence about backyard hockey is taken, is Dryden's thoughtful and moving account of nine typical days in the middle of his last season with the Canadiens.

Dryden's Backyard

KEN DRYDEN

 **I** get out of bed and pull back the curtains. It has snowed overnight and traces are still gently falling. For several minutes I stand there, my forehead pressed to the window, watching the snow, looking out at the backyards of the houses behind, where the Pritchards, the MacLarens, and the Carpenters lived, and down below at the winter's depth of snow, and at the backyard where I spent my childhood. 1

"Dryden's Backyard." That's what it was called in our neighbourhood. It was more than 70 feet long, paved curiously in red asphalt, 45 feet wide at "the big end," gradually narrowing to 35 feet at the flower bed, to 25 feet at the porch—our center line—to 15 feet at "the small end." While Steve Shutt and Guy Lafleur were in Willowdale and Thurso on backyard rinks their fathers built, while Larry Robinson was on a frozen stream in Marvelville and Réjean Houle on a road in Rouyn under the only street light that his street had, I was here. 2

3　　It was an extraordinary place, like the first swimming pool on the block, except there were no others like it anywhere. Kids would come from many blocks away to play, mostly "the big guys," friends of my brother, a year or two older than him, seven or eight years older than me. But that was never a problem. It was the first rule of the backyard that they had to let me play. To a friend who complained one day, Dave said simply, "If Ken doesn't play, you don't play."

4　　We played "ball hockey" mostly, with a tennis ball, its bounce deadened by the cold. A few times, we got out a garden hose and flooded the backyard to use skates and pucks, but the big end was slightly lower than the small end, and the water pooled and froze unevenly. More important, we found that the more literal we tried to make our games, the less lifelike they became. We could move across the asphalt quickly and with great agility in rubber "billy" boots; we could shoot a tennis ball high and hard. But with skates on, with a puck, we were just kids. So after the first few weeks of the first year, we played only ball hockey.

5　　Depending on the day, the time, the weather, there might be any number of kids wanting to play, so we made up games any number could play. With four and less than nine, we played regular games, the first team scoring ten goals the winner. The two best players, who seemed always to know who they were, picked the teams and decided on ends. First choice of players got second choice of ends, and because the size of the big end made it more fun to play in, the small end was the choice to defend. Each team had a goalie—one with goalie pads, a catching glove, and a goalie stick; the other with only a baseball glove and a forward's stick. When we had more than eight players, we divided into three or more teams for a round-robin tournament, each game to five. With fewer than four, it was more difficult. Sometimes we attempted a regular game, often we just played "shots," each player being both shooter and goalie, standing in front of one net, shooting in turn at the other. Most often, however, we played "penalty shots."

6　　But the backyard also meant time alone. It was usually after dinner when the "big guys" had homework to do and I would turn on the floodlights at either end of the house and on the porch, and play. It was a private game. I would stand alone in the middle of the yard, a stick in my hands, a tennis ball in front of me, silent, still, then suddenly dash ahead, stickhandling furiously, dodging invisible obstacles for a shot on net. It was Maple Leaf Gardens filled to wildly cheering capacity, a tie game, seconds remaining. I was Frank Mahovlich, or Gordie Howe, I was anyone I wanted to be, and the voice in my head was that of Leafs broadcaster Foster Hewitt: ". . . there's ten seconds left, Mahovlich, winding up at his own line, at center, eight seconds, seven, over the blueline, six—he winds up, he shoots, *he scores!*" The mesh that had been tied to the bottoms of our red metal goalposts until frozen in the ice had been ripped away to hang loose from the cross-bars, whipped back like a flag in a stiff breeze. My arms and stick flew into the air, I screamed a scream inside my head, and collected my ball to do it again— many times, for many minutes, the hero of all my own games.

It was a glorious fantasy, and I always heard that voice. It was what made my fantasy seem almost real. For to us, who attended hockey games mostly on TV or radio, an NHL game, a Leafs game, was played with a voice. If I wanted to be Mahovlich or Howe, if I moved my body the way I had seen them move theirs and did nothing else, it would never quite work. But if I heard the voice that said their names while I was playing out that fantasy, I could believe it. Foster Hewitt could make me them. 7

My friends and I played every day after school, sometimes during lunch and after dinner, but Saturday was always the big day. I would go to bed Friday night thinking of Saturday, waking up early, with none of the fuzziness I had other days. If it had snowed overnight, Dave and I, with shovels and scrapers, and soon joined by others, would pile the snow into flower beds or high against the back of the garage. Then at 9:00 A.M. the games would begin. 8

There was one team in the big end, another in the small; third and fourth teams sat like birds on a telephone wire, waiting their turn on the wall that separated the big end from Carpenter's backyard. Each team wore uniforms identical to the other's. It was the Canadian midwinter uniform of the time—long, heavy duffel coats in browns, grays, or blues; tuques in NHL team colors, pulled snug over the ears under the watchful eye of mothers, here rolled up in some distinctive personal style; leather gloves, last year's church gloves, now curling at the wrist and separating between fingers; black rubber "billy" boots over layers of heavy woolen socks for fit, the tops rolled down like "low cuts" for speed and style. 9

Each game would begin with a faceoff, then wouldn't stop again. Action moved quickly end to end, the ball bouncing and rolling, chased by a hacking, slashing scrum of sticks. We had sticks without tops on their blades—"toothpicks"; sticks with no blades at all—"stubs." They broke piece by heart-breaking piece, often quickly, but still we used them. Only at the start of a season, at Christmas (Dave and I routinely exchanged sticks until one year he gave me a stick and I gave him a pair of socks) and once or twice more, would we get new ones. All except John Stedelbauer. His father owned a car dealership and during the hockey season gave away hockey sticks to his customers as a promotion. Stedelbauer 10 got all the new sticks he needed, fortunately, as they weren't very good. One year he broke nineteen of them.

11   A goal would be scored, then another, and slowly the game would leapfrog to five. Bodies grew warm from exertion, fingers and toes went numb; noses ran, wiped by unconscious sleeves; coats loosened, tuques fell off; steam puffed from mouths and streamed from tuqueless heads. Sticks hacked and slashed; tennis balls stung. But in the euphoria of the game, the pain disappeared. Sitting on the wall that overlooked his backyard, Rick "Foster" Carpenter, younger and not very athletic, gave the play-by-play, but no one listened. Each of us had his own private game playing in his head. A fourth goal, then a fifth, a cheer and the first game was over. Quickly, four duffel coats, four tuques, four pairs of weathered gloves and rubber "billy" boots would jump from the wall to replace the losers; and the second game would begin. We paused at noon while some went home and others ate the lunch that they had brought with them. At 6:00 P.M., the two or three who remained would leave. Eighteen hours later, after church, the next game would begin.

12   When I think of the backyard, I think of my childhood; and when I think of my childhood, I think of the backyard. It is the central image I have of that time, linking as it does all of its parts: father, mother, sister, friends; hockey, baseball, and Dave—big brother, idol, mentor, defender, and best friend. Yet it lasted only a few years. Dave was already twelve when the backyard was built; I was six. He and his friends played for three or four years, then stopped; I played longer but, without them, less often. Yet until moments ago, I had never remembered that.

13   The backyard was not a training ground. In all the time I spent there, I don't remember ever thinking I would be an NHL goalie, or even hoping I could be one. In backyard games, I dreamed I *was* Sawchuk or Hall, Mahovlich or Howe; I never dreamed I would be like them. There seemed no connection between the backyard and Maple Leaf Gardens; there seemed no way to get to there from here. If we ever thought about that, it never concerned us; we just played. It was here in the backyard that we *learned* hockey. It was here we got close to it, we got *inside* it, and it got inside us. It was here that our inextricable bond with the game was made. Many years have now passed, the game has grown up and been complicated by things outside it, yet still the backyard remains—untouched, unchanged, my unseverable link to that time, and that game.

[   ]

Vocabulary

a. *paragraph 5:* round-robin tournament
b. *paragraph 10:* scrum
c. *paragraph 11:* euphoria
d. *paragraph 12:* mentor
e. *paragraph 13:* inextricable, unseverable

Questions

1. Dryden builds to general conclusions through his experiences with backyard hockey. How does he show that these conclusions are the main ideas of his essay?
2. How does Dryden blend fantasy, memory, and reality in his account? Where does the emphasis lie?
3. Why does he spend so much time on details (paragraphs 9, 10, and 11, for example)? How do these contribute to the overall effect of the essay?
4. Is this essay primarily about playing hockey as a child, or is it about something else?

Writing Assignments

1. Illustrate your reasons for playing a sport or a musical instrument or for performing a similar activity. Let your reader discover your reasons through the details of your essay.
2. Write an essay on one of the following topics or on one of your own choosing.
   a. the art of making friends
   b. on giving advice
   c. a formative event from childhood
   d. living away from home
   e. waiting in line

   Give your thesis emphasis by introducing it in a prominent place in the essay—perhaps at the end of the opening paragraph, or in the final paragraph. If you begin the essay with your thesis, you can give it emphasis by repeating or restating it at key points.

NORTHROP FRYE

One of the century's most influential literary critics, Northrop Frye (1912–1991) wrote seminal books on William Blake (*Fearful Symmetry*), literary theory (*The Anatomy of Criticism*), and the Bible and literature (*The Great Code*). Born at Sherbrooke, Quebec, and raised in Moncton, New Brunswick, he was educated at Victoria College, University of Toronto, and maintained, as professor of English, a lifelong association with the university. He had a lasting influence on such Canadian writers as Jay Macpherson, James Reaney, and Margaret Atwood. Always interested in education in the broadest sense, Frye speculated in the following essay on why the conception of literature that is presented to children in school is not what contemporary scholars regard as being the elementary principles of that subject as now conceived. Literature for Frye was particularly important because it "gives us not only a means of understanding, but a power to fight. . . . Advertising, propaganda, the speeches of politicians, popular books and magazines, the clichés of rumour, all have their own kind of pastoral myths, quest myths, hero myths, sacrificial myths, and nothing will drive these shoddy constructs out of the mind except the genuine forms of the same thing."

Elementary Teaching

NORTHROP FRYE

1   The first thing that university teachers want to know is: what is important in the pre-university study of literature? Most of us, when we complain about our freshmen, base our complaints on the theme of information or memorized knowledge: our students don't know enough; they haven't read enough: the chronology of literature is a vague haze in their minds; some of them could hardly distinguish Chaucer from Tennyson except by the spelling, and so on. But if students don't have enough information, it is a simple enough matter to supply it or provide the sources of supply. The trouble is that what they learn they learn within a mental structure of habits and assumptions, and university comes much too late in a student's life to alter that structure. For example: many students come to university assuming that convention is the opposite of originality, and is a sign that a poet is superficial and insincere. If they are writing poetry themselves, they are apt to get bristly and aggressive about this assumption. They can't be writing in a convention that all their friends are writing in: they must be conveying unique experiences, because their poems say that they are. Here is a result of illiterate teaching that makes the most scrambled nonsense out of all literary values, yet nothing can really be done about it. We tell them at university that literary sincerity is quite different from personal sincerity, that it can only be developed by craftsmanship working within a convention, and that it is the function of convention to set free the power of expressing emotions, not to provide formulas for ready-made emotions, though it may do this for dull writers. They listen; they understand; they may

even believe; but the effect on their mental habits is very like the effect of schoolmarm English on the little boy: "Dar ain't no 'ain't you', is dey? It's 'aren't you', ain't it?"

Or, again, I am at an educational conference listening to a speech by a high authority in the field. I know him to be a good scholar, a dedicated servant of society, and an admirable person. Yet his speech is a muddy river of clichés, flowing stickily into a delta of banalities at the peroration. The content of the speech does not do justice to his mind: what it does reflect is the state of his literary education. It is not that he has never read good literature, for he has the literary tastes that one would expect a cultivated man to have. But he has never been trained to think rhetorically, to visualize his abstractions, to subordinate logic and sequences to the insights of metaphor and simile, to realize that figures of speech are not the ornaments of language, but the elements of both language and thought. And because his main scholarly interests lie outside literature, he has never been compelled to make up for these deficiencies himself. The result is that he is fluent without being articulate, and cannot break out of an armour of ready-made phrases when he tries to express his real convictions. Once again, nothing can now be done for him: there are no courses in remedial metaphor. 2

The greatest fallacy in the present conception of literary education is the notion that prose is the normal language of ordinary speech, and should form the centre and staple of literary teaching. From prose in this sense we move out to utilitarian English on one side and to the more specialized literary study of poetry on the other. Few subjects can be more futile than a prose-based approach to poetry, an approach which treats poems as documents, to be analysed or summarized or otherwise translated into the language of communication. The root of the fallacy is the assumption that prose represents the only valid form of thought, and that poetry, considered as thought, is essentially decorated or distorted prose. When we suggest that young people try writing poetry, what most of them immediately produce are discontinuous prose statements about their emotions, or what they think their emotions ought to be, when confronted with the outside world. This is not merely because they have been taught to read poetry as a series of statements of this kind—"all that guff about nature," as one freshman expressed it—it is rather that they assume that all verbal expression derives from the attempt to describe something, and that poetry differs from prose, as a mode of thought, in being an attempt to describe subjective emotions. 3

The main principles of a coherently organized curriculum are simple enough, but very different from the one just mentioned. Poetry should be at the centre of all literary training, and literary prose forms the periphery. In a properly constructed curriculum there would be 4 no place for "effective communication" or for any form of utilitarian English. We still have textbooks on effective writing produced by people who have no notion how to write, mainly because they are trying to be effective about it, but one hopes that the market for them will disappear in our time. The styles employed by journalists and advertisers are highly conventionalized rhetorics, in fact practically trade jargons, and have to be learned as separate skills, without much direct reference to literature at all. A literary training is a considerable handicap in trying to understand, for example, the releases of public relations counsels. I am not saying this just to be ironic: I am stating a fact. I remember a *New Yorker* cartoon of a milkman who found the notice "no milk" on a doorstep, and woke up the household at four in the morning to enquire whether he meant that he had no milk or that he wanted no milk. I suspect that the milkman was a retired teacher of English: certainly he reflects the disadvantages of being sensitive to the nuances of expression. A literary person confronted with most of the verbal technologies of our time is in the position of a genuinely intelligent student confronted with an intelligence test which grossly oversimplifies its categories and calls for an arbitrary choice of half-truths. He is sure to fail the test simply because he is more intelligent than the creature who designed it. The primary function of education is to make one maladjusted to ordinary society; and literary education makes it more difficult to come to terms with the barbarizing of speech, or what *Finnegans Wake* calls the jinglish janglage.

5   The connections of literature are with the imagination, not with the reason, hence the ideal in literature is one of intensity and power rather than of precision or accuracy, as in science. There can be no intensity without precision, but to aim directly at precision is trying to seize the shadow. Poetry is one of the creative arts, in the context of music and painting, or rhythm and pattern. The rhythmical energy of poetry, its intimate connection with song and dance, is the elementary basis of its appeal, and the primary aspect of it to be presented to children, along with its affinity with the concrete and the sensational, its power of making things vivid by illustration, which has traditionally been expressed in the formula *ut pictura poesis*.

6   I am certainly no expert on the teaching of children, but it seems obvious that all such teaching has to follow the child's own rhythm of thought and development, and not project on him some half-baked adult mystique, whether that mystique claims to derive from the anti-intellectual left or the anti–anti-intellectual right. And it is clear that children recapitulate, as we should expect them to do, the experience of primitive literature, and turn most naturally and easily to the abstract and conventionalized, to riddles, conundrums, and stylized jingles. The authors of *The Lore and Language of School-children* quote an unremarkable verse:

Mrs. White had a fright
In the middle of the night,
She saw a ghost eating toast
Half-way up the lamp post

and append the comment of a nine-year-old critic: "I think what's so clever about this is the way it all rhymes." Later, in speaking of the child's fondness for tongue twisters and multiple puns, they remark: "It takes children a long time before they cease to be amazed that one word can have more than one meaning." One would hope that this amazement would last the rest of their lives. The speech of a small child is full of chanting and singing, and it is clear that the child understands what many adults do not, that verse is a more direct and primitive way of conventionalizing speech than prose is.

This principle, that the physical energy and concrete vividness   7
of verse should normally be presented earlier than the more complex and adulterated rhythm of prose, affects the training in both reading and writing. It is difficult to know how a child thinks, but it is less difficult to know how he talks, once one has gained his confidence, and how he talks might afford an educational clue. Any child who has talked to me has addressed me in an uninhibited stream of burble for which the nearest literary counterpart is the last chapter of *Ulysses*. This chapter has no punctuation, and neither has a child's speech. Surely in teaching writing one should begin by trying to channel this free current of verbal energy and start giving it some precision as it goes along. To teach a child to write as though he were deciphering something from linear B, proceeding from word to phrase, from phrase to sentence, from sentence to paragraph, is to ensure that what he eventually writes will be a dead language. Good writing has to be based on good speech, and good speech is a logical, though complex, development from natural speech. It is a striking feature of our culture that so much creative activity in literature, as in music and painting, should be either explicitly academic or explicitly resistant to education, a culture either of Brahmins or of Dharma bums. In Canada these two aspects of literary culture have reached a curious schizophrenia in which a constant polemic against academic poetry is carried on by poets who are nearly all employed by universities. It seems to me that the source of the feeling that education inhibits spontaneity may be somewhere in the region I have just indicated: in the reversal of the natural rhythms of thought and expression which a prose-based literary education is only too apt to produce.

Vocabulary

a. *paragraph 1:* convention, bristly
b. *paragraph 2:* delta, banalities, peroration, rhetorically, metaphor, remedial
c. *paragraph 3:* fallacy, utilitarian
d. *paragraph 4:* periphery, nuances, maladjusted, barbarizing
e. *paragraph 6:* mystique, conundrums, append
f. *paragraph 7:* Brahmins, Dharma bums

Questions

1. What points is Frye making about the way in which children are currently taught? How does the way in which Frye presents his main points contribute to his argument?
2. Frye is suggesting what is wrong with the current curriculum and how it might be changed. What are your views on the changes he proposes?
3. Frye ranges widely in his discussion of elementary teaching. Make a list of the subjects he covers and consider how they cohere.

Writing Assignment

Explain why a literary training can be a handicap in today's society, and show how Frye uses anecdotal humour to illustrate this point. Use your own humorous examples to illustrate an abstract point in a short essay.

DANIEL C. DENNETT

Daniel C. Dennett, the director of the Center for Cognitive Studies at Tufts University in Medford, Massachusetts, is the author of *Brainstorms, The Mind's I,* and *Consciousness Explained.* This essay is adapted from his book *Darwin's Dangerous Idea: Evolution and the Meanings of Life.* In it, he argues that we have refused to accept the implications of Darwinian theory for some of our most cherished beliefs.

Darwin's Dangerous Idea

DANIEL C. DENNETT

1   When I was a schoolboy, my friends and I used to amuse ourselves with fantasies about an imaginary chemical

we called universal acid. I have no idea whether we invented it or inherited it, along with Spanish fly and saltpeter, as part of underground youth culture. Universal acid is a liquid so corrosive that it will eat through *anything*. The problem with universal acid, of course, is what to keep it in. It dissolves glass bottles and stainless-steel canisters as readily as it does paper bags. What would happen if somehow you came upon a dollop of universal acid? Would the entire planet eventually be destroyed? If not, what would be left? After everything had been transformed by its encounter with universal acid, what would the world look like?

Our speculations were a diverting joke; none of us expected to come in contact with such corrosive material. Yet in only a few years I would encounter something bearing as close a likeness to universal acid as anyone could wish. It was not a chemical but an idea — one that eats through virtually every traditional concept, leaving in its wake a revolutionized world view, with most of the old landmarks still recognizable but transformed in fundamental ways. It was the idea that Charles Darwin, in 1859, unleashed on an unsuspecting world. 2

I was not the first to realize that I was dealing with dangerous stuff. From the moment of publication of *The Origin of Species*, Darwin's fundamental idea has inspired intense reactions, ranging from ferocious condemnation to ecstatic allegiance, sometimes tantamount to religious zeal. Darwin's theory has been abused and misrepresented by friend and foe alike. It has been misappropriated to lend scientific respectability to appalling political and social doctrines. It has been pilloried in caricature by opponents, some of whom would have it compete in the schools with "creation science," a pathetic hodgepodge of pious pseudoscience. 3

Almost no one is indifferent to Darwin, and no one should be. The Darwinian theory is a scientific theory, and a great one, but that is not all it is. The creationists who oppose it so bitterly are right about one thing: Darwin's dangerous idea cuts much deeper into the fabric of our most fundamental beliefs than many of its sophisticated apologists have yet admitted, even to themselves. Even today, more than a century after Darwin's death, many people still have not come to terms with its mind-boggling implications. Perhaps, they think, one can distinguish the parts of Darwin's idea that really are established beyond any reasonable doubt from the other, more speculative parts. Perhaps the rock-solid scientific facts would then turn out to have no stunning implications for religion, or human nature, or the meaning of life, whereas the parts of Darwin's ideas that get people so upset could be quarantined as controversial extensions, or mere interpretations, of the scientifically irresistible parts. That would be reassuring. 4

5   But alas, that is just about backward. There are vigorous controversies swirling around in contemporary evolutionary theory, but
people who feel threatened by Darwinism should not take heart
from that fact. Most—if not quite all—of the controversies concern
issues that are "just science"; no matter which side wins, the outcome will not undo the basic Darwinian idea. That idea, which is as
secure as any in science, really does have far-reaching implications
for visions of what the meaning of life is or could be. Among other
things, Darwin changed forever what it means to ask, and answer,
the question, Why?

The Great Chain of Being

6   To appreciate how deeply Darwin's universal acid has etched its
way into the intellectual landscape, it may help to see how the
world looked before Darwin inverted it. A passage written by the
English philosopher John Locke in his *Essay Concerning Human
Understanding*, published in 1690, perfectly illustrates the conceptual blockade that was in place before the Darwinian revolution:

> Let us suppose any parcel of Matter eternal, great or small,
> we shall find it, in it self, able to produce nothing. . . . Mat-
> ter then, by its own Strength, cannot produce in it self so
> much as Motion: the motion it has, must also be from Eter-
> nity, or else be produced, and added to Matter by some
> other Being more powerful than Matter. . . . But let us sup-
> pose Motion eternal too; yet Matter, *incogitative Matter* and
> Motion, whatever changes it might produce of Figure and
> Bulk, *could never produce Thought*. . . .
>
> So that if we will suppose nothing first, or eternal; *Mat-
> ter* can never begin to be: If we suppose bare Matter, with-
> out Motion, eternal; *Motion* can never begin to be: If we
> suppose only Matter and Motion first, or eternal; *Thought*
> can never begin to be.

7   The argument may seem strange and stilted to modern readers,
but Locke himself thought he was just reminding people of something obvious: mind must come first, or at least it must be tied for
first. And so it seemed to many brilliant and skeptical thinkers
before Darwin. Behind their thinking lay a top-to-bottom view of
things often described as a ladder, a tower, or, in the memorable
phrase of the American intellectual historian Arthur O. Lovejoy, a
"great chain of being." Locke's argument invoked a particularly
abstract version of the hierarchy, which I call the cosmic pyramid:

God

Mind

Design

O r d e r

C h a o s

N o t h i n g

Everything finds its place somewhere in the pyramid—even blank nothingness, the ultimate foundation. Not all matter is ordered; some is in chaos; only some ordered matter is also designed; only some designed things have minds; and, of course, only one mind is God.

What is the difference between order and design? As a first stab, I would say that order is mere regularity, mere pattern; design reflects Aristotle's *telos*, an exploitation of order for a purpose, as in a cleverly designed artifact. The solar system exhibits stupendous order, but (apparently) it has no purpose—it is not *for* anything. An eye, in contrast, is for seeing. Before Darwin, the distinction was not always clearly marked, but Darwin suggested a division. Give me order and time, he said, and I will give you design—without the aid of mind.

Kinds, Essence, and Change

Darwin did not set out to find an antidote to Locke's conceptual paralysis or to pin down a grand cosmological alternative. His aim was slightly more modest: he wanted to explain the origin of species. The naturalists of his day had amassed mountains of facts about living things and had succeeded in systematizing those facts along several dimensions. Two great sources of wonder emerged from that work. First were all the discoveries about the impressive adaptations of organisms. Second was the recognition of the prolific diversity of living things: it had begun to dawn on people that literally millions of kinds of plants and animals inhabit the earth. Why were there so many?

Even more striking were the patterns discernible within that diversity, particularly the huge gaps between many organisms. There were birds and mammals that swam like fish, but none with gills; there were dogs of many sizes and shapes, but no dogcats or dogcows or feathered dogs. The patterns cried out for classification. Aristotle taught that all things—not just living things—have two kinds of properties: essential properties, without which they fail to be the particular kind of thing they are, and accidental properties, which are free to vary within the kind. And along with each kind of thing came an essence. Essences for Aristotle were definitive: timeless, unchanging, all or nothing. A thing could not be *rather* silver or *quasi*-gold or a *semi*-mammal. Species of organisms were deemed to be as timeless and unchangeable as the perfect triangles and circles of Euclidean geometry.

11   On the outskirts of that deliciously crisp and systematic hierarchy lurked a plethora of awkward and puzzling facts. There were all manner of hard-to-classify intermediate creatures, which seemed to have parts of more than one essence. There were curious higher-order patterns of shared and unshared features: Why should it be backbones and not feathers that birds and fish share, and why should *creature with eyes* or *carnivore* not be as important a classifier as is *warm-blooded*? Which principle of classification should count? In Plato's famous image, which system "carved nature at the joints"?

12   What Darwin provided was the first background theory for showing why one classification scheme would get the joints right. The solution, he argued, was to take a historical approach. Species are not eternal and immutable; they have evolved over time and can give birth to new species in turn. The idea was not new; many versions of it had been seriously discussed since the time of the ancient Greeks. But there was a powerful Aristotelian bias against it: essences, after all, were unchanging; a thing could not change its essence, and new essences could not be born (except, of course, by God's command in episodes of Special Creation). Reptiles could no more turn into birds than copper could turn into gold.

13   To imagine how the idea of evolution must have struck Darwin's contemporaries, consider how you would react if someone announced that, long, long ago, the number 7 had been an even number and that it had gradually acquired its oddness by exchanging some properties with the ancestors of the number 10 (which was once a prime number). Utter nonsense, of course. Inconceivable. Yet that was just the kind of conceptual leap Darwin demanded of his peers. In *The Origin of Species* he set out both to prove *that* modern species were revised descendants of earlier species — species had evolved — and to show *how* that "descent with modification" had taken place. The book presented an overwhelmingly persuasive case for the first thesis and a tantalizing case in favor of the second. Suddenly the burden of proof shifted to the skeptics: Could they show that Darwin's arguments were mistaken? Could they show how natural selection would be incapable of giving rise to the effects he described? Given all the signs of historical process that Darwin had uncovered — all the brush marks of the artist, you might say — could anyone imagine how any process other than natural selection could have led to all those effects?

Algorithmic Processes

Darwin succeeded not only because he documented his ideas   14
exhaustively but also because he grounded them in a powerful theoretical framework. In modern terms, he had discovered the power
of an algorithm.

An algorithm is a formal process that can be counted on—   15
logically—to yield a certain kind of result whenever it is "run" or
instantiated. The idea that an algorithm is a foolproof and somehow
"mechanical" procedure has been around for centuries, but it was
the pioneering work of Alan M. Turing, Kurt Gödel and Alonzo
Church in the 1930s that more or less fixed the current understanding of the term. Three key features of algorithms are important
here:

1. *Substrate neutrality:* The power of the procedure is a result of its
   logical structure, not the materials that happen to be used in
   carrying it out. Long division works equally well with pencil or
   pen, paper or parchment, neon lights or skywriting, using any
   symbol system you like.
2. *Underlying mindlessness:* Although the overall design of the procedure may be brilliant, or may yield brilliant results, each constituent step is utterly simple. The recipe requires no wise decisions or delicate judgments on the part of the recipe reader.
3. *Guaranteed results:* Whatever it is an algorithm does, it always
   does it, provided the algorithm is executed without misstep. An
   algorithm is a foolproof recipe.

Algorithms need not have anything to do with numbers. Con-   16
sider the process of annealing a piece of steel. What could be more
physical, less "computational," than that? The blacksmith repeatedly heats the steel and then lets it cool, and somehow in the
process it becomes much stronger. How? Does the heat create special toughness atoms that coat the surface? Or does it suck out of
the atmosphere subatomic glue that binds all the iron atoms
together? No, nothing like that takes place.

The right level of explanation is the algorithmic level: As the   17
metal cools from its molten state, it begins to form a solid in many
spots at the same time, creating crystals that grow together until the
entire mass is solid. The first time that takes place, the arrangement
of the individual crystal structures is less than optimal; they are
weakly held together, with lots of internal stresses and strains. Heating the steel again—but not all the way to melting—partly breaks
down those structures, so that, when next they cool, the broken-up
bits adhere to the still-solid bits in a different arrangement. It can be

mathematically proved that the rearrangements tend to form a progressively stronger total structure, provided the heating and cooling are done just right.

18   To understand annealing in depth you have to learn the physics of all the forces operating at the atomic level. But the basic idea of how and why the process works can be lifted clear of those details and put in substrate-neutral terminology. For example, metallurgical annealing has inspired a general problem-solving technique in computer science known as simulated annealing, a way of getting a computer program to build, disassemble and rebuild a data structure (such as another program) over and over, blindly groping toward a better—sometimes even an optimal—version.

19   Similarly, Darwin's ideas about the powers of natural selection can be lifted out of their home base in biology. Darwin himself had few inklings about the microscopic processes of genetic inheritance (and those turned out to be wrong). Because of substrate neutrality, however, his basic insights have floated like a cork on the waves of subsequent research and controversy, from Mendel to molecular biology.

Universal Acid, Redux

20   Here, then, is Darwin's dangerous idea: the algorithmic level *is* the level that best accounts for the speed of the antelope, the wing of the eagle, the shape of the orchid, the diversity of species and all the other occasions for wonder in the world of nature. Incredible as it may seem, the entire biosphere is the outcome of nothing but a cascade of algorithmic processes feeding on chance. Who designed the cascade? Nobody. It is itself the outcome of a blind algorithmic process. As Darwin himself put it, in a letter to the British geologist Charles Lyell shortly after the publication of *Origin*:

> I would give absolutely nothing for the theory of Natural Selection, if it requires miraculous additions at any one stage of descent. . . . If I were convinced that I required such additions to the theory of natural selection, I would reject it as rubbish.

21   The idea of evolution by algorithm is still controversial. Today evolutionary biologists are engaged in a tug-of-war between those who are relentlessly pushing toward an algorithmic treatment and those who, for various submerged reasons, are resisting the trend. It is rather as if there were metallurgists around who were disappointed by the algorithmic explanation of annealing. "You mean that's all there is to it? No microscopic superglue especially created by the heating and cooling process?" Nobody denies that evolution,

like annealing, works; what is at issue is Darwin's radical vision of how and why it works. The forces of resistance can dimly see that their skirmish is part of a wider campaign. If the game is lost in evolutionary biology, where will it end?

Like universal acid, Darwin's idea quickly began to eat its way out of its original container. If the redesign of organisms could be a mindless, algorithmic process of evolution, why could that process itself not be the product of evolution, and so forth, all the way down the cosmic pyramid? And if mindless evolution could account for the breathtakingly clever artifacts of the biosphere, how could the products of our own minds be exempt from an evolutionary explanation? Darwin's idea thus also threatened to spread all the way up, dissolving the illusion of human authorship, our own divine spark of creativity and understanding. 22

In response, anxious thinkers have waged a number of failed campaigns to contain Darwin's idea within some acceptably safe, partial revolution. Cede some or all of modern biology to Darwin, perhaps, but hold the line there. Keep Darwinian thinking out of cosmology, out of psychology, out of human culture, out of ethics, politics and religion! (Among those who favour holding the line within biology itself, Stephen Jay Gould has offered several post-Darwinian counterrevolutions.) The forces of containment have won many battles and, to their credit, have exposed and discredited many flawed applications of Darwin's idea. But new, improved waves of Darwinian thinking keep coming. 23

Order and Design

Like any good revolutionary, Darwin did not simply topple the old system; he adapted as much of it as possible to his own purposes. Under his influence the cosmic pyramid took on a new meaning, hinging on a radically altered concept of design. Many philosophers had regarded the existence of design as proof of the existence of God. The late-eighteenth-century theologian William Paley compared the intricacy of the universe to that of a watch found on a heath in the wilderness. Where there is a watch, can there fail to be a watchmaker? 24

As Paley pointed out, a watch exhibits a tremendous amount of work done. Watches and other designed objects do not just happen: they are the product of what modern industry calls R&D—research and development—and R&D is costly, in both time and energy. Before Darwin the only model of a process whereby R&D could get done was one that invoked an intelligent artificer. What Darwin saw was that in principle the same work could be done by a different kind of process that distributed the work over huge amounts of time, thriftily conserving the design work that had been accomplished at each stage so that it did not have to be done over again. 25

26   Another way of looking at the difference—and the tight relation—between design and order was popularized by the Austrian
physicist Erwin Schrödinger. In physics, order or organization can
be measured as differences in heat between regions of space–time;
entropy is simply disorder, the opposite of order. According to the
second law of thermodynamics, the entropy of any isolated system
increases with time. In other words, things run down; the universe
is unwinding out of a more ordered state into the ultimately disor-
dered state called its heat death.

27   What, then, are living things? They are things that resist crumbling into dust, at least for a while, by not being isolated—by taking in from their environment the wherewithal to keep life and limb
together. The psychologist Richard L. Gregory of the University of
Bristol in England sums up the idea crisply:

> Time's arrow given by Entropy—the loss of organization,
> or loss of temperature differences—is statistical and is sub-
> ject to local small-scale reversals. Most striking: life is a sys-
> tematic reversal of Entropy, and intelligence creates struc-
> tures and energy differences against the supposed gradual
> "death" through Entropy of the physical Universe.

A designed thing, then, is either a living thing or a part of a living
thing, or the artifact of a living thing, organized in the service of the
battle against disorder.

28   It is not impossible to oppose the trend of the second law, but it
is costly, as Gregory dramatized with an unforgettable example.
Suppose you decided to reverse entropy by unscrambling an egg.
How much would it cost to make a device that takes scrambled
eggs as input and delivers unscrambled eggs as output? Even with
an unlimited budget the most brilliant engineers could not do it.
But there is a ready solution: a live hen. Feed it scrambled eggs, and
it will be able to make eggs for you—for a while—thanks to the
design built into it.

29   The more design a thing exhibits, the more R&D work must
have been done to make it. In Darwin's conception, the vertical
dimension of the cosmic pyramid becomes the measure of how much
design has gone into items at a given level. Minds still end up near
the top, but only because they are among the most advanced effects
(to date) of the creative process—not, as in the old version, its cause
or source. And the products of human minds, namely, human artifacts, must count as more designed still. That might seem counter-
intuitive at first; surely a paper clip is a trivial product of design
compared with any living thing, however rudimentary. But imagine yourself walking along an apparently deserted beach on an

alien planet. Which discovery would excite you more: a clam, or a clam rake?

Cranes and Skyhooks

Now imagine all the "lifting" that must have been needed to create 30 the magnificent organisms and (other) artifacts in the upper reaches of the cosmic pyramid. Vast distances must have been traversed since the dawn of life and the earliest, simplest self-replicating entities. Darwin has offered an account of the crudest, most rudimentary, stupidest imaginable lifting process: natural selection. By taking the smallest possible steps, the process can gradually, over eons, traverse those huge distances.

Could it really have happened that way? Can Darwin's mind- 31 lessly mechanical algorithms really get all the way to here (the world of wonders we all inhabit) from there (the world of chaos or utter undesignedness) in only a few billion years? Or did the process need a leg up now and then, if only at the very beginning, from some sort of "mind first" force or power or process? In short, does evolution need a skyhook?

> **skyhook.** orig. *Aeronaut*. An imaginary contrivance for attachment to the sky; an imaginary means of suspension in the sky.   —*Oxford English Dictionary*

The first use of the term noted by the *OED* dates from 1915, when an airplane pilot, commanded to remain aloft for an hour beyond the planned landing, replied, "Submitted: that this machine is not fitted with skyhooks."

Skyhooks would be wonderful things to have: miraculous lift- 32 ers, unsupported and insupportable, great for hauling unwieldy objects out of difficult circumstances and speeding up all sorts of construction projects. Sad to say, though, there are no skyhooks.

But there are cranes. Anyone who is, like me, a lifelong specta- 33 tor at construction sites surely has noticed with some satisfaction that it sometimes takes a small crane to set up a big crane. And it must have occurred to many other onlookers that, in principle, the big crane could be used to build a still more spectacular crane. In principle (if not in real-world construction projects), there is no limit to the cascade of cranes that could be organized to accomplish some mighty end. In the Darwinian context cranes are natural evolutionary subprocesses or features that speed up the basic, slow pace of natural selection. Cranes are expensive; they have to be designed and built from everyday parts already on hand; and they need to be erected on a firm base of existing ground. Once built, however, they are excellent lifters; they do their job in an honest, non–question-begging fashion; and they have the decided advantage of being real.

34   For more than a century skeptics have been trying to find a proof that Darwin's idea just cannot work, at least not all the way. Time and again they have come up with truly fascinating challenges: leaps and gaps and other marvels that do seem, at first, to need skyhooks. But then along have come the cranes—discovered, in many cases, by the very skeptics who were hoping to find a skyhook.

Sex

35   One extremely powerful crane, most evolutionary theorists agree, is sex. Species that reproduce sexually can move through the universe of possible, nonlethal designs—which might be called design space—much more rapidly than organisms that reproduce asexually. That cannot be the raison d'être of sex, however. Evolution cannot see far down the road; anything it builds must have an immediate payoff to counterbalance the cost. Some other, short-term benefit must have maintained the positive selection pressure required to make sexual reproduction an offer few species could refuse.

36   Another crane, one that was created to be a crane, is genetic engineering. Genetic engineers—people who engage in recombinant-DNA tinkering—can now take huge leaps through design space, creating organisms that would never have evolved by "ordinary" means. That is no miracle—provided the genetic engineers themselves (and the artifacts they use in their trade) are wholly the products of earlier, slower evolutionary processes.

37   In *The Descent of Man* Darwin made it clear that the cranes of evolution reach all the way up to the throne of mind. That idea was too revolutionary for many people—and it remains so, even among some of evolution's best friends. Alfred Russel Wallace, whom Darwin acknowledged as codiscoverer of the principle of evolution, never quite got the point. When, later in life, Wallace converted to spiritualism and exempted human consciousness altogether from the iron rule of evolution, Darwin wrote to him: "I hope you have not murdered too completely your own and my child."

38   More recently the physicist Paul Davies of the University of Adelaide in Australia proclaimed in his book *The Mind of God* that the reflective power of human minds can be "no trivial detail, no minor by-product of mindless purposeless forces." That familiar denial betrays an ill-examined prejudice. Why, one might ask Davies, would its being a by-product of mindless, purposeless forces make it trivial? Why couldn't the most important thing of all be something that arose from unimportant things? Darwin's inversion suggests that varieties of excellence, worth and purpose can emerge, bubbling up out of "mindless, purposeless forces."

People ache to believe that human beings are vastly different 39
from all other species—and they are right. We are different. We are
the only species that has access to an extra mode for preserving and
communicating design: culture. (Other species have some capacity
to transmit information "behaviourally" as well as genetically, but
they have not developed culture to the takeoff point that our species
has.) People have language, the primary medium of culture, and
language has opened up new regions of design space that only we
are privy to. In a few short millennia—a mere instant in biological
time—we have already launched our new exploration vehicles to
transform not only the planet but the very process of design development that created us.

Crane-Making Cranes

Human culture is not just a crane made up of cranes; it is a crane- 40
making crane, so powerful that its effects can swamp many (but not
all) of the earlier genetic pressures and processes that created it and
still coexist with it.

What kind of evolutionary revolution took place to set us apart 41
so decisively from all other products of the genetic revolution? The
explanation, I think, parallels the wonderful story told by the biologist Lynn Margulis of the University of Massachusetts at Amherst,
about the revolution that paved the way for all complex life. Once
upon a time, Margulis says, the only organisms on earth were cells
without nuclei, the prokaryotes. They were simple, solitary forms
of life, destined for nothing fancier than drifting around in an
energy-rich soup and reproducing themselves. Then, one day,
some prokaryotes were invaded by parasites. But the invaders
turned out to be beneficial; they joined forces with their hosts, creating a revolutionary new kind of entity, a eukaryotic cell. That
partnership opened up the vast space of possibilities known as
multicellular life.

A few billion years passed. Then one fine day another invasion 42
began. A single species of multicellular organism, a kind of primate,
had developed a variety of structures and capacities that happened
to make the organism particularly well suited for the invaders. In
fact, the primate hosts had created the invaders as well, in much the
way spiders create webs and birds create nests. In a twinkling—in
less than 100,000 years—the invaders transformed the apes who
were their unwitting hosts into something altogether new: *witting*
hosts, who, thanks to their huge stock of new-fangled invaders,
could imagine the heretofore unimaginable, leaping through design
space as nothing had ever done before. Following the evolutionary
biologist Richard Dawkins of the University of Oxford, I call the
invaders memes. The radically new kind of entity created when a

particular kind of animal is properly furnished (or infested) with memes is what is commonly called a person.

43   Roughly speaking, memes are ideas—specifically, the kind of complex ideas that form themselves into distinct memorable units, such as: *arch; wheel; wearing clothes; vendetta; right triangle; alphabet; calendar; the Odyssey; calculus; chess; perspective drawing; evolution by natural selection; impressionism; "Greensleeves"; deconstructionism.* In Dawkins's conception, memes represent units of cultural transmission analogous to the genes of biological evolution. Like genes, memes are replicators, subject to much the same principles of evolution as genes are. Their fate is determined by whether copies and copies of copies of them persist and multiply, and that depends on the selective forces that act directly on the various physical vehicles that embody them. Some thinkers have proposed that there could be a science of meme evolution—memetics—strongly parallel to genetics. Others consider the proposal absurd.

Emotional Aversions

44 Some people hate the very idea of explaining human culture in evolutionary terms. I think they are making a big mistake. They want to believe that the human way of life is radically different from that of all other living things—and so it is. But they also want to understand that difference as the result of a miracle, a gift from God, a skyhook, not a crane. Why? Why should people flinch from carrying Darwin's idea through to its logical conclusion?

45   The answer, I think, is fear. They are afraid that the idea will not just explain but will explain *away* the minds and purposes and meanings that everyone holds dear; that the universal acid will pass through their most cherished monuments, dissolving them into an unrecognizable and unlovable puddle of scientistic destruction.

46   I can sympathize with such concerns. But the damage, if damage it is, is already done. Even if Darwin's idea came to be rejected by science—utterly discredited and replaced by some vastly more powerful (and currently unimaginable) vision—it would still have irremediably demolished everything that came before it. Simply by making design without mind conceivable, Darwin rendered Locke's argument, and the thinking behind it, as obsolete as the quill pen with which it was written. There can be no returning to pre-Darwinian innocence.

47   We used to sing a lot when I was a child, at school and Sunday school, around the campfire at summer camp, or gathered around the piano at home. One of my favourite songs, simple but surprisingly beautiful, was "Tell Me Why":

Tell me why the stars do shine,
Tell me why the ivy twines,

Tell me why the sky's so blue,
Then I will tell you just why I love you.

Because God made the stars to shine,
Because God made the ivy twine,
Because God made the sky so blue,
Because God made you, that's why I love you.

That straightforward, sentimental declaration still brings a lump to my throat—so sweet, so innocent, so reassuring is its vision of life. But it is a vision most of us have outgrown, however fondly we may recall it. The kindly God who lovingly fashioned every one of us (all creatures great and small) and sprinkled the sky with shining stars for our delight—that God is, like Santa Claus, a myth of childhood, not anything a sane, undeluded adult could literally believe in.

I, too, cherish many of the ideas and ideals that Darwin seems 48 to challenge, and I want to protect them. I want to protect the campfire song, and what is beautiful and true in it, for my little grandson and his friends, and for their children. Many other, more magnificent ideas may also need protection. But the only good way to do that—the only way that has a chance in the long run—is to cut through the smoke screens and look at the idea as unflinchingly, as dispassionately, as possible.

There is no future in a sacred myth. Why not? Because of our 49 curiosity. Because, as the song reminds us, we want to know why. We may have outgrown the song's answer, but we will never outgrow the question. Whatever we hold precious, we cannot protect it from our curiosity, because being who we are, one of the things we deem precious is the truth. Our love of truth is surely a central element in the meaning we find in our lives. In any case, the idea that we might preserve meaning by kidding ourselves is a more pessimistic, more nihilistic idea than I for one can stomach. If that were the best that could be done, I would conclude that nothing mattered after all.

Vocabulary

a. *paragraph 3:* pilloried, caricature
b. *paragraph 11:* plethora
c. *paragraph 16:* annealing
d. *paragraph 17:* optimal
e. *paragraph 19:* substrate
f. *paragraph 30:* self-replicating
g. *paragraph 43:* vendetta, impressionism, deconstructionism, replicators
h. *paragraph 45:* scientistic

i. *paragraph 46:* irremediably
j. *paragraph 49:* nihilistic

Questions

1. Dennett devotes his essay to showing how Darwin's "dangerous idea" threatens our traditional beliefs. Write a one-sentence outline of each paragraph and trace the development of his argument.
2. As part of his explanation, Dennett rejects the creationist view expressed at the outset (paragraph 4). How does he show it to be wrong?
3. How does Dennett use the ideas of Paley, Schrödinger, and Gregory in paragraphs 24 to 28?
4. How important are the metaphors of "skyhooks" and "cranes" to Dennett's argument?
5. How effective is the use of the song lyrics in paragraph 47?
6. Why does Dennett characterize society as unwilling to accept the logical consequences of Darwin's theory?

Writing Assignments

1. Discuss how the creationist/evolutionist debate has influenced your own life. Has it changed your view of what Dennett calls the future of a "sacred myth"?
2. Analyze the uses to which other scientific discoveries have been put in our century. How do attitudes toward such discoveries vary?

JONATHAN RAUCH

Jonathan Rauch, currently a writer for *The Economist* in London, is the author of *Kindly Inquisitors: The New Attacks on Free Thought*. In the following much-discussed essay, he provocatively insists on freedom of speech for hatemongers. He argues that the intellectual pluralism we value in our culture is best defended by our right to say hateful things about each other.

In Defense of Prejudice: Why Incendiary Speech Must Be Protected

JONATHAN RAUCH

1   The war on prejudice is now, in all likelihood, the most uncontroversial social movement in America.

Opposition to "hate speech," formerly identified with the liberal left, has become a bipartisan piety. In the past year, groups and factions that agree on nothing else have agreed that the public expression of any and all prejudices must be forbidden. On the left, protesters and editorialists have insisted that Francis L. Lawrence resign as president of Rutgers University for describing blacks as "a disadvantaged population that doesn't have that genetic, hereditary background to have a higher average." On the other side of the ideological divide, Ralph Reed, the executive director of the Christian Coalition, responded to criticism of the religious right by calling a press conference to denounce a supposed outbreak of "name-calling, scapegoating, and religious bigotry." Craig Rogers, an evangelical Christian student at California State University, recently filed a $2.5 million sexual-harassment suit against a lesbian professor of psychology, claiming that anti-male bias in one of her lectures violated campus rules and left him feeling "raped and trapped."

In universities and on Capitol Hill, in workplaces and newsrooms, authorities are declaring that there is no place for racism, sexism, homophobia, Christian-bashing, and other forms of prejudice in public debate or even in private thought. "Only when racism and other forms of prejudice are expunged," say the crusaders for sweetness and light, "can minorities be safe and society be fair." So sweet, this dream of a world without prejudice. But the very last thing society should do is seek to utterly eradicate racism and other forms of prejudice. 2

I suppose I should say, in the customary I-hope-I-don't-sound-too-defensive tone, that I am not a racist and that this is not an article favoring racism or any other particular prejudice. It is an article favoring intellectual pluralism, which permits the expression of various forms of bigotry and always will. Although we like to hope that a time will come when no one will believe that people come in types and that each type belongs with its own kind, I doubt such a day will ever arrive. By all indications, *Homo sapiens* is a tribal species for whom "us versus them" comes naturally and must be continually pushed back. Where there is genuine freedom of expression, there will be racist expression. There will also be people who believe that homosexuals are sick or threaten children or— especially among teenagers—are rightful targets of manly savagery. Homosexuality will always be incomprehensible to most people, and what is incomprehensible is feared. As for anti-Semitism, it appears to be a hardier virus than influenza. If you want pluralism, then you get racism and sexism and homophobia, and communism and fascism and xenophobia and tribalism, and that is just for a start. If you want to believe in intellectual freedom and the progress of knowledge and the advancement of science and all those other good things, then you must swallow hard and accept this: for as 3 thick-headed and wayward an animal as us, the realistic question is how to make the best of prejudice, not how to eradicate it.

4   Indeed, "eradicating prejudice" is so vague a proposition as to be meaningless. Distinguishing prejudice reliably and non-politically from non-prejudice, or even defining it crisply, is quite hopeless. We all feel we know prejudice when we see it. But do we? At the University of Michigan, a student said in a classroom discussion that he considered homosexuality a disease treatable with therapy. He was summoned to a formal disciplinary hearing for violating the school's policy against speech that "victimizes" people based on "sexual orientation." Now, the evidence is abundant that this particular hypothesis is wrong, and any American homosexual can attest to the harm that the student's hypothesis has inflicted on many real people. But was it a statement of prejudice or of misguided belief? Hate speech or hypothesis? Many Americans who do not regard themselves as bigots or haters believe that homosexuality is a treatable disease. They may be wrong, but are they all bigots? I am unwilling to say so, and if you are willing, beware. The line between a prejudiced belief and a merely controversial one is elusive, and the harder you look the more elusive it becomes. "God hates homosexuals" is a statement of fact, not of bias, to those who believe it; "American criminals are disproportionately black" is a statement of bias, not of fact, to those who disbelieve it.

5   Who is right? You may decide, and so may others, and there is no need to agree. That is the great innovation of intellectual pluralism (which is to say, of post-Enlightenment science, broadly defined). We cannot know in advance or for sure which belief is prejudice and which is truth, but to advance knowledge we don't need to know. The genius of intellectual pluralism lies not in doing away with prejudices and dogmas but in channeling them—making them socially productive by pitting prejudice against prejudice and dogma against dogma, exposing all to withering public criticism. What survives at the end of the day is our base of knowledge.

6   What they told us in high school about this process is very largely a lie. The Enlightenment tradition taught us that science is orderly, antiseptic, rational, the province of detached experimenters and high-minded logicians. In the popular view, science stands for reason against prejudice, open-mindedness against dogma, calm consideration against passionate attachment—all personified by pop-science icons like the magisterially deductive Sherlock Holmes, the coolly analytic Mr. Spock, the genially authoritative Mr. Science (from our junior-high science films). Yet one of science's dirty secrets is that although science as a whole is as unbiased as anything human can be, scientists are just as biased as anyone else, sometimes more so. "One of the strengths of science," writes the

philosopher of science David L. Hull, "is that it does not require that scientists be unbiased, only that different scientists have different biases." Another dirty secret is that, no less than the rest of us, scientists can be dogmatic and pigheaded. "Although this pigheadedness often damages the careers of individual scientists," says Hull, "it is beneficial for the manifest goal of science," which relies on people to invest years in their ideas and defend them passionately. And the dirtiest secret of all, if you believe in the antiseptic popular view of science, is that this most ostensibly rational of enterprises depends on the most irrational of motives—ambition, narcissism, animus, even revenge. "Scientists acknowledge that among their motivations are natural curiosity, the love of truth, and the desire to help humanity, but other inducements exist as well, and one of them is to 'get that son of a bitch,'" says Hull. "Time and again, scientists whom I interviewed described the powerful spur that 'showing that son of a bitch' supplied to their own research."

Many people, I think, are bewildered by this unvarnished and all too human view of science. They believe that for a system to be unprejudiced, the people in it must also be unprejudiced. In fact, the opposite is true. Far from eradicating ugly or stupid ideas and coarse or unpleasant motives, intellectual pluralism relies upon them to excite intellectual passion and redouble scientific effort. I know of no modern idea more ugly and stupid than that the Holocaust never happened, nor any idea more viciously motivated. Yet the deniers' claims that the Auschwitz gas chambers could not have worked led to closer study and, in 1993, research showing, at last, how they actually did work. Thanks to prejudice and stupidity, another opening for doubt has been shut.

An enlightened and efficient intellectual regime lets a million prejudices bloom, including many that you or I may regard as hateful or grotesque. It avoids any attempt to stamp out prejudice, because stamping out prejudice really means forcing everyone to share the same prejudice, namely that of whoever is in authority. The great American philosopher Charles Sanders Peirce wrote in 1877: "When complete agreement could not otherwise be reached, a general massacre of all who have not thought in a certain way has proved a very effective means of settling opinion in a country." In speaking of "settling opinion," Peirce was writing about one of the two or three most fundamental problems that any human society must confront and solve. For most societies down through the centuries, this problem was dealt with in the manner he described: errors were identified by the authorities—priests, politburos, dictators—or by mass opinion, and then the error-makers were eliminated along with their putative mistakes. "Let all men who reject the established belief be terrified into silence," wrote Peirce, describing this system. "This method has, from the earliest times, been one of the chief means of upholding correct theological and political doctrines."

9   Intellectual pluralism substitutes a radically different doctrine: we kill our mistakes rather than each other. Here I draw on another great philosopher, the late Karl Popper, who pointed out that the critical method of science "consists in letting our hypotheses die in our stead." Those who are in error are not (or are not supposed to be) banished or excommunicated or forced to sign a renunciation or required to submit to "rehabilitation" or sent for psychological counseling. It is the error we punish, not the errant. By letting people make errors—even mischievous, spiteful errors (as, for instance, Galileo's insistence on Copernicanism was taken to be in 1633)—pluralism creates room to challenge orthodoxy, think imaginatively, experiment boldly. Brilliance and bigotry are empowered in the same stroke.

10   Pluralism is the principle that protects and makes a place in human company for that loneliest and most vulnerable of all minorities, the minority who is hounded and despised among blacks and whites, gays and straights, who is suspect or criminal among every tribe and in every nation of the world, and yet on whom progress depends: the dissident. I am not saying that dissent is always or even usually enlightened. Most of the time it is foolish and self-serving. No dissident has the right to be taken seriously, and the fact that Aryan Nation racists or Nation of Islam anti-Semites are unorthodox does not entitle them to respect. But what goes around comes around. As a supporter of gay marriage, for example, I reject the majority's view of family, and as a Jew I reject its view of God. I try to be civil, but the fact is that most Americans regard my views on marriage as a reckless assault on the most fundamental of all institutions, and many people are more than a little discomfited by the statement "Jesus Christ was no more divine than anybody else" (which is why so few people ever say it). Trap the racists and anti-Semites, and you lay a trap for me too. Hunt for them with eradication in your mind, and you have brought dissent itself within your sights.

11   The new crusade against prejudice waves aside such warnings. Like earlier crusades against antisocial ideas, the mission is fueled by good (if cocksure) intentions and a genuine sense of urgency. Some kinds of errors are held to be intolerable, like pollutants that even in small traces poison the water for a whole town. Some errors are so pernicious as to damage real people's lives, so wrongheaded that no person of right mind or goodwill could support them. Like their forebears of other stripe—the Church in its campaigns against heretics, the McCarthyites in their campaigns against Communists

—the modern anti-racist and anti-sexist and anti-homophobic campaigners are totalists, demanding not that misguided ideas and ugly expressions be corrected or criticized but that they be eradicated. They make war not on errors but on error, and like other totalists they act in the name of public safety—the safety, especially, of minorities.

The sweeping implications of this challenge to pluralism are not, I think, well enough understood by the public at large. Indeed, the new brand of totalism has yet even to be properly named. "Multiculturalism," for instance, is much too broad. "Political correctness" comes closer but is too trendy and snide. For lack of anything else, I will call the new anti-pluralism "purism," since its major tenet is that society cannot be just until the last traces of invidious prejudice have been scrubbed away. Whatever you call it, the purists' way of seeing things has spread though American intellectual life with remarkable speed, so much so that many people will blink at you uncomprehendingly or even call you a racist (or sexist or homophobe, etc.) if you suggest that expressions of racism should be tolerated or that prejudice has its part to play. 12

The new purism sets out, to begin with, on a campaign against words, for words are the currency of prejudice, and if prejudice is hurtful then so must be prejudiced words. "We are not safe when these violent words are among us," wrote Mari Matsuda, then a UCLA law professor. Here one imagines gangs of racist words swinging chains and smashing heads in back alleys. To suppress bigoted language seems, at first blush, reasonable, but it quickly leads to a curious result. A peculiar kind of verbal shamanism takes root, as though certain expressions, like curses or magical incantations, carry in themselves the power to hurt or heal—as though words were bigoted rather than people. "Context is everything," people have always said. The use of the word "nigger" in *Huckleberry Finn* does not make the book an "act" of hate speech—or does it? In the new view, this is no longer so clear. The very utterance of the word "nigger" (at least by a non-black) is a racist act. When a *Sacramento Bee* cartoonist put the word "nigger" mockingly in the mouth of a white supremacist, there were howls of protest and 1,400 canceled subscriptions and an editorial apology, even though the word was plainly being invoked against racists, not against blacks. 13

Faced with escalating demands of verbal absolutism, newspapers issue lists of forbidden words. The expressions "gyp" (derived from "Gypsy") and "Dutch treat" were among the dozens of terms stricken as "offensive" in a much-ridiculed (and later withdrawn) *Los Angeles Times* speech code. The University of Missouri journalism school issued a *Dictionary of Cautionary Words and Phrases*, which included "*Buxom*: Offensive reference to a woman's 14 chest. Do not use. See 'Woman.' *Codger*: Offensive reference to a senior citizen."

15   As was bound to happen, purists soon discovered that chasing around after words like "gyp" or "buxom" hardly goes to the roots of the problem. As long as they remain bigoted, bigots will simply find other words. If they can't call you a kike then they will say Jewboy, Judas, or Hebe, and when all those are banned they will press words like "oven" and "lampshade" into their service. The vocabulary of hate is potentially as rich as your dictionary, and all you do by banning language used by cretins is to let them decide what the rest of us may say. The problem, some purists have concluded, must therefore go much deeper than laws: it must go to the deeper level of ideas. Racism, sexism, homophobia, and the rest must be built into the very structure of American society and American patterns of thought, so pervasive yet so insidious that, like water to a fish, they are both omnipresent and unseen. The mere existence of prejudice constructs a society whose very nature is prejudiced.

16   This line of thinking was pioneered by feminists, who argued that pornography, more than just being expressive, is an act by which men construct an oppressive society. Racial activists quickly picked up the argument. Racist expressions are themselves acts of oppression, they said. "All racist speech constructs the social reality that constrains the liberty of nonwhites because of their race," wrote Charles R. Lawrence III, then a law professor at Stanford. From the purist point of view, a society with even one racist is a racist society, because the idea itself threatens and demeans its targets. They cannot feel wholly safe or wholly welcome as long as racism is present. Pluralism says: There will always be some racists. Marginalize them, ignore them, exploit them, ridicule them, take pains to make their policies illegal, but otherwise leave them alone. Purists say: That's not enough. Society cannot be just until these pervasive and oppressive ideas are searched out and eradicated.

17   And so what is now under way is a growing drive to eliminate prejudice from every corner of society. I doubt that many people have noticed how far-reaching this anti-pluralist movement is becoming.

18   *In universities*: Dozens of universities have adopted codes proscribing speech or other expression that (this is from Stanford's policy, which is more or less representative) "is intended to insult or stigmatize an individual or a small number of individuals on the basis of their sex, race, color, handicap, religion, sexual orientation or national and ethnic origin." Some codes punish only persistent harassment of a targeted individual, but many, following the purist doctrine that even one racist is too many, go much further. At Penn,

an administrator declared: "We at the University of Pennsylvania have guaranteed students and the community that they can live in a community free of sexism, racism, and homophobia." Here is the purism that gives "political correctness" its distinctive combination of puffy high-mindedness and authoritarian zeal.

In school curricula: "More fundamental than eliminating racial   19 segregation has to be the removal of racist thinking, assumptions, symbols, and materials in the curriculum," writes theorist Molefi Kete Asante. In practice, the effort to "remove racist thinking" goes well beyond striking egregious references from textbooks. In many cases it becomes a kind of mental engineering in which students are encouraged to see prejudice everywhere; it includes teaching identity politics as an antidote to internalized racism; it rejects mainstream science as "white male" thinking; and it tampers with history, installing such dubious notions as that the ancient Greeks stole their culture from Africa or that an ancient carving of a bird is an example of "African experimental aeronautics."

In criminal law: Consider two crimes. In each, I am beaten bru-   20 tally; in each, my jaw is smashed and my skull is split in just the same way. However, in the first crime my assailant calls me an "asshole"; in the second he calls me a "queer." In most states, in many localities, and, as of September 1994, in federal cases, these two crimes are treated differently: the crime motivated by bias — or deemed to be so motivated by prosecutors and juries—gets a stiffer punishment. "Longer prison terms for bigots," shrilled Brooklyn Democratic Congressman Charles Schumer, who introduced the federal hate-crimes legislation, and those are what the law now provides. Evidence that the assailant holds prejudiced beliefs, even if he doesn't actually express them while committing an offense, can serve to elevate the crime. Defendants in hate-crimes cases may be grilled on how many black friends they have and whether they have told racist jokes. To increase a prison sentence only because of the defendant's "prejudice" (as gauged by prosecutor and jury) is, of course, to try minds and punish beliefs. Purists say, Well, they are dangerous minds and poisonous beliefs.

In the workplace: Though government cannot constitutionally   21 suppress bigotry directly, it is now busy doing so indirectly by requiring employers to eliminate prejudice. Since the early 1980s, courts and the Equal Employment Opportunity Commission have moved to bar workplace speech deemed to create a hostile or abusive working environment for minorities. The law, held a federal court in 1988, "does require that an employer take prompt action to prevent . . . bigots from expressing their opinions in a way that abuses or offends their co-workers," so as to achieve "the goal of eliminating prejudices and biases from our society." So it was, as

UCLA law professor Eugene Volokh notes, that the EEOC charged that a manufacturer's ads using admittedly accurate depictions of samurai, kabuki, and sumo were "racist" and "offensive to people of Japanese origin"; that a Pennsylvania court found that an employer's printing Bible verses on paychecks was religious harassment of Jewish employees; that an employer had to desist from using gender-based job titles like "foreman" and "draftsman" after a female employee sued.

22   On and on the campaign goes, darting from one outbreak of prejudice to another like a cat chasing flies. In the American Bar Association, activists demand that lawyers who express "bias or prejudice" be penalized. In the Education Department, the civil-rights office presses for a ban on computer bulletin board comments that "show hostility toward a person or group based on sex, race or color, including slurs, negative stereotypes, jokes or pranks." In its security checks for government jobs, the FBI takes to asking whether applicants are "free of biases against any class of citizens," whether, for instance, they have told racist jokes or indicated other "prejudices." Joke police! George Orwell, grasping the close relationship of jokes to dissent, said that every joke is a tiny revolution. The purists will have no such rebellions.

23   The purist campaign reaches, in the end, into the mind itself. In a lecture at the University of New Hampshire, a professor compared writing to sex ("You and the subject become one"); he was suspended and required to apologize, but what was most insidious was the order to undergo university-approved counseling to have his mind straightened out. At the University of Pennsylvania, a law lecturer said, "We have ex-slaves here who should know about the Thirteenth Amendment"; he was banished from campus for a year and required to make a public apology, and he, too, was compelled to attend a "sensitivity and racial awareness" session. Mandatory re-education of alleged bigots is the natural consequence of intellectual purism. Prejudice must be eliminated!

24   Ah, but the task of scouring minds clean is Augean. "Nobody escapes," said a Rutgers University report on campus prejudice. Bias and prejudice, it found, cross every conceivable line, from sex to race to politics: "No matter who you are, no matter what the color of your skin, no matter what your gender or sexual orientation, no matter what you believe, no matter how you behave, there is somebody out there who doesn't like people of your kind." Charles Lawrence writes: "Racism is ubiquitous. We are all racists." If he means that most of us think racist thoughts of some sort at one time or another, he is right. If we are going to "eliminate prejudices and biases from our society," then the work of the prejudice police is unending. They are doomed to hunt and hunt and hunt, scour and scour and scour.

What is especially dismaying is that the purists pursue preju- 25
dice in the name of protecting minorities. In order to protect people
like me (homosexual), they must pursue people like me (dissident).
In order to bolster minority self-esteem, they suppress minority
opinion. There are, of course, all kinds of practical and legal problems with the purists' campaign: the incursions against the First
Amendment; the inevitable abuses by prosecutors and activists who
define as "hateful" or "violent" whatever speech they dislike or can
score points off of; the lack of any evidence that repressing prejudice
eliminates rather than inflames it. But minorities, of all people,
ought to remember that by definition we cannot prevail by numbers, and we generally cannot prevail by force. Against the power of
ignorant mass opinion and group prejudice and superstition, we
have only our voices. If you doubt that minorities' voices are powerful weapons, think of the lengths to which Southern officials went to
silence the Reverend Martin Luther King Jr. (recall that the city commissioner of Montgomery, Alabama, won a $500,000 libel suit, later
overturned in *New York Times v. Sullivan* [1964], regarding an advertisement in the *Times* placed by civil-rights leaders who denounced
the Montgomery police). Think of how much gay people have
improved their lot over twenty-five years simply by refusing to
remain silent. Recall the Michigan student who was prosecuted for
saying that homosexuality is a treatable disease, and notice that he
was black. Under that Michigan speech code, more than twenty
blacks were charged with racist speech, while no instance of racist
speech by whites was punished. In Florida, the hate-speech law was
invoked against a black man who called a policeman a "white
cracker"; not so surprisingly, in the first hate-crimes case to reach the
Supreme Court, the victim was white and the defendant black.

In the escalating war against "prejudice," the right is already 26
learning to play by the rules that were pioneered by the purist
activists of the left. Last year leading Democrats, including the
President, criticized the Republican Party for being increasingly in
the thrall of the Christian right. Some of the rhetoric was harsh
("fire-breathing Christian radical right"), but it wasn't vicious or
even clearly wrong. Never mind: when Democratic Representative
Vic Fazio said Republicans were "being forced to the fringes by the
aggressive political tactics of the religious right," the chairman of
the Republican National Committee, Haley Barbour, said, "Christian-bashing" was "the left's preferred form of religious bigotry."
Bigotry! Prejudice! "Christians active in politics are now on the
receiving end of an extraordinary campaign of bias and prejudice,"
said the conservative leader William J. Bennett. One discerns, here,
where the new purism leads. Eventually, any criticism of any group
will be "prejudice."

27   Here is the ultimate irony of the new purism: words, which pluralists hope can be substituted for violence, are redefined by purists *as* violence. "The experience of being called 'nigger,' 'spic,' 'Jap,' or 'kike' is like receiving a slap in the face," Charles Lawrence wrote in 1990. "Psychic injury is no less an injury than being struck in the face, and it often is far more severe." This kind of talk is commonplace today. Epithets, insults, often even polite expressions of what's taken to be prejudice are called by purists "assaultive speech," "words that wound," "verbal violence." "To me, racial epithets are not speech," one University of Michigan law professor said. "They are bullets." In her speech accepting the 1993 Nobel Prize for Literature in Stockholm, Sweden, the author Toni Morrison said this: "Oppressive language does more than represent violence; it is violence."

28   It is not violence. I am thinking back to a moment on the subway in Washington, a little thing. I was riding home late one night and a squad of noisy kids, maybe seventeen or eighteen years old, noisily piled into the car. They yelled across the car and a girl said, "Where do we get off?"

29   A boy said, "Farragut North."

30   The girl: "*Faggot* North!"

31   The boy: "Yeah! Faggot North!"

32   General hilarity.

33   First, before the intellect resumes control, there is a moment of fear, an animal moment. Who are they? How many of them? How dangerous? Where is the way out? All of these things are noted preverbally and assessed by the gut. Then the brain begins an assessment: they are sober, this is probably too public a place for them to do it, there are more girls than boys, they were just talking, it is probably nothing.

34   They didn't notice me and there was no incident. The teenage babble flowed on, leaving me to think. I became interested in my own reaction: the jump of fear out of nowhere like an alert animal, the sense for a brief time that one is naked and alone and should hide or run away. For a time, one ceases to be a human being and becomes instead a faggot.

35   The fear engendered by these words is real. The remedy is as clear and as imperfect as ever: protect citizens against violence. This, I grant, is something that American society has never done very well and now does quite poorly. It is no solution to define words as violence or prejudice as oppression, and then by cracking down on words or thoughts pretend that we are doing something about violence and oppression. No doubt it is easier to pass a speech code or hate-crimes law and proclaim the streets safer than actually to make the streets safer, but the one must never be confused with the other.

Every cop or prosecutor chasing words is one fewer chasing criminals. In a world rife with real violence and oppression, full of Rwandas and Bosnias and eleven-year-olds spraying bullets at children in Chicago and in turn being executed by gang lords, it is odious of Toni Morrison to say that words are violence.

Indeed, equating "verbal violence" with physical violence is a treacherous, mischievous business. Not long ago a writer was charged with viciously and gratuitously wounding the feelings and dignity of millions of people. He was charged, in effect, with exhibiting flagrant prejudice against Muslims and outrageously slandering their beliefs. "What is freedom of expression?" mused Salman Rushdie a year after the ayatollahs sentenced him to death and put a price on his head. "Without the freedom to offend, it ceases to exist." I can think of nothing sadder than that minority activists, in their haste to make the world better, should be the ones to forget the lesson of Rushdie's plight: for minorities, pluralism, not purism, is the answer. The campaigns to eradicate prejudice—all of them, the speech codes and workplace restrictions and mandatory therapy for accused bigots and all the rest—should stop, now. The whole objective of eradicating prejudice, as opposed to correcting and criticizing it, should be repudiated as a fool's errand. Salman Rushdie is right, Toni Morrison wrong, and minorities belong at his side, not hers.

36

Vocabulary

a. *paragraph 1:* bipartisan
b. *paragraph 2:* homophobia
c. *paragraph 6:* icon, manifest, animus
d. *paragraph 8:* putative
e. *paragraph 11:* pernicious
f. *paragraph 13:* shamanism
g. *paragraph 15:* insidious
h. *paragraph 19:* egregious
i. *paragraph 24:* Augean, ubiquitous
j. *paragraph 26:* thrall
k. *paragraph 27:* epithets

Questions

1. What is Rauch's unifying idea? What makes the essay more than a collection of examples?
2. How does Rauch's view of human nature determine his thesis and the development of his argument?
3. Why in paragraphs 6 through 9 does Rauch introduce ideas from science and philosophy? How do they help him undermine the ideal of objectivity?

4. How does he use personal experience to argue for the rights of dissenters?
5. How does Rauch handle the apparent contradiction at the heart of his argument—namely, that a pluralistic society must safeguard the rights of those opposed to pluralism?

Writing Assignments

1. Rauch argues that racists can be controlled if we "marginalize them, ignore them, exploit them, ridicule them, take pains to make their policies illegal, but otherwise leave them alone." This assumes that justice will always triumph in a pluralistic society. Can you think of any examples from history that argue against this assumption?
2. "Sticks and stones may break your bones, but names will never hurt you." Explore the implications of the idea expressed in this nursery rhyme with reference to your own experience.

Beginnings, Middles, and Endings

To make your ideas convincing, you need to capture the attention of your readers and hold it. You will lose their attention if, in beginning the essay, you describe in too much detail how you intend to proceed. Usually you need to indicate a point of view and briefly suggest how you will develop the essay. The following is an ineffective way of doing so:

> I am going to describe how we played bare-handed softball when I was young. I will illustrate with one particular event.

Compare these sentences with the following paragraph from Harry Bruce's essay "The Softball Was Always Hard." Bruce states his subject and suggests how he will develop his essay without directly stating his purpose:

> When I tell young softball players I played the game bare-handed, they regard me warily. Am I one of those geezers who's forever jawing about the fact that, in his day, you had to walk through six miles of snowdrifts just to get to school? Will I tediously lament the passing of the standing broad jump, and the glorious old days when the only football in the Maritimes was English rugger, and when hockey was an outdoor art rather than indoor mayhem, and, at decent yacht clubs, men were gentlemen and women were *personae non grata*? No, but I will tell today's softball players that—with their fancy uniforms, batters' helmets, dugouts, manicured diamonds, guys to announce who's at bat over public-address systems and, above all, gloves for every fielder—the game they play is more tarted-up and sissy than the one I knew.

If you need to state your purpose and outline the discussion to follow, you can do so with a minimum of personal reference and without sounding stuffy. Here is a paragraph that both states the purpose of the author and outlines the book introduced by the paragraph:

> The aim of this book is to delineate two types of clever schoolboy: the converger and the diverger. The earlier chapters offer a fairly detailed description of the intellectual abilities, attitudes, and personalities of a few hundred such boys. In the last chapters, this description is then used as a basis for a more speculative discussion—of the nature of intelligence and originality and of the ways in which intellectual and personal qualities interact. Although the first half of the book rests heavily on the results of psychological tests, and the last two chapters involve psychoanalytic theory, I have done my best to be intelligible, and, wherever possible, interesting to everyone interested in clever schoolboys: parents, schoolteachers, dons, psychologists, administrators, clever schoolboys. (Liam Hudson, *Contrary Imaginations*)

This author directly engages the interest of his reader. The bonus, this introductory paragraph promises, will be the wit of the author, evident in the humorous discussion of a seemingly dry subject.

By contrast, the author of the following paragraph eases his readers into the subject without an immediate statement of purpose. But he does make an immediate appeal to an important concern of the reader—the problem of how to deal with personal failures and those of friends and family members:

> The administration of criminal justice and the extent of individual moral responsibility are among the crucial problems of a civilized society. They are indissolubly linked, and together they involve our deepest emotions. We often find it hard to forgive ourselves for our own moral failures. All of us, at some time or other, have faced the painful dilemma of when to punish and when to forgive those we love—our children, our friends. How much harder it is, then, to deal with the stranger who transgresses. (David L. Bazelon, "The Awesome Decision")

Notice that personal references are not out of place in an opening paragraph—or anywhere else in an essay. The risk of such references is that they can divert the reader from the subject of the essay to the author. For this reason they should be kept to a minimum.

Transitions

In the middle, or body, of paragraphs and essays, transitional words and phrases help us to connect ideas and details. We especially need them when we change the subject or course of discussion, as in the following passage:

> For the main chemical action is to get energy for the muscles by burning sugar there; but three-quarters of that is lost as heat. And there is *another* limit, on the runner and the gazelle equally, which is *more* severe. At this speed, the chemical burn-up in the muscles is too fast to be complete. The waste products of incomplete burning, chiefly lactic acid, now foul up the blood. (Jacob Bronowski, "The Athlete and the Gazelle"; italics added)

The transitional words *another* and *more* show the course of the writer's thinking in the sentence: *another* tells us he is adding a detail to intensify his explanation of why muscles tire; *more* shows he is about to compare the effect of lactic acid on the muscles' functioning with the inefficiency of the chemical action in the muscles.

Words like *after* and *since* express relationships of time; words like *above* and *below* express relationships of space. Here are some important transitions that show the relationship of ideas:

- qualification: *however, nevertheless, nonetheless*
- illustration and explanation: *for example, so, thus*
- comparison: *similarly, in the same way, by comparison, likewise*
- contrast: *by contrast, on the one hand, on the other hand*
- consequence: *thus, as a result, consequently, therefore*
- concession: *admittedly, nevertheless, however*
- amplification: *moreover, furthermore, also, in addition, indeed*
- summation: *in conclusion, to sum up, all in all, finally*

Punctuation also shows us how ideas are related. A colon tells us that an expansion, explanation, or illustration follows; a semicolon tells us that the ideas joined are closely related or of the same importance.

The opening paragraphs build the expectations of the reader. The body of the essay sustains the reader's interest. An effective ending will not let the discussion drop: the reader should not finish the essay with a sense of loose ends, of lines of thought left uncompleted. In the formal essay, the ending may restate the thesis or perhaps even state it for the first time — if you build to the thesis through explanation and details. One of the most effective conclusions, the reference back to ideas that opened the essay, gives the reader a sense of completion.

> I have my own cabin on that shore now, and though most of those farmyard ballplayers of thirty-seven summers ago have moved away I still see one of them occasionally. He's a mere forty-six, and I like him now as I liked him then.

Sometimes I walk along the gravel beach to a patch of grass, from which a footpath once led to a general store. The Ball-maker's shack is gone, but gray planks and ribs and rusty boat nails still endure the lashing of the salt wind that ceaselessly sweeps the bay. They're all that's left of his schooner. Wrecked by time, like bare-handed softball. (Harry Bruce, "The Softball Was Always Hard")

JOHN POSTGATE

John Postgate is Emeritus Professor of Microbiology at the University of Sussex. In the following essay, he draws on his knowledge of science to argue that it has been unfairly blamed for the horrors of our century. Proper credit for those, he insists, goes to religious fanatics of various persuasions.

Religion: Are We Better Off without It?

JOHN POSTGATE

1   Why is it that a society that has reaped such enormous benefits from science should have developed such a widespread suspicion and dislike of it?

2   Consider, for example, the following from a columnist in the *The Oldie* magazine. "Modern science has become a lucrative, prestigious racket, maintaining its hold over us by force and propaganda. . . . It is expensive, dirty and dangerous. It is eating up the world's resources, spreading filth over its surface and creating ever more lethal devices. . . . Despite the billions that have been lavished on medical research, there has been . . . no significant reduction in deaths from cancer and heart disease."

3   This shows all the petulant silliness that has informed much recent anti-science writing, and reflects a widespread outlook, which almost always includes a Christian or Islamic bias. Why has the old dispute between religion and science resurfaced in so crude a form?

4   The reason, I suggest, is that science has come to occupy the high ground of morality, which has prompted bizarre attacks against it. Moral superiority may seem an odd defence against accusations that science is responsible for almost all of the environmental and social

problems of the modern world, but the effect of science is not the central issue. It is an old truth that science is neutral, that its applications are as good, or as evil, as people make them.

Some recent attacks on science have been more subtle. It has been argued that the neutrality of science means that it is dehumanising. Being neutral, it imposes no spiritual or moral value. It denies the existence of God and rejects any transcendental purpose to justify our existence. It belittles mankind's status in the universe, and threatens a reductionist, materialist interpretation of our thinking and being; it dismisses the possibility of rewards and retribution in an after-life, and enjoins no imperatives towards goodness, kindness, altruism, or even considerate behaviour towards one's fellows. In short, it is amoral as well as inhuman.

I will not rehearse the counter-arguments, that science is as spiritually rewarding as a religious experience. Arguments about spirituality are sterile, but those about morality are not. And science is far from being amoral; it imposes a stern, austere morality on its practitioners, one which pervades their lives and results from the fundamental nature of science.

Science is a continual linking together of observations and experiences, codified as self-consistent logical structures (catalogues, hypotheses and theories) into what we call knowledge. It requires a particular way of thinking about the world, which we call reasoning.

This is not to say that scientific inspiration is necessarily rational; often it is not. But before an observation or concept becomes part of the logical structures of science, it must be seen to be rational when dovetailed into the existing body of knowledge.

Those structures are constantly open to challenge and modification, which is the crucial difference between science and religion. There are no dogmas, no absolute certainties, in science; what are thought and spoken of as scientific truths are simply probabilities so high that we can treat them as if they were certainties. Science approaches ever closer to the truth, but never gets there. So for a scientist there is no absolute truth.

Why, then, does anyone bother to seek knowledge? For the same reasons that a baby or a puppy explores the world around it; there is no other way. The more we understand our surroundings and can foresee opportunities and events, the safer and happier we feel. This search for what we call scientific truth imposes its own morality of honesty, co-operation and sharing.

These virtues are imposed not by priests or mystical authority, but by utterly practical considerations. You do not, as a scientist, advance knowledge or your own reputation if you are guilty of deception, or self-deception; nor if you disregard unwelcome or inconsistent evidence, nor yet if you conceal rather than share data.

12   Why? Because deception, plagiarism and falsification of evidence will be found out, usually very soon; self-deception will engender contempt; concealment, such as failure to publish, will be self-defeating through loss of scientific credit; but above all such behaviour will delay scientific progress.

13   Of course, there are scientific cheats and fraudsters, but they are happily rare. The most common transgression today is probably concealment. It happens for reasons ranging from industrial or military secrecy to gaining an advantage in a race for publication. It rarely amounts to more than a delay in announcing one's findings, and it is always shaming. Fudging results to support a point of view is probably the next most common transgression, but it is rare because every scientist knows it is ultimately pointless.

14   Of course, scientific communities have their share of jealousy, greed, prejudice and envy, but all scientists know that in the end progress depends on openness and the sharing of data. Opinions and convictions may be held as strongly as in any walk of life, but a window of open-mindedness and self-criticism is essential.

15   This becomes a general outlook which can make scientists exasperating to live with; it is also the reason why so few scientists are to be found in politics, or hold religious beliefs. Those scientists who are religious have to think in compartments, closing down for religious thought the critical faculties that they would use for scientific work.

16   Yet in spite of the strong moral foundation of science and the material progress which it has delivered, scientists must be careful not to underestimate the benefits of the world's religions. They have given purpose, morality and social coherence to people's lives. They have nurtured art, learning and literature and, in earlier times, produced the substantial technical and material benefits which stemmed from religious architecture and land use.

17   So if one counts up the benefits of science and religion, the score is roughly equal. But the world's religions have also brought the horrors of human sacrifice, crusades, pogroms and inquisitions. In the modern world this darker side of religion has become dangerous. For unlike science, religion is not neutral; it tells people what to do. And one of the things it tells them is, "Kill the infidel."

18   Just consider, for example, Ulster, Yugoslavia, Israel, Iran, Iraq, Sudan, Kashmir, Armenia and Azerbaijan today; observe Protestant, Catholic, Serbian and Russian Orthodox Christians, Jews, Shia and Suni Moslems, Hindus, Sikhs, and minor sects, in their tens and hundreds of thousands, murdering each other, often in revoltingly medieval ways. All in the name of their god or gods.

19   It is sometimes claimed that the conflicts are not religious but ethnic, tribal, nationalist or political. A few surely are—especially in Africa, for example, where genuine tribalism persists—but try asking

those who are sniping and shelling in Bosnia, shouting slogans in Tehran and Baghdad, sacking temples in Kashmir, shooting tourists in Egypt, planting bombs in British shopping malls.

Some say that these fundamentalist killers are deviants, distorting the true teachings of their religion and perverting its morality; that these modern-day holy wars are a negative fall-out of religion, analogous to the pollution, environmental damage and unethical experiments which disfigure the applications of science. 20

There is something in this, but it does not stand up to close examination. Most religions do indeed forbid killing; a few of the belligerents are mindless thugs, sadistically disobeying this injunction; but most such fighters are ordinary people, following a religious imperative. They find support from their myths and texts, among their priests and their silent co-religionists, because retribution is part of religion. In some devious way they are convinced that they are carrying out their god's will. 21

Therein lies the moral advantage of science. Its morality is incompatible with such imperatives: scientific principles, and logic, cannot be construed as incitement to mass killing, or even individual murder. Science has had its back-sliders: a few scientists have shown themselves capable of murder in the name of research, as happened in Nazi Germany and Japanese prison camps during the second world war. Doubtless, too, there are enthusiastic participants in the current spate of religious conflicts who, in another compartment of their minds, are moral and dedicated scientists. 22

Every walk of life has its aberrants, but can you imagine scientists, in hundreds, thousands, tens of thousands even, arming themselves and murdering, torturing and maiming their fellow beings for some scientific principle or "truth"? Many people will need religion for decades to come, probably for centuries, because science is comparatively young and the morality it imposes, by example and not precept, is still inaccessible to many people. But today religion, with its backbone of retribution, *jihad*, crusade and battle, presents a threat to mankind that is quite as serious as any of the environmental and social perils attributed to science, and much more immediate. 23

A couple of years ago, I remember a scholar of Byzantine history saying he hoped that "mankind will soon learn that religion is too important a matter to kill each other about." It took me two days to realise how tragically mistaken that thought was. I wished him to say: "If only mankind would learn that religion is too *unimportant* a matter to kill each other about." 24

Vocabulary

a. *paragraph 3:* petulant
b. *paragraph 5:* transcendental, altruism
c. *paragraph 13:* transgression
d. *paragraph 17:* pogroms
e. *paragraph 23:* aberrants, *jihad*

Questions

1. Why does Postgate begin with a question? How does it determine the organization of what follows?
2. Why does he establish an opposition between science and religion?
3. How do paragraphs 10, 12, and 16 provide transitions in the middle of the essay?
4. How is his conclusion in paragraph 24 introduced and justified?

Writing Assignments

1. Do you believe that science enjoys the moral ascendancy that Postgate attributes to it?
2. Compare Postgate's view of science with the one expressed in Jonathan Rauch's essay.

BARBARA EHRENREICH

In the following essay, Barbara Ehrenreich offers a humorous appraisal of gluttony, links it with fanatical exercising, and reaches some provocative conclusions about our values.

Food Worship

BARBARA EHRENREICH

1   Ethiopia reminds us that there are still people for whom food is primarily a means to biological survival. Here, to judge from the rapid conversion of real estate into takeout shops for gourmets and the sudden prominence of vegetables that begin with the letter *a*, food has come to mean much more: status, authority, entertainment, style, possibly religion. Among the up-scale, trend-setting people who are held up for our admiration in commercials for credit cards and wine coolers, food appears to be

more fascinating than either sex or trivia games. An evening on the town, which used to mean dinner and a show, now means a showy dinner, followed perhaps by a chaste gelato.

In fact, in anticipation of the time when food will have surpassed all other ingredients of high culture and when upward mobility will hinge on a mastery of puff pastry rather than a familiarity with computers or great books, I am thinking of substituting food emporiums for museums on my children's Sunday outings. Already, food has gained an equal footing with fashion and skin care in the men's magazines, driven diet books to the remainder shelves, and—as food history, food criticism, etc.—gained a foothold in academia. Those areas of artistic and intellectual endeavor that wish to survive may have to take up food themes or be content to make the same kind of accommodation to the restaurant that music has made to the piano bar.

2

As a longtime admirer of foods that outrank me in social status, I am not complaining. Thanks to the food fixation of the upwardly mobile, pita bread and salad bars have sedimented down to Burger King, suggesting that cold poached salmon may not be far behind. And I will admit to having occasionally dined—on other people's expense accounts—at establishments so tony that the dishes are reportedly rinsed in Perrier and the beef has graduated from stress-free, organic grazing environments. So it is without envy or ingratitude that I have been wondering, why food? Why food of all the obsessions—sex, astrology, real estate, tropical bird feeding—available to those in the Gold Card bracket?

3

The first explanation I have come up with is a straightforward biological one. Upscale people are fixated with food simply because they are now able to eat so much of it without getting fat, and the reason they don't get fat is that they maintain a profligate level of calorie expenditure. The very same people whose evenings begin with melted goat cheese and wind up, hours later, with raspberries cushioned on a lascivious crème à l'anglaise get up at dawn to run, break for a midmorning aerobics class, and watch the evening news while racing on a stationary bicycle.

4

This explanation assumes that past generations of dieters—the mothers and grandmothers of today's big-time eaters—left a large proportion of our contemporaries genetically imprinted with a hunger of deep and savage proportions. After having been teased for so long with grapefruit halves and celery sticks, this vast hunger quite justifiably demands plates heaping with Tex-Mex, three-course lunches and between-meal pasta primavera pick-me-ups. Paradoxically, of course, the very occupations that pay well enough to finance gastronomic intake on such a scale—corporate law, international

5

banking, cocaine retailing—involve almost zero energy expenditures in the course of a day's work. Hence the wild aerobic flailings and desperate five-mile runs required to maintain a fast-track metabolism. Exercise is the yuppie version of bulimia.

6   Not to push this theory too far, you might say that exercise is to eating in the eighties as contraception was to sex in the sixties. The pill, IUDs and eventually legalized abortion freed sex from its ancient biological consequences and helped usher in the sexual revolution. In the same way, jogging, jazzercise, and Jane Fonda's videotape have uncoupled gluttony from obesity and thus made possible what may someday be called the gastrointestinal revolution.

7   But hunger, revived hourly by workouts and runs, only explains why people eat, not what they eat. People who are merely hungry have been known to eat almost anything—bologna sandwiches, bowls of millet, unripe Brie. Something larger than hunger sends young account executives rushing out of their condos after dark to pick up an extra bottle of walnut oil or raspberry vinegar. And that can only be the drive to impress, intimidate, and inspire insecurity in one's dinner guests.

8   As a way of establishing one's own status or gauging another's, food has obvious advantages over our former cultural obsession, sex. A sexual encounter can only give you insight into your partner's personal warmth, generosity, capacity for whimsy, and so forth. But a bout of competitive eating, as it is now called, gives you fairly precise information about your dining partner's current and anticipated income, social class or origin, and probable taste in home furnishings. Does your date think sushi is still stylish? Then he has probably been passed over for promotion and squeezed out when his apartment went co-op. If, on the other hand, he goes unhesitatingly for the baby bass en croute, he may have a Harvard MBA and a flair for currency speculation, just the kind of things that should, in the world of culinary high-rollers, make you want to eat out with him more often.

9   The fact that physical exercise—at least when performed with no thought of wages or other compensation and preferably at some expense to the exerciser—is itself a high-status activity only heightens the necessity of conspicuous eating. Whereas a decade or so ago, the woman who ordered an abstemious chef's salad for lunch placed herself on a moral plane above her sister diners, today she would only be suspected of sloth. Clearly, one would have to be a dancercise dropout or a marathon reject to get by on less than two thousand calories at midday. In fact, when has anyone last seen chef's salad on a menu of any importance? Nor is it fashionable any longer to claim to require only coffee for breakfast: friends would suspect you of failing to jog to work and wonder where you even got the strength to grind the beans. Conversely, of course, anyone

who makes a point of getting about town without running shoes risks being suspected of secret abstentions from béarnaise sauce and mousse. No one stays on the fast track these days without developing the metabolic capacity of the shrew, that tiny mammal that consumes three times its weight in food each day.

I hesitate to moralize about how this upscale metabolic speed-up might look to a resident of a sub-Saharan refugee camp, for I remember all too well how I responded, as a child, to any dinnertable reference to children so unfortunate that they would feel blessed to encounter my plate of fried Spam and potatoes. (So wrap it up and send it to India then.) Yet our parents' point sunk in: we all know that there is a connection between waste in one location and simultaneous starvation in another, between the gluttony of a few and the chronic hunger of the world's many. Perhaps if we could get our minds off the next meal and the caloric residue of the last one, we might figure out what to do about it.   10

> [ ]

Vocabulary

a. *paragraph 1:* gelato
b. *paragraph 2:* emporiums, academia
c. *paragraph 4:* profligate, lascivious
d. *paragraph 5:* gastronomic, metabolism, bulimia
e. *paragraph 7:* millet
f. *paragraph 8:* gauging, sushi, culinary
g. *paragraph 9:* conspicuous, abstemious
h. *paragraph 10:* chronic

Questions

1. Why does Ehrenreich begin and end with references to Ethiopia?
2. How successfully does Ehrenreich answer the questions posed at the end of paragraph 3? To what extent do these answers structure the essay?
3. What is Ehrenreich's point when she says that "exercise is the yuppie version of bulimia"? What other use does she make of witty phrases?
4. What do you make of her proposition that there is a link between one's taste in food and social status?

Writing Assignments

1. Compose a humorous essay on a serious subject, as Ehrenreich does.
2. Describe an activity similar to food worship and proceed to draw conclusions about human behaviour.

> [ ]

WAYNE GRADY

Wayne Grady was editor of the highly respected *Penguin Book of Modern Canadian Short Stories* and the equally successful *Harrowsmith* magazine. In 1984 he won the John Glassco Translation Prize, and translating French-Canadian fiction continues to be a distinguished part of his work. In 1994 he published *The Nature of Coyotes: Voice of the Wilderness*. In the following essay on the coyote he discusses how these denizens of the natural world can tell us much about both our private and our public ecologies, and he does so in a style that is as light as it is profoundly engaging.

The Haunting Powers of God's Dog

WAYNE GRADY

1   With my finger, I smear a small dab of crunchy peanut butter on the release mechanism, then pry back the spring-loaded snap bar and set the pin into the cog. Then I place the loaded trap on the floor, tight against the cabin wall. We've been having mouse problems in the cabin. A whole colony of them seems to have moved in for the winter. Every night we hear them scrabbling at the log walls and clicking across the sink, and every morning there are mouse turds on the drainboard; claw and tooth marks in the soap. This morning I'd noticed, just after brushing my teeth, that the entire bristled end of my toothbrush was cross-hatched with tiny incisor marks.

2   When I check my trap the next morning, it is upside down and a pair of tiny white feet are sticking out from under it. I pick it up and turn it over, noting the creamy brown fur on the upper body, the delicate, almost human feet with long, thin toes and wrinkled palms like those of a newborn baby. The mouse's black eyes define beadiness—they *are* beads, like the shiny heads of tailor's pins, staring at nothing with astonished concentration. White-footed mouse, *Peromyscus leucopus*. I carry it outside by the tail and toss it into the trees. It bounces on the frozen grass as though it has no weight at all.

3   We are all victims of our own mythologies. In all the stories we tell about ourselves, human beings are the losers. I have been struck by this during the year I've spent doing research on the coyote and its place in North America. We all know coyotes kill sheep—just as

rodents carry plague, and wolves attack people. There is enough truth in each of the stories to make us believe the lies. Some coyotes kill sheep, yes, and some people rob banks.

A friend of mine tells me about Scott Gilmore, a sheep farmer just outside Tamworth, in eastern Ontario, who says that so far this year, he's lost 45 sheep to coyotes. He has only 60 ewes left, and he says he's getting out of farming. "Coyotes done me in," he told my friend. When I call him, he sounds robust, even cheerful. 4

"Did you really lose 45 sheep?" I ask him. 5

"Yes, I did," he booms. "Lambs and ewes. Actually, it's 55 now. Nobody seems to want to do anything about it, either. All those do-gooders out there trying to save coyotes, and here I am, feedin' 'em." He laughs. He doesn't sound like someone who is getting out of farming. "Are you?" I ask. 6

"Hell, no! I'm 75 years old. What else would I do?" 7

I tell him I'd like to come out to talk to him. "Good enough," he says. 8

Where do truth and myth collide? When did they part company? In 1861, Mark Twain, travelling west, saw his first coyote from the window of the train. He didn't like what he saw. "The coyote," he wrote in *Roughing It*, "is a long, slim, sick and sorry-looking skeleton with a gray wolf skin stretched over it, a tolerably bushy tail that forever sags down with a despairing expression of forsakenness and misery, a furtive and evil eye, and a long, sharp face with slightly lifted lip and exposed teeth. He has a general slinking expression all over. The coyote is a living, breathing allegory of Want." 9

Roughing It was published in 1872, the same year Yellowstone National Park was established in Wyoming "for the pleasure and enjoyment of the people." Park officials, under the impression that pleasure and enjoyment were a matter of pastoral views of elk, immediately set about ridding the park of wolves and coyotes. Biologist Adolph Murie noted sourly in 1940 that coyote and wolf eradication began as soon as hunting became so wanton as to imperil the existence of game animals. By the time Murie's book appeared, every wolf and thousands of coyotes had been trapped or poisoned, and as a result, the elk herd had declined until it was, in Murie's words, "hovering on the brink of disaster." 10

One day last summer, as I was hiking along a trail in Yellowstone, I sat down to eat my lunch on a ridge overlooking a wide valley. My foot jangled something metallic, a length of chain that ran into a crevice between two rocks. Using a stick, I dug out a pair of rusted leg-hold traps, the kind that, until 1935, government agents used to capture coyotes. I stepped on the spring bar and opened the jaws of one of the traps, and the release pin held. I poked a stick into it, and the jaws snapped shut and broke off the 11 end of the stick. There was a large "V" in the middle of the foot pad and, around it, the words "Victor, Made in the USA." I meant to turn the traps in at the ranger station in Mammoth, but I never got around to it. Now they sit on my desk, reminders of how the mechanism of myths can linger on long after the truth that set them in motion has died.

12   I check my mousetraps every morning—I put out two of them now —and every morning, I have two more mice, each looking eerily unharmed except for a deep crease across the back of the neck where the snap bar is buried. The head juts up at a natural angle, and the staring eyes and the small open mouth look as though the mouse has been caught in mid-sentence. One morning, though, one of the mice is creased across the middle of its back. It must have been licking a smear of peanut butter near the top of the trap's wooden base and inadvertently stepped on the trigger. It is no less dead than the other mouse, but the trap is several centimetres from where I set it the night before. I wonder whether the mouse struggled before it died or if its spinal cord continued to send contract-and-expand signals to its legs for a while after death. As I remove the body, something familiar in the design of the words stamped in red ink on the wood catches my attention. They are arranged around a large "V" and say "Victor. Woodstream Corp., Lititz, Pa., USA."

13   Gordon Hewitt was Canada's consulting zoologist at the end of the past century, a century that had seen the disappearance of the bison, the grey wolf, the mountain lion, the bald eagle, the osprey, and the grizzly from most of their former ranges and of the passenger pigeon and the great auk from the face of the earth. Hewitt wrote the revision to the Northwest Game Act in 1917 and published a book in 1921 called *The Conservation of the Wild Life of Canada*. The chapter "The Value of Wild Life to the Nation" begins ominously enough from the point of view of, say, deer: "One of the most serious problems of the present day is the gradually increasing cost of food, particularly meat."

14   Wildlife for Hewitt meant "game animals"—ungulates, for the most part—although he also included swans, polar bears, barrenground grizzlies, and the rare white kermode bear. His purpose was to show that "wild life" could be economically useful to the Dominion: he proposed schemes for the domestication of bison, caribou, and muskox and wrote about "the decorative value of our wild life."

15   Wolves, cougars, and coyotes had a chapter all to themselves: it was called "The Enemies of Wild Life." "Any rational system of wild-life protection," it began, "must take into account the control

of the predatory species of mammals and birds." In most Canadian provinces, predator control was accomplished by means of a bounty system: local authorities were required to pay $1 to anyone who brought in a coyote "scalp"—both ears joined by an isthmus of skin. Between 1907 and 1917 in Saskatchewan alone, this system accounted for the slaughter of 204,424 coyotes, for which municipalities paid $232,000 in bounties. Oddly enough, in Hewitt's view, the huge number of dead coyotes was proof the bounty system wasn't working. To him, so many coyotes trapped meant only that there were too many coyotes out there.

Hewitt wanted to replace bounties with something like the American system. He would divide the entire country west of Ontario into districts and put an inspector in each district to supervise a squad of full-time, salaried agents whose sole job it would be to hunt coyotes. The beauty of this system, Hewitt wrote, was that the agents would have to turn their pelts over to the Crown, and coyote pelts at the time were worth $10 to $15 on the fur market. If all the coyotes killed in Saskatchewan had been taken by federal employees and sold at the annual Hudson's Bay Company fur auction, the government would have made $3 million instead of spending $232,000 in bounties. 16

Fortunately for everyone, coyotes included, Hewitt's scheme went nowhere. Bounties continued and increased for the next 50 years. They were officially banned in Ontario in 1972, but at least three counties—Grey, Bruce, and Simcoe, the three primary sheep-farming regions—still pay hunters to kill coyotes. One Simcoe County hunter created a sensation in 1992 when he drove into Barrie with his entire winter kill of 50 coyotes in the back of his pickup truck, parked in front of City Hall, and went in to claim his bounty. Actually, they don't call it a bounty any more, because bounties are illegal. They call it "reimbursement for control of predators." As one Ministry of Natural Resources biologist told me, "I guess that's sort of like paying someone to hunt for you, which is also illegal in Ontario. But it's a big province." 17

The Navajo word for coyote means "God's dog," the ancient palindrome. When the Navajo hunted a coyote that had been preying on their sheep, they did so with great ceremony. As they trailed the coyote across the desert, they sprinkled its tracks with corn pollen, their symbol of long life and health. When they found the coyote, they apologized for having to kill it and then did so with as little violence as they could manage. Then they buried it, placing a small turquoise bead in each nostril to aid the return of God's dog to its master. 18

In native myth, the world is an imperfect place, and Coyote the Trickster was sent "to make things right." He accomplishes this in a 19 bumbly sort of way. He peoples the earth, gives names to the animals, places some clans here and others there, creates hills where there had been only water, islands where there once were turtles. He brings fire down from the mountains. But then things begin to go wrong. Coyote is greedy and curious. He steals tobacco from Crow. He steals Chickadee's magic arrows and then loses them. He stretches his penis across a river so that he can have intercourse with the Mallard Duck girl. He is indeed an allegory of Want. He is nature incarnate. To the Navajo, there is no separation between truth and myth. To the Navajo, all history is natural history.

20   For example, the Navajo word for mouse, *na'atoosi*, means "the one that sucks on things," and traditional teaching warns against contact with mice. They must be kept out of houses and away from food, and clothing touched by a mouse must be burned. According to Ben Muneta, a Navajo doctor in New Mexico, mice were thought to be the bearers of disease, which is spread through their droppings and saliva. In a closed room, Navajo legend says, the power of the mouse would take over and destroy you if it got in your eyes or nose or mouth.

21   I am reading this in a magazine article about a new illness called Four Corners disease that was first diagnosed in a Navajo community in the American Southwest in 1993. The disease, which killed 25 people in two months, is caused by a previously unknown species of hantavirus. It takes the form of haemorrhagic fever—first you feel as if you're getting the flu, then your lungs fill up with blood, then you die. There are 200 known species of hantaviruses, all carried by rodents. The rodent carrying the Four Corners virus was the deer mouse—*Peromyscus maniculatus*. There had been a population explosion of deer mice in the past year, partly, the article points out, because a wet summer had produced bumper crops of seeds and berries. But I also knew there had been a massive coyote-eradication program throughout the Southwest. In 1992, government agents there had killed nearly 100,000 coyotes and 100,000 coyotes could have eaten one hell of a lot of deer mice.

22   A few hours after reading the article, sitting in the cabin, I begin to feel the flu coming on. My head aches, there is a pinched feeling in my sinuses, and when I stand up, I feel dizzy. I remember my toothbrush, which must have been coated with mouse saliva, and the dried mouse droppings in the cupboard. My forehead feels hot. Pulling on my coat, I stumble outside to fill my lungs with fresh air, and after a while, my pulse rate goes back down and I feel better.

23   I also feel foolish. But this night, when I set my two traps against the cabin wall, I wear gloves.

We are accustomed to thinking of myths as lies. That allowing coy- 24
otes to run with deer herds will improve the health of the herd, we
say, is a myth, by which we mean it is not true. At the same time, we
know that myths are the foundation stories of our culture. They are
the basis of our beliefs. That humans have dominion over the creatures of the earth is, we believe, true. What happens to a society
when it knows that everything it believes to be true is based on a lie?

We declare war on ourselves. In the legends of the Navajo and 25
the Okanagan and the Blackfoot and the Nez Percé, when Coyote is
killed, he is always brought back to life. In our world, coyotes also
keep coming back. Although millions of coyotes have been killed
by ranchers, sheep farmers, and federal agents over the past century and a half, there are more of them now than ever. Their range,
once confined to the flat, arid grasslands of the Great Plains, now
extends south to the Panama Canal, north to Alaska, west to Vancouver, and east to Nova Scotia. When coyotes become victims of
our myths, they just go over the hill and have more coyotes.

When we become victims, even of our own mythologies, we 26
seek our own forms of revenge. After World War I, we threw
cyanide canisters into coyote dens, as if the dens were bunkers.
We've run them down with snowmobiles until their hearts burst.
We've sawed off their lower jaws and then let them go so that they
would starve to death. We've wrapped them in burlap bags soaked
in gasoline, set torches to them, and turned them loose in the
desert. After World War II, we used new poisons. Compound 1080,
which works on the central nervous system, causes its victims to
age and die within a few hours. Coyotes have been found lying on
their sides, slavering, their legs running at full gallop.

One story I heard has the quality of myth. A sheep rancher in 27
Arizona caught a coyote, tied a stick of dynamite to its side, lit the
dynamite, and let the coyote run off into the desert, hoping it
would enter its den and blow up its own pups. Instead, Coyote ran
straight under the rancher's brand-new pickup truck.

At Scott Gilmore's farm, the side road veers sharply to the right. 28
There is a small garage near the road, then a short lane to the white
frame house, and beyond that, the barns. In the yard beside the
house, a black and white Border collie is gnawing busily on something and doesn't look up when I pass. The whole yard is strewn
with bones, fresh sheep bones, some with flesh attached. Two of the
skulls still have teeth in them and something in the eye sockets I
don't want to look at. Two glistening spinal columns lie in an explosion of white wool and blood, as though someone has just broken
open a David Cronenberg pillow.

29   "The dog drags them up here," Gilmore says. He is standing in the doorway behind a screen door. "Yesterday, she came back with a deer femur, don't know where the hell she got that." He opens the door and steps out onto the porch, a big man: big hands, big face, big neck, barrel chest, and cavernous voice. He doesn't look anywhere near 75.

30   We go through the door into the dining room, a small wallpapered room nearly taken up by a huge pedestalled table and six chairs. He starts talking about coyotes, except he doesn't call them coyotes, he calls them wolves. One of the myths coyotes suffer from is that they are really small wolves. Brush wolves. They aren't. They have their own DNA. They are older than wolves.

31   "Three years ago," he says, "I began losing lambs to wolves early in the spring, and I tried to get the township to do something about it. I asked that they arrange to send a Natural Resources trapper in before the real damage started. Well, two months went by, and I lost eight more lambs, so I contacted the local MPP, that was on a Thursday afternoon, and he immediately called the Natural Resources offices in Tweed, and on Friday morning, the township clerk called me to tell me the trapper would be here the following Tuesday. That trapper came and got 22 wolves off my land."

32   "How do you mean, 'got'?" I asked him.

33   "Trapped," says Gilmore. "Killed. And I never lost another lamb after that. So this year when it started up again, I just wrote straight to the Minister of Natural Resources. That was in June, and a letter came from his office saying he'd get back to me at his earliest convenience. It hasn't come yet, and I've lost 55 sheep that I know of and probably more that I don't know of."

34   "What about compensation?" I ask. "Have you applied for that?"

35   "Oh, I put my application in to the township," he says. "I've been paid for maybe 32 lambs out of the 55 I've lost—the ones the wolves pick up and carry away, you've got no evidence, you see— so it leaves me without much income from my sheep. I've slaughtered only 12 lambs this year. But the $3,000 the township's paid me in compensation, well, they could've trapped out every wolf in the township for that."

36   "Have you tried trapping them out yourself?" I ask.

37   "Well, it seems to me that that's not my job, is it. There was a fella from Napanee came out one day, asked me if he could set some traps. I said go ahead. He set out four or five traps, came back the next day, and he'd caught my dog and one of the neighbour's cats. You have to know what you're doing to catch a wolf."

38   The dog is still in the yard when I leave, still gnawing on what is left of two or three sheep. I'm trying to separate the truth from the myths in what Gilmore has told me. I stop, meaning to ask him what

it's like to be a sheep farmer with a dog that has developed such an obvious taste for mutton, but when I turn around, the door is closed.

It's dark when I get back to the cabin. There are no mice in the traps because this morning I decided not to set them. It wasn't a huge decision; I'd just lost the taste for it. Maybe tomorrow, I'll try to find where they get in and nail a tin-can lid over the hole. I light two kerosene lamps, put the kettle on the stove for tea, and step back outside to look at the stars. 39

The sound comes from the other side of a granite ridge that cuts across the south end of the muskrat swamp, just under Orion. Coyotes, howling. It isn't so much a howling as an ululation, a talking in tongues; it rises and falls, weaves and curls, seems to hover at the edge of speech, and it brings my eyes down from the stars with a snap. Coyotes, howling. 40

As I stand here in the dark, trying to fix the sound in my memory, there comes the whistle of a train filtering through the trees, and I think, Yes, that's it exactly. Coyote howls and train whistles are not so much single sounds as braids of sound, one chord made up of a whole range of notes. Coyotes and trains both speak to us of somewhere else, some distant place where we are not and may never be. Some mythical place. They convey an intelligence, a sense of longing and regret, a wistfulness, as if they know they are the voice of the unattainable. They leave us standing in the frozen woods with our ears straining and our hearts burdened with an undefinable feeling of loss. And not their loss, either, but ours. 41

Vocabulary

a. *paragraph 9:* furtive, allegory
b. *paragraph 10:* pastoral, wanton, imperil
c. *paragraph 12:* inadvertently
d. *paragraph 13:* zoologist, ominously
e. *paragraph 14:* ungulates
f. *paragraph 15:* isthmus
g. *paragraph 17:* reimbursement
h. *paragraph 19:* incarnate
i. *paragraph 21:* haemorrhagic
j. *paragraph 30:* pedestalled
k. *paragraph 40:* ululation

Questions

1. How important to Grady's essay is the first-person point of view?
2. How does the opening description of baiting the mousetrap relate to Grady's subject?

3. What use does Grady make of native myth? How do these stories influence your own view of his subject?

4. How appropriate is the shift in tone at the end of the essay? What purpose does Grady's lyrical flight serve?

5. What exactly are Grady's feelings about how we treat wild animals? Does he state them for us or instead imply them in the essay?

Writing Assignments

1. Write a characterization of Wayne Grady on the basis of what he reveals about himself in this essay. Consider what he chooses to emphasize as well as his selection of details.

2. Write a narrative describing a similar experience of your own—a fight, the killing of an animal, facing up to an unpleasant duty. Clarify both the physical and the psychological points of view for your reader.

MICHAEL IGNATIEFF

Michael Ignatieff is a Canadian writer and broadcaster, currently living in England. He is the author of *A Just Measure of Pain: The Penitentiary in the Industrial Revolution*, *The Needs of Strangers* (with Hugh Brody), *Nineteen Nineteen*, *The Russian Album*, and most recently, *Blood and Belonging*. He has also written two novels, *Asya* and *Scar Tissue*. In the following essay about his mother's degenerative illness, he displays his considerable talent for sympathetic portraiture.

Deficits

MICHAEL IGNATIEFF

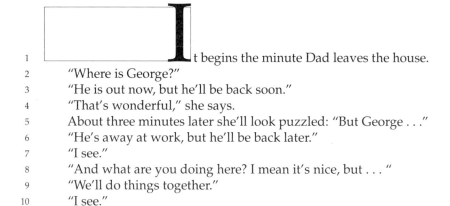

1   **I**t begins the minute Dad leaves the house.
2   "Where is George?"
3   "He is out now, but he'll be back soon."
4   "That's wonderful," she says.
5   About three minutes later she'll look puzzled: "But George . . ."
6   "He's away at work, but he'll be back later."
7   "I see."
8   "And what are you doing here? I mean it's nice, but . . . "
9   "We'll do things together."
10 "I see."

P A R T

Methods of Development

Introduction

Essays traditionally have been classified as *narrative, descriptive, expository,* and *argumentative.* These labels broadly describe essays that narrate events, describe a scene, explain an idea, or argue a point. We customarily refer to novels as narratives, word pictures as descriptions, sets of directions as expositions, and summaries of reasons as arguments. This traditional classification does not, however, tell us everything about narration, description, exposition, and argument. For these also serve other purposes. The novel that depends on narrative seeks to entertain us, or, as with Hugh MacLennan's *Two Solitudes,* to move us or persuade us to take action. Descriptions like Vladimir Nabokov's impression of a classroom or Margaret Atwood's of the Canadian North serve these same purposes and others. Argument is an essential means to persuasion, and so is exposition, as in an advertisement that explains what a product does and gives us reasons for buying it.

The paragraphs and essays in this part illustrate narration and description as well as exposition and argument. In particular, they distinguish several methods of development common in exposition —example, comparison and contrast, analogy, classification and division, definition, process, and cause and effect. These methods of analysis occur both in exposition and in argument, as we will see in the next section.

As in a paragraph, you can use these methods of analysis singly or in combination in an essay. The more methods your essay requires, the more attention you must give to your organization and transitions. The reader should understand at every point in the essay why you are using a particular method of analysis and how it develops the thesis. Transitions are needed to make these uses clear.

Keep in mind that you know more about the subject than do most of your readers: you are illustrating and analyzing ideas for their clarification. Obviously the kind and number of examples you choose depend on how much help you judge that your readers need. How you organize the essay depends, too, on this judgement. Where you place the thesis in an explanatory essay depends on how much information your readers need to understand it; where you place it in the persuasive essay depends on how disposed they are to accept it.

These essays by no means show all the possible ways of organizing and developing ideas. But they do illustrate the choices writers have today in dealing with their experiences and with current ideas and issues. They are models of effective ways to write about experiences and ideas, and can serve as resources to which you can return in planning and revising your own essays.

Description

Descriptive writing concerns itself with what we see, and is useful in all forms of writing. There are two categories of description: objective and impressionistic. In its choice of words, objective description aims for the value-free and the non-connotative, to approximate scientific writing as far as is possible. Impressionistic description, on the other hand, in its use of language, reveals the writer's reaction to the subject described. In the former, the writer selects details with a view to achieving complete fidelity to the subject; in the latter, with a view to creating a dominant impression. When describing something, it is advisable to order the details spatially, that is, describe the subject as you wish the reader to see it: top to bottom, left to right, and so on. The direction of a spatial description can be signalled by the use of such words as *above, on the right, next, adjacent, across, down.*

In a descriptive paragraph or essay, you must be careful to specify the place from which the observation is made. Indeed, you may need to specify even the angle of observation. Notice how carefully the writer controls point of view in describing what lying in bed feels like:

> Later I lay open-mouthed in bed, my arms flung wide at my sides to steady the whirling darkness. At this latitude I'm spinning 836 miles an hour round the earth's axis; I often fancy I feel my sweeping fall as a breakneck arc like the dive of dolphins, and the hollow rushing of wind raises hair on my neck and the side of my face. In orbit around the sun I'm moving 64,800 miles an hour. The solar system as a whole, like a merry-go-round unhinged, spins, bobs, and blinks at the speed of 43,200 miles an hour along a course set east of Hercules. (Annie Dillard, "At Tinker Creek")

Something more than the point of view is suggested in these sentences: a dominant mood or attitude.

If you fail to clarify the point of view from which you make the observation, or fail to clarify a change in position, details will seem blurred. Avoid abrupt or unexpected shifts in mood or attitude, which can confuse your reader.

VLADIMIR NABOKOV

Novelist, translator, poet, critic, professor, and professional lepidopterist, Vladimir Nabokov (1899–1977) was born in St. Petersburg and educated at Cambridge. As an émigré in Germany and France, Nabokov wrote nine novels in Russian. He escaped with his wife and son from France when it was invaded by the Nazis in 1940, and sailed to America. His English novels include *Lolita, Pale Fire,* and *Ada.* The following description is taken from *Strong Opinions,* a collection of interviews and essays.

The Exam Room

VLADIMIR NABOKOV

For some reason my most vivid memories concern examinations. Big amphitheater in Goldwin Smith. Exam from 8:00 A.M. to 10:30. About 150 students — unwashed, unshaven young males and reasonably well-groomed young females. A general sense of tedium and disaster. Half-past eight. Little coughs, the clearing of nervous throats, coming in clusters of sound, rustling of pages. Some of the martyrs plunged in meditation, their arms locked behind their heads. I meet a dull gaze directed at me, seeing in me with hope and hate the source of forbidden knowledge. Girl in glasses comes up to my desk to ask: "Professor Kafka, do you want us to say that . . . ? Or do you want us to answer only the first part of the question?" The great fraternity of C-minus, backbone of the nation, steadily scribbling on. A rustle arising simultaneously, the majority turning a page in their bluebooks, good teamwork. The shaking of a cramped wrist, the failing ink, the deodorant that breaks down. When I catch eyes directed at me, they are forthwith raised to the ceiling in pious meditation. Windowpanes getting misty. Boys peeling off sweaters. Girls chewing gum in rapid cadence. Ten minutes, five, three, time's up.

Questions

1. How does Nabokov organize his description of the classroom?
2. Nabokov uses a number of sentence fragments. Why are these appropriate? Contrast their use at the beginning and end of the paragraph.
3. What does the tone tell us about Nabokov's attitude to teaching?
4. Why does Nabokov have a student address him as Professor Kafka?

Writing Assignment

Look around your classroom and write a description of how it changes during a class. Use different sentence lengths and, like Nabokov, find some way to compress the entire experience into a paragraph or two.

VIRGINIA WOOLF

Virginia Woolf (1882–1941) was born in London, the daughter of Sir Leslie Stephen, a distinguished man of letters. She educated herself in her father's library and through her contacts with the London intelligentsia. Her most important novels, *Jacob's Room, Mrs. Dalloway, To the Lighthouse,* and *The Waves,* constitute an important contribution to modern fiction. Her numerous, elegantly written essays on a variety of topics are part of her enduring legacy to twentieth-century literature.

The Death of the Moth

VIRGINIA WOOLF

Moths that fly by day are not properly to be called moths; they do not excite that pleasant sense of dark autumn nights and ivy-blossom which the commonest yellow underwing asleep in the shadow of the curtain never fails to rouse in us. They are hybrid creatures, neither gay like butterflies nor sombre like their own species. Nevertheless the present specimen, with his narrow hay-coloured wings, fringed with a tassel of the same colour, seemed to be content with life. It was a pleasant morning, mid-September, mild, benignant, yet with a keener breath than that of the summer months. The plough was already scoring the field opposite the window, and where the share had been, the earth was pressed flat and gleamed with moisture. Such vigour came rolling in from the fields and the down beyond that it was difficult to keep the eyes strictly turned upon the book. The rooks too were keeping one of their annual festivities; soaring round the tree-tops until it looked as if a vast net with thousands of black knots in it had been cast up into the air; which, after a few moments sank slowly down upon the trees until every twig seemed to have a knot at the end of it. Then, suddenly, the net would be thrown into the air again in a wider circle this time, with the utmost clamour and vociferation, as though to be thrown into the air and settle slowly down upon the tree-tops were a tremendously exciting experience.

2   The same energy which inspired the rooks, the ploughmen, the horses, and even, it seemed, the lean bare-backed downs, sent the moth fluttering from side to side of his square of the window-pane. One could not help watching him. One was, indeed, conscious of a queer feeling of pity for him. The possibilities of pleasure seemed that morning so enormous and so various that to have only a moth's part in life, and a day moth's at that, appeared a hard fate, and his zest in enjoying his meagre opportunities to the full, pathetic. He flew vigorously to one corner of his compartment, and, after waiting there a second, flew across to the other. What remained for him but to fly to a third corner and then to a fourth? That was all he could do, in spite of the size of the downs, the width of the sky, the far-off smoke of houses, and the romantic voice, now and then, of a steamer out at sea. What he could do he did. Watching him, it seemed as if a fibre, very thin but pure, of the enormous energy of the world had been thrust into his frail and diminutive body. As often as he crossed the pane, I could fancy that a thread of vital light became visible. He was little or nothing but life.

3   Yet because he was so small, and so simple a form of the energy that was rolling in at the open window and driving its way through so many narrow and intricate corridors in my own brain and in those of other human beings, there was something marvellous as well as pathetic about him. It was as if someone had taken a tiny bead of pure life and, decking it as lightly as possible with down and feathers, had set it dancing and zigzagging to show us the true nature of life. Thus displayed one could not get over the strangeness of it. One is apt to forget all about life, seeing it humped and bossed and garnished and cumbered so that it has to move with the greatest circumspection and dignity. Again, the thought of all that life might have been had he been born in any other shape caused one to view his simple activities with a kind of pity.

4   After a time, tired by his dancing apparently, he settled on the window ledge in the sun, and the queer spectacle being at an end, I forgot about him. Then, looking up, my eye was caught by him. He was trying to resume his dancing, but seemed either so stiff or so awkward that he could only flutter to the bottom of the window-pane; and when he tried to fly across he failed. Being intent on other matters I watched these futile attempts for a time without thinking, unconsciously waiting for him to resume his flight, as one waits for a machine, that has stopped momentarily, to start again

without considering the reason for its failure. After perhaps a seventh attempt he slipped from the wooden ledge and fell, fluttering his wings, on to his back on the window-sill. The helplessness of his attitude roused me. It flashed upon me that he was in difficulties; he could no longer raise himself; his legs struggled vainly. But, as I stretched out a pencil, meaning to help him to right himself, it came over me that the failure and awkwardness were the approach of death. I laid the pencil down again.

The legs agitated themselves once more. I looked as if for the 5 enemy against which he struggled. I looked out of doors. What had happened there? Presumably it was midday, and work in the fields had stopped. Stillness and quiet had replaced the previous animation. The birds had taken themselves off to feed in the brooks. The horses stood still. Yet the power was there all the same, massed outside, indifferent, impersonal, not attending to anything in particular. Somehow it was opposed to the little hay-coloured moth. It was useless to try to do anything. One could only watch the extraordinary efforts made by those tiny legs against an oncoming doom which could, had it chosen, have submerged an entire city, not merely a city, but masses of human beings; nothing, I knew, had any chance against death. Nevertheless after a pause of exhaustion the legs fluttered again. It was superb this last protest, and so frantic that he succeeded at last in righting himself. One's sympathies, of course, were all on the side of life. Also, when there was nobody to care or to know, this gigantic effort on the part of an insignificant little moth, against a power of such magnitude, to retain what no one else valued or desired to keep, moved one strangely. Again, somehow, one saw life, a pure bead. I lifted the pencil again, useless though I knew it to be. But even as I did so, the unmistakable tokens of death showed themselves. The body relaxed, and instantly grew stiff. The struggle was over. The insignificant little creature now knew death. As I looked at the dead moth, this minute wayside triumph of so great a force over so mean an antagonist filled me with wonder. Just as life had been strange a few minutes before, so death was now as strange. The moth having righted himself now lay most decently and uncomplainingly composed. O yes, he seemed to say, death is stronger than I am.

```
┌─────────────────────────┐
│                         │
│                         │
└─────────────────────────┘
```

Vocabulary

a. *paragraph 1:* hybrid, benignant, vociferation
b. *paragraph 2:* diminutive
c. *paragraph 3:* cumbered, circumspection
d. *paragraph 5:* animation, antagonist

Questions

1. In her description of the moth, Woolf develops and illustrates several major ideas that build to her central or topic idea. What are they?
2. Why does Woolf begin by describing the world outside her room? What is the significance of the details she chooses?
3. Does Woolf successfully avoid sentimentality?
4. Study the eight sentences in paragraph 1 and observe the variation in sentence lengths. To what purpose does Woolf vary sentence length here? What effect does she achieve by doing so?

Writing Assignments

1. Write a description of a seemingly insignificant event and link it to larger concerns.
2. Using Woolf's essay as a model, write a closely observed description in which you emphasize the uniqueness of individual detail.

HUGH MacLENNAN

Hugh MacLennan (1907–1990) was a novelist whose nationalist concerns made him a central figure in the continuing debate about Canada's identity. He was educated at Dalhousie University, at Oxford as a Rhodes scholar, and at Princeton University, where he was awarded a PhD in Classics in 1935. He taught in McGill's Department of English from 1951 to 1981. His first novel, *Barometer Rising,* and collection of essays, *Cross-Country,* established MacLennan as an important interpreter of Canada, a reputation that he was to confirm with subsequent books of essays and such novels of national concerns as *Two Solitudes* and *The Precipice.* MacLennan won the Governor General's Award three times for fiction and twice for non-fiction. In the following selection from *Barometer Rising,* he mixes fiction and reportage to re-create the suspense, effects, and sheer pyrotechnical display of a munitions ship explosion, crafting a prose that doesn't compete with the event itself so much as provide a literary medium through which readers can approach the experience.

The Halifax Explosion

HUGH MacLENNAN

1   The *Mont Blanc* was now in the Narrows and a detail of men went into her chains to unship the anchor. It

would be dropped as soon as she reached her appointed station in the Basin. A hundred yards to port were the Shipyards and another hundred yards off the port bow was the blunt contour of Richmond Bluff; to starboard the shore sloped gently into a barren of spruce scrub. During the two minutes it took the *Mont Blanc* to glide through this strait, most of Bedford Basin and nearly all its flotilla of anchored freighters were hidden from her behind the rise of Richmond Bluff.

Around the projection of this hill, less than fifty fathoms off the port bow of the incoming *Mont Blanc*, another vessel suddenly appeared heading for the open sea. She flew the Norwegian flag, and to the startled pilot of the munitioner the name *Imo* was plainly visible beside the hawse. She was moving at half-speed and listing gently to port as she made the sharp turn out of the Basin to strike the channel of the Narrows. And so listing, with white water surging away from her fore-foot, she swept across the path of the *Mont Blanc*, exposing a gaunt flank labeled in giant letters BELGIAN RELIEF. Then she straightened, and pointed the bow directly at the fore-quarter of the munitioner. Only at that moment did the men on the *Imo*'s bridge appear to realize that another vessel stood directly in their path. 2

Staccato orders broke from the bridge of the *Mont Blanc* as the two ships moved toward a single point. Bells jangled, and megaphoned shouts came from both bridges. The ships sheered in the same direction, then sheered back again. With a violent shock, the bow of the *Imo* struck the plates of the *Mont Blanc* and went grinding a third of the way through the deck and forward hold. A shower of sparks splashed out from the screaming metal. The canisters on the deck of the *Mont Blanc* broke loose from their bindings and some of them tumbled and burst open. Then the vessels heeled away with engines reversed and the water boiling out from their screws as the propellers braked them to a standstill. They sprawled sideways across the Narrows, the *Mont Blanc* veering in toward the Halifax shore, the *Imo* spinning about with steerageway lost entirely. Finally she drifted toward the opposite shore. 3

For a fraction of a second there was intense silence. Then smoke appeared out of the shattered deck of the *Mont Blanc*, followed by a racing film of flame. The men on the bridge looked at each other. Scattered shouts broke from the stern, and the engine-room bells jangled again. Orders were half-drowned by a scream of rusty metal as some sailors amidships followed their own inclination and twisted the davits around to lower a boat. The scurry of feet grew louder as more sailors began to pour out through the hatches onto the deck. An officer ran forward with a hose, but before he could connect it his men were ready to abandon ship. 4

5   The film of flame raced and whitened, then it became deeper like an opaque and fulminant liquid, then swept over the canisters of benzol and increased to a roaring tide of heat. Black smoke billowed and rolled and engulfed the ship, which began to drift with the outgoing tide and swing in toward the graving-dock of the Shipyards. The fire trembled and leaped in a body at the bridge, driving the captain and pilot aft, and there they stood helplessly while the tarry smoke surrounded them in greasy folds and the metal of the deck began to glow under their feet. Both men glanced downward. Underneath that metal lay leashed an incalculable energy, and the bonds which checked it were melting with every second the thermometers mounted in the hold. A half-million pounds of trinitrotoluol and twenty-three hundred tons of picric acid lay there in the darkness under the plates, while the fire above and below the deck converted the hollow shell of the vessel into a bake-oven.

6   If the captain had wished to scuttle the ship at that moment it would have been impossible to do so, for the heat between decks would have roasted alive any man who tried to reach the sea-cocks. By this time the entire crew was in the lifeboat. The officers followed, and the boat was rowed frantically toward the wooded slope opposite Halifax. There, by lying flat among the trees, the sailors hoped they would have a chance when their ship blew up. By the time they had beached the boat, the foredeck of the *Mont Blanc* was a shaking rampart of fire, and black smoke pouring from it screened the Halifax waterfront from their eyes. The sailors broke and ran for the shelter of the woods.

7   By this time men were running out of dock sheds and warehouses and offices along the entire waterfront to watch the burning ship. None of them knew she was a gigantic bomb. She had now come so close to the Shipyards that she menaced the graving-dock. Fire launches cut out from a pier farther south and headed for the Narrows. Signal flags fluttered from the Dockyard and the yard-arms of ships lying in the Stream, some of which were already weighing anchor. The captain of the British cruiser piped all hands and called for volunteers to scuttle the *Mont Blanc*; a few minutes later the cruiser's launch was on its way to the Narrows with two officers and a number of ratings. By the time they reached the burning ship her plates were so hot that the seawater lapping the plimsoll line was simmering.

8   The *Mont Blanc* had become the center of a static tableau. Her plates began to glow red and the swollen air inside her hold heated the cargo rapidly towards the detonation point. Launches from the harbour fire department surrounded her like midges and the water from their hoses arched up with infinite delicacy as they curved

into the rolling smoke. The *Imo*, futile and forgotten, was still trying to claw her way off the farther shore.

Twenty minutes after the collision there was no one along the entire waterfront who was unaware that a ship was on fire in the harbor. The jetties and docks near the Narrows were crowded with people watching the show, and yet no warning of danger was given. At that particular moment there was no adequate centralized authority in Halifax to give a warning, and the few people who knew the nature of the *Mont Blanc*'s cargo had no means of notifying the town or spreading the alarm, and no comfort beyond the thought that trinitrotoluol can stand an almost unlimited heat provided there is no fulminate or explosive gas to detonate it.

Bells in the town struck the hour of nine, and by this time nearly all normal activity along the waterfront had been suspended. A tug had managed to grapple the *Mont Blanc* and was towing her with imperceptible movement away from the Shipyards back into the channel of the Narrows. Bluejackets from the cruiser had found the bosun's ladder left by the fleeing crew, and with flesh shrinking from the heat, were going over the side. Fire launches surrounded her. There was a static concentration, and intense expectancy in the faces of the firemen playing the hoses, a rhythmic reverberation in the beat of the flames, a gush from the hose-nozzles and a steady hiss of scalding water. Everything else for miles around seemed motionless and silent.

Then a needle of flaming gas, thin as the mast and of a brilliance unbelievably intense, shot through the deck of the *Mont Blanc* near the funnel and flashed more than two hundred feet toward the sky. The firemen were thrown back and their hoses jumped suddenly out of control and slashed the air with S-shaped designs. There were a few helpless shouts. Then all movement and life about the ship were encompassed in a sound beyond hearing as the *Mont Blanc* opened up. . . .

Three forces were simultaneously created by the energy of the exploding ship, an earthquake, an air-concussion, and a tidal wave. These forces rushed away from the Narrows with a velocity varying in accordance with the nature of the medium in which they worked. It took only a few seconds for the earthquake to spend itself and three minutes for the air-expansion to slow down to a gale. The tidal wave traveled for hours before the last traces of it were swallowed in the open Atlantic.

When the shock struck the earth, the rigid ironstone and granite base of Halifax peninsula rocked and reverberated, pavements split and houses swayed as the earth trembled. Sixty miles away in the town of Truro windows broke and fell to the ground, tinkling in

9

10

11

12

13

the stillness of the streets. But the ironstone was solid and when the shock had passed, it resumed its immobility.

14   The pressure of the exploding chemicals smashed against the town with the rigidity and force of driving steel. Solid and unbreathable, the forced wall of air struck against Fort Needham and Richmond Bluff and shaved them clean, smashed with one gigantic blow the North End of Halifax and destroyed it, telescoping houses or lifting them from their foundations, snapping trees and lamp posts, and twisting iron rails into writhing, metal snakes; breaking buildings and sweeping the fragments of their wreckage for hundreds of yards in its course. It advanced two miles southward, shattering every flimsy house in its path, and within thirty seconds encountered the long, shield-like slope of the Citadel which rose before it.

15   Then, for the first time since it was fortified, the Citadel was able to defend at least a part of the town. The airwall smote it, and was deflected in three directions. Thus some of its violence shot skyward at a twenty-degree angle and spent itself in space. The rest had to pour around the roots of the hill before closing in on the town for another rush forward. A minute after the detonation, the pressure was advancing through the South End. But now its power was diminished, and its velocity was barely twice that of a tornado. Trees tossed and doors broke inward, windows split into driving arrows of glass which buried themselves deep in interior walls. Here the houses, after swaying and cracking, were still on their foundations when the pressure had passed.

16   Underneath the keel of the *Mont Blanc* the water opened and the harbor bottom was deepened twenty feet along the channel of the Narrows. And then the displaced waters began to drive outward, rising against the town and lifting ships and wreckage over the sides of the docks. It boiled over the shores and climbed the hill as far as the third cross-street, carrying with it the wreckage of small boats, fragments of fish, and somewhere, lost in thousands of tons of hissing brine, the bodies of men. The wave moved in a gigantic bore down the Stream to the sea, rolling some ships under and lifting others high on its crest, while anchor-chains cracked like guns as the violent thrust snapped them. Less than ten minutes after the detonation, it boiled over the breakwater off the park and advanced on McNab's Island, where it burst with a roar greater than a winter storm. And then the central volume of the wave rolled on to sea, high and arching and white at the top, its back glossy like the plumage of a bird. Hours later it lifted under the keel of a steamer far out in the Atlantic and the captain, feeling his vessel heave, thought he had struck a floating mine.

But long before this, the explosion had become manifest in new forms over Halifax. More than two thousand tons of red hot steel, splintered fragments of the *Mont Blanc*, fell like meteors from the sky into which they had been hurled a few seconds before. The ship's anchor soared over the peninsula and descended through a roof on the other side of the Northwest Arm three miles away. For a few seconds the harbor was dotted white with a maze of splashes, and the decks of raddled ships rang with reverberations and clangs as fragments struck them.

17

Over the North End of Halifax, immediately after the passage of the first pressure, the tormented air was laced with tongues of flame which roared and exploded out of the atmosphere, lashing downwards like a myriad blowtorches as millions of cubic feet of gas took fire and exploded. The atmosphere went white-hot. It grew mottled, then fell to the streets like a crimson curtain. Almost before the last fragments of steel had ceased to fall, the wreckage of the wooden houses in the North End had begun to burn. And if there were any ruins which failed to ignite from falling flames, they began to burn from the fires in their own stoves, onto which they had collapsed.

18

Over this part of the town, rising in the shape of a typhoon from the Narrows and extending five miles into the sky, was poised a cloud formed by the exhausted gases. It hung still for many minutes, white, glossy as an ermine's back, serenely aloof. It cast its shadow over twenty miles of forest land behind Bedford Basin.

19

```



```

Vocabulary

a. *paragraph 1:* starboard, flotilla
b. *paragraph 2:* fathoms, munitioner, hawse, listing
c. *paragraph 3:* staccato, sheered, steerageway
d. *paragraph 4:* davits
e. *paragraph 5:* fulminant, benzol, graving-dock, aft, trinitrotoluol, picric acid
f. *paragraph 6:* sea-cocks, rampart
g. *paragraph 7:* yardarms, plimsoll line
h. *paragraph 8:* tableau, midges
i. *paragraph 9:* jetties
j. *paragraph 10:* grapple, bosun
k. *paragraph 15:* smote
l. *paragraph 16:* brine
m. *paragraph 17:* manifest
n. *paragraph 18:* myriad
o. *paragraph 19:* ermine

Questions

1. Is MacLennan's description organized chronologically or spatially, or some combination of the two?
2. Why does paragraph 11 end with an ellipsis (. . .)? What does this contribute to the structure of the passage?
3. Where does MacLennan evoke senses other than the visual, and what do they contribute to the overall impression?
4. The narrator assumes a number of different perspectives on the explosion. Locate these and comment on their effect.
5. How does MacLennan create suspense?

Writing Assignment

Use MacLennan's description of the explosion as a model for an account of a catastrophe with which you are familiar. Develop an overall impression or an attitude, and let your selection of details reveal it.

HUGH GRAHAM

Hugh Graham is a free-lance writer who lives in Toronto. In the following essay he remembers an Ontario family that made a strong impression on him when he was a boy.

Life and Death in Ontario County

HUGH GRAHAM

1   I was seven in the winter of 1959 when my parents and I went to look at a farm house near Greenbank, about twenty-five miles north of Whitby, Ontario. It was occupied by a ferretish old man with faded blue eyes, and his wife, and their sixty-year-old son. They lived in one large room and my mother discovered that they slept under coats upstairs. Everything they had was old and worn out. The ceiling was low and buckled, the blistered wall-paper was from the twenties, and the air thick and dry with stove heat. Puzzles of Scottish castles had been framed and hung on the wall. Everything that could be saved was stacked in another room behind a door closed and stuffed with rags.

We returned several times that winter, sometimes after dark, and entering that house was to cross into a warm and dim place that was otherworldly and unsettling. The son, a lumbering giant of a man, shaved in front of us beside the stove in his undervest and suspenders using a cracked mirror, a straight razor, and a basin with steaming water from a blackened kettle. The old man sat idly in a rocking chair among other chairs around the stove with flattened torn cushions. The old woman was the only one who was moving, large and bird-like, giving me and my friends candy and pictures. Out in the back, on the unfinished planks of the woodshed wall there was a tattered collage of pasted-up magazine illustrations that included a painted thirties advertisement of an old countryman in a suit playing a violin. The evening light in the picture seemed to be like the light in their house, the night sky was the color of his suit, and for a long time I was certain that the fictional fiddler was the old man. Beyond the woodshed a track through the snow led to a hand pump. In the depths of that hard winter when they were snow-bound, food had to be brought them from the village. I had never seen such people. My mother explained to me that it was poverty. They maintained the land for a beef farmer, their name was Beedon, and I later realized they were the forgotten; tenants of a type commonly associated with the American south.

When we took possession and began work on the farm house, they had moved down two concession lines to a solid ancient field stone house on high and bald melancholy farm land. The old man, John Beedon, and his son Alf put in our garden, built livestock fencing, and taught us how to manage our woodlot and sixty acres of pasture. And now we seemed to be visiting in the new place, where they had brought the same heavy smell of mildew and stove heat, just as we had visited the old. Mrs. Beedon still had a miniature museum she had created in an aquarium that displayed a growing and changing collection of postcards, dolls, doll furniture, miniature flags, and buttons, which she called her "funny box."

I had been afraid of them at first. They were crude, spoke with "don't" and "ain't." Beedon was slight, bantam-like, testy, and irascible, and the son, haunted and moronic, towered over his parents. The three looked alike, with sharp eyes and big noses and thin flat mouths and the two men had abscess scars in the right cheek, which gave them a look of wild inhaling. One winter Mrs. Beedon was talking to my mother, when, in a moment of womanly confidence, steadying her thick glasses, she pulled down a black stocking and then pulled up a leg of long underwear and showed a faint blue mark where the old man had given her a kick.

5   The son, Alf, as Beedon told us outright, was dim, subnormal, while Alf himself, with his monumental craggy face and deepset gray eyes, seemed to agree with equanimity. All his life he had held menial jobs and worked with his father in laboring or picking up highway tree-trimmings in a horse and wagon for Ontario Hydro. Alf spoke with a solemn nodding expertise about cutting post tops to a slant to keep out rot and expounded with an air of grave foreboding on the common details of maintaining the property. He had a high hearse-like black '48 Dodge and at every opportunity he opened the hood to display the engine with my father listening and nodding politely while trying to get on with things. But when his father was discussing the plans for the day with mine, and Alf attempted to add a detail, the old man snapped, "There, we heard enough from you," with a swift short kick in the shin.

6   On weekends Alf drove home from a cleaning job in Milton and spent the time with a case of twenty-four in front of the television mildly sloshed; the program, which he highly recommended, was *Popeye.* "I've courted every girl in Reach Township," he told us, with the implication he'd turned them all down, but it was when my mother hired him to drive her into Port Perry to do shopping that he talked. My mother, who was easily bored, was impressed with his skill as a raconteur as he told his stories with reverence and amazement, saying he'd been overseas during the war and that an English girl had slapped him for proposing they go to Petticoat Lane. His father told us flatly that Alf had never been out of the country and had been turned down for the service "because of bad nerves." My mother later gathered that Alf had taken stories he'd heard from braggarts, farmers, and servicemen, and honed them into his own imaginary past.

7   In the summers when I got to know the old man, he was eighty and cycling six miles a day to our place over hilly gravel concession roads. I recall him always in indigo twill trousers with suspenders, a light-colored fedora he never took off, hawk-like without teeth and with alert pale eyes that never seemed to change; an expression of amused, open-mouthed, almost delectable outrage, as if he had caught you doing something he had predicted you would do. In those summers I was a city kid with no friends in the country and I spent my days with the old man. He taught me how to build livestock fencing, to use an axe and a scythe, to cut and trim timber and till a garden. He worked slowly and with certainty and economy. He used an axe gently and perfectly, everything he had was immaculate and shop-worn, his tools white with wear, fastidiously sharp and clean. He had nothing new, but rather items that seemed to be part of the derelict inside of our barn: rags, pegs, bottles, wire, and a jealously guarded enamel drinking ladle. For stretches of sum-

mers running, my only life was his, as we replaced rods of fencing in hot dry pasture ringing with crickets. He stretched fence wire by hand, strand by strand with a crowbar, set posts in straight, dug-out stones four feet in the ground, planted solid anchor posts, and cut exact and tightly notching brace poles. With a pale wild eye he could line up posts so that lengthwise they appeared as one from here to the horizon. I stayed with him while he ate his gum-soft lunch out of the same old Wonderbread bag and drank Pepsi (Coca-Cola was "poison") in the noon shade of the driving shed.

He and his family had lived dirt poor with no plumbing in the same kinds of houses for close to sixty years. He had visited no city since he'd been to Toronto in 1908. He had gone to see the Exhibition, then a celebrated agricultural fair, disliked the city, condemned the fair, which was nowhere near as good as the one in Lindsay, and went home quickly never to return. His time was that of teams and traces; he operated no machinery, would not even touch a tractor. He had no use for television, found football ridiculous, could just read headlines and sign his name, and kept their money in cash at the post office. But all his life seemed to have been lived in a struggle to prove he was, or had been, right. He argued tooth and nail with my mother about putting in the garden and was always vindicated; when my father's car arrived on weekends, Beedon looked up with a smile, ready to show him his errors. The old man's tales were of cleverness and cheating, triumphant accounts of meanness and dishonesty and in these he seemed to stand alone in a world of rural propriety. Where the conversation of the farm wives and close-mouthed farmers that we knew was filled with righteous anodynes, tact, and caution, Beedon's eyes lit up at recollections of incompetence and shabbiness. Perhaps he had nothing to lose by such stories; he seemed to have fought with every employer he had ever had; he walked out on fence-building jobs because the farmer insisted on hanging the wire upside down. His suspicions of malice were often senseless and extravagant, for example, that a shovel of ours found in the pond had been thrown there by a man we hardly knew, for spite. 8

We on the other hand were city middle-class, devoid of the natural suspicion of farmers, and since we had the money to pay him what he wanted without welshing, he seemed, for that practical reason, to respect us—even if he always told us we were wrong, or was amused by our ignorance and capriciousness. After my father hung a stark contemporary conceptual piece over the mantel, the old man smiled toothlessly and said, "What you doing with a picture of a shovel?" His affections were indeed practical and determined his loyalty, and yet when local painters accidentally set our house on fire, he ran in alone through dense smoke and tried to drag out the furniture before he was pulled out by firemen. 9

10   He had lived and worked longer in the county than almost anyone and yet for all his stories no one seemed to know him. In turn, the world he described seemed to have passed, a spectral place devoid of witnesses where he fought two men to court a woman, where he had been able single-handedly to lift a full-grown heifer into the back of a wagon. When he'd dart in laughing and jab at the tail of my pony just to make him kick, he seemed very much of another age. Likewise, his entertainment was in talking: in denials, claims, and tales; the brush with death riding the famous long slope at Sandy Hook after his bicycle chain broke; a renowned giant elm near Goodwood, which he said had yielded seventy-odd cords of wood in its death, and then regretted, "I never did get down to see that tree."

11   The stories he told were redolent of the abandoned farm houses that were scattered around Greenbank, of suicide, fraud, and arson, of vandalized, trashed, melancholy places where frozen overalls still hung by the door over boots ghosted with dust and among the mites and mildew of a medicine cabinet where you could find a dusky tin of brilliantine, still viscous and marked by the scoop of fingers; where the son of a man whose farm had a broken dam decorated with a cow skull had died drinking strychnine. Those very places that smelled of mildew and damp plaster but hadn't fallen to dereliction were the places lived in by Beedon and his family. In a house rented in Uxbridge the attic had been closed and several nights running he heard a heavy chain dragged the length of the house across the floor above. In the daytime he investigated and found nothing; it was bare and completely sealed, but a few days later he learned that two years before the butcher who lived there had hanged himself. There was a story of the thirties that began with a column of smoke he had seen over near Uxbridge and ended with the owner of a blazing house tearing out of the front door with a baby carriage draped for protection with heavy blankets. And what made Beedon look at you as if he dared you to believe anyone could be courageous or honest, was the fact that the carriage had concealed no baby but four expensive folded suits. The implication, of course, was insurance fraud.

12   After five years I could scarcely remember the time when I had been afraid of him and now he was the first person the prospect of whose death made me sad. By then I knew he didn't mind me, and his gone world, which seemed to live on in the stillness before thunderstorms and the dry decay of barns, had become mine as well, a ghost world of Reach Township which followed me back to the city and to school.

┌─────────────────────────┐
│   │
└─────────────────────────┘

Vocabulary

a. *paragraph 1:* ferretish
b. *paragraph 4:* irascible
c. *paragraph 5:* equanimity
d. *paragraph 7:* indigo, twill
e. *paragraph 8:* anodynes
f. *paragraph 11:* redolent, brilliantine

Questions

1. How does Graham's division of the essay into sections contribute to his portrayal of the Beedon family? What details add most to his description of them?
2. How does the account of the setting complement the presentation of character?
3. How does Graham use chronology to convey his changing relation with the Beedons?
4. What is the dominant impression that Graham creates in the essay? Explain how he does it.

Writing Assignment

Write an essay that opens with your response to a remembered event, and then develop this impression through details.

MORDECAI RICHLER

Although he occasionally gains notoriety for his controversial journalism analyzing the state of contemporary Canadian culture, Mordecai Richler will continue to be best known as the author of some of the funniest and most important comic novels in recent decades: *The Apprenticeship of Duddy Kravitz, St. Urbain's Horseman, Joshua Then and Now,* and *Solomon Gursky Was Here.* His books of non-fiction include *Hunting Tigers under Glass; O Canada, O Québec;* and *This Year in Jerusalem.* The following passage displays his skill for detailed description and his ability to capture a particular milieu, in this instance his native Montreal in the 1930s. In fact, Richler has claimed that he views his literary vocation as the challenge to bear accurate witness to his time and place, to "get it right."

Main Street

MORDECAI RICHLER

1   If the Main was a poor man's street, it was also a dividing line. Below, the French Canadians. Above, some distance above, the dreaded WASPs. On the Main itself there were some Italians, Yugoslavs and Ukrainians, but they did not count as true Gentiles. Even the French Canadians, who were our enemies, were not entirely unloved. Like us, they were poor and coarse with large families and spoke English badly.

2   Looking back, it's easy to see that the real trouble was there was no dialogue between us and the French Canadians, each elbowing the other, striving for WASP acceptance. We fought the French Canadians stereotype for stereotype. If many of them believed that the St. Urbain Street Jews were secretly rich, manipulating the black market, then my typical French Canadian was a moronic gum-chewer. He wore his greasy black hair parted down the middle and also affected an eyebrow moustache. His zoot trousers were belted just under the breastbone and ended in a peg hugging his ankles. He was the dolt who held up your uncle endlessly at the liquor commission while he tried unsuccessfully to add three figures or, if he was employed at the customs office, never knew which form to give you. Furthermore, he only held his liquor commission or customs or any other government job because he was the second cousin of a backwoods notary who had delivered the village vote to the Union Nationale for a generation. Other French Canadians were speed cops, and if any of these ever stopped you on the highway you made sure to hand him a folded two-dollar bill with your licence.

3   Actually, it was only the WASPs who were truly hated and feared. "Among them," I heard it said, "with those porridge faces, who can tell what they're thinking?" It was, we felt, their country, and given sufficient liquor who knew when they would make trouble?

4   We were a rude, aggressive bunch round the Main. Cocky too. But bring down the most insignificant, pinched WASP fire insurance inspector and even the most arrogant merchant on the street would dip into the drawer for a ten spot or a bottle and bow and say, "Sir."

5   After school we used to race down to the Main to play snooker at the Rachel or the Mount Royal. Other days, when we chose to avoid school altogether, we would take the No. 55 streetcar as far as St. Catherine Street, where there was a variety of amusements

two-piece suits. Yet they broke into spontaneous applause. They, too, were saying no to the Superwoman myth.

That moment is as good as any to stop and assess, to review and preview.

For all the social change in the past decade, all the rhetoric and action, we have moved from one national ideal of True Womanhood to another—from Supermom to Superwoman. The girl who was told that when she grew up she should get married and have children and keep house is now a grown-up woman being told that she should be married, have children, keep house and a job, or better yet, a career.

While mothers at home have felt increasingly pressured for "not working," mothers in the work force feel increasingly pressured by the double burden. They have been "liberated" to the Russian model—have a new role on top of an old one.

Every study shows the same things. The overwhelming number of working mothers do the overwhelming amount of housework and child care. They may not have it all, but they seem to do it all.

Why has the change been so lopsided? I have asked that question a hundred times and heard a dozen different answers, ranging from the psychological to the economic. One feminist psychiatrist says that women spent the decade proving themselves. A sociologist believes that the person who initiates the change—the person who goes to work even out of necessity—accepts the personal responsibility for it.

A woman from a working-class neighborhood in Baltimore tells me that women are stretching their own energy to cover both their traditional and nontraditional values: the desire or demand to make Christmas pudding and a salary. An economist offers a different theory: "The average woman earns fifty-nine cents to her husband's dollar. She sees her time as worth less and overworks herself. She gets it twice."

And last week a union leader said: "Remember three things. One: A lot of women with lousy jobs hope they'll be able to quit. By doing everything, they think they're keeping their options open. Two: The home is the only place some women have any power. They sure don't want to let go of that. Three: Never underestimate the power of the men in their lives to resist."

Perhaps single mothers were the first to wipe off the upbeat Superwoman makeup that covered the lines of fatigue. But now it seems to many women that the Superwoman model who looked so chic at the beginning of the decade looks worn at the end.

In 1970, women had just begun to agitate collectively for new choices. But in 1980, the "daughters" who were to "have it all" face new choices that are still limited, frightening as well as attractive.

12   Many women, especially those "up against the clock" of their thirties, approach motherhood with fear and trembling. Those for whom homemaking, even temporary, is not a psychological or economic possibility see only two choices: superdrudge or childlessness.

13   In Washington, a forty-five-year-old woman says ironically, "I saw my mother frustrated at home. My daughter sees me overworked. I'm not such a great role model myself."

14   Superwoman was in part a creation of the self-help, self-reliant, self-improvement seventies. This was the flip side of the so-called Me Decade. It was not new narcissism, but new isolation masked as independence.

15   "I used to take pride in being a Superwoman," said a Manhattan woman listening to Friedan that afternoon. "Now I see it, not as a personal victory but as a failure. A failure of my relationship with my husband, a failure of the work world, maybe even a failure of the society that just isn't adjusting to the way we live."

16   The Superwoman myth is exploding like an overstuffed sofa. Women are no longer willing to look inside themselves for all the answers and all the energy. At the turn of the decade, they don't want a Superwoman pep talk any more. They long for something more precious and more realistic: a support system—of families, the workplace and the community—to fend off this cultural kryptonite.

Vocabulary

   a. *paragraph 4:* rhetoric
   b. *paragraph 14:* narcissism

Questions

   1. What audience is Goodman addressing—young women, unsympathetic males, the common reader? How do you know?
   2. How does Goodman use the history of the women's movement to make her case? What is the effect of the testimonial evidence she marshals?
   3. How does Goodman's idea of a "support system" provide an alternative to the superwoman myth?

Writing Assignments

   1. Drawing on your own experiences or those of friends, write an essay on some aspects of the women's movement.
   2. Goodman describes the myth of the superwoman as the "new isolation masked as independence." Write an essay discussing the extent to which this phrase describes the situations of women you know.

Sometimes I try to count the number of times she asks me these questions but I lose track. 11

I remember how it began, five or six years ago. She was 66 then. She would leave a pot to boil on the stove. I would discover it and find her tearing through the house, muttering, "My glasses, my glasses, where the hell are my glasses?" 12

I took her to buy a chain so that she could wear her glasses around her neck. She hated it because her mother used to wear *her* glasses on a chain. As we drove home, she shook her fist at the windscreen. 13

"I swore I'd never wear one of these damned things." 14

I date the beginning to the purchase of the chain, to the silence that descended over her as I drove her home from the store. 15

The deficits, as the neurologists call them, are localized. She can tell you what it felt like when the Model T Ford ran over her at the school gates when she was girl of seven. She can tell you what a good-looking man her grandfather was. She can tell you what her grandmother used to say, "A genteel sufficiency will suffice," when turning down another helping at dinner. She remembers the Canadian summer nights when her father used to wrap her in a blanket and take her out to the lake's edge to see the stars. 16

But she can't dice an onion. She can't set the table. She can't play cards. Her grandson is five, and when they play pairs with his animal cards, he knows where the second penguin will be. She just turns up cards at random. 17

He hits her because she can't remember anything, because she keeps telling him not to run around quite so much. 18

Then I punish him. I tell him he has to understand. 19

He goes down on the floor, kisses her feet, and promises not to hit her again. 20

She smiles at him, as if for the first time, and says, "Oh, your kiss is so full of sugar." 21

After a week with him, she looks puzzled and says, "He's a nice little boy. Where does he sleep? I mean, who does he belong to?" 22

"He's your grandson." 23

"I see." She looks away and puts her hand to her face. 24

My brother usually stays with her when Dad is out of town. Once or twice a year, it's my turn. I put her to bed at night. I hand her the pills—small green ones that are supposed to control her moods—and she swallows them. I help her out of her bra and slip, roll down her tights, and lift the nightie over her head. I get into the bed next to hers. Before she sleeps she picks up a Len Deighton and reads a few paragraphs, always the same paragraphs, at the place where she has folded down the page. When she falls asleep, I pick the book off her chest and I pull her down in the bed so that her 25 head isn't leaning against the wall. Otherwise she wakes up with a crick in her neck.

26   Often when I wake in the night, I see her lying next to me, staring into the dark. She stares and then she wanders. I used to try to stop her, but now I let her go. She is trying to hold on to what is left. There is a method in this. She goes to the bathroom every time she wakes, no matter if it is five times a night. Up and down the stairs silently, in her bare feet, trying not to wake me. She turns the lights on and off. Smooths a child's sock and puts it on the bed. Sometimes she gets dressed, after a fashion, and sits on the downstairs couch in the dark, clutching her handbag.

27   When we have guests to dinner, she sits beside me at the table, holding my hand, bent forward slightly to catch everything that is said. Her face lights up when people smile, when there is laughter. She doesn't say much any more; she is worried she will forget a name and we won't be able to help her in time. She doesn't want anything to show. The guests always say how well she does. Sometimes they say, "You'd never know, really." When I put her to bed afterward I can see the effort has left her so tired she barely knows her own name.

28   She could make it easier on herself. She could give up asking questions.

29   "Where we are now, is this our house?"

30   "Yes."

31   "Where is our house?"

32   "In France."

33   I tell her: "Hold my hand, I'm here. I'm your son."

34   "I know."

35   But she keeps asking where she is. The questions are her way of trying to orient herself, of refusing and resisting the future that is being prepared for her.

36   She always loved to swim. When she dived into the water, she never made a splash. I remember her lifting herself out of the pool, as sleek as a seal in a black swimsuit, the water pearling off her back. Now she says the water is too cold and taking off her clothes is too much of a bother. She paces up and down the poolside, watching her grandson swim, stroking his towel with her hand, endlessly smoothing out the wrinkles.

37   I bathe her when she wakes. Her body is white, soft, and withered. I remember how, in the changing-huts, she would bend over as she slipped out of her bathing suit. Her body was young. Now I see her skeleton through her skin. When I wash her hair, I feel her skull. I help her from the bath, dry her legs, swathe her in towels, sit her on the edge of the bath and cut her nails: they are horny and yellow. Her feet are gnarled. She has walked a long way.

When I was as old as my son is now I used to sit beside her at the bedroom mirror watching her apply hot depilatory wax to her legs and upper lip. She would pull her skirt up to her knees, stretch her legs out on the dresser, and sip beer from the bottle, while waiting for the wax to dry. "Have a sip," she would say. It tasted bitter. She used to laugh at the faces I made. When the wax had set, she would begin to peel it off, and curse and wince, and let me collect the strips, with fine black hairs embedded in them. When it was over, her legs were smooth, silky to touch. 38

Now I shave her. I soap her face and legs with my shaving brush. She sits perfectly still; as my razor comes around her chin we are as close as when I was a boy. 39

She never complains. When we walk up the hill behind the house, I feel her going slower and slower, but she does not stop until I do. If you ask her whether she is sad, she shakes her head. But she did say once, "It's strange. It was supposed to be more fun than this." 40

I try to imagine what the world is like for her. Memory is what reconciles us to the future. Because she has no past, her future rushes toward her, a bat's wing brushing against her face in the dark. 41

"I told you. George returns on Monday." 42

"Could you write that down?" 43

So I do. I write it down in large letters, and she folds it in her white cardigan pocket and pats it and says she feels much less worried. 44

In half an hour, she has the paper in her hand and is showing it to me. 45

"What do I do about this?" 46

"Nothing. It just tells you what is going to happen." 47

"But I didn't know anything of this." 48

"Now you do," I say and I take the paper away and tear it up. 49

It makes no sense to get angry at her, but I do. 50

She is afraid Dad will not come back. She is afraid she has been abandoned. She is afraid she will get lost and never be able to find her way home. Beneath the fears that have come with the forgetting, there lie anxieties for which she no longer has any names. 51

She paces the floor, waiting for lunch. When it is set before her, she downs it before anyone else, and then gets up to clear the plates. 52

"What's the hurry?" I ask her. 53

She is puzzled. "I don't know," she says. She is in a hurry and she does not know why. She drinks whatever I put before her. The wine goes quickly. 54

"You'll enjoy it more if you sip it gently." 55

"What a good idea," she says and then empties the glass with a gulp. 56

I wish I knew the history of this anxiety. But I don't. All she will tell me is about being sprawled in the middle of Regent Street amid 57 the blood and shop glass during an air raid, watching a mother sheltering a child, and thinking: I am alone.

58   In the middle of all of us, she remained alone. We didn't see it. She was the youngest girl in her family, the straggler in the pack, born cross-eyed till they straightened her eyes out with an operation. Her father was a teacher and she was dyslexic, the one left behind.

59   In her wedding photo, she is wearing her white dress and holding her bouquet. They are side by side. Dad looks excited. Her eyes are wide open with alarm. Fear gleams from its hiding place. It was her secret and she kept it well hidden. When I was a child, I thought she was faultless, amusing, regal. My mother.

60   She thinks of it as a happy family, and it was. I remember them sitting on the couch together, singing along to Fats Waller records. She still remembers the crazy lyrics they used to sing:

> There's no disputin'
> That's Rasputin
> The high-falutin loving man.

I don't know how she became so dependent on him, how she lost so many of the wishes she once had for herself, and how all her wishes came to be wishes for him.

61   She is afraid of his moods, his silences, his departures, and his returns. He has become the weather of her life. But he never lets her down. He is the one who sits with her in the upstairs room, watching television, night after night, holding her hand.

62   People say: it's worse for you, she doesn't know what is happening. She used to say the same thing herself. Five years ago, when she began to forget little things, she knew what was in store, and she said to me once, "Don't worry. I'll make a cheerful old nut. It's you who'll have the hard time." But that is not true. She feels everything. She has had time to count up every loss. Every night, when she lies awake, she stares at desolation.

63   What is a person? That is what she makes you wonder. What kind of a person are you if you only have your habits left? She can't remember her grandson's name, but she does remember to shake out her tights at night and she never lets a dish pass her by without trying to clean it, wipe it, clear it up, or put it away. The house is littered with dishes she is putting away in every conceivable cupboard. What kind of a person is this?

64   It runs in the family. Her mother had it. I remember going to see her in the house with old carpets and dark furniture on Prince Arthur Avenue. The windows were covered with the tendrils of plants growing in enormous Atlas battery jars, and the parquet

floors shone with wax. She took down the giraffe, the water buffalo, and the leopard — carved in wood — that her father had brought back from Africa in the 1880s. She sat in a chair by the fire and silently watched me play with them. Then — and it seems only a week later—I came to have Sunday lunch with her and she was old and diminished and vacant, and when she looked at me she had no idea who I was.

I am afraid of getting it myself. I do ridiculous things: I stand   65
on my head every morning so that the blood will irrigate my brain; I compose suicide notes, always some variant of Captain Oates's: "I may be gone for some time." I never stop thinking about what it would be like for this thing to steal over me.

She has taught me something. There are moments when her   66
pacing ceases, when her hunted look is conjured away by the stillness of dusk, when she sits in the garden, watching the sunlight stream through all the trees they planted together over 25 years in this place, and I see something pass over her face which might be serenity.

And then she gets up and comes toward me looking for a glass   67
to wash, a napkin to pick up, a child's toy to rearrange.

I know how the story has to end. One day I return home to see   68
her and she puts out her hand and says: "How nice to meet you." She's always charming to strangers.

People say I'm already beginning to say my farewells. No, she   69
is still here. I am not ready yet. Nor is she. She paces the floor, she still searches for what has been lost and can never be found again.

She wakes in the night and lies in the dark by my side. Her face,   70
in profile, against the pillow has become like her mother's, the eye sockets deep in shadow, the cheeks furrowed and drawn, the gaze ancient and disabused. Everything she once knew is still inside her, trapped in the ruined circuits—how I was when I was little, how she was when I was a baby. But it is too late to ask her now. She turns and notices I am awake too. We lie side by side. The darkness is still. I want to say her name. She turns away from me and stares into the night. Her nightie is buttoned at the neck like a little girl's.

Questions

1. Ignatieff begins his essay with dialogue. What in this exchange prepares us for the world he proceeds to portray? Are the other uses of dialogue also significant?
2. Why does the writer conclude with a scene set in the middle of the night?

3. What is the thesis of the essay? Does the essay introduce the thesis early or build to a statement of it?

4. What impression do you have of the writer, and how is this impression created? Does the writer seek to be objective in reporting events? In general what does the point of view contribute to the essay?

Writing Assignments

1. Notice how Ignatieff sketches in scenes from daily life with a series of typical but specific details—paragraphs 63–66, for example. Paying as much attention to detail, write an account of a relationship in your own life.

2. Describe a photograph in your family album. What do the details— clothing, hairstyle, pose, background—tell you about the era in which it was taken?

ELLEN GOODMAN

Ellen Goodman was born in Massachusetts and graduated from Radcliffe College. She has worked as a reporter for *Newsweek, The Detroit Free Press,* and *The Boston Globe,* where she has been an associate editor since 1986. Her syndicated column, "At Large," is carried by more than 200 newspapers. Her books of essays include *Close to Home, Turning Points, Keeping in Touch,* and *Making Sense.* The following essay is taken from "At Large."

Superwoman, Supertired

ELLEN GOODMAN

1   In one moment, she wrapped it all up, the whole decade of change, the remaining problems, the new anxieties. Betty Friedan, the founding mother, the astute and caring observer of the women's movement, stood in front of a New York audience last month and said: "We told our daughters you can have it all. Well, can they have it all? Only by being Superwoman. Well, I say *no* to Superwoman!"

2   By any media calculation, the audience was a collection of superwomen. They wore their raised consciousness layered with

offered. We could play the pinball machines and watch archaic strip-tease movies for a nickel at the Silver Gameland. At the Midway or the Crystal Palace we could see a double feature and a girlie show for as little as thirty-five cents. The Main, at this juncture, was thick with drifters, panhandlers and whores. Available on both sides of the street were "Tourist Rooms by Day and Night," and everywhere there was the smell of french fried potatoes cooking in stale oil. Tough, unshaven men in checked shirts stood in knots outside the taverns and cheap cafés. There was the promise of violence.

As I recall it, we were always being warned about the Main. ₆ Our grandparents and parents had come there by steerage from Rumania or by cattleboat from Poland by way of Liverpool. No sooner had they unpacked their bundles and cardboard suitcases than they were planning a better, brighter life for us, the Canadian-born children. The Main, good enough for them, was not to be for us, and that they told us again and again was what the struggle was for. The Main was for *bummers*, drinkers, and (heaven forbid) failures.

Vocabulary

a. *paragraph 1:* WASPs
b. *paragraph 2:* stereotype, zoot, notary
c. *paragraph 5:* archaic, juncture
d. *paragraph 6:* steerage

Questions

1. Richler's description of a Montreal neighbourhood depends on an accretion of detail. How would you describe the point of view?
2. How does Richler characterize the typical French Canadian in paragraph 2? The typical WASP in paragraphs 3 and 4? How does the combination of specific details and general comment contribute to the overall impression?
3. How does the sequence of details in paragraph 5 control the reader's perceptions?
4. How would you characterize the shift in emphasis in the concluding paragraph? Does this shift result from the details, the point of view, the tone?

Writing Assignment

Create a scene in which you evoke both character and setting without describing the character. Make the concrete details reveal the character and impression you wish to convey.

Narration

Narration is an account of a sequence of events. Narrative writing describes an action; it answers the question, "What happened?" For example, the following report of a boxing match captures the intensity of the fight's climactic moment:

> In the twelfth, Griffith caught him. Paret got trapped in a corner. Trying to duck away, his left arm and his head became tangled on the wrong side of the top rope. Griffith was in like a cat ready to rip the life out of a huge boxed rat. He hit him eighteen right hands in a row, an act which took perhaps three or four seconds. (Norman Mailer, "The Death of Benny Paret")

Because narration deals with action in time, the events are usually controlled by verb tenses and the use of such signalling words as *now, when, while, then, before, after, next,* and so on. Consider the use of these techniques in E.B. White's "Once More to the Lake," an account of revisiting a summer camp:

> But when I got back there, with my boy, and we settled into a camp near a farmhouse and into the kind of summertime I had known, I could tell that it was going to be pretty much the same as it had been before—I knew it, lying in bed the first morning, smelling the bedroom, and hearing the boy sneak quietly out and go off along the shore in a boat. I began to sustain the illusion that he was I, and therefore, by simple transposition, that I was my father.

Writers often find the flashback technique helpful, either in explaining an action more fully or in providing necessary motivation or context. In White's essay, an event in the present triggers a recollection of his own boyhood:

> My boy loved our rented outboard, and his great desire was to achieve singlehanded mastery over it, and authority, and he soon learned the trick of choking it a little (but not too much), and the adjustment of the needle valve. Watching him I would remember the things you could do with the old one-cylinder engine with the heavy flywheel, how you could have it eating out of your hand if you got really close to it spiritually. Motor boats in those days didn't have

clutches, and you would make a landing by shutting off the motor at the proper time and coasting in with a dead rudder. But there was a way of reversing them, if you learned the trick, by cutting the switch and putting it on again exactly on the final dying revolution of the flywheel, so that it would kick back against compression and begin reversing.

When narrating an action, avoid passive verb forms. Note how the writer uses active verbs to convey movement succinctly:

This fight had its turns. Griffith won most of the early rounds, but Paret knocked Griffith down in the sixth. Griffith had trouble getting up, but made it, came alive and was dominating Paret again before the round was over. Then Paret began to wilt. In the middle of the eighth round, after a clubbing punch had turned his back to Griffith, Paret walked three disgusted steps away, showing his hindquarters. (Norman Mailer, "The Death of Benny Paret")

Precise detail is the soul of good narrative. Note the specificity of White's description of handling the motorboat. Writing that lapses into generalities loses its hold not only on the reader but also on the real world.

ERIC NICOL

Three-time winner of the Stephen Leacock Medal for humour, Eric Nicol was born in Kingston, Ontario, in 1919, and has spent most of his life in Vancouver. He has published many collections of the daily column he writes for *The Vancouver Province,* and has written many radio plays and television scripts as well. His subject is often the middle-class anxieties of contemporary urban life. "Parents Night," for example, explores the comic consequences of an adult's revisiting elementary school in a new role.

Parents Night

ERIC NICOL

It was Parents Night at the school, and since I was a parent, I was able to get in.   1

Usually my wife attends these meetings in which the teachers   2
try to communicate with the peer group of Cro-Magnon man. This time I went to spell her off. (I was always a pretty fair speller.)

3   Entering the school was not all that easy because the main doors were locked. I was delighted to see this tradition being carried on despite the revolution in education methods and goals. At any school I ever attended as a child (and that was several years ago), the main doors were always locked. Tight.

4   Schools have a phobia about anybody getting in or out except by the side doors or windows.

5   They will open the big front doors only in the event of fire, flood or earthquake. A major earthquake. Over the principal's dead body.

6   Having tried the main doors I entered by the side door and faced another survivor of the old school: the dismembered hand painted on the stairwall, pointing sternly down. The hand never points up. No matter what floor of the school you wish to reach, you follow the unfickle finger downward. Space is curved, in the school as in the universe, and "up" is a concept having reality only in the mind of the janitor.

7   I followed the finger. It led me through the smells that are peculiar to a school; the basic uric, the occasional whiff of brine from the room where the women teachers dry their tears and blow their noses before going back for another crack at the boy with the pink beard, and the pervasive aroma of something that died in a student's locker.

8   I passed the inevitable wall covered with framed photos of former principals, each portrait retouched with highlights on the eyes to create the semblance of the will to live.

9   At the door of the auditorium a teacher placed literature in the hands of the parents filing past. She appeared to be grateful that we were able to grasp the material physically if not mentally.

10   But what grabbed *me*, as proof of the changeless element of education, was the way the parents seated themselves in the auditorium. The first ten rows were empty. Silver-haired couples sat as far to the rear, away from the ominous microphone, as they could without violating the ropes with which the school had denied them the last ten rows.

11   Besides sitting at a maximum distance from the source of information, the parents occupied aisle seats, for a faster exit when the buzzer sounded. As I took a seat near the back of the aisle, I realized that this was what we parents had learned best at school: the logistics of laying back and getting the hell out.

12   This was what stuck in our minds. Algebra, history, French—all that stuff had perished in the grey cells, but the defence mechanism against being nailed with a question was as well-oiled as ever.

13   After the principal had, with a blend of resignation and infinite patience, explained the school curriculum to us parents, and we had failed to understand a word, we made for the side doors. There

was some good-natured grumbling. Confessions of lack of comprehension. Satisfaction at seeing parents older than oneself.

But nobody thought to go up and thank the principal for his   14
gallant effort to instruct us in what was happening in education. We were getting out of school, our ignorance intact. That was enough to make Parents Night a success.

Vocabulary

a. *paragraph 2:* peer group
b. *paragraph 4:* phobia
c. *paragraph 6:* dismembered, unfickle
d. *paragraph 10:* ominous
e. *paragraph 11:* logistics

Questions

1. How is Nicol's narrative organized? Divide it into its constituent parts.
2. What does Nicol conclude about "parents night"? What do the last two paragraphs show about this conclusion?
3. Nicol's sentence structure reflects the rhythms of ordinary speech. Analyze his story with a view to determining how he achieves this effect. Consider sentence length and structure in your answer.
4. Discuss the blend of colloquial and learned diction in paragraphs 6, 7, and 10. What does Nicol achieve with this kind of shift?
5. What is Nicol's tone in the essay? Is he simply pleasantly satiric about his experience, or is the tone more complex?
6. Nicol uses pronouns, conjunctions, and repetition of key words to make transitions between paragraphs. Give some examples of each.

Writing Assignment

Imagine a reunion of your grade-eight class and write a short narrative about how this reunion evokes old patterns of behaviour—that is, show your classmates at nineteen still behaving as they did at thirteen.

HOWARD WHITE

Howard White is a West Coast writer born in 1945. His books include *Raincoast Chronicles, Spilsbury's Coast, The Accidental Airline, A Hard Man to Beat,* and *The Men There Were Then.* He has received numerous awards for his writing, including the Canadian Media Club Award and the Canadian Historical Association Career Award for Regional History. In 1991 his *Writing in the Rain: Stories, Essays, and Poems,* from which "My Experience with

Greatness" is taken, won the Stephen Leacock Medal for humour. In this essay, White constructs a tight narrative about a freewheeling, death-defying dash to catch a ferry—to illustrate the everyday heroic achievements of this not-so-common man.

My Experience with Greatness

HOWARD WHITE

1   When I was a kid I wanted to be great. A great man. Didn't matter at what, my ideas changed daily on that score, but I just had this very sure feeling I'd be great at it, whatever it was.

2   As it turned out, I was right. I did get to be great at a number of things, or at least pretty great. But there are a lot of problems with greatness I never suspected as a kid, and the main one grew out of that fuzziness about the chosen field, or perhaps more accurately unchosen field, you get to play your greatness out in.

3   I guess the lesson greatness has taught me can be summed up in two simple points, two things they don't tell you about greatness in school that when you found out about them tended to turn the whole thing into a kind of hollow victory. Number one is that greatness is a lot more common than they would have you think. Number two is, the process of selecting outstanding people for public celebration is rigged against the vast majority of people who do truly brilliant, herculean, heroic things. There are all sorts of people locked in obscure struggle whose ultimate triumph we will never read about, who, but for fate, might have demonstrated the same mettle on the world stage amid international acclaim.

4   Take me.

5   I'm a really unfortunate case, in that even my peers ignore my accomplishments because they're in fields where I'm the only guy there. For instance I am the undisputed world champion at catching the Langdale ferry from Pender Harbour in forty-seven minutes in a 1973 Volvo with no brakes and eight cases of books in the back. I proved this last Thursday.

6   The distance from Pender Harbour to Langdale is forty-eight miles so I must have averaged a touch under sixty, which isn't a qualifying speed at the Indy, but I'd give a lot to see A.J. Foyt try and duplicate my feat. For one thing, the stretch from Pender to

Halfmoon Bay follows an old logging road. I know the guy who pushed it in, Art Shaw. He had one of these weird cats with the controls up ahead of the engine and a blade that lifted right up over the cab, and old Art was kind of a passive resister when it came to obstacles like rock knobs, skunk cabbage patches or big stumps—his strategy was to go around. A lot of the skunk cabbage patches have dried up and a lot of the stumps have since rotted down, but Art's loops are still there, immortalized in six inches of cracking asphalt. They have loops at Indy too, but I doubt they have reverse banks, changes of radius midway through and six-inch breaks in the pavement like the Sunshine Coast Highway does north of Halfmoon Bay. Most Pender Harbourites give themselves an hour and a quarter to an hour and a half for the Langdale run, and the all-time record, as far as I know, is forty-one minutes. But that was set in a new Porsche.

The thing about a 1973 Volvo is, this story takes place in 1984.   7
Volvos are good cars. I've had two of them now. One '62 fastback that I bought off Walter Ibey for four hundred dollars in 1971, and this 1973 wagon I bought off Edith Daly two years ago. But there's one thing you have to keep in mind about a Volvo, and that is they're only built to last eleven years. The ads all say get a Volvo and it'll last eleven years, and that's true. But what the ads don't tell you is that immediately on its eleventh birthday a Volvo gives up like the one-hoss shay and becomes a deadly risk to anyone attempting to run a further mile.

I'd had a driveshaft out of this Volvo once and I'd replaced the   8
clutch once and put a new set of used rotors and calipers on the front axle, but apart from some rattles and clatters and flaking-away fenders, it kept going pretty steady. But last January it had its eleventh birthday. The first clue was it abruptly started using a quart of oil a day. I noticed a black puddle underneath it the size of a medium pizza and traced the trouble to a loose tappet cover. I buttoned that up and it stopped using oil for about three days, when I found a puddle under it the size of an extra-large pizza. This time it was a front main bearing seal. Still not realizing what the car was trying to tell me, I spent a very unhappy day and a half installing a new seal. A few fill-ups went by without my needing to add oil, then I brought it home with the tappets clacking like the Four Horsemen of the Apocalypse and found the oil level right off the stick. I looked underneath, but there was no puddle.

Actually the first thing that should have tipped me off was the   9
rear wiper conking out. The older Volvo wagons were famous for that deliciously luxurious rear-window wiper—it had a lot to do with my buying one—and I had always been impressed at the way this frivolous extra kept stiffly wiping, long after other unessentials like the radio, heater, trunk latch, and emergency brake had

corroded into oblivion. Blind Bob Wolpert, who runs an illegal junk yard up by the Spinnaker Road subdivision and is something of a purveyor of the new urban mythology, told me a Volvo is no good once that wiper stops and should be immediately abandoned on the roadside, but I have never been able to admit the supernatural into my real-life decision-making process.

10   Anyway, one day after the extra-large oil puddle, I got tired of driving without rear vision and remembered to turn the hose on the now completely socked-in rear window. The water from the hose didn't have the slightest effect on it. I took a close look and discovered the entire back end of the car was coated with a tarry amalgam of black crankcase oil and dust about three-eighths of an inch thick. I had to use a paint scraper and gasoline to cut a peephole. The next time I took it out, with clear vision of the road behind me for the first time in a month, it all came home to me. The road behind me appeared clouded in a bluish mist, where the road ahead was bright and clear. It was hard on the twists and dips around Pender to see more than a car-length behind, but going up the mile-long straight stretch outside Halfmoon Bay, the bluish mist became an inky smog completely obscuring the Peninsula Transport semi I'd passed seconds earlier. Thwarted from leaking her vital fluids away onto the ground, the old girl was now spewing it out of the exhaust with the emphasis of a sick whale spouting blood. I knew it was over then.

11   Having realized this, I also realized it would be a waste of time to fix any of the innumerable things that started now going wrong at the rate of one or two a trip—a strange lumpiness in the rear brakes, a half-turn or so of slack somewhere in the drive chain so it jolted like a coal train every time you touched the gas, a buck in the motor that would express itself going up hills and act on the drive chain lurch in a most alarming way—I knew I was going to have to get up to the car dump while it would still make the trip under its own power, but I kept waiting for something good in the eight-hundred-dollar range to show up in the *Coast News* want ads, and kept thinking I could get one more little trip out of the Volvo.

12   This was how matters stood at 9:30 the morning of March 11, 1984, when Jake Willett woke me up with a phone call wanting to know how come I wasn't in Horseshoe Bay to meet him for our work poetry reading tour of Vancouver Island pulp mills. I had been supposed to take the 8:30 ferry from Langdale, meet him in Horseshoe Bay at 9:15, then take the 11:30 ferry from Horseshoe Bay to Vancouver Island and drive up to start our tour in Gold River that evening.

13   "Jake, you wouldn't believe this, but I just slept through the alarm." This was a fair enough lie considering it was the first thing

I said that day, but it wasn't so good considering we have kids who wake up at 7:00 and go to school at 8:30, which Jake knew. The truth was I'd forgotten about our rendezvous, and about the entire four-day reading tour, and had been sleeping in quite determinedly with a pillow over my head.

"There's another ferry at 10:30. Can you make that?" 14

Jake is perhaps the most organized and reliable person on the 15 Pacific Slope of Western America, at least among the work poets. He would be constitutionally incapable of missing a ferry. My only hope was that, as a labour writer of middle-class origin, he would understand what a working-class thing this was I'd done.

"Sure Jake. No prob," I said. "See you at . . . " I made my voice 16 sound convincingly alert, I thought, but it was still too early in the day to add 10:30 and 1.

"11:30," he said firmly. "Don't forget the books." 17

"Right." 18

In a way it was lucky I didn't have any time to think, or speak 19 to my wife. It probably would have ended in bloodshed. This wasn't the first time I'd done something like this, just perhaps the worst time. I stuffed a spare shirt and toothbrush into my briefcase and bolted for the door patting down my hair. Mary stopped me with my wallet and watch, and a look made up of equal parts of pity and fury, not safe to kiss.

On the front porch I halted with a realization that this rather 20 typical screwup had just taken on a truly horrifying dimension. There before me in the yard hunched my blighted Volvo. The sight chilled me. A poem I planned to read later that day, about the death of a logger, came into my mind:

events
in themselves ordinary,
in combination deadly . . .

Not only was I about to attempt the twisty morning run to 21 Langdale in a completely unrealistic time, I was going to try it in a disintegrating eleven-year-old Volvo that was unsafe to sit in let alone drive, and not only was I going to ask God to forgive me this temptation to fate, I was going to load the car up with eight heavy cases of books. I couldn't take my wife's good little Toyota, because I had to leave it parked four days at the Langdale terminal and her constitution couldn't support life for over thirty minutes without her Toyota.

The logical solution was to have her drive me and I could sense 22 she was just waiting for me to fall to my knees and ask, but somehow the trial presented by the Volvo, with its risk of almost certain death, seemed easier to face.

23   Going over the first hill I discovered the lumpy rear wheel brakes had now totally given up, leaving me with brakes only on one front wheel, which not only failed to much alter the car's forward momentum, but almost ripped the steering wheel out of my hands and pitched me into a granite bluff. So now in addition to making the hour-long Langdale run in an unsafe wreck overloaded with books, I was going to do it with only one locking front wheel for brakes.

24   I recognized that this was going to be one of the greatest tests I'd ever faced, one that demanded every ounce of concentration, of heroic nerve, that a person could ever be expected to muster. I snuck up carefully on the big hills, coasting over their crests at a near stall, nursing my shred of braking capacity along as far as I dared test that shrieking, shuddering left front wheel, then letting the old beast fly sixty, seventy, eighty miles an hour, making up the time I lost bucking up the grades at the head of my ever-thickening black storm cloud of oil smoke.

25   I stopped religiously every ten miles to throw another quart or two of oil into the smoking hot motor, no doubt setting the world speed record for pouring two quarts of oil too, and kept my ear so attuned to every new rattle and throb I was able to just keep the motor on the edge where I was getting everything it had left without giving it the excuse it desperately wanted to pack up totally. Talk about living on the edge, no Edmund Hillary inching along a Himalayan ice shelf was ever so exposed and vulnerable as I was streaking through the intersection at the bottom of the Norwest Bay hill in that smoking, pounding missile of rust, grease and steam. And yet I was on top of the problem. Nothing caught me by surprise. When an elderly woman in a fifteen-miles-an-hour Pinto pulled out in front of me on a corner with a car in the oncoming lane, I just cranked it for the shoulder and streaked past, skidding in the gravel. If I had given in to the instinct to even touch the brake, that left wheel would have jerked me into the oncoming car so fast no one would ever have known what happened. There were a hundred factors, all matters of life and death, which I had to keep juggling in my mind, never missing a one. I even remembered to slow down at the speed trap outside Sechelt, letting the Pinto overtake me and get nailed. Does an astronaut at his bank of blinking controls have so much to keep track of? No, all his equipment is forgiving and reliable and all his decisions neat and simple. Gus Grissom would never have made it past the hairpin at Silver Sands. But I made it to the ferry with thirty seconds to spare.

26   As it happened, there was a two-sailing wait and cars were lined up for a mile, but after what I'd been through nothing the BC Ferry Corp could throw at me could give me even a moment's

pause. I just pulled into the oncoming lane, leaned on the horn and streaked through the lineup, yelling at the fluorescent-gloved attendant, "Emergency work—poetry mercy run! Gangway!", drove up in front of the baggage van and had six boxes moved before the fat lady from the toll booth had time to come puffing down.

"What do you think you're doing! You get back to the end of the line!" she barked. I smiled sweetly.

"Just loading baggage, ma'am."

Her buggy eyes followed the boxes from the drooping, dripping, hissing Volvo to the otherwise completely empty baggage van.

"That's not baggage! That van is reserved for hand baggage!"

"Are you telling me there's no room, ma'am?" I was done anyway. Her bosom was heaving under the blue Ferry Corp blazer as she struggled to contain her outrage, and before she could think up another institutional imperative to fling at me, I was into the car and gone back up the road. I just ran the old heap into the brush outside the compound and left the keys in it. Then I made for the ferry at a dead run.

It wasn't until I was leaning over the rail as the boat pulled away, watching the toll booth lady still waving her arms and regaling the man with orange gloves, that I let go. Waves of relief washed over me. I beamed at the luminous prop wash, the pale blue terminal buildings, the left-behind lines of cars, the dark slopes of Mount Elphinstone behind. And I just felt—great.

Vocabulary

a. *paragraph 3:* mettle
b. *paragraph 7:* shay
c. *paragraph 8:* rotors, calipers, tappet
d. *paragraph 9:* purveyor
e. *paragraph 10:* amalgam

Questions

1. What is White's purpose in the essay? How do you interpret its title?
2. Of what importance are the other characters in White's essay? What techniques does he use to introduce and portray them?
3. What device does White use to structure his narrative?
4. What sort of emotions does this essay convey? What response does it seek to evoke in the reader?

Writing Assignments

1. Write an essay that begins in the present, then recounts an episode from the past that illustrates the present mood. Reveal your feelings

through the details rather than simply stating them.

2. Compare Howard White's essay with E.B. White's "Once More to the Lake."

DAVID MACFARLANE

David Macfarlane was born in Hamilton in 1952 and received his BA from the University of Toronto in 1975. He has been a regular contributor to *Saturday Night* magazine since 1983, rising to the post of Associate Editor for the year 1987–88, and the winner of numerous National Magazine Awards for his contributions to various magazines. He is also the author of *The Danger Tree*, which won the Canadian Authors Association Award for non-fiction and was short-listed for Ontario's Trillium Award. In the following essay he constructs a complex narrative to tell the highly suggestive story of his relationship to the legendary city of light.

Love and Death

DAVID MACFARLANE

1   The first dead body I ever saw was one I found hanging under a bridge in Paris. It was late at night. I remember being impressed with its stillness and with the calm, unprotesting way its unbound hands rested at its sides. The face, a young man's, was swollen black. When I saw it I let out a little yelp I hadn't heard come from inside me before.

2   Fourteen years later, I was back in Paris for a brief visit. My friend Bernard Grégoire, who is a Parisian, found occasion to remind me of the night I found the body. It was my last evening in the city, and an odd thing just had happened.

3   Bernard and I were playing chess at the Old Navy, an unfashionable and undistinguished café on the boulevard St-Germain. Walking past our table, slowly swaying her graceful hips, a young woman smiled. At me. And this inspired Bernard—a man who prides himself on his rakish good looks and his way with women— to remind me of the suicide.

4   We weren't supposed to be at the Old Navy. Bernard and I had planned to play in style at Les Deux Magots, the elegant café at the corner of the place St-Germain-des-Prés. But when we opened our chessboard there we were informed by a white-aproned waiter that

playing games at the tables was not allowed. We moved down the street. The Old Navy wasn't so choosy.

Bernard, who also prides himself on his aggressive chess, was 5 beating me badly. He lined up my defeated pieces beside his glass of Cointreau on ice. It was a lovely evening, just after the dinner hour, and the sidewalks were crowded with the sauntering passers-by who, more than any other characteristic of the city, make Paris Paris. The smell of the place — a combination of hot, ancient air from the métro and black tobacco from everywhere, exhaust fumes and flowers, stone walls and coffee, gutters and ironed linen—took me back fourteen years to when I was twenty-five and had an apartment on the rue de Saussure. The smell, and also the strange, disproportionate noise of the place—the way that the clatter of ice or the laughter of a woman can be heard across a café in spite of the loud rush of traffic only a few feet away — saddened me the way the passage of time always will, and, at the same time, delighted me with the simple fact of my being in Paris.

"You're still a terrible player," Bernard said. 6

I had to agree. Bernard is decisive and methodical, bent, from 7 his first move, on destroying his opposition. My strategy amounts to little more than vaguely hoping for the best. But that night at the Old Navy, Bernard's offensive was interrupted at a crucial moment by the strolling tap of high heels on pavement. The rhythm was seductively slow. We both looked up, and we were both surprised to see a peerlessly beautiful young lady, arm in arm with a well-dressed young man, smiling warmly and directly at me.

Her brown hair was pulled back in a thick ponytail. It shone 8 like satin in the light from the café. Her face had a fine, Pre-Raphaelite quality. Her hands were long and graceful. Her nails were red, and her eyes were wide and exotic. She was wearing an elegantly tailored silk suit, and her neck was wrapped in an ivory scarf. Her sophistication was obvious and unquestionably Parisian. She moved, swaying gracefully off the axis of her narrow toes, with a steady, measured pace.

When I realized who she was I smiled back. Only a few hours 9 before, while waiting for Bernard, I had shared a curious moment with her. For two and a half hours I had been drinking thirty-franc Ricards at Les Deux Magots, and daydreaming happily about Paris. I was staring at a handsome young couple seated a few tables away. The light around them seemed golden in the late glow of a Paris afternoon. (Such is the effect of three Ricards.) She was beautiful. He was quiet and attentive. She was laughing and they were drinking champagne. Eventually, she sensed my steady gaze and turned towards me. Her young man was looking the other way, across St-Germain.

10   She didn't seem insulted by my stare. Apparently, we understood one another. She seemed to realize, or so I imagined, that I
was someone who, in a guileless and slightly drunken way, was
simply enjoying the pleasure she was taking in the remarkable
coincidence of her being alive and happy, in love and in Paris. She
leaned across the table to kiss the young man—in one of those protracted and passionate public embraces that only Parisians have the
panache to pull off—and as she did she smiled at me as if we were
old friends.

11   But when she strolled by our table at the Old Navy a few hours
later and our eyes met again, I saw no reason to explain our brief
and innocent past to Bernard. I preferred to leave him puzzled. "Ah
Paris," I said, just cryptically and just archly enough to annoy him.
"A city of coincidence."

12   Bernard wasn't going to be impressed. He wasn't even going to
be curious. "Sometimes," he said, "I think North Americans do
nothing but think of stupidities to say about Paris."

13   "But Bernard," I said, "it's true."

14   Bernard and I had met in the spring of 1976 on the train to Paris
from Chartres. Then, by coincidence, we ran into one another two
weeks later on the wide stone steps of the Luxembourg Gardens. In
an odd, Parisian way this didn't surprise me. I had already come to
realize that the city, in spite of its sprawling and exhausting size,
encouraged chance encounters. The chairs of its cafés face out to the
sidewalks and to the happenstance of passers-by. Its oldest streets
turn back on one another in reunions of convoluted circles. And
because the city's greatest pleasures are its public ones—strolls
along the grand boulevards, explorations through winding streets,
promenades through the parks, drinks in cafés, and walks by the
Seine—it's not surprising in all of Paris to see someone you know
from somewhere else, or someone you noticed that morning at a
cheese stall, or perhaps just someone you remember from the lineup for taxis at the airport.

15   "Coincidence?" Bernard asked. He was staring glumly at me over
the chessboard. "Like that time you got into trouble with *le pendu*."

16   "I guess."

17   "What was her name? That Polish girl?"

18   "Gabrielle."

19   "Now that," Bernard said, "was bizarre."

20   Bernard used to have a *vélo*. He has a car now. It's a green, five-
year-old Peugeot that bears the battle scars of parking in Paris. During my visit we drove everywhere, and the car changed the city for
me. I won't think of Paris the same way again.

21   When I lived in Paris, I walked. Endlessly. Gabrielle used to
chide me about the time I spent in plodding, pedestrian transit. I

would set out hours in advance for a film or a gallery or a quarter of Paris I had not yet seen. Even the métro was a luxury—the less money I spent, the longer I could stay, and I had no plans of leaving.

Exploring Paris on foot gave it an oddly disunified aspect—or this, at least, was the image that persisted in my memory once I left. The city seemed less a single entity than a gray solar system of destinations—the Cinémathèque, the Jeu de Paume, place des Vosges, the rue St-Denis, Sacré-Coeur, the Marché aux Puces, Père Lachaise, Le Grand Palais—orbiting at incredible distances my little apartment. I happen to read maps the way I play chess, and my most common memory of Paris is of heading in what I thought was the general direction of somewhere and finding myself, unperturbed and unhurried, back at the corner of a grand terraced boulevard and an askew little street I thought I'd left far behind. 22

But on this visit, I hardly walked at all. We drove, and Bernard proved to be an excellent driver—in the Parisian manner. He was fast and accurate and ruthless. "You must ignore pedestrians," he told me in the midst of his guided tour. "If you slow for them you might cause an accident." 23

Bernard insisted on using the car for our every outing. In fact, the only distances we ever walked were the inevitable four or five blocks from wherever we could park to wherever we were going. Once, on our way to the Musée d'Orsay to see Millet's *The Gleaners,* Manet's *Le Déjeuner sur l'herbe,* and Cézanne's *Apples and Oranges*— "You're only here for two days," Bernard said. "Three masterpieces should be enough"—we found a miraculous parking spot directly behind the museum. "For a Parisian," Bernard said, "this is better than an orgasm. I will now not need sex for a week." And my most Parisian memory of the trip—not a meal, nor a vista, nor a monument—was a glimpse of two young men on motor scooters. In front of us, they wove through traffic at breakneck speed and then, whirling around place d'Italie, shook hands without slowing down and went their separate ways. 24

This, I realized, was the Paris most Parisians know—the Paris of traffic jams, exhaust fumes, noise, and, in spite of all this, the civility of handshakes. I would prefer, I suppose, a Paris without cars, but Bernard scoffed at what he called touristic nostalgia for the *belle époque.* "Paris is Paris," he said. "Regrettably we are alive in the present tense." He shrugged and shifted to fourth, cutting through the place de l'Alma and heading across the river. We cut over the steel gray water of the Seine. That was when I saw the black iron bridge I had walked under one night fourteen years before. 25

On that evening, Gabrielle was supposed to go with me to the Cinémathèque. We'd spent the day at my apartment, but by the 26 afternoon she'd changed her mind. Gabrielle, from the day I met her, was in the process of breaking up with her boyfriend. I'd never met him. I knew he was a student. From what Gabrielle told me I knew he was a poet and a political activist—romantic and darkly impossible. The break-up had been going on for months. When it seemed that they had finally ended things, Gabrielle spent time with me. Then, afraid because he got so upset, she'd go back to his place in the Marais. Her description of where he lived always made me think of *La Bohème*.

27   But the last movie at the Cinémathèque that night was *La Nuit américaine*, one of my favorite Truffauts. And that afternoon, in the little enclosure outside the apartment, Gabrielle and I had our one and only argument. We stood beside two crumbling terracotta pots of red geraniums. We both shouted our terrible French while my landlady, proper as a correctly declined noun, listened and pretended to sweep her doorstep.

28   I went to the movie myself. Afterwards, I had an espresso in a café behind the Palais de Chaillot. I watched the passersby at the place Wilson. An hour or so passed. It was a lovely, moonlit night. I decided to walk home partway along the cobbled banks of the Seine.

29   The river was black and smooth, only wrinkled here and there with the reflection of the yellow lights on the *quais*. The noise of traffic droned in the distance. My soft-soled walking shoes slopped along the bricks of the embankment. I could smell the river. Occasionally, a little wave slapped the dark stone wall below me. I approached the narrow bridge that crossed from the avenue de New York on the Right Bank to the quai Branly on the Left. I stepped out of the soft light of a full moon and, beneath the network of iron struts, walked straight into a pair of dangling feet.

30   Since Bernard was the only Parisian I knew during the time I lived in Paris, the night after I found the body I met him at Le Sélect and told him the story. I had imagined this would calm me down, but Bernard listened with growing consternation. He was horrified. Not horrified because I'd found a body hanging underneath a bridge; Bernard was a Parisian. Bernard was horrified because I'd called the police.

31   In those days Bernard smoked Gitanes *jaunes*. He lit one, and as he waved out the match he pushed his other hand through his lank brown hair. "This is very serious, man." he said. "The police here can be very weird."

32   I explained. I had called the police; I had waited forty-five minutes for their arrival; I had put up with two hours of their questioning while they'd taken endless photographs of the corpse—only to save someone else the trauma of finding the body. Bernard

shrugged his shoulders, arched his eyebrows, and blew out a gust of smoke in the single gesture that Parisians reserve for the stupidities of anyone who, obviously not from Paris, isn't even from France. "Pfft," he said. "You should have kept walking."

Bernard was right. *Le pendu*, as the police called the body, was a ³³ young Polish student. He was in Paris studying French at the Alliance Française. By an extremely unhappy coincidence studying French at the Alliance Française was my excuse for being in Paris as well. The fact that I almost never went to classes didn't help. Neither, apparently, did he. Worse, the three hours a week that both of us spent our time avoiding were the same three hours. We were in the same class. And worse still, there were only a few Poles in the class. Gabrielle was one.

I learned this the morning after I found the body. I was taken ³⁴ from my apartment by two policemen for further questioning. Standing in the courtyard with her broom, my landlady acknowledged my escorted departure with the same icy formality with which she kept careful track of all my comings and goings. The police, presumably, had asked her which apartment was mine. They had, perhaps, even explained to her why they were interested. This hadn't altered her impression of me. Being a foreign student and being arrested, possibly for murder, amounted to pretty much the same thing.

"*Au revoir, monsieur,*" she said. ³⁵

"*Au revoir, madame,*" I replied. ³⁶

The investigating officer was a Detective Lévy. He sat behind a ³⁷ neatly ordered desk. The photographs the police had taken of the hanging body were in an envelope in front of him. To his left was an ancient typewriter. The walls of his office were a dirty beige, and his tall windows opened onto a courtyard. The only decorations in the room were a row of six different gauges of shotgun shells lined up across the top of a metal cabinet and a poster for a Goya exhibition at the Orangerie. The illustration was Saturn eating his children.

Detective Lévy passed me the photographs and watched me ³⁸ carefully as I looked at them. He told me what the police had learned. As he spoke I felt my face flush. He rested his chin thoughtfully between his thumb and forefinger. I passed the pictures back. I couldn't tell if he knew anything about Gabrielle. He asked me what I had been doing down by the river alone so late at night. He listened to my reply with the slightly pained expression that typically greeted my French in Paris. I told him I liked walking.

Detective Lévy sat back in his chair. He had a round face and ³⁹ gleaming, brilliantined hair. Almost certainly, he said, the case was a suicide. It was not, in a city the size of Paris, an uncommon thing. But there were, he went on, gazing up to the flaking ornamental molding in the ceiling, a few things that worried him. The first, of course, was the strange coincidence that in all of Paris it had been a classmate who'd happened upon the body.

40   And there was the knot. The knot would have been difficult for someone to tie by himself. Detective Lévy swivelled in his chair and considered the height of his windows. He didn't want to bother me with technicalities, but it happened that there was something a bit odd about the position of the feet.

41   *"Monsieur,"* he said. *"Est-ce que vous avez touché le cadavre?"*

42   *"Non, monsieur."*

43   Detective Lévy sighed. He held a pencil as if it were a cigarette holder and he were a movie star. He regretted the inconvenience but wondered if I could stay in Paris for the next few days. Just in case. He wanted to make further inquiries at the school. A formality, really. The family might ask about certain details.

44   I said that I would stay. Detective Lévy acknowledged his thanks and his regret with a slight shrug. It was, his expression managed to convey, just a question of bad luck that I was involved in this. A regrettable coincidence. I agreed and shrugged back. We both stood.

45   *"Vous aimez Paris?"* he asked as we shook hands.

46   *"Oui, monsieur. Beaucoup."*

47   The next day I was on the train to London.

Vocabulary

a. *paragraph 3:* rakish
b. *paragraph 8:* Pre-Raphaelite
c. *paragraph 10:* guileless, protracted, panache
d. *paragraph 11:* cryptically, archly
e. *paragraph 14:* happenstance, convoluted
f. *paragraph 22:* askew
g. *paragraph 30:* consternation

Questions

1. Make a list of the key elements in Macfarlane's narrative. Why are they ordered in this way? Could you change the sequence of events without sacrificing the essay's impact?
2. Locate the essay's climax. What is gained by delaying it? How does the concluding sentence affect the resolution?
3. Consider the descriptive details in paragraph 5. What overall impression do they create?
4. Macfarlane uses pronouns, conjunctions, and repetitions of key words to make transitions between paragraphs. Give some examples of each.

5. How does the tone contribute to the impression of Paris Macfarlane seeks to convey?

Writing Assignment

Imagine revisiting a place you enjoyed and recount the experience. Try to make your essay as detailed as Macfarlane's.

E.B. WHITE

E.B. White (1899–1985) was one of America's most distinguished writers—an essayist, a poet, a writer of books for children. His life-long association with *The New Yorker* magazine began in 1926. The columns that appeared in *Harper's* under the title "One Man's Meat" were collected in 1942 and published in a book of the same name. Other essays are found in *The Second Tree from the Corner, The Points of My Compass,* and *Essays of E.B. White.* In all of these books there is much about Maine, where White lived for many years. The following essay is a poignant evocation of childhood and the passage of time. In his account of a trip to the summer camp of his youth, E.B. White meditates on continuity and change.

Once More to the Lake

E.B. WHITE

One summer, along about 1904, my father rented a camp on a lake in Maine and took us all there for the month of August. We all got ringworm from some kittens and had to rub Pond's Extract on our arms and legs night and morning, and my father rolled over in a canoe with all his clothes on; but outside of that the vacation was a success and from then on none of us ever thought there was any place in the world like that lake in Maine. We returned summer after summer—always on August 1st for one month. I have since become a salt-water man, but sometimes in summer there are days when the restlessness of the tides and the fearful cold of the sea water and the incessant wind which blows across the afternoon and into the evening make me wish for the placidity of a lake in the woods. A few weeks ago this feeling got so strong I bought myself a couple of bass hooks and a spinner and returned to the lake where we used to go, for a week's fishing and to revisit old haunts.

2   I took along my son, who had never had any fresh water up his nose and who had seen lily pads only from train windows. On the journey over to the lake I began to wonder what it would be like. I wondered how time would have marred this unique, this holy spot— the coves and streams, the hills that the sun set behind, the camps and the paths behind the camps. I was sure that the tarred road would have found it out and I wondered in what other ways it would be desolated. It is strange how much you can remember about places like that once you allow your mind to return into the grooves which lead back. You remember one thing, and that suddenly reminds you of another thing. I guess I remembered clearest of all the early mornings, when the lake was cool and motionless, remembered how the bedroom smelled of the lumber it was made of and of the wet woods whose scent entered through the screen. The partitions in the camp were thin and did not extend clear to the top of the rooms, and as I was always the first up I would dress softly so as not to wake the others, and sneak out into the sweet outdoors and start out in the canoe, keeping close along the shore in the long shadows of the pines. I remembered being very careful never to rub my paddle against the gunwale for fear of disturbing the stillness of the cathedral.

3   The lake had never been what you would call a wild lake. There were cottages sprinkled around the shores, and it was in farming country although the shores of the lake were quite heavily wooded. Some of the cottages were owned by nearby farmers, and you would live at the shore and eat your meals at the farmhouse. That's what our family did. But although it wasn't wild, it was a fairly large and undisturbed lake and there were places in it which, to a child at least, seemed infinitely remote and primeval.

4   I was right about the tar: it led to within half a mile of the shore. But when I got back there, with my boy, and we settled into a camp near a farmhouse and into the kind of summertime I had known, I could tell that it was going to be pretty much the same as it had been before—I knew it, lying in bed the first morning, smelling the bedroom, and hearing the boy sneak quietly out and go off along the shore in a boat. I began to sustain the illusion that he was I, and therefore, by simple transposition, that I was my father. This sensation persisted, kept cropping up all the time we were there. It was not an entirely new feeling, but in this setting it grew much stronger. I seemed to be living a dual existence. I would be in the middle of some simple act, I would be picking up a bait box or laying down a table fork, or I would be saying something, and suddenly it would be not I but my father who was saying the words or making the gesture. It gave me a creepy sensation.

We went fishing the first morning. I felt the same damp moss covering the worms in the bait can, and saw the dragonfly alight on the tip of my rod as it hovered a few inches from the surface of the water. It was the arrival of this fly that convinced me beyond any doubt that everything was as it always had been, that the years were a mirage and there had been no years. The small waves were the same, chucking the rowboat under the chin as we fished at anchor, and the boat was the same boat, the same color green and the ribs broken in the same places, and under the floor-boards the same fresh-water leavings and débris — the dead helgramite, the wisps of moss, the rusty discarded fish-hook, the dried blood from yesterday's catch. We stared silently at the tips of our rods, at the dragonflies that came and went. I lowered the tip of mine into the water, tentatively, pensively dislodging the fly, which darted two feet away, poised, darted two feet back, and came to rest again a little farther up the rod. There had been no years between the ducking of this dragonfly and the other one — the one that was part of memory. I looked at the boy, who was silently watching his fly, and it was my hands that held his rod, my eyes watching. I felt dizzy and didn't know which rod I was at the end of.

We caught two bass, hauling them in briskly as though they were mackerel, pulling them over the side of the boat in a businesslike manner without any landing net, and stunning them with a blow on the back of the head. When we got back for a swim before lunch, the lake was exactly where we had left it, the same number of inches from the dock, and there was only the merest suggestion of a breeze. This seemed an utterly enchanted sea, this lake you could leave to its own devices for a few hours and come back to, and find that it had not stirred, this constant and trustworthy body of water. In the shallows, the dark, water-soaked sticks and twigs, smooth and old, were undulating in clusters on the bottom against the clean ribbed sand, and the track of the mussel was plain. A school of minnows swam by, each minnow with its small individual shadow, doubling the attendance, so clear and sharp in the sunlight. Some of the other campers were in swimming, along the shore, one of them with a cake of soap, and the water felt thin and clear and unsubstantial. Over the years there had been this person with the cake of soap, this cultist, and here he was. There had been no years.

Up to the farmhouse to dinner through the teeming, dusty field, the road under our sneakers was only a two-track road. The middle track was missing, the one with the marks of the hooves and the splotches of dried, flaky manure. There had always been three tracks to choose from in choosing which track to walk in; now the choice was narrowed down to two. For a moment I missed terribly the middle alternative. But the way led past the tennis court, and something about the way it lay there in the sun reassured me; the tape had loosened along the backline, the alleys were green with plantains and other weeds, and the net (installed in June and removed in September) sagged in the dry noon, and the whole place steamed with midday heat and hunger and emptiness. There was a choice of pie for dessert, and one was blueberry and one was apple, and the waitresses were the same country girls, there having been no passage of time, only the illusion of it as in a dropped curtain — the waitresses were still fifteen; their hair had been washed, that was the only difference—they had been to the movies and seen the pretty girls with the clean hair.

8   Summertime, oh summertime, pattern of life indelible, the fadeproof lake, the woods unshatterable, the pasture with the sweetfern and the juniper forever and ever, summer without end; this was the background, and the life along the shore was the design, the cottages with their innocent and tranquil design, their tiny docks with the flagpole and the American flag floating against the white clouds in the blue sky, the little paths over the roots of the trees leading from camp to camp and the paths leading back to the outhouses and the can of lime for sprinkling, and at the souvenir counters at the store the miniature birch-bark canoes and the post cards that showed things looking a little better than they looked. This was the American family at play, escaping the city heat, wondering whether the newcomers in the camp at the head of the cove were "common" or "nice," wondering whether it was true that the people who drove up for Sunday dinner at the farmhouse were turned away because there wasn't enough chicken.

9   It seemed to me, as I kept remembering all this, that those times and those summers had been infinitely precious and worth saving. There had been jollity and peace and goodness. The arriving (at the beginning of August) had been so big a business in itself, at the railway station the farm wagon drawn up, the first smell of the pine-laden air, the first glimpse of the smiling farmer, and the great importance of the trunks and your father's enormous authority in such matters, and the feel of the wagon under you for the long ten-mile haul, and at the top of the last long hill catching the first view of the lake after eleven months of not seeing this cherished body of water. The shouts and cries of the other campers when they saw you, and the trunks to be unpacked, to give up their rich burden. (Arriving was less exciting nowadays, when you sneaked up in your car and parked it under a tree near the camp and took out the bags and in five minutes it was all over, no fuss, no loud wonderful fuss about trunks.)

Peace and goodness and jollity. The only thing that was wrong   10
now, really, was the sound of the place, an unfamiliar nervous
sound of the outboard motors. This was the note that jarred, the
one thing that would sometimes break the illusion and set the years
moving. In those other summertimes all motors were inboard; and
when they were at a little distance, the noise they made was sedative, an ingredient of summer sleep. They were one-cylinder and
two-cylinder engines, and some were make-and-break and some
were jump-spark, but they all made a sleepy sound across the lake.
The one-lungers throbbed and fluttered, and the twin-cylinder ones
purred and purred, and that was a quiet sound too. But now the
campers all had outboards. In the daytime, in the hot mornings,
these motors made a petulant, irritable sound; at night, in the still
evening when the afterglow lit the water, they whined about one's
ears like mosquitoes. My boy loved our rented outboard, and his
great desire was to achieve singlehanded mastery over it, and
authority, and he soon learned the trick of choking it a little (but not
too much), and the adjustment of the needle valve. Watching him I
would remember the things you could do with the old one-cylinder
engine with the heavy flywheel, how you could have it eating out
of your hand if you got really close to it spiritually. Motor boats in
those days didn't have clutches, and you would make a landing by
shutting off the motor at the proper time and coasting in with a
dead rudder. But there was a way of reversing them, if you learned
the trick, by cutting the switch and putting it on again exactly on
the final dying revolution of the flywheel, so that it would kick
back against compression and begin reversing. Approaching a dock
in a strong following breeze, it was difficult to slow up sufficiently
by the ordinary coasting method, and if a boy felt he had complete
mastery over his motor, he was tempted to keep it running beyond
its time and then reverse it a few feet from the dock. It took a cool
nerve, because if you threw the switch a twentieth of a second too
soon you would catch the flywheel when it still had speed enough
to go up past center, and the boat would leap ahead, charging bull-
fashion at the dock.

We had a good week at the camp. The bass were biting well   11
and the sun shone endlessly, day after day. We would be tired at
night and lie down in the accumulated heat of the little bedrooms
after the long hot day and the breeze would stir almost impercepti-
bly outside and the smell of the swamp drift in through the rusty
screens. Sleep would come easily and in the morning the red squir-
rel would be on the roof, tapping out his gay routine. I kept remembering everything, lying in bed in the mornings—the small steam-
boat that had a long rounded stern like the lip of a Ubangi, and

how quietly she ran on the moonlight sails, when the older boys played their mandolins and the girls sang and we ate doughnuts dipped in sugar, and how sweet the music was on the water in the shining night, and what it had felt like to think about girls then. After breakfast we would go up to the store and the things were in the same place — the minnows in a bottle, the plugs and spinners disarranged and pawed over by the youngsters from the boys' camp, the fig newtons and the Beeman's gum. Outside, the road was tarred and cars stood in front of the store. Inside, all was just as it had always been, except there was more Coca-Cola and not so much Moxie and root beer and birch beer and sarsaparilla. We would walk out with a bottle of pop apiece and sometimes the pop would backfire up our noses and hurt. We explored the streams, quietly, where the turtles slid off the sunny logs and dug their way into the soft bottom; and we lay on the town wharf and fed worms to the tame bass. Everywhere we went I had trouble making out which was I, the one walking at my side, the one walking in my pants.

12   One afternoon while we were there at the lake a thunderstorm came up. It was like the revival of an old melodrama that I had seen long ago with childish awe. The second-act climax of the drama of the electrical disturbance over a lake in America had not changed in any important respect. This was a big scene, still the big scene. The whole thing was so familiar, the first feeling of oppression and heat and a general air around camp of not wanting to go very far away. In midafternoon (it was all the same) a curious darkening of the sky, and a lull in everything that had made life tick; and then the way the boats suddenly swung the other way at their moorings with the coming of a breeze out of the new quarter, and the premonitory rumble. Then the kettle drum, then the snare, then the bass drum and cymbals, then cracking light against the dark, and the gods grinning and licking their chops in the hills. Afterward the calm, the rain steadily rustling in the calm lake, the return of light and hope and spirits, and the campers running out in joy and relief to go swimming in the rain, their bright cries perpetuating the deathless joke about how they were getting simply drenched, and the children screaming with delight at the new sensation of bathing in the rain, and the joke about getting drenched linking the generations in a strong indestructible chain. And the comedian who waded in carrying an umbrella.

13   When the others went swimming my son said he was going in too. He pulled his dripping trunks from the line where they had hung all through the shower and wrung them out. Languidly, and with no thought of going in, I watched him, his hard little body, skinny and bare, saw him wince slightly as he pulled up around his

vitals the small, soggy, icy garment. As he buckled the swollen belt, suddenly my groin felt the chill of death.

```

```

Vocabulary

a. *paragraph 1:* incessant
b. *paragraph 2:* gunwale
c. *paragraph 3:* primeval
d. *paragraph 4:* transposition
e. *paragraph 5:* helgramite
f. *paragraph 6:* undulating
g. *paragraph 7:* teeming, plantains
h. *paragraph 8:* indelible
i. *paragraph 10:* sedative, petulant
j. *paragraph 11:* sarsaparilla
k. *paragraph 12:* melodrama, premonitory
l. *paragraph 13:* languidly, vitals

Questions

1. How does White, at the beginning of his essay, set his narrative in a specific time and place?
2. What senses does he appeal to in the essay? Cite specific examples.
3. Why does he use phrases such as "blows across the afternoon" (paragraph 1), "doubling the attendance" (paragraph 6), and "ingredient of summer sleep" (paragraph 10)? How do such details affect the mood of the essay?
4. Discuss the effectiveness of the depiction of the storm in paragraph 12. Why does he use the drama metaphor to describe the incident?
5. Study and comment on the complex stylistic uses of the word "and" in paragraphs 7 and 11.
6. What other points does his narrative make about the "indestructible chain" linking the generations?

Writing Assignment

Using comparison and contrast, tell the story of revisiting a place you knew as a child. Avoid generalizing about impressions by using as many specific details as possible.

Example

The word *example* originally referred to a sample or typical instance. The word still has this meaning, and for many writers it is an outstanding instance—even one essential to the idea under discussion, as in the following explanation of right- and left-handedness in the world:

> The world is full of things whose right-hand version is different from the left-hand version: a right-handed corkscrew as against a left-handed, a right snail as against a left one. Above all, the two hands; they can be mirrored one in the other, but they cannot be turned in such a way that the right hand and the left hand become interchangeable. That was known in Pasteur's time to be true also of some crystals, whose facets are so arranged that there are right-hand versions and left-hand versions. (Jacob Bronowski, *The Ascent of Man*)

Examples are essential when we are presenting ideas. Those that seem clear to us might not be clear to our readers. Therefore, we must be very careful in selecting the examples we choose to include in an essay. The examples must be typical of the subject, representing the qualities we wish to illustrate. For instance, the crimes Walter Stewart describes in "Good Old Us" were committed by ordinary people, not psychotic criminals.

The examples chosen must be related clearly to the topic. If Walter Stewart had described a riot during the Winnipeg General Strike, it would not illustrate "typical" behaviour but rather the frustration brought on by a particular event. The examples chosen must also be limited in number. Doubtless, Stewart had access to many more examples of crime and corruption in Canada, but chose to use only a select few. We must decide how many examples are needed to illustrate the point and elicit the desired response from the audience.

Examples make ideas concrete and point to the experiences and observations that formed these ideas. Almost all essays depend on examples; some consist entirely of examples.

MEREDITH CHILTON

Meredith Chilton is the curator of the George R. Gardiner Museum of Ceramic Art, located in Toronto. In the following essay, she shows how the

EXAMPLE   149

history of perfume containers can provide insights into the mores and hygienic practices of entire cultural epochs.

A Fugitive Pleasure: Perfume in the 18th Century

MEREDITH CHILTON

To recall the ephemeral pleasures of the privileged in the 18th century is to invoke the Rococo period, marked by its frivolity, lightness, and hedonism. The art of Boucher offers intimate glimpses of nymphs and shepherdesses. There were water gardens and chinoiserie pavilions, the fleeting delights of taking tea alfresco, witty conversations and flirtation in the salon or the boudoir, the refinement of charm and elegance of manner, and of course, the elusive scent of perfume.

In France, the Court of Louis XV, where the pursuit of pleasure was paramount, became known as *La Cour Parfumée*. Good taste became the principal concern of the aristocracy. Perfume, like porcelain, was a symbol of luxury and fashion. No one in France had more influence on fashion and taste than Louis's mistress, Mme de Pompadour. She was a prolific user of perfume, purchasing hundreds of thousands of livres worth each year from merchant-traders such as Lazare Duvaux, whose records show that she bought *Eau de Portugal* and *Huile de Venus* from his shop "Au Chagrin de Turquie" (The Turkish Lament) on the rue Saint-Honoré.

Perfume became an intrinsic part of fashionable life. It was used in a wide variety of products, one of the most popular of which was perfumed gloves, a conceit introduced during the 16th century. *Neroli*, a scent made from bitter-orange blossoms, named for the Duchess of Neroli, was the favored fragrance for gloves of the period. A prohibitive tax on hides, introduced in the 1760s, devastated the industry, which was centered in Grasse and Montpellier. Many *gantiers-parfumeurs*, or perfumed-glove makers, moved to Paris to become simply perfumers. One, Jean-Louis Fargeon, became Louis XV's perfumer.

Perfume was also an important ingredient in cosmetics and hairdressing. Upon rising, the lady of fashion would attend to her toilette. "The role of a young Beauty is much more serious than you can imagine. Nothing is more important than what happens at her toilette in the morning," wrote Montesquieu. First a foundation called *plâtre*, or plaster, was applied. It often consisted of fine white clay, ground pearls, honey, and gum. In spite of criticism from the medical profession, many recipes called for powdered white lead. It was combined with pomade, a thick paste similar to modern cold cream made from a mixture of pure white lard and essential oils of violets, jasmine, or lilies-of-the-valley. This foundation was then carefully applied to the skin to conceal wrinkles.

5   Rouge came next. A typical recipe for *Carmin rouge* involved pulverizing a mixture of talc and cochineal, and then stirring in olive oil and gum. Rosewater was then added before the rouge was transferred to small pots. It was applied to the face with a small brush or a spherical suede tampon.

6   Finally, beauty spots were applied. These were small pieces of black fabric, cut in a variety of fanciful shapes such as hearts and crescent moons, which were stuck onto the face with gum. The placing of patches was an art in itself and involved much discussion at the dressing table. While dressing, a lady might be joined in her boudoir by her paramour, friends, and relatives, as well as by tradesmen, musicians, and hairdressers. Advice would be given on the position of a curl or the placing of a beauty spot. Each location of a beauty spot on the face had a name and a significant meaning. Thus a lady might inform everyone of her moods and intentions by wearing "the discreet," "the passionate," or "the coquette."

7   However, lovers of artifice in Britain had to be wary since an act of the British Parliament in 1774 declared: "Any woman of any age or rank found deceiving, seducing, or leading into matrimony any of His Majesty's subjects through the use of perfume, wigs or any cosmetics shall incur the penalties laid down for sorcery, and the marriage shall be declared null and void."

8   After dressing and the application of cosmetics came the arranging of the hair. Wigs had been introduced by Louis XIII and were initially worn only by men, who sported cascading curls of brown or black human hair or horsehair in the latter years of the 17th century. Under Louis XVI the fashion changed and extraordinarily elaborate wigs were worn by both men and women. Ladies' wigs became so extreme that hairdressers were obliged to use small ladders to arrange the topmost curls. Wigs were usually powdered either gray or white. The powder was made of talc, a soft mineral that was ground, purified, and sometimes supplemented with china clay or starch. It was sifted through silk screens and scented with essential oils. The most popular perfume for wigs in the 18th century was orris root, which smelt slightly of violets. Powder would be applied to a lightly pomaded wig in a "powder room." Ladies and gentlemen would protect their clothes with large dust

EXAMPLE 151

cloths, and hold cone-shaped masks over their faces to prevent the powder from settling on their make-up.

This elaborate toilette required several hours of preparation in the boudoir. Most ladies of fashion never appeared in public before noon. Consequently, small meals were eaten while dressing took place. Elegant ewers and basins were made so that ladies and gentlemen might rinse their fingers in rosewater after partaking of a light repast in the bedroom upon rising, or later in the boudoir. A fine Sèvres example of these articles is in the collection of the George R. Gardiner Museum of Ceramic Art. The factory was established at Vincennes in 1738 and moved to Sèvres in 1756, where it became the Royal French Porcelain Manufactory under the patronage of Louis XV. 9

Of course, ladies and gentlemen did not only wear scented gloves, wigs, and cosmetics. They also applied large quantities of perfume directly to their bodies. Perfume was not an 18th-century invention but had been used as scent for the body, in medicine, and for religious purposes for thousands of years. The art of making perfume had been greatly enhanced by the introduction of distillation in the 2nd century. Much experimentation in perfumery was carried out by early Islamic scientists, and Europeans benefited from this knowledge. By 1370 the first European perfume, in the modern sense, appeared. It was a mixture of essential plant oils and alcohol, originally based on oil of rosemary but later with additions of oil of lavender. The perfume was named for Queen Elizabeth of Hungary and was called *Hungary Water*. 10

The most famous perfume of the 18th century was *Eau de Cologne*. It had been invented in 1732 by two Italians, Gian Paolo Feminis and Giovanni Maria Farina, whose business was established in Cologne. *Eau de Cologne* was the perfume preferred by Mme du Barry, another mistress of Louis XV. Other perfumers experimented with a wide variety of extractions of precious oils, including bergamot, lavender, and rosemary, which were the principal ingredients of *Eau de Cologne*. However, most perfumes of the period had only a single floral ingredient, such as jasmine or orange blossom. For example, Marie Antoinette's favorite perfumes were rosewater and a water of violets. 11

Some of the perfume companies still in existence today were established at this time: in London, Floris in 1730 and Yardley in 1770, in Paris, Houbigant in 1775. In North America, Caswell-Massey was founded in Newport, Rhode Island, in 1752. Clients included George Washington and Captain Kidd, who shared a fondness for Caswell-Massey's perfume number six. 12

All these perfumes needed to be stored in containers, usually of glass or porcelain. The growing fashionability of perfume led to a 13 parallel production of exquisite tiny porcelain bottles, called "toys," just one among many miniature items, such as needle cases and snuff boxes, made for the delectation of the aristocracy. The earliest European porcelain perfume bottles were made at Meissen, the first factory in Europe to produce true, or hardpaste, porcelain. Initially, Meissen's perfume bottles were made in traditional "pilgrim bottle" or flask shapes, but by the 1740s whimsical forms were introduced resembling the larger porcelain figures made at the factory. Sometimes the heads of the figures became the stoppers for the perfume bottles.

14   After the secret of making porcelain became widely known in the 1750s, many small porcelain factories were established all over Europe. Most of these made perfume bottles. However, the main center for the production of scent bottles was in England, at Chelsea and in several other London factories that have not yet been positively identified. One of them was the mysterious "Girl-in-a-Swing" factory, which may have been established by Charles Gouyn, one of the original partners of the Chelsea factory. The real name of the "Girl-in-a-Swing" factory remains unknown. It is named for the figure of a girl in a swing, one of the first pieces attributed to the factory.

15   The perfume bottles made at Chelsea during the red-anchor period (1752–58) were wonderful whimsical creations, often shaped like clusters of fruit or flowers or simple and charming figures. Naturalistic animals and birds were also popular. Later Chelsea bottles, made during the gold-anchor period (1758–69), are more elaborate. They were often sold with small shagreen or sharkskin cases. (The colored anchors refer to the marks painted on the bottoms of the pieces.) A collection of one hundred English and Continental porcelain scent bottles in the Gardiner Museum includes some bottles with containers for more than one perfume, and others that have tiny mirrored compartments for storing beauty spots.

16   Perfumes were used not only in the boudoir but also in the drawing room. Pot-pourri was made from dried flowers, such as roses, orange blossoms, lavender, myrtle, oakmoss, and orris root, layered with salt and left to macerate in the sun for several days. It was then placed in porcelain containers vented with airholes. Sèvres became particularly well known for its exquisite pot-pourri containers. Each shape was named, and many came in different sizes. A pot-pourri Pompadour in the Gardiner collection was made at Vincennes about 1750.

17   Rooms were also scented with perfumed pastilles that were burnt to release their aromatic smoke. At Louis XV's court, these were called *oiselets de Chypre*, or "little birds of Cyprus," a curious name of unknown origin. The pastilles were formed by hand by rolling gum

EXAMPLE   153

mixed with laudanum, storax, cloves, sandalwood, camphor, aloes, and sugar of valerian. They were lit like candles and placed inside small vented porcelain figures or special containers. At Meissen, oriental figures were made with pierced ears and open mouths for the perfumed smoke to escape. One of the most important porcelain objects in the Gardiner collection is a wonderful pastille burner in the shape of a Magot, an oriental figure. It was made at Chantilly, France, in 1740. Between the Magot's knees is a porcelain globe lined in ormolu, with a detachable ormolu lid. A pastille may be placed inside the globe and ignited, and the lid replaced. Perfumed smoke will then waft through the holes in the lid. Originally, the Magot's hands were on pivots and they would have been set in motion to help fan the fragrant aroma throughout the room.

Perhaps the most frivolous and extravagant use of perfume is recounted in a story based upon a malicious rumor spread by the Marquis d'Argenson, one of Mme de Pompadour's most outspoken opponents. In 1750, he accused Louis XV's mistress of a "scandalous extravagance," by her squandering of 800,000 livres on Vincennes porcelain flowers.   18

Vincennes had become famous for naturalistic porcelain flowers: they formed a substantial part of the factory's production in the early days. In 1748, 45 women were employed solely to create flowers. These were made of porcelain, assembled petal by petal, and were fitted either onto painted stems or onto wire ones wrapped in green silk.   19

The story gradually evolved from the Marquis's rumor. Apparently Mme de Pompadour planted a winter garden filled with thousands of these artificial porcelain flowers, at her Château de Bellevue, near Paris. Each flower was said to have been perfumed correctly; roses were scented with rosewater, carnations with carnations, lilies with lilies-of-the-valley—all this just to amuse the king at a time when most of the population was impoverished. Only recently has Mme de Pompadour been exonerated in this matter. Careful scrutiny of the records of her purchases revealed that the king's mistress purchased only 24 vases embellished with 88 flowering porcelain plants in 1750. She spent 32,696 livres at Vincennes that year, far less than the rumored 800,000 livres. For his calumny, the unwise Marquis d'Argenson lost his ministerial position. Mme de Pompadour remains, nonetheless, the most conspicuous patron of precious perfumes and delicate porcelain of her age.   20

And after all, who would not agree with Cowley when he wrote: 21

Who that has reason, and his smell,
Would not among the roses and jasmine dwell,

Rather than all his spirits choke
With exhalations of dirt and smoke?

```


```

Vocabulary

a. *paragraph 1:* ephemeral, chinoiserie, alfresco
b. *paragraph 6:* couette
c. *paragraph 7:* artifice
d. *paragraph 8:* orris, pomaded
e. *paragraph 9:* ewers, repast
f. *paragraph 11:* bergamot
g. *paragraph 16:* oakmoss, macerate
h. *paragraph 17:* pastilles, laudanum, storax, cloves, sandalwood, camphor, aloes, sugar of valerian, ormolu

Questions

1. What is the primary purpose of Chilton's essay? Does she also use her examples to say something about eighteenth-century history?
2. What effect does she achieve with the examples in paragraphs 11 and 17? How does her narrative example concerning Mme de Pompadour epitomize the theme of the essay?
3. Why does she conclude by quoting the verse from Cowley?
4. How general an audience is Chilton addressing, and how do you know?

Writing Assignments

1. Narrate an experience that illustrates the injustice or pointlessness of a social code or rule of etiquette in our society.
2. Using examples as Chilton does, argue for the unconventional position in a debate about the merits of higher education, democracy, or sexual equality.

```


```

BRONWEN WALLACE

Bronwen Wallace (1945–1989) was born in Kingston, Ontario, where she lived most of her life. She was a poet, essayist, and short story writer whose literary life was closely identified with her home town and a group of writers associated with *Quarry* magazine and Quarry Press. Her books of poetry include *Signs of the Former Tenant, Common Magic, The Stubborn Particulars of Grace,* and *Keep that Candle Burning Bright;* her short stories are collected in *People You'd Trust Your Life To;* and her essays are available in *Arguments with the World,* which was edited by Joanne Page. In the following essay, Wallace writes about gender inequities and, particularly, the disadvantages suffered traditionally by women in their role as mother.

EXAMPLE   155

An Auction at Mother's Childhood Home

BRONWEN WALLACE

Last week, my mother and I went to an auction sale in Enterprise, Ontario. It was one of many such sales I will attend this summer, though I seldom buy anything. I just like to look at the jumble of things—and I like to watch the auctioneers in action, their singsong patter one of the sounds that mean summer to me.

Last week's sale was no different than any other. There was the usual collection of everything from canning jars to double beds, a wonderful set of wicker lawn furniture, some beautiful old tools— you know, the sort of stuff that just seems to grow from 40-odd years of living in one place. And there was that strangely familiar silence in the empty house, as if the house itself were wondering what—or rather, who—would happen to it next.

This sale did have one major difference, though. The house we were visiting was the house my mother had lived in as a girl, the house where my father had courted her and where their wedding luncheon had been served after the ceremony. She took me through all the rooms, telling me how they had looked back then — my grandfather had sold the place 40 years ago—describing the views out the various windows, as she remembered them. We ran into old school chums of hers and the talk drifted, as it does among women, until various members of various families, their antecedents and connections, their current states of health, their children and grandchildren, were all satisfactorily accounted for.

It was strange to stand in that house, where I had never stood before, and to realize how little I knew of my mother's early life. My father's boyhood home is very familiar to me, as is his family. My mother's is not. Some of this, in my case, is simply a result of circumstance—my maternal grandmother died before I was born, whereas my father's mother lived until I was in my 20s. Both my grandfathers died when I was a child.

But there is a cultural factor here as well. In a patriarchy, the primacy of the father is taken for granted. And what this often means, in everyday life, is the loss of our mothers' families and our mothers' childhoods. It is a loss—or rather, a renunciation—that is symbolized when a married woman takes her husband's name, a situation that, until recently, was assumed as a matter of course. It is also a loss that every woman I know speaks of—sometimes with bitterness and pain.

6   My first book of poems, *Marrying into the Family*, explored this loss in many ways. I began to write the poems in the first place because I was struck by how little I knew about any of my female ancestors. I was struck, too, by how many had died young, either in childbirth or from TB, and how quickly they had been succeeded by second wives, stepmothers. And since contact was not always maintained with the first wife's family, the natural, hereditary links seemed doubly lost to me.

7   "As a woman," writes poet Lorna Crozier in an essay, "I cannot take my mother's name, my mother has no name; as a woman, I cannot take my mother's country, my mother has no country. As a woman, my country has no name, my name is no one's country."

8   Often this loss includes the loss of material links as well. Many, many women I know, whose mothers have died, complain of losing precious reminders of her—dishes, furniture, jewelry—when their fathers remarry and these are taken over by his new wife. Under this grief is also a current of anger, too. Anger that the mother can be so easily replaced and all trace of her existence lost to her children.

9   This loss is compounded by the lack of information available to us about past women's lives. If I want to get a sense of my father's life, for example, I have lots of easily available books, movies, television programs. Not so my mother's. One of the advantages of Women's Studies programs, and other sorts of feminist research, is that they act as reclamation projects, returning to us at least some of what has been lost.

10   We all begin with a mother. We all begin with a mother who is the center of our world, the most powerful person we know. It is amazing that so much power and importance can be lost so quickly or that it can come to be perceived only as negative, as when mothers alone are blamed for the failings of their children or when we speak disparagingly of someone who is "too close" to his or her mother.

11   Indeed, our culture has spent a lot of time finding ways to curtail the power of the mother. The increasing intervention of more and more technology in the birthing process is one example. The fate that many mothers meet in the courts is another. Phyllis Chesler's book *Mothers on Trial* provides excellent documentation for the numerous situations in which women lose custody disputes, often to abusive men, because they are seen to be "unfit" by patriarchal standards. Another way of "blaming mother." Or think of mother-in-law jokes, culturally accepted ways of diminishing her power.

12   And yet that power can never be entirely diminished. Even when men's lives and men's doings are the center of our culture, there are thousands of oblique, often subversive, references to the

EXAMPLE   157

power of the mother. Indeed, it is almost as if these references have to be oblique in order not to be censored. Some feminist scholars argue that they are all that is left of a rich and complex matriarchal literature which we have lost.

Take *Cinderella,* for example, one of the oldest fairy tales known. 13 Like many of these tales, it comes from an ancient oral tradition and this particular story is known in many languages, including Chinese. In all versions, the presence of Cinderella's dead mother's spirit is remarkable. In the familiar Grimm version she is a little bird who lives in the tree which grows on her grave, and it is she who provides Cinderella with the clothes that she wears to the ball. In one sense, she is far more powerful than the prince, and it is by her power that Cinderella is delivered to a life of wealth and safety. It is interesting to note, too, that the stepmother, the usurper, is seen as "evil" in this tale because she shows no affection for another woman's child. The fact that all this power gets diminished, in the Walt Disney version, to a silly fairy godmother says a great deal.

This reading of Cinderella is only one, of course, but it's one to 14 think about. Many feminists dismiss Cinderella as being only about how girls should grow up to marry princes. We must remember, first of all, that most of these tales have peasant origins and that, from this point of view, marrying a prince might be just fine. We might also reread this tale—and others—to find out what it says about mothers and their power. Some scholars argue that earlier versions of these tales give even more power to the mother, power that has been curtailed in later, patriarchal versions.

Or think of stories like *Anne of Green Gables* and *Jane Eyre* in the 15 light of what they say about the sorrow and dislocation of mother-less children. And in the great southern black spiritual, "Sometimes I Feel Like a Motherless Child," the loss of the mother becomes a metaphor for the loss of a country, for being sold into slavery in an alien and hostile place.

In modern literature by women, the search for the mother and 16 what she means is a constant theme. Grace Paley comes to mind, as does Jamaica Kincaid, Margaret Laurence, Adrienne Rich, and many, many others. I'll end with one of my favorite quotes from "The Ottawa Valley," a story by Alice Munro in which a woman remembers a journey she made, as a young girl with her mother, to her mother's birthplace. A story in which she tries to come to terms with everything her mother means to her and with her own con-flicting feelings about her mother, feelings which, until recently, we have not been given the language to explore:

> The problem, the only problem, is my mother. And she is the one of course that I am trying to get; it is to reach her that this

whole journey has been undertaken. With what purpose? To mark her off, to describe, to illuminate, to celebrate, to get rid of her, and it did not work, for she looms too close, just as she always did. She is heavy as always, she weighs everything down, and yet she is indistinct, her edges melt and flow. Which means she has stuck to me as close as ever and refused to fall away, and could go on and on, applying what skills I have, using what tricks I know, and it would always be the same.

```
┌──────────────────────┐
│                      │
│                      │
└──────────────────────┘
```

Vocabulary

a. *paragraph 3:* antecedents
b. *paragraph 5:* patriarchy, renunciation
c. *paragraph 9:* compounded, reclamation
d. *paragraph 10:* disparagingly
e. *paragraph 11:* intervention
f. *paragraph 12:* oblique, subversive, matriarchal
g. *paragraph 14:* usurper

Questions

1. List Wallace's examples of the ill effects of life in the patriarchy. Are they ordered in a specific manner?
2. Do the many instances of inequity cited by Wallace prove that women suffer from a sexist bias in the system?
3. Why does she use examples from fairy tales? What relationship does Wallace establish between reality and fiction?
4. Wallace ends her essay with examples of women writers who have explored the importance of mother–daughter relationships. What is the effect of this conclusion?

Writing Assignments

1. Compare Wallace's examination of sexism with Walter Stewart's account of Canada's racist past.
2. Write an essay about examples of relations between men and women that prove or disprove Wallace's thesis.

```
┌──────────────────────┐
│                      │
│                      │
└──────────────────────┘
```

WALTER STEWART

Walter Stewart is a professor and the director of the School of Journalism at the University of King's College, Halifax. His essays and journalism have earned him a national reputation as one of the most clear-sighted and

EXAMPLE 159

honest observers of Canadian national life. Among his best-known books are *Shrug: Trudeau in Power, But Not in Canada, Strike!, True Blue: The Loyalist Legend,* and *Tower of Gold, Feet of Clay: The Canadian Banks.* In the following selection, Stewart argues that we as Canadians "are held captive by the myth of the reasonable citizen," despite all the evidence that Canadians can be as violent, racist, and antidemocratic as Americans.

Good Old Us

WALTER STEWART

Williams Lake, British Columbia, 1966. An 1
Indian girl met some youths in a beverage room, and they agreed to give her a lift to her aunt's place. Of course, they didn't take her to her aunt's; they took her to a garbage dump, where the three whites thought they would get a little free loving. Everybody knows about Indian girls.

Unfortunately, this girl didn't. She was found dead the next 2
morning, naked and dead by the roadside. The youths, all of good families, admitted that they had wrestled her around some, got fed up with her, and pitched her out of the car into the cold April night. She died of a broken neck, but they said she was alive when they last saw her. What they did wasn't right, maybe, but it wasn't murder, either. A white jury agreed; two of the youths were convicted of assault, and fined $200; the charge against the third was dismissed.

The House of Commons, Ottawa, 1938. Premier Maurice Dup- 3
lessis of Quebec had brought in a law, the Padlock Law, that permitted the seizure and closing of any premises suspected of being used to propagate communism. No proof was required, no defence was permitted, and "communism" was never defined. The law was used against all of Duplessis's political opponents. In Ottawa, J.S. Woodsworth, leader of the CCF, rose in his place in Parliament and, his voice shaking with emotion, declared, "Twice every day for six months the provincial police have carried out execution without judgment, dispossession without due process of law; twenty times a month they have trampled on liberties as old as Magna Carta." Woodsworth was shouted down. Ernest Lapointe, Minister of Justice, told him, "In spite of the fact that the words are so unpleasant to the honourable member for Winnipeg North Centre, I do desire to say that the reign of law must continue in this country, that peace and order must prevail."

Outside Vancouver, 1887. A mob of whites, disturbed that in- 4
dentured Chinese coolie labourers had taken jobs in the mines that

God meant white men to have, rushed the Chinese camp and drove the workers out into the January night. There was a twenty-foot cliff behind the camp, and the coolies were driven over it; you could hear them going plump, plump, plump, into the freezing sea.

5   Toronto, 1945. E.B. Jolliffe, provincial leader of the CCF, charged that the Ontario Provincial Police were being used as political spies by the Conservative government, that a special squad was gathering private information for Premier George Drew, and that this information was being used to harass Liberals and CCFers. Jolliffe said the OPP was acting as a private "Gestapo"—an emotive word for that time. He had an impressive amount of evidence, including the testimony of Alvin Rowe, an OPP officer who had worked on the secret squad and who had come to Jolliffe because, he said, he was being used as a political spy, and didn't like it. A royal commission was called to inquire into Jolliffe's charges, but its terms of reference were so narrow that it was barred from conducting a real investigation. Then Alvin Rowe was killed in a plane crash; Jolliffe's party was badly punished at the polls.

6   Sydney, Nova Scotia, 1971. The Sydney police went on strike for higher wages. They had barely left their posts when gangs of toughs took over the town and began drag-racing up and down the main street. Fights, looting, then a general riot broke out; the town was in a state bordering on anarchy until the strike was settled.

7   Near Seven Oaks, Manitoba, 1816. A disagreement arose between fur traders of the North West Company and settlers brought in by Lord Selkirk to found a permanent community. So the company arranged to have the settlement attacked, and twenty people were murdered. When Selkirk tried to exact justice, he was blocked by the political manoeuvrings of his opponents, defeated in court, and eventually driven into near bankruptcy.

8   Near Wymark, Saskatchewan, 1967. A man who had complained that the RCMP was slow in acting on his earlier charges that he was being harassed by obscene telephone calls was working in his pasture. An RCMP car pulled up, two constables piled out, and he was taken away and held for forty days, under the Saskatchewan Mental Health Act, without ever being charged, or convicted, or even told what he had done wrong.

9   During the forty days he was subjected to shock treatments and drug therapy and then, one day, he was turned loose as suddenly as he had been locked up.

10   Montreal, 1949. A university professor's house blew up, and his wife and daughter were killed, while he was injured. He was clapped into jail and held for three months under the provincial Coroner's Act. Police had discovered that he had a mistress some time previously, and they assumed, without a shred of proof, that

EXAMPLE   161

he had blown up his own house. He was not charged; he was simply held, while the press seethed with stories of his infidelity, his callousness, his savagery. Eventually, it turned out that the house had been destroyed by a natural gas explosion. He was released.

Toronto, 1974. An American sociologist, a controversial figure 11 alleged to hold strong and wrong views on the subject of race, had been invited to speak at the University of Toronto. A group of left-wing students and teachers decreed that he was an inappropriate speaker; they stormed the lectern, staged a minor riot, and drove the sociologist away. His speech was never made. Months later, two students were suspended for their part in the affair; it can be argued that freedom of speech remains suspended at the university.

I am in favour of smugness, to a point; it rounds the figure, deepens 12 the dimples, and aids the digestive process. I believe, too, that Canadians have a certain amount to be smug about; by and large, we have been a reasonable and prosperous people; by and large, we have avoided mass murder, organized tyranny, and the more public forms of corruption. However, since 1972, since Watergate, smugness has become a national religion, a national disease. Nothing that has happened on the North American continent since our side sacked Washington in 1814 has given Canadians such unalloyed pleasure as Watergate. While the Americans wallow in guilt and self-doubt, we bubble with joy and self-righteousness. Thank God, we say, for our British traditions and innate Canadian decency. There may be rot and racism, inequity and injustice, among those fractious, rebellious Yankees, but not in Canada.

Well, we have never had anything quite like Watergate, but that 13 is a claim we share with most nations of the world. We have, however, had major political corruption involving our highest figures—remember Sir John A. and the Pacific Scandal, remember the McGreevy brothers, remember the Beauharnois Scandal, remember the Ontario Highways Scandal?—and we have had extensive cover-ups, political dirty tricks, pay-offs, and—God knows—thousands of examples of the abuse of power.

A major difference between us and the Americans—besides the 14 size, the pervasiveness, the sheer bloody-mindedness of Watergate —is our diffidence. Except for the Pacific Scandal (after all, that was a long time ago), Canadian outbursts of corruption, venality, brutality, racism, and oppression have gone largely unrecorded. It's not that we don't want to hear about such subjects—we do—but we don't want to hear them when they happen in Canada. During the spring of 1975, Canadians flocked to their theatres to see an American film about authoritarianism in the U.S., called *Hearts and Minds*. At the same time, they stayed away in droves from a Canadian film about authoritarianism in Canada, called *Les Ordres*. There are some things we would rather not know.

15   We view ourselves as a superior people, a sober, peaceable people, a people of extraordinarily decent instincts and firmly entrenched liberties, and we reject any contrary evidence. Thus, when our federal government comes along, as it did in October 1970, and throws 435 people into jail without charge or trial, when it makes it a crime ever to have belonged to a political organization that was legal five minutes before the law was passed, we are not shocked or upset; we applaud. If the government chooses to establish retroactive crime, our reaction is not to say that our civil liberties are in jeopardy, but that the government must have powerful reasons, secret reasons, reasons that remain secret to this day, to act so arbitrarily. Indeed, some officers of the Canadian Civil Liberties Association give their approval—although the Association itself does not. Because we know we are decent, reasonable people, because our government would never do anything really wrong, really suppressive, whatever is done must, of necessity, be reasonable and right. Indeed, some Canadians are still half-expecting the government to produce secret reasons, one of these days, that will explain the whole thing satisfactorily (just as some of us still wait around on Easter morn for a bunny to drop off a clutch of eggs).

16   One of the problems we face as a nation, perhaps in greater measure than other nations, is that we are held captive by the myth of the reasonable citizen. The Canadian as we see him, the Canadian in the mind of God, is a man who never gives in to extremism; he is a patient man (who shuns violence), a neighbourly man (who spurns racism), a democratic man (who supports free speech, civil liberties, and honesty in politics). He is, in short, all the things your average wild-eyed, gun-toting, bigoted, loud-mouthed, venal, aggressive, tyrannical bastard of an American is not. What is more, his history has made him the gentle citizen he is today. There have been blots on the copybook—things like the Winnipeg General Strike, the Regina Riot, the incarceration of Japanese Canadians during World War II—but these are minor slips, casually recorded or missed entirely in our history of ourselves.

17   Enough. Canadians, as a people, are no better and no worse than anyone else. We were slavers in the eighteenth and early nineteenth centuries, and our treatment of minorities, from Indians to Jehovah's Witnesses, is only marginally different from that of the Americans. We have staged some of the bigger and more bloody-minded riots on the continent, from the Bytown Riots of the 1840s ("Them Bytown days was fightin' days") to the Kenora race riots of 1974. We have not only passed, but applauded, viciously repressive legislation, and our gun laws, to take only one minor example of

EXAMPLE   163

wrong-headed self-congratulation, are in fact looser and dumber than those in most U.S. states.

```

```

Vocabulary

a. *paragraph 3:* dispossession, Magna Carta
b. *paragraph 4:* indentured
c. *paragraph 5:* Gestapo, emotive
d. *paragraph 6:* anarchy
e. *paragraph 10:* infidelity, callousness
f. *paragraph 12:* unalloyed, fractious
g. *paragraph 14:* venality
h. *paragraph 16:* tyrannical, incarceration

Questions

1. What is Stewart's purpose in beginning with an account of a series of incidents?
2. Consider how Stewart has organized his material. Does it cohere or is it simply a random sample?
3. Why does he include date and place names at the beginning of each example? How does the tone shift in the second part of the essay?
4. What persuasive purposes might Stewart's account serve? How effective do you find his commentary on the examples he cites?
5. Why does he include a comparison with the United States (paragraph 12)? How does this comparison advance his argument?

Writing Assignment

Stewart lists instances of Canadian lawlessness, violence, and racism that have not been widely publicized, and uses them to challenge Canadians' assumptions about themselves and their country. Investigate other aspects of Canadian society that people are reluctant to face up to. Report your findings in a descriptive narrative. Include information on observed or scientifically documented effects and give the sources of your findings.

```

```

ROBERTSON DAVIES

Robertson Davies (1913–1995) was born in Thamesville, Ontario, and educated at Upper Canada College, Queen's University, and Balliol College, Oxford. Journalist, editor, dramatist, director, and professor, Davies is best known for his brilliant novels and accomplished essays. He gained his reputation as one of Canada's foremost novelists with *Fifth Business,* *The Manticore,* and *World of Wonders—the Deptford Trilogy—*in which he uses the characters from his small-town Ontario world to explore the realms of magic, Jungian psychology, and the nature of evil; along the way he provides his typical wealth of arcana in details about matters as diverse as saints' lives and travelling theatre companies. In essays like this one on superstition, he explores one of his interests by classifying and defining it.

A Few Kind Words for Superstition

ROBERTSON DAVIES

1 In grave discussions of "the renaissance of the irrational" in our time, superstition does not figure largely as a serious challenge to reason or science. Parapsychology, UFOs, miracle cures, transcendental meditation and all the paths to instant enlightenment are condemned, but superstition is merely deplored. Is it because it has an unacknowledged hold on so many of us?

2 Few people will admit to being superstitious; it implies naïveté or ignorance. But I live in the middle of a large university, and I see superstition in its four manifestations, alive and flourishing among people who are indisputably rational and learned.

3 You did not know that superstition takes four forms? Theologians assure us that it does. First is what they call Vain Observances, such as not walking under a ladder, and that kind of thing. Yet I saw a deeply learned professor of anthropology, who had spilled some salt, throwing a pinch of it over his left shoulder; when I asked him why, he replied, with a wink, that it was "to hit the Devil in the eye." I did not question him further about his belief in the Devil: but I noticed that he did not smile until I asked him what he was doing.

4 The second form is Divination, or consulting oracles. Another learned professor I know, who would scorn to settle a problem by tossing a coin (which is a humble appeal to Fate to declare itself), told me quite seriously that he had resolved a matter related to university affairs by consulting the *I Ching*. And why not? There are thousands of people on this continent who appeal to the *I Ching*, and their general level of education seems to absolve them of superstition. Almost, but not quite. The *I Ching*, to the embarrassment of rationalists, often gives excellent advice.

5 The third form is Idolatry, and universities can show plenty of that. If you have ever supervised a large examination room, you know how many jujus, lucky coins and other bringers of luck are placed on the desks of the candidates. Modest idolatry, but what else can you call it?

EXAMPLE   165

The fourth form is Improper Worship of the True God. A while   6
ago, I learned that every day, for several days, a 1/2 bill (in Canada
we have 1/2 bills, regarded by some people as unlucky) had been
tucked under a candlestick on the altar of a college chapel. Investigation revealed that an engineering student, worried about a girl,
thought that bribery of the Deity might help. When I talked with
him, he did not think he was pricing God cheap, because he could
afford no more. A reasonable argument, but perhaps God was
proud that week, for the scientific oracle went against him.

Superstition seems to run, a submerged river of crude religion,   7
below the surface of human consciousness. It has done so for as
long as we have any chronicle of human behavior, and although I
cannot prove it, I doubt if it is more prevalent today than it has
always been. Superstition, the theologians tell us, comes from the
Latin *supersisto*, meaning to stand in terror of the Deity. Most people keep their terror within bounds, but they cannot root it out, nor
do they seem to want to do so.

The more the teaching of formal religion declines, or takes a   8
sociological form, the less God appears to great numbers of people
as a God of Love, resuming his older form of a watchful, minatory
power, to be placated and cajoled. Superstition makes its appearance, apparently unbidden, very early in life, when children fear
that stepping on cracks in the sidewalk will bring ill fortune. It may
persist even among the greatly learned and devout, as in the case of
Dr. Samuel Johnson, who felt it necessary to touch posts that he
passed in the street. The psychoanalysts have their explanation, but
calling a superstition a compulsion neurosis does not banish it.

Many superstitions are so widespread and so old that they   9
must have risen from a depth of the human mind that is indifferent
to race or creed. Orthodox Jews place a charm on their doorposts;
so do (or did) the Chinese. Some peoples of Middle Europe believe
that when a man sneezes, his soul, for that moment, is absent from
his body, and they hasten to bless him, lest the soul be seized by the
Devil. How did the Melanesians come by the same idea? Superstition seems to have a link with some body of belief that far ante-
dates the religions we know — religions which have no place for
such comforting little ceremonies and charities.

People who like disagreeable historical comparisons recall that   10
when Rome was in decline, superstition proliferated wildly, and
that something of the same sort is happening in our Western world
today. They point to the popularity of astrology, and it is true that
sober newspapers that would scorn to deal in love philters carry
astrology columns and the fashion magazines count them among
their most popular features. But when has astrology not been popular? No use saying science discredits it. When has the heart of man
given a damn for science?

11   Superstition in general is linked to man's yearning to know his fate, and to have some hand in deciding it. When my mother was a child, she innocently joined her Roman Catholic friends in killing spiders on July 11, until she learned that this was done to ensure heavy rain the day following, the anniversary of the Battle of Boyne, when the Orangemen would hold their parade. I knew an Italian, a good scientist, who watched every morning before leaving his house, so that the first person he met would not be a priest or a nun, as this would certainly bring bad luck.

12   I am not one to stand aloof from the rest of humanity in this matter, for when I was a university student, a gypsy woman with a child in her arms used to appear every year at examination time, and ask a shilling of anyone who touched the Lucky Baby; that swarthy infant cost me four shillings altogether, and I never failed an examination. Of course, I did it merely for the joke—or so I thought then. Now, I am humbler.

>

Vocabulary

a. *paragraph 1:* renaissance, parapsychology, transcendental
b. *paragraph 2:* naïveté, manifestations
c. *paragraph 3:* theologians
d. *paragraph 4:* oracles, absolve, rationalists
e. *paragraph 5:* jujus
f. *paragraph 8:* minatory, placated, cajoled
g. *paragraph 10:* proliferated, philters

Questions

1. On what basis does Davies divide superstitions? What are the four forms he distinguishes?
2. What point is he making through these divisions?
3. In referring to superstitions as a "submerged river of crude religion," what point is Davies making about human nature? What do his examples of the *I Ching,* lucky charms, and bribing the Deity show?
4. What is the order of ideas in the twelve paragraphs? Why does Davies save the example of the gypsy woman and her child for last?
5. Can you think of examples of other kinds of superstitions?

Writing Assignment

Analyze the significance of a superstition in your own life. Discuss the ways in which you have attempted to rationalize this superstition.

>

EXAMPLE   167

WILFRID SHEED

Wilfrid Sheed was born in London in 1930 and moved to the United States in 1947. He has worked as a movie critic for various magazines, and as a cultural commentator. His books include *A Middle-Class Education*, *The Three Mobs: Labor, Church, and Mafia*, *The Good Word*, *The Boys of Winter*, and *Essays in Disguise*, from which the following humorous look at a few of the seven deadly sins is taken.

A Few of My Favorite Sins

WILFRID SHEED

P ride, Anger, Lust . . . no, I mean Envy, Covetousness, Lust . . . and [pause for mind to empty completely] did I mention Lust? That makes seven, doesn't it?" Naming the deadly sins is uncannily like trying to remember the seven dwarfs. The first person to say "Doc" three times figures he's made it. (In my own case, the Taj Mahal serves the same purpose for the Seven Wonders of the World.)

Since Doc has been written about quite enough lately, I thought I'd look in on some of the more neglected seven deadlies, including my own special pet, Sloth, the totally negative sin, the Great Zilch. All the other sins are about something, and they all smack suspiciously of hard work. Gluttony, for instance, can be grueling: long hours nailed to the same chair, gobbling your way to acute discomfort. By the eighth course, the very idea of food makes you sick. It is your mortal enemy, yet you soldier on.

Stout fellow. The very definition of sin, as of virtue, includes persistence after you've lost interest, and only the ideal keeps you going. Avarice is another example. Does Lord so-and-so really *want* another newspaper? He's hardly had time to enjoy the fifty he already owns. But Avarice is a brutal taskmaster, and it never permits you to enjoy anything; there is no peak to its mountains, no finish line, no place even to sit down.

Envy is another mean mother. You have to be in tip-top shape for Envy. Because again, you can never relax for a minute—not so long as one other writer (if this sin occurs in other professions, I can't picture it) is out there trying maliciously to steal your championship from behind your back. (Yes, we have our championships—and little award ceremonies, every night.)

5   And that isn't the worst of it with the green-eyed monster. Since Envy has a kind of cheap, moldy taste to it (even for the practitioner), you must labor mightily to disguise it, especially from yourself. "You've always envied so-and-so and you know it," says your spouse breezily, and you fairly rend your garments to deny it, dragging in decent, God-fearing words like "honest" and "objective" and "in my judgment" in a ludicrously sincere voice to defend your crummy obsession. (Okay, I'm only trying to make it sound as exciting as Doc.) There is no sight more touching than an Envy victim trying to hide his complaint, which is like covering up an advanced case of poison ivy.

6   After such a workout, simple Pride can seem positively relaxing. You suddenly don't give a damn how the competition is doing, because there is no competition. The death of God in the sixties removed the last hurdle, and now you've got the track to yourself. You're number one, *numero uno*, the top and only banana. Why, you even get to decide what's a sin around here, so your worries are over on that score too. Outside of a trifling risk of going — or already being — completely insane, the proud man has it made in the shade.

7   Or so it seems. But in execution, Pride can be as taxing as any other love affair. How do you keep interested in yourself day after day? What is there left to impress yourself with? Being the only boy in the world must put quite a strain on your charm, and veteran peacocks can be as bored and tetchy as old couples who have worked too hard at saving the marriage.

8   And so it goes, through the rigors of Anger and the fatigues of what's-his-name, the one I can never remember. But we are now approaching Sloth—the Big One, the Abyss, the Afternoon Devil, as they used to call it—the sin against being alive.

9   When it comes to Sloth, words fail me. The pencil drops from my hand, unsharpened. Is Sloth really worth writing about? Is *anything* worth writing about? Having breezed through the other sins, I find myself staring at the page in gloomy paralysis. That was okay for the first hour or so, but it's been two days now.

10   Sloth, like the other deadly no-no's, becomes acutely uncomfortable after the first fine flush, and — sure proof of its sincerity — frequently works against your own interests. It not only won't pay your bills, but it won't fill in applications for grants or phone up appropriate women. It won't even close windows when you're freezing to death. It is stoical because it is too lazy to be anything else.

11   On the other hand, it does keep you out of mischief. *All* its sins are the sins of omission, because it isn't up to anything more strenuous, but such sins can pile to the sky: sick friends unvisited, troubling letters unanswered. They then proceed to sit on your chest,

EXAMPLE 169

making further movement out of the question. Although they are made out of absolutely nothing, their dead weight would pinion Hercules, or keep even Joyce Carol Oates from writing.

Sloth can probably afflict anyone who isn't Japanese, but it is an 12 occupational hazard of artists and saints—part of their kit—and for them it hardly even pretends to be fun. (You must not equate Sloth with writer's block, which is perfectly normal Terror and should be practiced more often.) It is more like a spiritual hangover. After the ecstasy of creation or religious vision, everything else seems flat and gray, an endless walking of the dog. Incidentally, drinking can at least fake the ecstasy for you in fits and starts, and it kills some of the long, dead hours before you're "on" again. But if you thought life was flat and gray before, try waking up with *two* hangovers. By then you can't even do what you want most in the world to do, and you are in hell.

To your average bustling citizen, Sloth may seem just too flabby 13 to make the team. But it passes the important tests: it wears you out from sheer rage and frustration, and however rotten it makes you feel, you can't imagine anything better. This is what finally makes a sin a sin: the willful exclusion of everything else in the universe in favor of one false idol, whether it be the next meal or the next merger or thy neighbor's lawn mower. The sinner cannot watch flowers bloom or sniff the breeze without envisaging his pet sin. Sloth takes this to the end of the line by eliminating even the idol and leaving the altar empty.

This brutally negative aspect of sin has been much overlooked 14 by those hearty souls who believe that the whole thing was created by preachers to keep us from having fun; it was more likely invented by mankind to save its skin. In the old days, sin was defined as an offense against God and neighbor. Now, in tune with our changing interests, it would probably be called an offense against self. It is certainly all three. Any one of the deadlies, in sufficient dosage, could rip open a community in minutes and leave it to the vultures. But since providence has spread the sins fairly evenly, we are obliged to work on smaller units: friends, families, selves.

The Devil, who thought all this up in the first place, and whose 15 existence can be proved by literary references alone (a very necessary character), is not a notorious fun-lover. But he does like his bit of death, in all its forms, and clearly he gets his own special kind of bang out of watching us have fun, and then turning the fun deadly.

Every vice has some good in it. Pride, for instance, is simply 16 self-respect gone mad, and Envy is just a vicious twist on admiration. I trust I don't have to tell my readers what's good about Doc. And as for Sloth, it is not really all that far from nirvana, the garden of Allah, or Abraham's bosom; it is just a mite premature. Rest in peace, but not yet.

17   I still think it is one hell of a sin.

Vocabulary

a. *paragraph 7:* tetchy
b. *paragraph 10:* stoical
c. *paragraph 13:* envisaging

Questions

1. How does Sheed rank the sins he considers?
2. In paragraphs 8 through 13, how does Sheed organize his discussion of Sloth? Why does he devote so much of the essay to this discussion?
3. Why does Sheed repeatedly refer to one of the seven dwarfs?
4. What is the tone of the essay, and what impression do you get of Sheed from the essay?

Writing Assignment

Divide another class of things—for example, virtues, pets, leisure activities —and, like Sheed, discuss the implications of your division.

Comparison

Comparison shows the similarities between people, things, or ideas; contrast shows the differences. The word *comparison* sometimes refers to both kinds of analysis, as in this block comparison of President Franklin Roosevelt with Great Britain's wartime prime minister, Winston Churchill:

> Roosevelt, as a public personality, was a spontaneous, optimistic, pleasure-loving ruler who dismayed his assistants by the gay and apparently heedless abandon with which he seemed to delight in pursuing two or more totally incompatible policies, and astonished them even more by the swiftness and ease with which he managed to throw off the cares of office during the darkest and most dangerous moments. Churchill too loves pleasure, and he too lacks neither gaiety nor a capacity for exuberant self-expression, together with the habit of blithely cutting Gordian knots in a manner which often upset his experts, but he is not a frivolous man. His nature possesses a dimension of depth — and a corresponding sense of tragic possibilities — which Roosevelt's light-hearted genius instinctively passed by. (Sir Isaiah Berlin, "Mr. Churchill")

Block comparisons present the details of the first subject as a whole and then the details of the second. But the author may choose to develop the comparison point by point, as in this second paragraph on Roosevelt and Churchill:

> Roosevelt played the game of politics with virtuosity, and both his successes and his failures were carried off in splendid style; his performance seemed to flow with effortless skill. Churchill is acquainted with darkness as well as light. Like all inhabitants and even transient visitors of inner worlds, he gives evidence of seasons of agonized brooding and slow recovery. Roosevelt might have spoken of sweat and blood, but when Churchill offered his people tears, he spoke a word which might have been uttered by Lincoln or Mazzini or Cromwell, but not by Roosevelt, great-hearted, generous and perceptive as he was. (Sir Isaiah Berlin, "Mr. Churchill")

Both paragraphs build from similarities to differences. Were the similarities more important, the author would probably have built to them instead. Notice also that the purpose of the comparison is to arrive at a relative estimate of the two men as leaders. We discover the qualities of Roosevelt through Churchill, and those of Churchill through Roosevelt.

Relative estimates are useful in explaining abstract concepts such as nationhood, as in the following extended comparison of Canada and the United States:

> The United States was a revolutionary society which had a Declaration of Independence and a belief in self-evident truths about man's inalienable rights to "life, liberty and the pursuit of happiness." Canada was a conservative society with a British North America Act committed to "peace, order, and good government." The United States was a society that had evolved from history, and took its self-image from the past. For Canada borders were important—they defined its separateness from the United States. Greg Curnoe's "Close the 49th Parallel, etc.," could have been painted in the 1850s as easily as in the 1960s, though the style would have been British Imperial rather than American Pop. For Americans not borders but "frontiers" were what was important. Frontiers were not boundaries, but places to go, to expand. (Ramsay Cook, "Canadian and American Culture")

Although the author is concerned with defining the status of Canada as a country, he does so through a relative estimate that illuminates the special situation of each nation. Only through comparison with other countries that have different histories will we understand Canada better.

The whole essay may use comparison and contrast as one of several methods of analysis or as the single method. As with the paragraph, the analysis may consist of a point-by-point comparison or a block comparison—a comparison of wholes. It is best to use one kind of comparison only; mixing the two kinds can produce a disorganized essay. The essays in this section combine comparison with examples, such as illustrative analogy and other methods of analysis.

Illustrative analogy is a special kind of example, a comparison of two quite different things or activities for the purpose of explanation—a child growing like a tender plant and needing sun, water, and a receptive soil as well as proper care from a skilled gardener. The comparison may be point by point. But there are differences also, and if there is danger of the analogy being carried too far (children are not so tender that they need as much protection as plants from the hazards of living), the writer may state these differences to limit the inferences readers may draw. The writer has chosen the analogy for the sake of vivid illustration and nothing more. We will see later that analogy is often used in argument: children *should* be fully protected from various hazards because they are tender plants. The argument will stand or fall depending on how convinced we are of the similarities and of the unimportance of the differences.

Analogy is often used in explanations of scientific ideas. One of the most famous is Fred Hoyle's analogy between the moving apart of the galaxies in the universe and an expanding raisin cake, in *The Intelligent Universe*:

> Suppose the cake swells uniformly as it cooks, but the raisins themselves remain of the same size. Let each raisin represent a cluster of galaxies, and imagine yourself inside one of them. As the cake swells, you will observe that all the other raisins move away from you. Moreover, the farther away the raisin, the faster it will seem to move. When the cake has swollen to twice its initial dimensions, the distance between all the raisins will have doubled itself—two raisins that were initially an inch apart will now be two inches apart; two raisins that were a foot apart will have moved two feet apart. Since the entire action takes place within the same time interval, obviously the more distant raisins must move apart faster than those close at hand. So it happens with the clusters of galaxies.

And Hoyle draws a further conclusion from his analogy:

> No matter which raisin you happen to be inside, the others will always move away from you. Hence the fact that we observe all the other galaxies to be moving away from us does not mean that we are situated at the center of the universe. Indeed, it seems certain that the universe has no center. A cake may be said to have a center only because it has a boundary. We must imagine the cake to extend outward without any boundary, an infinite cake, so to speak, which means that however much cake we care to consider there is always more.

Hoyle points out the limits of the analogy in these final sentences. One advantage of the raisin analogy is the disparity of size between a raisin and a galaxy—a system of sometimes billions of stars occupying an enormous amount of space. The disparity in size provides a relative estimate of size in the universe.

Reasoning about everyday decisions and choices also often uses analogy, as in the decision to buy a book similar in subject and setting to an author's earlier book you enjoyed. Since arguments from analogy make predictions only, you cannot be certain that you will in fact enjoy the book. But you can increase the probability that you will enjoy it—by making the comparison with several books of the author and not just one, and by looking for as many similarities as possible.

These are two important characteristics of good arguments from analogy. A candidate for federal office may argue that she has the same record and personal characteristics as a much admired former member of Parliament. This analogical argument will be even stronger if she makes the comparison with several former MPs instead of with one. Thus she points out that, like them, she was mayor of a large city, held office in years of economic hardship, and had a successful career as a provincial legislator.

Dissimilarities between the candidate and the people cited must not be significant enough to weaken the argument. Differences in height or colour of hair are obviously insignificant and not relevant to the conclusion. But the candidate may have to argue that her being a woman is an insignificant difference, too. She may even use other dissimilarities to strengthen her case. If the MPs cited have the same record of service as the candidate yet are different in gender, race, and background—some coming from small towns and some from large cities—the probability increases that qualifications have to do with the similarities she has cited, despite the differences in gender, race, or background.

Finally the points of similarity must be relevant to the conclusion and give strength to it: the analogy would be weak if the candidate used the similarities cited to claim she had the same kind of education as did previous MPs. But the analogy does support the limited conclusion that she has the experience to deal with unemployment and the federal deficit intelligently. A limited conclusion could be drawn from a limited analogy if the points of similarity are clearly specified or agreed on, if these points are relevant to the conclusions, and if inferences are drawn from these points only.

SIR JAMES JEANS

Sir James Jeans (1877–1946), British mathematician and physicist, was educated at Cambridge University. He taught at Cambridge and Princeton in the United States, and worked at the Mount Wilson Observatory in California, where he studied the structure of stars. As well as being an expert in a number of scientific fields, he is a master of the informal essay. In the following essay, he draws on his scientific expertise and his popularizing skill to explain a natural phenomenon.

Why the Sky Looks Blue

SIR JAMES JEANS

Imagine that we stand on an ordinary sea- 1
side pier, and watch the waves rolling in and striking against the iron columns of the pier. Large waves pay very little attention to the columns —they divide right and left and reunite after passing each column, much as a regiment of soldiers would if a tree stood in their road; it is almost as though the columns had not been there. But the short waves and ripples find the columns of the pier a much more formidable obstacle. When the short waves impinge on the columns, they are reflected back and spread as new ripples in all directions. To use the technical term, they are "scattered." The obstacle provided by the iron columns hardly affects the long waves at all, but scatters the short ripples.

We have been watching a sort of working model of the way in 2
which sunlight struggles through the earth's atmosphere. Between us on earth and outer space the atmosphere interposes innumerable obstacles in the form of molecules of air, tiny droplets of water, and small particles of dust. These are represented by the columns of the pier.

The waves of the sea represent the sunlight. We know that sun- 3
light is a blend of many colors—as we can prove for ourselves by passing it through a prism, or even through a jug of water, or as nature demonstrates to us when she passes it through the raindrops of a summer shower and produces a rainbow. We also know that light consists of waves, and that the different colors of light are produced by waves of different lengths, red light by long waves and blue light by short waves. The mixture of waves which constitutes sunlight has to struggle past the columns of the pier. And these obstacles treat the light waves much as the columns of the pier treat the sea-waves. The long waves which constitute red light are hardly affected but the short waves which constitute blue light are scattered in all directions.

Thus the different constituents of sunlight are treated in different 4
ways as they struggle through the earth's atmosphere. A wave of blue light may be scattered by a dust particle, and turned out of its course. After a time a second dust particle again turns it out of its course, and so on, until finally it enters our eyes by a path as zigzag as that of a flash of lightning. Consequently the blue waves of the sunlight enter our eyes from all directions. And that is why the sky looks blue.

Vocabulary

a. *paragraph 1:* impinge
b. *paragraph 2:* interposes
c. *paragraph 4:* constituents

Questions

1. Writers use analogies to make something abstract and difficult concrete and simple. How does Jeans succeed in doing this here?
2. Since light waves and ocean waves are different in many respects, what are the limits of Jeans's analogy? What would happen if he pushed it too far—if, for example, he considered tidal waves or choppy seas or whitecaps in his account?
3. Contrast the ways in which the analogy illustrates Jeans's point here and the way McEwan's analogy (in his essay "The Plot Thickens for the Century's Final Chapter") controls his argument.

Writing Assignment

Consult a science column in *Omni, Scientific American,* or *The Economist* and note how often science writers use analogies to aid in explanation. Develop your own analogy to explain a complex idea from a discipline you know well.

WILLIAM J. MITCHELL

William J. Mitchell is Dean of the School of Architecture and Planning at Massachusetts Institute of Technology. He is the author of *City of Bits: Space, Place and the Infobahn.* In the following essay, he argues that the information explosion will rapidly transform every aspect of our lives.

The Parable of the Pizza Parlor

WILLIAM J. MITCHELL

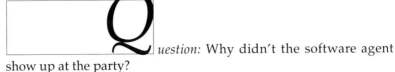

1   *Question:* Why didn't the software agent show up at the party?
Answer: Because it had no body to go with.

2   This nerdy variant on the old Halloween joke about the skeleton neatly encapsulates some commonly expressed hopes and flip-side

fears about the Information Superhighway—that it will inexorably replace transportation with telecommunication, face-to-face meetings with transactions in cyberspace, and human secretaries and assistants with disembodied software agents. In reality, a robust infobahn is likely to produce a considerably more complex and subtle redistribution of functions among buildings, transportation systems and computer networks. Let me illustrate this point with a homely story I call "The Parable of the Pizza Parlor."

Not so long ago pizza parlors were mostly found on Main Street. They had advertising signs out front to pull in customers, counters where those customers placed orders and handed over cash, kitchens where pizza was baked, and an eating space containing tables and seats. All these components were wrapped up in one small building. 3

In the era of the automobile, a competing configuration emerged. The pizza parlor (by now perhaps part of a chain) did not rely just on its sign; it also advertised in the Yellow Pages and in the mass media. It moved from Main Street to a location beside the highway, and it acquired a parking lot. Many customers now telephoned in their orders and had them delivered by car to their homes and offices. Transportation and telecommunication systems began to play significant roles in the pizza parlor's workings, and its architectural unity fragmented as consumption shifted from a single seating area to the many different locations where customers ate their delivered pizzas. 4

Main Street began to die as the pizza parlor and other businesses left for more attractive sites. Soon the old, familiar Main Street was no longer the place where people went to hang out. 5

Sometime in the mid-1990s the pizza parlor went on-line on the World Wide Web. The street address turned into a network address, and the counter became a screen display that allowed a customer at any computer terminal to design a virtual pizza and pay using some form of digital cash. The kitchen transmuted into a nationwide collection of food preparation centers at locations carefully selected to provide maximum coverage of the market. Each order was automatically routed to the preparation point nearest to the customer. There the local kitchen produced and packaged the pizza, which was then delivered via a radio-controlled vehicle. 6

The old advertising signs gradually disappeared, and soon there was no newspaper or television advertising either. Instead customers were attracted through graphic "storefronts" in on-line virtual malls and through network "Yellow Pages" listings. 7

The electronic pizza parlor, some future observer might note, was a big hit. Pizza suppliers reached a much larger market than ever before, and because customers now consumed the product at home, the suppliers did not have to build and maintain restaurant facilities in expensive locations. 8

9   The customers also liked the new setup; they could always get exactly what they wanted, quickly, reliably and inexpensively. But they sometimes missed the atmosphere of the ramshackle old parlors, the conversations that unfolded there, and the opportunities that the pizzerias afforded to get out of the house and feel like part of a local community.

10   The pizza parlor may seem like a minor institution, but this story illustrates a more general trend. Using sophisticated telecommunications, for example, office workers may now telecommute from home or simply rely on personal electronic devices to set up virtual workplaces anywhere. Retailers that combine on-line interactive catalogues with direct delivery from the warehouse can now compete with pedestrian shopping streets and automobile-oriented malls. And increasingly effective distance-learning and telemedicine systems are reducing the need to go to school or visit the doctor's office.

11   In short, cities will be transformed as the Information Superhighway develops. We will have to rethink the spatial relationships, transportation connections and telecommunication linkages among homes, workplaces and service providers. Housing will have to be reconfigured as a wide range of transactions that once took place elsewhere moves back into domestic space.

12   The weakening or disappearance of traditional gathering places will require the creation of different foci for community life—both physical places and on-line, virtual locations. Offices, hospitals, schools and shopping centers will fragment and recombine in surprising ways as virtual transactions and telepresence relax traditional requirements of proximity. Perhaps reinvigorated local communities will cluster around restaurants, parks and health clubs while also benefiting from strong electronic connections to the wider world.

13   This restructuring will take place on a massive scale. Depending on the design and policy choices we make in the coming years, it could produce more equitable access to services and economic opportunities, or it could yield electronically serviced islands of privilege, surrounded by zones of disinvestment, unemployment and poverty. The stakes are huge.

14   Cities will certainly not disappear as an increasing amount of human interaction shifts into cyberspace; they will evolve into complex hybrids of physical spaces and on-line locations. They will have places where you need a body to go and places where you don't.

```
┌─────────────────────────────┐
│                             │
└─────────────────────────────┘
```

Vocabulary

    a. *paragraph 2:* inexorably
    b. *paragraph 12:* foci
    c. *paragraph 14:* cyberspace, hybrids

Questions

1. Where in the opening paragraph does Mitchell state his thesis? How does he proceed to illustrate it?
2. Why does Mitchell call his essay a parable? What kind of comparison does the use of this term imply?
3. How convincing do you find his comparison of real space and cyberspace?
4. How plausible are Mitchell's predictions about the organization of communities in the coming decades?

Writing Assignment

Compare your vision of neighbourhoods in the future with Mitchell's. Defend your conception with examples, as he does.

IAN McEWAN

Ian McEwan was born in 1948 and currently lives in Oxford, England, with his wife and four children. His first book of stories, *First Love, Last Rites* (1975), won the Somerset Maugham Award for fiction. In it he already displays the boldness of imagination that has distinguished his fictional worlds as places where the improbable happens without apology. His novels include *The Cement Garden, The Comfort of Strangers, The Child in Time, The Innocent,* and *Black Dogs.* Some of his plays for television have been collected in *The Imitation Game and Other Plays.* In the following essay, he constructs an extended metaphor for twentieth-century history as a book we read while we write it, as a fiction to be analyzed for its patterns, and as a text to be deconstructed for a better understanding of the ideologies that shape the context of our lives.

The Plot Thickens for the Century's Final Chapter

IAN McEWAN

L isten, my friend," a French academic once said to me in the early 1980s, "you are talking as if history actually happened."

We were speaking of the Suez Crisis of 1956, which I had written about in a film. "But didn't it?" I said to the pitying smiles and good-natured shrugs of a roomful of Continental European critics.

Did I not know, they asked, that history was a text to be deconstructed? It had no other reality.

3   Ten years later, I met the same group and this time we were talking about the fall of the Berlin Wall, which I had written about in a novel. "You lot," I said, hoping to tease, "don't believe that anything actually happened in Berlin at all." Once again, the same pitying smiles. Oh that! No one believes that old stuff anymore . . .

4   But don't mock. Fashion is the very breath of our cultural energy, and we should no more deny it to intellectuals than we do to teenagers or dress designers. Spawn a thousand creatures of thought, and time and usage will select out those fittest to survive. And it is in this spirit that I want to revive the mental miniskirt or skateboard of yesteryear and consider history as a text.

5   We have all been reading an immensely long novel and, though we are in the final pages, no one quite knows how it is going to end.

6   Its accounts of human misery and courage make the works of Primo Levi pale; its least unlovely characters could only be drawn by a godly Dostoyevsky; it has moments of invention that would have made Calvino weep with envy, and it attains peaks of tragic absurdity that would have sent Kafka cowering for solace into the arms of his father.

7   The pages teem with interlacing plots in the manner of *A Thousand and One Nights* and the reader has to pick a way through. Like that classic, and like *The Canterbury Tales*, this book has about it a democratic plenitude because everyone gets to tell a story. The title is a little dull, but don't be put off; it is, after Márquez: *A Hundred Years of Europe*. Or shall we simply call this novel, *The Twentieth Century*?

8   It's pretty hard to begin talking about a book this long. We all have our favourite bits, so why not be anecdotal? Personally, I like that moment near the beginning when the obscure young clerk with specs twirls his conceptual lasso and binds time, matter, space and gravity into two beautiful theories from which springs a whole new scientific paradigm.

9   I was on the edge of my seat for the first performance of *The Rite of Spring*, and I was stirred by the tale of the young doctor who, one grey afternoon on an Oxford running track, pushed himself to the first four-minute mile.

10   In fact, if you only read the chapters on scientific discovery, artistic expression and sporting achievement and skipped the rest, you would end the novel beaming with pride and love for modern Europeans. What tumultuous intellectual energy and curiosity! What humour, and brave, beautiful barings of the soul! What physical prowess and courage! What a people!

11   But what you would have to skip is long, hard to read, and harder to understand. There are world wars, slaughter, torture,

induced famine, forced migration, lies, propaganda and crazy ideologies, and every cruelty and barbarity imaginable, with corpses
piled a million deep page after page.

The reader is insulted and disgusted by a mad and sickeningly   12
repetitious tale of frenzied genocide in central Europe, of death factories and bureaucratic evil that seems finally to demolish his self-
esteem, and cause him to damn all modern literature as an indulgent
obscenity. Are we Europeans, with our "Demoiselles d'Avignon," our
heroic discovery of DNA, our European Cup, truly as bad as this? If
so, can we ever forgive ourselves? And might we do it again? Troubled readers will suspect that applauding or deploring disparate
episodes will take us no nearer to an understanding of this mighty
novel. What we need is to discern the plot of all the plots, and we
could do worse than try to think of a shape.

A few years ago, when we were three-quarters of the way   13
through, a plausible pattern for many was in the form of a *V*. From the
imperial certainties and prosperity of the late 19th century, we descend
into the mayhem of two world wars, reaching rock-bottom degrada-
tion with the Holocaust; from this point, roughly mid-century, we rise
through postwar reconstruction, social stability, the German and Italian economic miracles, the entrenchment of liberal democracies,
and European integration.

True, there are the grey tyrannies of the east, but even here opti-   14
mistic readers thought they could detect slow, if erratic, liberalisation.
This simple, satisfying plot appears triumphantly vindicated by the
events symbolised by the fall of the Berlin Wall. The second world
war is finally over. Liberal democracies are inevitable everywhere. It
is the end of history, some readers proclaimed, the end of this novel.

But unread chapters remained, and to some the *V* is beginning   15
to look like a zigzag, plunging from the peak of 1989 as the old
viruses of the European disease, frozen to inaction by the Cold War,
begin to swarm back into the bloodstream; on the fringes are
racism, nationalism, xenophobia, and anti-semitism.

Among the political elites, there is a new nervousness about the   16
European project, and helplessness before genocide in former
Yugoslavia; there is unemployment, homelessness and recession;
and everywhere that deep pessimism and ungenerosity of spirit
known as the far right.

Even as our novel squares up to its resolution, we may yet see   17
this zigzag transformed into an asymmetrical *W*, for in these days of
the information revolution we cram far more on the page, and events
move quickly. Also, it seems unlikely that the postwar generations of
Europeans, with the nightmares behind them, will easily abandon
the consensual ideas that brought them prosperity and peace.

18   Besides, the plots I have been talking of here belong to the mainstream of the political culture, and there are almost certainly other grand patterns that may turn out to be more important.

19   The lives of women have been transformed, as have those of many working people. The environment has been degraded even as our anguish about it intensifies. Our electronic machines are becoming ever more interesting. The old are getting older, and migration is on the increase, as are anti-rational cults and religions of all kinds, with their attendant consolations and intolerance.

20   According to literary fashion, it is for every reader to deconstruct this text. As we begin to turn to the final chapters we had better start thinking about the reviews we will prepare, not for newspapers and journals, but for bars, cafés, kitchens and bedrooms.

21   Our chosen literary form is democratic: the more we listen to the reckonings of others, hear how they shuffle the priorities and try to see the different shapes of plots they discern, the better we will understand for ourselves this gigantic sprawling novel that no one can put down.

Vocabulary

a. *paragraph 2:* deconstructed
b. *paragraph 6:* solace
c. *paragraph 7:* plenitude
d. *paragraph 8:* anecdotal, paradigm
e. *paragraph 10:* prowess
f. *paragraph 11:* ideologies
g. *paragraph 12:* genocide
h. *paragraph 13:* entrenchment
i. *paragraph 14:* vindicated
j. *paragraph 15:* xenophobia
k. *paragraph 17:* asymmetrical, consensual

Questions

1. List the similarities between twentieth-century history and a book that we are reading as we write it. What differences weaken the analogy?
2. Does McEwan begin the essay with a statement of his thesis, or does he build to it? How would you summarize his thesis?
3. What do the terms of McEwan's analogy assume about his audience's level of education?
4. What other analogies does McEwan introduce to support his reading of history?

Writing Assignments

1. Think of other analogies for understanding twentieth-century history: a computer game, a soap opera, a sports competition. Write an essay that illustrates the appropriateness of your choice.
2. Write an essay on one of the following analogies, discussing points of similarity and dissimilarity, and using this discussion to argue a thesis.
   a. The family is a small nation.
   b. The nation is a large family.
   c. Choosing a university or college is like buying a car.
   d. Voting is like selecting a video.

JAMES GORMAN

James Gorman is an American humorist whose books include *First Aid for Hypochondriacs* and *The Total Penguin*. He writes a monthly column called "Light Elements" for *Discover* magazine; some of these columns have been collected in *The Man with No Endorphins: And Other Reflections on Science*. The following essay on an old friend and the new technology admirably represents the writer, who has said, "It's nice to know that while there may not be justice in the world, at least there's irony."

Man, Bytes, Dog

JAMES GORMAN

Many people have asked me about the Cairn 1
Terrier. How about memory, they want to know. Is it IBM-compatible? Why didn't I get the IBM itself, or a Kaypro, Compaq, or Macintosh? I think the best way to answer these questions is to look at the Macintosh and the Cairn head on. I almost did buy the Macintosh. It has terrific graphics, good word-processing capabilities, and the mouse. But in the end I decided on the Cairn, and I think I made the right decision.

Let's start out with the basics: 2

MACINTOSH:
Weight (without printer): 20 lbs.
Memory (RAM): 128K
Price (with printer): $3,090

CAIRN TERRIER:
Weight (without printer): 14 lbs.
Memory (RAM): Some
Price (without printer): $250

3   Just on the basis of price and weight, the choice is obvious. Another plus is that the Cairn Terrier comes in one unit. No printer is necessary, or useful. And—this was a big attraction to me—there is no user's manual.

4   Here are some of the other qualities I found put the Cairn out ahead of the Macintosh:

PORTABILITY: To give you a better idea of size, Toto in *The Wizard of Oz* was a Cairn Terrier. So you can see that if the young Judy Garland was able to carry Toto around in that little picnic basket, you will have no trouble at all moving your Cairn from place to place. For short trips it will move under its own power. The Macintosh will not.

RELIABILITY: In five to ten years, I am sure, the Macintosh will be superseded by a new model, like the Delicious or the Granny Smith. The Cairn Terrier, on the other hand, has held its share of the market with only minor modifications for hundreds of years. In the short term, Cairns seldom need servicing, apart from shots and the odd worming, and most function without interruption during electrical storms.

COMPATIBILITY: Cairn Terriers get along with everyone. And for communications with any other dog, of any breed, within a radius of three miles, no additional hardware is necessary. All dogs share a common operating system.

SOFTWARE: The Cairn will run three standard programs, SIT, COME, and NO, and whatever else you create. It is true that, being microcanine, the Cairn is limited here, but it does load the programs instantaneously. No disk drives. No tapes.

5   Admittedly, these are peripheral advantages. The real comparison has to be on the basis of capabilities. What can the Macintosh and Cairn do? Let's start on the Macintosh's turf — income-tax preparation, recipe storage, graphics, and astrophysics problems:

	Taxes	Recipes	Graphics	Astrophysics
Macintosh	yes	yes	yes	yes
Cairn	no	no	no	no

At first glance it looks bad for the Cairn. But it's important to look beneath the surface with this kind of chart. If you yourself are leaning toward the Macintosh, ask yourself these questions: Do you want to do your own income taxes? Do you want to type all your recipes into a computer? In your graph, what would you put on the x axis? The y axis? Do you have any astrophysics problems you want solved? 6

Then consider the Cairn's specialties: playing fetch and tug-of-war, licking your face, and chasing foxes out of rock cairns (eponymously). Note that no software is necessary. All these functions are part of the operating system: 7

	Fetch	Tug-of-War	Face	Foxes
Cairn	yes	yes	yes	yes
Macintosh	no	no	no	no

Another point to keep in mind is that computers, even the Macintosh, only do what you tell them to do. Cairns perform their functions all on their own. Here are some of the additional capabilities that I discovered once I got the Cairn home and housebroken: 8

WORD PROCESSING: Remarkably, the Cairn seems to understand every word I say. He has a nice way of pricking up his ears at words like "out" or "ball." He also has highly tuned voice-recognition.

EDUCATION: The Cairn provides children with hands-on experience at an early age, contributing to social interaction, crawling ability, and language skills. At age one, my daughter could say "Sit," "Come," and "No."

CLEANING: This function was a pleasant surprise. But of course cleaning up around the cave is one of the reasons dogs were developed in the first place. Users with young (below age two) children will still find this function useful. The Cairn Terrier cleans the floor, spoons, bib, and baby, and has an unerring ability to distinguish strained peas from ears, nose, and fingers.

PSYCHOTHERAPY: Here the Cairn really shines. And remember, therapy is something that computers have tried. There is a program that makes the computer ask you questions when you tell it your problems. You say, "I'm afraid of foxes." The computer says, "You're afraid of foxes?"

9   The Cairn won't give you that kind of echo. Like Freudian analysts, Cairns are mercifully silent; unlike Freudians, they are infinitely sympathetic. I've found that the Cairn will share, in a nonjudgmental fashion, disappointments, joys, and frustrations. And you don't have to know BASIC.

10   This last capability is related to the Cairn's strongest point, which was the final deciding factor in my decision against the Macintosh—user-friendliness. On this criterion, there is simply no comparison. The Cairn Terrier is the essence of user-friendliness. It has fur, it doesn't flicker when you look at it, and it wags its tail.

```

```

Vocabulary

a. *paragraph 4:* superseded
b. *paragraph 5:* peripheral
c. *paragraph 7:* eponymously

Questions

1. What is Gorman's thesis, and where does he first state it? Where does he restate it later in the essay?
2. How does he organize the comparison between the computer and the dog? Does he contrast the computer and dog point by point, or instead deal with one set of patterns first, another set afterwards? Or does he mix these methods of organization?
3. Why is information already given in the essay repeated in the boxes?
4. Despite his humorous tone, is Gorman making a serious point?

Writing Assignments

1. Using the comparison-and-contrast technique, write a short essay about comparable people or things: your parents, two close friends, Canada and Russia, hockey and baseball.
2. Write an essay comparing Gorman's and Wendell Berry's attitudes to computers.

```

```

RICHARD M. RESTAK

Richard M. Restak is a neurologist at the Georgetown University School of Medicine. He prefaces a recent book on the infant brain by saying that, in the area of neurology, "anyone who waxes 'definitive' can depend on earning for himself the snickers of those a decade or two hence." The tentative but provocative suggestions in the essay that follows provide a fine example of Restak's willingness to take a controversial position based on his own research.

The Other Difference between Boys and Girls

RICHARD M. RESTAK

There is no denying it: Boys think differ- 1
ently from girls. Even though recent brain-research evidence is controversial, that conclusion seems inescapable. I know how offensive that will sound to feminists and others committed to overcoming sexual stereotypes. But social equality for men and women really depends on recognizing these differences in brain behavior.

At present, schooling and testing discriminate against both 2
sexes, ignoring differences that have been observed by parents and educators for years. Boys suffer in elementary-school classrooms, which are ideally suited to the way girls think. Girls suffer later, when they must take scholarship tests that are geared for male performance.

Anyone who has spent time with children in a playground or 3
school setting is aware of differences in the way boys and girls respond to similar situations. For example, at a birthday party for five-year-olds it's not usually the girls who pull hair, throw punches or smear each other with food.

Typically, such differences are explained on a cultural basis. 4
Boys are expected to be more aggressive and play rough games, while girls are presumably encouraged to be gentle and non-assertive. After years of exposure to such expectations, the theory goes, men and women wind up with widely varying behavioral and intellectual repertoires. As a corollary, many people believe that if child-rearing practices could be equalized and sexual stereotypes eliminated, most of these differences would eventually disappear. The true state of affairs is not that simple.

Undoubtedly, many differences traditionally believed to exist 5
between the sexes are based on stereotypes. But evidence from recent brain research indicates that some behavioral differences between men and women are based on differences in brain functioning that are biologically inherent and unlikely to be changed by cultural factors alone.

One clue to brain differences between the sexes came from obser- 6
vation of infants. One study found that from shortly after birth, females are more sensitive to certain types of sounds, particularly to a mother's voice. In a laboratory, if the sound of the mother's voice is

displaced to another part of the room, female babies react while males usually seem oblivious to the displacement. Female babies are also more easily startled by loud noises.

7   Tests show girls have increased skin sensitivity, particularly in the fingertips, and are more proficient at fine motor performance. Females are also generally more attentive to social contexts—faces, speech patterns, subtle vocal cues. By five months, a female can distinguish photographs of familiar people, a task rarely performed well by boys of that age. At five and eight months, girls will babble to a mother's face, seemingly recognizing her as a person, while boys fail to distinguish between a face and a dangling toy, babbling equally to both.

8   Female infants speak sooner, have larger vocabularies and rarely demonstrate speech defects. (Stuttering, for instance, occurs almost exclusively among boys.) Girls exceed boys in language abilities, and this early linguistic bias often prevails throughout life. Girls read sooner, learn foreign languages more easily and, as a result, are more likely to enter occupations involving language mastery.

9   Boys, in contrast, show an early visual superiority. They are also clumsier, performing poorly at something like arranging a row of beads, but excel at other activities calling on total body coordination. Their attentional mechanisms are also different. A boy will react to an inanimate object as quickly as he will to a person. A male baby will often ignore the mother and babble to a blinking light, fixate on a geometric figure and, at a later point, manipulate it and attempt to take it apart.

10   A study of preschool children by psychologist Diane McGuinness of Stanford University found boys more curious, especially in regard to exploring their environment. Her studies also confirmed that males are better at manipulating three-dimensional space. When boys and girls are asked to mentally rotate or fold an object, boys overwhelmingly outperform girls. "I folded it in my mind" is a typical male response. Girls are likely to produce elaborate verbal descriptions which, because they are less appropriate to the task, result in frequent errors.

11   There is evidence that some of these differences in performance are differences in brain organization between boys and girls. Overall, verbal and spatial abilities in boys tend to be "packaged" into different hemispheres: the right hemisphere for nonverbal tasks, the left for verbal tasks. But in girls nonverbal and verbal skills are likely to be found on both sides of the brain. The hemispheres of women's brains may be less specialized for these functions.

12   These differences in brain organization and specialization are believed by some scientists to provide a partial explanation of why members of one sex or the other are underrepresented in certain

professions. Architects, for example, require a highly developed spatial sense, a skill found more frequently among men. Thus, the preponderance of male architects may be partially caused by the more highly developed spatial sense that characterizes the male brain.

Psychological measurements of brain functioning between the sexes also show unmistakable differences. In 11 subtests of the most widely used general intelligence test, only 2 (digit span and picture arrangement) reveal similar mean scores for males and females. These sex differences are so consistent that the standard battery of this intelligence test now contains a masculinity–femininity index to offset sex-related proficiencies and deficiencies. 13

Most thought-provoking of all are findings by Eleanor Maccoby and Carol Nagy Jacklin of Stanford University on personality traits and intellectual achievement. They found that intellectual development in girls is fostered among individuals who are assertive and active, and have a sense that they can control, by their own actions, the events that affect their lives. These factors appear to be less important in the intellectual development of boys. 14

Recent studies even suggest that high levels of intellectual achievement are associated with cross-sex typing: the ability to express traits and interests associated with the opposite sex. Educational psychologist E.P. Torrance of the University of Georgia suggests that sexual stereotypes are a block to creativity, since creativity requires sensitivity—a female trait—as well as autonomy and independence—traits usually associated with males. M.P. Honzik and J.W. Mcfarlane of the University of California at Berkeley support Torrance's speculation with a 20-year follow-up on subjects who demonstrated significant IQ gains. Those with the greatest gains displayed less dependency on traditional sex roles than those whose IQs remained substantially the same. 15

It's important to remember that we're not talking about one sex being generally superior or inferior to another. In addition, the studies are statistical and don't tell us a lot about individuals. The findings are controversial, but they can help us establish true social equity. 16

One way of doing this might be to change such practices as nationwide competitive examinations. If boys, for instance, truly excel in right-hemisphere tasks, scholastic aptitude tests should be substantially redesigned to assure that both sexes have an equal chance. Some of the tests now are weighted with items that virtually guarantee superior male performance. 17

Attitude changes are also needed in our approach to "hyperactive" or "learning disabled" children. The evidence for sex differences here is staggering: More than 90 percent of hyperactives are 18 males. This is not surprising since the male brain is primarily visual, while classroom instruction demands attentive listening. The male brain learns by manipulating its environment, yet the typical student is forced to sit still for long hours in the classroom. There is little opportunity, other than during recess, for gross motor movements or rapid muscular responses. In essence, the classrooms in most of our nation's primary grades are geared to skills that come naturally to girls but develop very slowly in boys. The result shouldn't be surprising: a "learning disabled" child who is also frequently "hyperactive."

19   We now have the opportunity, based on emerging evidence of sex differences in brain functioning, to restructure elementary grades so that boys find their initial educational contacts less stressful. At more advanced levels of instruction, teaching methods could incorporate verbal and linguistic approaches to physics, engineering and architecture (to mention only three fields where women are conspicuously underrepresented).

20   The alternative is to do nothing about brain differences. There is something to be said for this approach, too. In the recent past, enhanced social benefit has usually resulted from stressing the similarities between people rather than their differences. We ignore brain-sex differences, however, at the risk of confusing biology with sociology, and wishful thinking with scientific fact.

Vocabulary

a. *paragraph 4:* repertoires, corollary
b. *paragraph 9:* fixate
c. *paragraph 12:* preponderance
d. *paragraph 15:* autonomy
e. *paragraph 19:* conspicuously

Questions

1. In what ways does Restak use comparison and contrast to establish the basis of his comparison of how boys and girls learn?
2. In paragraphs 6 through 15, Restak establishes an important difference between the ways in which boys and girls process information. How would you describe that difference?
3. What importance does Restak's survey have for teaching children in schools?
4. Where does Restak attempt to deal with the political implications of the differences he discusses?

Writing Assignments

1. Write an essay in the form of a debate between those who would emphasize the differences between the sexes and those who would stress the similarities.
2. Write a polemical essay that considers the similarities and differences between the male and female attitudes toward sports, children, home, or a subject of your own choosing. Consider the sex stereotyping associated with your chosen subject and comment on its effects.

Definition

There are many ways of defining something, and the way we choose depends on our purpose. If we are in a store that advertises "Submarine Sandwiches" and a visitor asks what these are, we can point to one on the counter. But pointing may not be enough: we may have to explain or "denote" what a submarine sandwich is—that is, single the submarine out from all other things like it. In a denotative definition, we can start with a classification of things like food and single the submarine out from all other kinds. But since the visitor knows a submarine is something to eat, we can limit our class to sandwiches.

A dictionary definition usually gives us a denotative definition of this sort—first identifying the class or genus of objects to which the word belongs and then distinguishing the word by its specific difference. As we noted, the class or genus may be broad (*food*) or it may be narrow (*sandwich*). The following dictionary definition of a submarine chooses a narrow genus:

> **Sub•ma•rine**[2] . . . a large sandwich consisting of a long roll that is split lengthwise and filled with a variety of cold meats, cheese, tomatoes, onions, coleslaw, etc. (*Gage Canadian Dictionary*)

Sometimes we want to do more than merely name or identify an object: we want to present ideas and impressions, the emotional aura we associate with it. The word *rose* has a precise denotation—a particular flower with describable properties. It also has a range of connotations or associations. Thus roses are often associated with success or happiness, and we recognize this association in the popular expression "a rosy future." Connotations may be positive in their implication, or negative. Though the words *inexpensive* and *cheap* both mean low in price, *cheap* usually carries the connotation of poor quality or of something contemptible. *Inexpensive* is an emotionally neutral word; *cheap* is not.

Denotative and connotative definitions tell us how words are used currently. Sometimes we find it helpful to give the original meaning, or etymology, to clarify the current meaning—for example, to explain that the word *gravity* comes from the Latin *gravitas*, meaning weight or heaviness. But we must be careful not to assume that a current word possesses, or should possess, its original meaning. The word *sinister* originally meant "of or on the left," but this meaning is rare today, and we would certainly be misunderstood if we used *sinister* to refer to a left-handed person. But notice how the etymology of *sinister* helps us to explain an expression like "a left-handed compliment."

We can use definition to clarify the meanings of words that have become indefinite or confused in popular usage. We sometimes call this kind of definition *precising*. Another use of definition is to stipulate or propose a name or term for a newly discovered phenomenon so that we can refer to it. An example is the term *quasar*, proposed in the 1960s for newly discovered "quasi-stellar" sources of light in the sky that seem not to be stars. Stipulative definitions are proposed with the understanding that the term may change later as more is discovered. By contrast, theoretical definitions propose an explanation or theory of the phenomenon: they do not merely propose a term for discussion and further research. Most textbook definitions of democracy and similar ideas are theoretical. In giving definitions, we should be clear about the use we are making of them. It will matter to the reader whether we are trying to make a commonly used word more exact in its usage or proposing a definition without claiming to know the whole truth about it.

HUGH RAWSON

A word buff since childhood, Hugh Rawson is the author of *A Dictionary of Euphemisms and Other Doubletalk* and *Wicked Words: A Treasury of Curses, Insults, Put-Downs and Other Formerly Unprintable Terms from Anglo-Saxon Times to the Present.* In the second book he traces the origin and uses of personal insults, ethnic slurs, political attacks, and swearing generally. He also shows how these terms reveal class and cultural differences.

Wicked Words

HUGH RAWSON

dog. The first of the animals to be domesticated and also a standard symbol of inferiority, abused linguistically in so many ways that one prefers to pass by in silence the question of what it says about man that he is so ready, in effect, to kick his oldest and best friend in the teeth. Stubb: "I will not tamely be called a dog, sir." Ahab: "Then be called ten times a donkey, and a mule, and an ass, and begone, or I'll clear the world of thee!" (Herman Melville, *Moby Dick*, 1851). Among the many extensions of the epithet's meaning:

2   A *dog* is a racehorse that doesn't run very fast, and a failure of any sort ("So many movies are *dogs*," *New Yorker*, 8/15/70); an ugly person, often a woman (see also MUTT); a worthless person, as in "Am I a dog that thou comest to me with staves?" (Goliath's complaint to the Hebrews when they sent a slip of a boy, David, to fight him (I Samuel, 17: 43)), or an untrustworthy person, as in Queen Margaret's warning of the treachery of the Duke of Gloucester, the future Richard III: "O Buckingham, take heed of yonder dog! Look, when he fawns, he bites, and when he bites, His venom will rankle [cause festering] to the death" (William Shakespeare, *Richard III*, 1592–93). And at the end of the play, after Richard has been slain, his conqueror, the future Henry VII, announces: "The day is ours—the bloody dog is dead."

3   Today, the canine epithet often is applied to one's favorite enemies. Thus, Marxists speak of *capitalist running dogs, mad dogs,* or *stray dogs* (Libyan leader Muammar el-Qaddafi also used the latter on the British in 1984); Moslems refer to *Christian dogs*, as in Lebanon when gunmen came to a woman's house, "calling out, among other things, 'Open the door, Christian dogs'" (*New York Times*, 2/17/84); and Christians have used the term, too, as in — addressing a venerable Jew — "Dog of an unbeliever, whelp of a she-wolf; darest thou press upon a Christian, and a Norman gentleman . . ." (Sir Walter Scott, *Ivanhoe*, 1820).

4   But the denigration has never been limited to members of other groups, e.g., "COTTON MATHER, *You Dog, Dam you, I'l inoculate you with this, with a Pox to you*" (message attached to a grenade, tossed through the reverend's window, 11/14/1721, in retaliation for his advocacy of smallpox inoculations in Boston; from Kenneth Silverman, *The Life and Times of Cotton Mather*, 1984). The word doesn't even have to be articulated for the point to be made, as when a Florida prosecutor said of a murder defendant, "He shouldn't be out of his cell unless he has a leash on him and a prison guard at the other end of that leash" (the man was convicted but the prosecutor's choice of words led to a series of appeals that reached the Supreme Court, where it was finally decided, five to four, that the characterization was not quite poisonous enough to require a retrial; *New York Times*, 6/24/86).

5   Only rarely is *dog* used affectionately. *Dogged* persistence usually is construed as a commendable quality. As Samuel Johnson pointed out, "a man may write at any time, if he will set himself doggedly to it" (James Boswell, *The Life of Samuel Johnson, LL.D.*, 1791) Trouble is, not everyone may approve of the result: "*Ulysses* is a dogged attempt to cover the universe with mud" (E.M. Forster, *Aspects of the Novel*, 1927). Others may sneer at those who *put on the dog* by getting all dressed up, though the display of finery is at

worst a venial sin. The phrase may have a humble origin, however, deriving from the *dog collar*, the allusion being to the high, stiff collar that people wore when decking themselves out for special occasions in the 1890s. Also on the good side, young men about town used to be known as *gay dogs* (this was before *gay* acquired its present sexual orientation). Other members of this pack included *handsome dog*, *lucky dog*, and *old dog* (as well as *sad dog* and *sick dog*, especially on mornings after). Sometimes the simple *dog* suffices, as when two of Samuel Johnson's friends knocked on his door at three o'clock one morning, and asked him to come carousing with them. Johnson readily agreed, saying: "What, is it you, you dogs! I'll have a frisk with you." And the three stayed up drinking the whole night through, proving that not all dictionary makers are drudges all the time (Boswell, *op. cit.*). Such friendly *dogs* are in the minority, however. The connotations of mediocrity, worthlessness, and even cowardice are much more common.

Vocabulary

a. *paragraph 1:* epithet
b. *paragraph 4:* denigration
c. *paragraph 5:* construed, commendable, connotations

Questions

1. What is the difference between the denotative definition of *dog* and the connotations Rawson analyzes?
2. How does Rawson use authority in establishing the etymological history of *dog*?
3. Why do you suppose so many of the connotations Rawson cites are pejorative? That is, why does man insist on kicking his "oldest and best friend in the teeth"?
4. What is the tone of the paragraph—the voice of the writer that you hear in reading it? Serious, sarcastic, bemused, ironic? What evidence in the passage supports your description of its tone?

Writing Assignments

1. Consult a dictionary of slang and write a couple of paragraphs on a favourite expression.
2. First give the denotative meaning of the name of a rock group. Then give its connotations and, if you can, explain their origin. Use your definition to make a point.

JOSEPH BRODSKY

Joseph Brodsky (1940–1996) is one of Russia's most talented writers. Persecuted and thrown into jail in the sixties, he left the Soviet Union in 1972 and thereafter made his home in the West. The author of numerous books of poetry, in Russian and English, he received the Nobel Prize for Literature in 1987. The following is adapted from "In Praise of Boredom," which is included in *On Grief and Reason*, a collection of recent essays and speeches. In the following essay, he advocates a passive attitude to the tedium that is the bane of so much of modern life. The text was originally delivered as a commencement address at Dartmouth College.

Listening to Boredom

JOSEPH BRODSKY

1   **A** substantial part of what lies ahead of you is going to be claimed by boredom. The reason I'd like to talk to you about it today, on this lofty occasion, is that I believe no liberal arts college prepares you for that eventuality. Neither the humanities nor science offers courses in boredom. At best, they may acquaint you with the sensation by incurring it. But what is a casual contact to an incurable malaise? The worst monotonous drone coming from a lectern or the most eye-splitting textbook written in turgid English is nothing in comparison to the psychological Sahara that starts right in your bedroom and spurns the horizon.

2   Known under several aliases—anguish, ennui, tedium, the doldrums, humdrum, the blahs, apathy, listlessness, stolidity, lethargy, languor, etc.—boredom is a complex phenomenon and by and large a product of repetition. It would seem, then, that the best remedy against it would be constant inventiveness and originality. That is what you, young and newfangled, would hope for. Alas, life won't supply you with that option, for life's main medium is precisely repetition.

3   One may argue, of course, that repeated attempts at originality and inventiveness are the vehicle of progress and, in the same breath, civilization. As benefits of hindsight go, however, this one is not the most valuable. For if we divide the history of our species by scientific discoveries, not to mention new ethical concepts, the result will not be very impressive. We'll get, technically speaking, centuries of boredom. The very notion of originality or innovation spells out the monotony of standard reality, of life.

The other trouble with originality and inventiveness is that they literally pay off. Provided that you are capable of either, you will become well-off rather fast. Desirable as that may be, most of you know firsthand that nobody is as bored as the rich, for money buys time, and time is repetitive. Assuming that you are heading for poverty, one can expect your being hit by boredom as soon as the first tools of self-gratification become available to you. Thanks to modern technology, those tools are as numerous as boredom's symptoms. In light of their function—to render you oblivious to the redundancy of time—their abundance is revealing. 4

As for poverty, boredom is the most brutal part of its misery, and escape from it takes more radical forms: violent rebellion or drug addiction. Both are temporary, for the misery of poverty is infinite; both, because of that infinity, are costly. In general, a man shooting heroin into his vein does so largely for the same reason you rent a video: to dodge the redundancy of time. The difference, though, is that he spends more than he's got, and that his means of escaping become as redundant as what he is escaping from faster than yours. On the whole, the difference in tactility between a syringe's needle and a stereo's push button roughly corresponds to the difference between the acuteness of time's impact upon the have-nots and the dullness of its impact on the haves. But, whether rich or poor, you will inevitably be afflicted by monotony. Potential haves, you'll be bored with your work, your friends, your spouses, your lovers, the view from your window, the furniture or wallpaper in your room, your thoughts, yourselves. Accordingly, you'll try to devise ways of escape. Apart from the self-gratifying gadgets I mentioned before, you may take up changing your job, residence, company, country, climate; you may take up promiscuity, alcohol, travel, cooking lessons, drugs, psychoanalysis. 5

In fact, you may lump all these together, and for a while that may work. Until the day, of course, when you wake up in your bedroom amidst a new family and a different wallpaper, in a different state and climate, with a heap of bills from your travel agent and your shrink, yet with the same stale feeling toward the light of day pouring through your window. You'll put on your loafers only to discover that they're lacking bootstraps by which to lift yourself up from what you recognize. Depending on your temperament and your age, you will either panic or resign yourself to the familiarity of the sensation, or else you'll go through the rigmarole of change once more. Neurosis and depression will enter your lexicon; pills, your medicine cabinet. 6

Basically, there is nothing wrong with turning life into the constant quest for alternatives, into leapfrogging jobs, spouses, and surroundings, provided that you can afford the alimony and jumbled memories. This predicament, after all, has been sufficiently glamorized on-screen 7 and in Romantic poetry. The rub, however, is that before long this quest turns into a full-time occupation, with your need for an alternative coming to match a drug addict's daily fix.

8   There is yet another way out of boredom, however. Not a better one, perhaps, from your point of view, and not necessarily secure, but straight and inexpensive. When hit by boredom, let yourself be crushed by it; submerge, hit bottom. In general, with things unpleasant, the rule is: The sooner you hit bottom, the faster you surface. The idea here is to exact a full look at the worst. The reason boredom deserves such scrutiny is that it represents pure, undiluted time in all its repetitive, redundant, monotonous splendor.

9   Boredom is your window on the properties of time that one tends to ignore to the likely peril of one's mental equilibrium. It is your window on time's infinity. Once this window opens, don't try to shut it; on the contrary, throw it wide open. For boredom speaks the language of time, and it teaches you the most valuable lesson of your life: the lesson of your utter insignificance. It is valuable to you, as well as to those you are to rub shoulders with. "You are finite," time tells you in the voice of boredom, "and whatever you do is, from my point of view, futile." As music to your ears, this, of course, may not count; yet the sense of futility, of the limited significance of even your best, most ardent actions, is better than the illusion of their consequences and the attendant self-aggrandizement.

10   For boredom is an invasion of time into your set of values. It puts your existence into its proper perspective, the net result of which is precision and humility. The former, it must be noted, breeds the latter. The more you learn about your own size, the more humble and the more compassionate you become to your likes, to the dust aswirl in a sunbeam or already immobile atop your table.

11   If it takes will-paralyzing boredom to bring your insignificance home, then hail the boredom. You are insignificant because you are finite. Yet infinity is not terribly lively, not terribly emotional. Your boredom, at least, tells you that much. And the more finite a thing is, the more it is charged with life, emotions, joy, fears, compassion.

12   What's good about boredom, about anguish and the sense of meaninglessness of your own, of everything else's existence, is that it is not a deception. Try to embrace, or let yourself be embraced by, boredom and anguish, which are larger than you anyhow. No doubt you'll find that bosom smothering, yet try to endure it as long as you can, and then some more. Above all, don't think you've goofed somewhere along the line, don't try to retrace your steps to correct the error. No, as W.H. Auden said, "Believe your pain." This awful bear hug is no mistake. Nothing that disturbs you ever is.

Vocabulary

a. *paragraph 2:* stolidity
b. *paragraph 5:* tactility

Questions

1. How important to your reading is it to know that Brodsky's original audience was a graduating class?
2. Where does he state his thesis? Does the essay build an argument on it or simply offer a series of illustrations of it?
3. What does the shift in paragraph 8 do to extend Brodsky's definition of boredom?
4. Why does Brodsky use humour in his essay? Does this detract from the serious side of the subject?

Writing Assignments

1. Write an essay similar to Brodsky's on one of the following:
   a. joy   d. jealousy
   b. fatigue   e. hatred
   c. anger   f. admiration
2. Write an essay exploring Brodsky's claim that boredom is "an invasion of time into your set of values."

JANE SMILEY

Jane Smiley won the Pulitzer Prize in 1992 for her novel *A Thousand Acres.* Her most recent novel is *Moo.* In the following excerpt from her essay "Idle Hands," published originally in *Hungry Mind Review,* she encourages us to re-examine our definition of "work" and to adopt a view arising more naturally from enlightened self-interest.

The Case against Chores

JANE SMILEY

I've lived in the upper Midwest for twenty-one years now, and I'm here to tell you that the pressure to put your children to work is unrelenting. So far I've squirmed out from under it, and my daughters have led a life of almost tropical idleness, much to their benefit. My son, however, may not be so lucky. His father was himself raised in Iowa and put to work at an early age, and you never know when, in spite of all my husband's best intentions, that early training might kick in.

2   Although "chores" are so sacred in my neck of the woods that almost no one ever discusses their purpose, I have over the years gleaned some of the reasons parents give for assigning them. I'm not impressed. Mostly the reasons have to do with developing good work habits or, in the absence of good work habits, at least habits of working. No such thing as a free lunch, any job worth doing is worth doing right, work before play, all of that. According to this reasoning, the world is full of jobs that no one wants to do. If we divide them up and get them over with, then we can go on to pastimes we like. If we do them "right," then we won't have to do them again. Lots of times, though, in a family, that *we* doesn't operate. The operative word is *you*. The practical result of almost every child-labor scheme that I've witnessed is the child doing the dirty work and the parent getting the fun: Mom cooks and Sis does the dishes; the parents plan and plant the garden, the kids weed it. To me, what this teaches the child is the lesson of alienated labor: not to love the work but to get it over with; not to feel pride in one's contribution but to feel resentment at the waste of one's time.

3   Another goal of chores: the child contributes to the work of maintaining the family. According to this rationale, the child comes to understand what it takes to have a family, and to feel that he or she is an important, even indispensable member of it. But come on. Would you really want to feel loved primarily because you're the one who gets the floors mopped? Wouldn't you rather feel that your family's love simply exists all around you, no matter what your contribution? And don't the parents love their children anyway, whether the children vacuum or not? Why lie about it just to get the housework done? Let's be frank about the other half of the equation too. In this day and age, it doesn't take much work at all to manage a household, at least in the middle class — maybe four hours a week to clean the house and another four to throw the laundry into the washing machine, move it to the dryer, and fold it. Is it really a good idea to set the sort of example my former neighbors used to set, of mopping the floor every two days, cleaning the toilets every week, vacuuming every day, dusting, dusting, dusting? Didn't they have anything better to do than serve their house?

4   Let me confess that I wasn't expected to lift a finger when I was growing up. Even when my mother had a full-time job, she cleaned up after me, as did my grandmother. Later there was a housekeeper. I would leave my room in a mess when I headed off for

school and find it miraculously neat when I returned. Once in a while I vacuumed, just because I liked the pattern the Hoover made on the carpet. I did learn to run water in my cereal bowl before setting it in the sink.

Where I discovered work was at the stable, and, in fact, there is no housework like horsework. You've got to clean the horses' stalls, feed them, groom them, tack them up, wrap their legs, exercise them, turn them out, and catch them. You've got to clip them and shave them. You have to sweep the aisle, clean your tack and your boots, carry bales of hay and buckets of water. Minimal horsekeeping, rising just to the level of humaneness, requires many more hours than making a few beds, and horsework turned out to be a good preparation for the real work of adulthood, which is rearing children. It was a good preparation not only because it was similar in many ways but also because my desire to do it, and to do a good job of it, grew out of my love of and interest in my horse. I can't say that cleaning out her bucket when she manured in it was an actual joy, but I knew she wasn't going to do it herself. I saw the purpose of my labor, and I wasn't alienated from it.

Probably to the surprise of some of those who knew me as a child, I have turned out to be gainfully employed. I remember when I was in seventh grade, one of my teachers said to me, strongly disapproving, "The trouble with you is you only do what you want to do!" That continues to be the trouble with me, except that over the years I have wanted to do more and more.

My husband worked hard as a child, out-Iowa-ing the Iowans, if such a thing is possible. His dad had him mixing cement with a stick when he was five, pushing wheelbarrows not long after. It's a long sad tale on the order of two miles to school and both ways uphill. The result is, he's a great worker, much better than I am, but all the while he's doing it he wishes he weren't. He thinks of it as work; he's torn between doing a good job and longing not to be doing it at all. Later, when he's out on the golf course, where he really wants to be, he feels a little guilty, knowing there's work that should have been done before he gave in and took advantage of the beautiful day.

Good work is not the work we assign children but the work they want to do, whether it's reading in bed (where would I be today if my parents had rousted me out and put me to scrubbing floors?) or cleaning their rooms or practicing the flute or making roasted potatoes with rosemary and Parmesan for the family dinner. It's good for a teenager to suddenly decide that the bathtub is so disgusting she'd better clean it herself. I admit that for the parent, this can involve years of waiting. But if she doesn't want to wait, she can always spend her time dusting.

Vocabulary

a. *paragraph 2:* gleaned, alienated
b. *paragraph 3:* rationale
c. *paragraph 5:* tack

Questions

1. How would you summarize Smiley's attitude toward work?
2. What are the effects of the shift to the second-person pronoun in paragraph 5? What does the terse style here suggest?
3. How does Smiley use personal experience to support her redefinition of the term *work*? How does she contrast her upbringing in this regard with her husband's?
4. How have attitudes toward "chores" changed in your own lifetime?

Writing Assignments

1. Smiley challenges our attitudes toward work. Write an essay similar to hers on the concept of play.
2. Use the *Gage Canadian Dictionary,* the *Oxford English Dictionary,* or the *Dictionary of American English,* and other reference books in the library to trace the history of one of the following terms:

a. anarchist	e. fascist	h. socialist
b. communiste.	f. mugwump	i. tory
c. Creole	g. republican	j. Yankee
d. democrat		

MARGARET ATWOOD

Margaret Atwood was born in Ottawa and educated at the University of Toronto and Harvard. As poet, novelist, short story writer, essayist, and activist in such organizations as PEN International, she has gained an international reputation of high standing, earning a world-wide readership equalled by few Canadian writers. Some of her best-known novels are *Surfacing, Lady Oracle, The Handmaid's Tale, Cat's Eye,* and *The Robber Bride.* She has published some ten books of poetry, eight novels, two books of criticism and essays, and several books of short stories—in all of them displaying an eye for telling and often estranging detail, an intellect that can't help but express itself wittily, and a dedicated writer's way with a polished sentence. In the following essay, she explores the bush country of northern

Quebec that she discovered as a child on field trips with her father, an ento-mologist, and ponders the metaphor of urban wilderness.

True North

MARGARET ATWOOD

Where is the north, exactly? It's not only a place but a direction, and as such its location is relative: to the Mexicans, the United States is the north, to Americans Toronto is, even though it's on roughly the same latitude as Boston.

Wherever it is for us, there's a lot of it. You stand in Windsor and imagine a line going north, all the way to the pole. The same line going south would end up in South America. That's the sort of map we grew up with, at the front of the classroom in Mercator projection, which made it look even bigger than it was, all that pink stretching on forever, with a few cities sprinkled along the bottom edge. It's not only geographical space, it's space related to body image. When we face south, as we often do, our conscious mind may be directed down there, towards crowds, bright lights, some Hollywood version of fame and fortune, but the north is at the back of our minds, always. There's something, not someone, looking over our shoulders; there's a chill at the nape of the neck.

The north focuses our anxieties. Turning to face north, face the north, we enter our own unconscious. Always, in retrospect, the journey north has the quality of dream.

The Acid Rain Dinner, in Toronto's Sheraton Centre, in 1985. The first of these fund-raising events was fairly small. But the movement has grown, and this dinner is huge. The leaders of all three provincial parties are here. So is the minister of the environment from the federal government. So are several labour leaders, and several high-ranking capitalists, and representatives of numerous northerly chambers of commerce, summer residents' associations, tourist-camp runners, outfitters. Wishy-washy urban professionals who say "frankly" a lot bend elbows with huntin', shootin', fishin', and cussin' burnt-necks who wouldn't be caught dead saying "frankly." This is not a good place to be overheard saying that actually acid rain isn't such a bad thing because it gets rid of all that brown scum and leeches in the lake, or who cares because you can water-ski anyway. Teddy Kennedy, looking like a bulky sweater, is the guest-speaker. Everyone wears a little gold pin in the shape of a rain drop. It looks like a tear.

5   Why has acid rain become the collective Canadian nightmare?
Why is it—as a good cause—bigger than baby-seal bashing? The
reasons aren't just economic, although there are lots of those, as the
fishing-camp people and foresters will tell you. It's more than that,
and cognate with the outrage aroused by the uninvited voyage of
the American icebreaker *Polar Sea* through the Northwest Passage,
where almost none of us ever goes. It's territorial, partly; partly a
felt violation of some area in us that we hardly ever think about
unless it's invaded or tampered with. It's the neighbours throwing
guck into our yard. It's our childhood dying.

6   In Europe, every scrap of land has been claimed, owned, re-
owned, fought over, captured, bled on. The roads are the only no-
man's land. In northern Canada, the roads are civilization, owned
by the collective human *we*. Off the road is *other*. Try walking in it,
and you'll soon find out why all the early traffic here was by water.
"Impenetrable wilderness" is not just verbal.

7   And suppose you get off the road. Suppose you get lost. Getting lost, elsewhere and closer to town, is not knowing exactly
where you are. You can always ask, even in a foreign country. In the
north, getting lost is not knowing how to get out.

8   One way of looking at a landscape is to consider the typical ways of
dying in it. Given the worst, what's the worst it could do? Will it be
delirium from drinking salty water on the high seas, shrivelling in the
desert, snakebite in the jungle, tidal waves on a Pacific Isle, volcanic
fumes? In the north, there are several hazards. Although you're
probably a lot safer there than you are on the highway at rush hour,
given the odds, you still have to be a little wary.

9   Like most lessons of this sort, those about the north are taught
by precept and example, but also, more enjoyably, by cautionary
nasty tale. There is death by blackfly, the one about the fellow who
didn't have his shirt cuffs tight enough in the spring and undressed
at night only to find he was running with blood, the ones about the
lost travellers who bloated up from too many bites and who, when
found, were twice the size, unrecognizable, and dead. There is
death from starvation, death by animal, death by forest fire; there is
death from something called "exposure," which used to confuse me
when I heard about men who exposed themselves: why would they
intentionally do anything that fatal? There's death by thunderstorm, not to be sneered at: on the open lake, in one of the excessive
northern midsummer thunderstorms, a canoe or a bush plane is a
vulnerable target. The north is full of Struwwelpeter-like stories
about people who didn't do as they were told and got struck by
lightning. Above all, there are death by freezing and death by
drowning. Your body's heat-loss rate in the water is twenty times

that in air, and northern lakes are cold. Even in a life jacket, even holding on to the tipped canoe, you're at risk. Every summer the numbers pile up.

Every culture has its exemplary dead people, its hagiography of landscape martyrs, those unfortunates who, by their bad ends, seem to sum up in one grisly episode what may be lurking behind the next rock for all of us, all of us who enter the territory they once claimed as theirs. I'd say that two of the top northern landscape martyrs are Tom Thomson, the painter who was found mysteriously drowned near his overturned canoe with no provable cause in sight, and the Mad Trapper of Rat River, also mysterious, who became so thoroughly bushed that he killed a Mountie and shot two others during an amazing wintertime chase before being finally mowed down. In our retelling of these stories, mystery is a key element. So, strangely enough, is a presumed oneness with the landscape in question. The Mad Trapper knew his landscape so well he survived in it for weeks, living off the land and his own bootlaces, eluding capture. One of the hidden motifs in these stories is a warning: maybe it's not so good to get *too* close to Nature.

I remember a documentary on Tom Thomson that ended, rather ominously, with the statement that the north had taken him to herself. This was, of course, pathetic fallacy gone to seed, but it was also a comment on our distrust of the natural world, a distrust that remains despite our protests, our studies in the ethics of ecology, our elevation of "the environment" to a numinous noun, our save-the-tree campaigns. The question is, would the trees save us, given the chance? Would the water, would the birds, would the rocks? In the north, we have our doubts.

A different part of the north. We're sitting around the table, by lamplight—it's still the old days here, no electricity—talking about bad hunters. Bad hunters, bad fishers, everyone has a story. You come upon a campsite, way in the back of beyond, no roads into the lake, they must have come in by float plane, and there it is, garbage all over the place, beer cans, blobs of human poop flagged by melting toilet paper, and twenty-two fine pickerel left rotting on a rock. Business executives who get themselves flown in during hunting season with their high-powered rifles, shoot a buck, cut off the head, fill their quota, see another one with a bigger spread of antlers, drop the first head, cut off the second. The woods are littered with discarded heads, and who cares about the bodies?

New way to shoot polar bear: you have the natives on the ground finding them for you, then they radio the location in to the base camp, the base camp phones New York, fellow gets on the plane, gets himself flown in, they've got the rifle and the clothing

10

11

12

13

all ready for him, fly him to the bear, he pulls the trigger from the plane, doesn't even get out of the g.d. *plane*, they fly him back, cut off the head, skin it, send the lot down to New York.

14   These are the horror stories of the north, one brand. They've replaced the ones in which you got pounced upon by a wolverine or had your arm chewed off by a she-bear with cubs or got chased into the lake by a moose in rut, or even the ones in which your dog got porcupine quills or rolled in poison ivy and gave it to you. In the new stories, the enemies and the victims of old have done a switch. Nature is no longer implacable, dangerous, ready to jump you; it is on the run, pursued by a number of unfair bullies with the latest technology.

15   One of the key nouns in these stories is "float plane." These outrages, this banditry, would not be possible without them, for the bad hunters are notoriously weak-muscled and are deemed incapable of portaging a canoe, much less paddling one. Among their other badnesses, they are sissies. Another key motif is money. What money buys these days, among other things, is the privilege of no-risk slaughter.

16   As for us, the ones telling the stories, tsk-tsking by lamplight, we are the good hunters, or so we think. We've given up saying we only kill to eat; Kraft dinner and freeze-dried food have put paid to that one. Really there's no excuse for us. However, we do have some virtues left. We can still cast a fly. We don't cut off heads and hang them stuffed on the wall. We would never buy an ocelot coat. We paddle our own canoes.

17   We're sitting on the dock at night, shivering despite our sweaters, in mid-August, watching the sky. There are a few shooting stars, as there always are at this time in August, as the earth passes through the Perseids. We pride ourselves on knowing a few things like that, about the sky; we find the Dipper, the North Star, Cassiopeia's Chair, and talk about consulting a star chart, which we know we won't actually do. But this is the only place you can really *see* the stars, we tell each other. Cities are hopeless.

18   Suddenly, an odd light appears, going very fast. It spirals around like a newly dead firecracker, and then bursts, leaving a cloud of luminous dust, caught perhaps in the light from the sun, still up there somewhere. What could this be? Several days later, we hear that it was part of an extinct Soviet satellite, or that's what they say. That's what they would say, wouldn't they? It strikes us that we don't really know very much about the night sky at all any more. There's all kinds of junk up there: spy planes, old satellites, tin cans, man-made matter gone out of control. It also strikes us that we are totally dependent for knowledge of these things on a few people who don't tell us very much.

Once, we thought that if the balloon ever went up we'd head   19
for the bush and hide out up there, living—we naively supposed—
off the land. Now we know that if the two superpowers begin hurl-
ing things at each other through the sky, they're likely to do it
across the Arctic, with big bangs and fallout all over the north. The
wind blows everywhere. Survival gear and knowing which moss
you can eat is not going to be a large help. The north is no longer a
refuge.

Driving back towards Toronto from the Near North, a small reprise   20
runs through my head:

> Land of the septic tank,
> Home of the speedboat,
> Where still the four-wheel-drive
> Wanders at will,
> Blue lake and tacky shore,
> I will return once more:
> Vroom-diddy-vroom-vroom
> Vroom-diddy-vroom-vroom
> Vroo-OO-oo-oom

Somehow, just as the drive north inspires saga and tragedy, the
drive south inspires parody. And here it comes: the gift shops
shaped like teepees; the maple-syrup emporiums that get themselves up like olde-tyme sugaring-off huts; and, farther south, the
restaurants that pretend to offer wholesome farm fare, the stores
that pretend to be general stores, selling quilts, soap shaped like
hearts, high-priced fancy conserves done up in frilly cloth caps, the
way Grandma (whoever she might be) was fondly supposed to
have made them.

And then come the housing developments, acres of prime   21
farmland turning overnight into Quality All-Brick Family Homes;
and then come the Industrial Parks; and there, in full anti-bloom, is
the city itself, looming like a mirage or a chemical warfare zone on
the horizon. A brown-grey scuzz hovers above it, and we think, as
we always do when facing re-entry, we're going into *that*? We're
going to breathe *that*?

But we go forward, as we always do, into what is now to us the   22
unknown. And once inside, we breathe the air, not much bad happens to us, we hardly notice. It's as if we've never been anywhere
else. But that's what we think, too, when we're in the north.

Vocabulary

a. *paragraph 2:* Mercator
b. *paragraph 3:* retrospect
c. *paragraph 5:* cognate
d. *paragraph 9:* precept, Struwwelpeter-like
e. *paragraph 10:* hagiography
f. *paragraph 11:* pathetic fallacy, ecology, numinous
g. *paragraph 12:* quota
h. *paragraph 14:* in rut, implacable
i. *paragraph 15:* portaging
j. *paragraph 17:* Perseids, Cassiopeia's Chair
k. *paragraph 18:* luminous
l. *paragraph 20:* reprise, saga, parody, emporiums
m. *paragraph 21:* scuzz

Questions

1. Atwood's definition of *north* is a precising definition. How does she try to persuade us of the need for this definition?
2. Atwood begins paragraph 1 with a question. How far does this question take her in the definition of *north*? Why do you think she begins this way?
3. What are Atwood's various strategies for defining *north*?
4. In paragraphs 13 and 14, Atwood offers two versions of "horror stories of the north." To what purpose?

Writing Assignment

Select some value-laden term or concept, such as "democracy," "obscenity," "freedom," or "work," and write your own definition.

Process

Like classification and division, process analysis is an essential method in technical writing, as in essays and books that describe how to assemble or repair machinery.

A process is a series of connected actions, each developing from the preceding one and leading to a result of some kind: a product, an effect, even a decision. Mechanical processes are probably the kind we deal with the most, and the examples in this section feature these—the risky business of playing the commodities market, or the craft or plastering a wall. A mechanical process is one that we create. By contrast, a natural process, such as that outlined in the following description of an athlete, is one we may initiate but do not create:

> He seems all animal in action. The heartbeat goes up; when he sprints at top speed the heart is pumping five times as much blood as normal, and ninety per cent of it is for the muscles. (Jacob Bronowski, "The Athlete and the Gazelle")

Both mechanical and natural processes are repeatable. A particular historical process—the events that led to the Riel Rebellion or those that produce an economic depression—is not, though the general circumstances may repeat themselves at another time.

Although we are committed in describing a process to presenting the steps chronologically—in the order they occur—we may interrupt the account to discuss the implications or details of a particular stage. In describing a complex process, we need to distinguish the main stages and the steps and procedures each of these contain. Process and causal analysis, discussed in the next section, are closely related and are often combined.

DIAN COHEN

Among her many positions of public-trust and private-sector responsibility, Dian Cohen includes those of president of Couture Associates, financial editor of *CTV News,* and regular columnist for *Maclean's* magazine. She also heads an economic communications consulting firm (and can be reached on the Internet at 70571.3702@compuserve.com). The following essay on how to play the commodities market is from her book *Money,* and is typical of the clarity and directness that characterize all her financial writing and commentary.

Trading Commodities

DIAN COHEN

If you bet on a horse, that's gambling. If you bet you can make Three Spades, that's entertainment. If you bet cotton will go up three points, that's business. See the difference?

(Blackie Sherrode)

1   If gold is the bedrock of financial security, then commodities, with their promises of huge trading profits, are the will-o'-the-wisps dancing seductively above it. Yes, it is possible to lose money in gold, if you really work at it, and it is also possible to make a bundle in commodities trading. But over the long term, gold is literally safer than money in the bank, whereas in the commodities game, 85% of the players are losers, while only 15% are winners—about the same odds as horse-racing or gambling. This fact doesn't have to keep you out of commodities. But you have to remember that commodity trading is a technique—a tool—to help you reach your financial goals.

2   Commodities are basic goods produced by primary producers. They are the raw materials consumed by secondary producers such as manufacturers. The most common examples of commodities include precious metals, like gold, silver, and platinum; other metals such as copper and nickel, produced by mine owners; agricultural goods such as wheat, corn, oats, soybeans, pork bellies (from which bacon is made), produced by farmers; and materials such as lumber and plywood, produced by sawmills.

3   There are three principal players involved in commodities markets: the producer, the consumer, and the commodities investor, or speculator. The attraction of commodities trading is the tremendous leverage that is possible. You don't put very much money down— 5% to 10% of the purchase price is average. In addition, there is no interest charged on the balance as there is with stock margins. With this kind of leverage, a very small change in the price of the commodity has a great effect on your profit or loss.

4   If you purchased $10,000 worth of a stock from your broker, and put up the full $10,000, then a $1,000 move in the value of that stock would increase or decrease your investment by 10%. If you margined

the stock at 50%, and thus put up only $5,000, then the $1,000 gain or loss would be 20%. That's leverage. But if you put up only $500 for a $10,000 purchase, as with the commodities market, then a $1,000 move up would show a 200% gain, while a movement downward would lose you *double* your money. That's really leverage!

You don't actually buy the commodities, and though you have the right, you are not obligated to take delivery of them. You are trading *contracts* to buy or sell the commodities in the future. What you are assuming is that at some point in a specific period in the future, the price of the commodity will have changed. If you feel it will be higher then than it is now, you contract to buy; if you feel it will be lower, you contract to sell.

How do you contract to sell something you don't own? When you make the contract, you are not required to deliver until the future date specified. That gives you plenty of time to get the commodity. In practice, you will never have to, since your plan is to offset that contract before delivery is required. Offsetting is a procedure by which your contract to deliver a commodity is cancelled. You do this by selling what you have bought, or by buying what you have sold. When you are in a "long" position, that is, you own a contract to *buy* a commodity, you offset this by obtaining another contract to *sell* the same commodity. If you start out by buying someone else's contract to sell it, you are in a "short" position and must buy a contract, to offset your position.

There are a number of commodity futures exchanges which operate in a similar manner to stock exchanges. There is the Chicago Board of Trade, which deals chiefly in grains, plywood, broilers (chickens), and silver; the Comex in New York, dealing only in metals; the Chicago Mercantile, which handles eggs, pork bellies, cattle, and lumber; the London Terminal Market, dealing in cocoa and sugar; and the London Metal Exchange, for copper and silver. There are several others, including the Winnipeg Commodity Exchange, which handles, among other things, canola and gold. These exchanges regulate the contracted amounts so that they are the same for all traders. This eliminates opportunities for big-time speculators to edge out the little guys. It also makes offsetting possible. The exchanges record and report the price during each day of trading. Unlike stocks, commodity futures prices are allowed to move only so far each day. This is to prevent trading activity from causing massive price moves. Once the price of a commodity future has moved to its permissible daily limit, no trading can take place outside that limit. It can still take place within the limit, however, and the next day it can move to a new limit. This regulates the futures market, but if spot prices — that is, the price at which the commodity is being bought and sold in the present — are extremely volatile, you may not be able to buy or sell your futures contract until the limited price movements catch up to the spot prices.

8   Consumers and producers of commodities are also active traders. Chocolate manufacturers, for example, trade in cocoa bean futures as a hedge against changes in the world price of cocoa, though they seldom take delivery. Nor are they as much interested in making money on the trade as they are in maintaining a uniform price for cocoa beans for manufacturing purposes. Thus, if world prices go up, and they hold a futures contract at a lower price, they can sell that contract, take their profit, and apply it to their operations back at the plant.

9   Producers hedge as well. The cocoa bean producer might be unsure of what his beans will bring on the market a year from now, and he would like to be assured of a reasonable price. So, he sells a contract at a price that will provide him with a profit, and insures him against a drop in world prices. Then he watches the market carefully, and hedges where he can.

10   How do you compete against these insiders? They may know chocolate, but like you, they don't know which way the price is going. All any of you can do is make an informed guess. Say a manufacturer calculates that to make his profit six months from now he needs to be able to buy cocoa at that time for 30 cents a pound. He will buy a contract to take delivery at that price on a specific date.

11   But the effect of that transaction is to establish the two sides of an argument. The buyer says that in six months' time cocoa will be worth 30 cents a pound or higher. The seller says it will be worth 30 cents or lower. It will certainly be one or the other, and that's where the speculator enters the picture. He backs one or the other by placing what is, in effect, a side bet with another speculator.

12   Some people feel that since they do not produce anything, speculators must make their money on the misfortunes of those who do produce. Others feel that speculators are essential to trading, since they will often take risks that others won't. Suppose a farmer wants to sell his eggs for future delivery, and needs to make 40 cents a dozen to cover his costs and make a profit. He may find that none of the users around will pay him more than 35 cents. He would be losing money, and obviously wouldn't sell. Enter the speculator. He is betting that sooner or later a user will have to give in to the farmer's required price. He buys the eggs now at the 40-cent price, in the hope that when the users give in, the price will be 40 cents or higher. In that way, speculators serve a useful function in the marketplace.

13   Another theory says that speculators tend to drive prices up or down out of all proportion to reality. For example, in the above case, the speculators may drive the price up to 50 cents. The farmer will

see that the speculators are way off base, and rush in to sell, thereby getting more than he could otherwise expect. Other farmers will see what is happening and rush in too. This action will tend to drive prices down. Of course, the ideal theory holds that if all buyers and sellers are fully knowledgeable, the market will always find its proper level. But since people are never fully knowledgeable, especially about the future, the market sometimes does get out of whack with reality. Therein lies the challenge of commodity trading.

So, how does an amateur who knows little or nothing about a particular industry get involved in commodities trading? Very carefully. 14

In order to trade successfully in the commodities market, you must know when the price of a commodity is going to move up or down, and that's not easy. The best available knowledge about a commodity and its market is essential. Your broker might help. Watching what other traders are doing will give some indications as well. For example, if the further you look into the future, the progressively lower the price of the commodity gets, then the market, strangely enough, is tending to rise. Conversely, if the furthest futures price is progressively higher than the closest price, the market is tending to fall. These indicators are more clearly seen when a market is about to change from being a discounted (lower future price) to a premium (higher future price) market. 15

Qualifying as a bona fide trader depends on the amount of money you have, and the tolerance threshold of your broker. Most houses won't touch you unless you have a net worth of $50,000 or more. But you can find brokers who will make transactions for you, even if you don't have more than $2,000 to trade. The best rule of thumb to follow is *never* put up more than you can afford to lose. 16

The cost of the commodity you wish to trade depends on the commodity, and on the exchange's policy that is in effect at that time. A contract for 5,000 bushels of wheat, or 40,000 pounds of cattle, costs about $1,500. A contract for 25,000 pounds of copper costs $1,300. The amount of money you stand to make also depends on the contract. A two-cent-per-bushel move upward in wheat will make you $100—more than enough to cover the $65 commission. A one-cent-a-pound rise in copper amounts to $250, again more than enough to cover the $80 commission. 17

Like all highly leveraged transactions, commodity trading is risky for speculators. But that's also why there are generous rewards. Commodities should be avoided unless the rest of your investment portfolio is in good shape, and you are prepared to lose everything you put into commodities. It is purely and simply highly leveraged risk taking. 18

Vocabulary

a. *paragraph 1:* will-o'-the-wisps
b. *paragraph 4:* margined
c. *paragraph 16:* bona fide
d. *paragraph 18:* portfolio

Questions

1. How is Cohen's essay organized? Identify the various parts and explain their purpose.
2. Identify the topic sentences in paragraphs 3, 5, 7, 9, 11, and 13. How do the paragraphs develop the topic sentences?
3. What techniques does Cohen use to assist the non-specialist reader?
4. Would you feel confident investing in the commodities market on the basis of the information Cohen provides?

Writing Assignments

1. Discuss experiences of your own with a process that you have learned. Make the language as simple and lucid as Cohen's.
2. In view of what the epigraph from Sherrode suggests about the nature of the market, discuss some other ways in which the free-enterprise system encourages risk taking.

ALEXANDER PETRUNKEVITCH

Alexander Petrunkevitch (1875–1964) was born in Russia and emigrated to America in 1903. He taught at Yale University and published two seminal works on spiders. A highly cultured man who worked also in history and philosophy, he translated poetry both from and into Russian. In the following essay, he describes in meticulous detail a curious and deadly battle between a spider and a wasp.

The Spider and the Wasp

ALEXANDER PETRUNKEVITCH

1   In the feeding and safeguarding of their progeny, insects and spiders exhibit some interesting analogies to

reasoning and some crass examples of blind instinct. The case I propose to describe here is that of the tarantula spiders and their arch-enemy, the digger wasps of the genus Pepsis. It is a classic example of what looks like intelligence pitted against instinct—a strange situation in which the victim, though fully able to defend itself, submits unwittingly to its destruction.

Most tarantulas live in the tropics, but several species occur in   2
the temperate zone and a few are common in the southern U.S. Some varieties are large and have powerful fangs with which they can inflict a deep wound. These formidable-looking spiders do not, however, attack man; you can hold one in your hand, if you are gentle, without being bitten. Their bite is dangerous only to insects and small mammals such as mice; for man it is no worse than a hornet's sting.

Tarantulas customarily live in deep cylindrical burrows, from   3
which they emerge at dusk and into which they retire at dawn. Mature males wander about after dark in search of females and occasionally stray into houses. After mating, the male dies in a few weeks, but a female lives much longer and can mate several years in succession. In a Paris museum is a tropical specimen which is said to have been living in captivity for 25 years.

A fertilized female tarantula lays from 200 to 400 eggs at a time;   4
thus it is possible for a single tarantula to produce several thousand young. She takes no care of them beyond weaving a cocoon of silk to enclose the eggs. After they hatch, the young walk away, find convenient places in which to dig their burrows, and spend the rest of their lives in solitude. The eyesight of tarantulas is poor, being limited to a sensing of change in the intensity of light and to the perception of moving objects. They apparently have little or no sense of hearing, for a hungry tarantula will pay no attention to a loudly chirping cricket placed in its cage unless the insect happens to touch one of its legs.

But all spiders, and especially hairy ones, have an extremely deli-   5
cate sense of touch. Laboratory experiments prove that tarantulas can distinguish three types of touch: pressure against the body wall, stroking of the body hair, and riffling of certain very fine hairs on the legs called trichobothria. Pressure against the body, by the finger or the end of a pencil, causes the tarantula to move off slowly for a short distance. The touch excites no defensive response unless the approach is from above, where the spider can see the motion, in which case it rises on its hind legs, lifts its front legs, opens its fangs and holds this threatening posture as long as the object continues to move.

The entire body of a tarantula, especially its legs, is thickly   6
clothed with hair. Some of it is short and wooly, some long and stiff. Touching this body hair produces one of two distinct reactions.

When the spider is hungry, it responds with an immediate and swift attack. At the touch of a cricket's antennae the tarantula seizes the insect so swiftly that a motion picture taken at the rate of 64 frames per second shows only the result and not the process of capture. But when the spider is not hungry, the stimulation of its hairs merely causes it to shake the touched limb. An insect can walk under its hairy belly unharmed.

7   The trichobothria, very fine hairs growing from disclike membranes on the legs, are sensitive only to air movement. A light breeze makes them vibrate slowly, without disturbing the common hair. When one blows gently on the trichobothria, the tarantula reacts with a quick jerk of its four front legs. If the front and hind legs are stimulated at the same time, the spider makes a sudden jump. This reaction is quite independent of the state of its appetite.

8   These three tactile responses—to pressure on the body wall, to moving of the common hair, and to flexing of the trichobothria—are so different from one another that there is no possibility of confusing them. They serve the tarantula adequately for most of its needs and enable it to avoid most annoyances and dangers. But they fail the spider completely when it meets its deadly enemy, the digger wasp Pepsis.

9   These solitary wasps are beautiful and formidable creatures. Most species are either a deep shiny blue all over, or deep blue with rusty wings. The largest have a wing span of about four inches. They live on nectar. When excited, they give off a pungent odor—a warning that they are ready to attack. The sting is much worse than that of a bee or common wasp, and the pain and swelling last longer. In the adult stage the wasp lives only a few months. The female produces but a few eggs, one at a time at intervals of two or three days. For each egg the mother must provide one adult tarantula, alive but paralyzed. The mother wasp attaches the egg to the paralyzed spider's abdomen. Upon hatching from the egg, the larva is many hundreds of times smaller than its living but helpless victim. It eats no other food and drinks no water. By the time it has finished its single Gargantuan meal and become ready for wasphood, nothing remains of the tarantula but its indigestible chitinous skeleton.

10   The mother wasp goes tarantula-hunting when the egg in her ovary is almost ready to be laid. Flying low over the ground late on a sunny afternoon, the wasp looks for its victim or for the mouth of a tarantula burrow, a round hole edged by a bit of silk. The sex of the spider makes no difference, but the mother is highly discriminating as to species. Each species of Pepsis requires a certain species of tarantula, and the wasp will not attack the wrong species. In a cage with a tarantula which is not its normal prey, the wasp avoids the spider and is usually killed by it in the night.

Yet when a wasp finds the correct species, it is the other way   11
about. To identify the species the wasp apparently must explore the
spider with her antennae. The tarantula shows an amazing tolerance
to this exploration. The wasp crawls under it and walks over it without evoking any hostile response. The molestation is so great and so
persistent that the tarantula often rises on all eight legs, as if it were
on stilts. It may stand this way for several minutes. Meanwhile the
wasp, having satisfied itself that the victim is of the right species,
moves off a few inches to dig the spider's grave. Working vigorously
with legs and jaws, it excavates a hole 8 to 10 inches deep with a
diameter slightly larger than the spider's girth. Now and again the
wasp pops out of the hole to make sure that the spider is still there.

When the grave is finished, the wasp returns to the tarantula to   12
complete her ghastly enterprise. First she feels it all over once more
with her antennae. Then her behavior becomes more aggressive.
She bends her abdomen, protruding her sting, and searches for the
soft membrane at the point where the spider's legs join its body—
the only spot where she can penetrate the horny skeleton. From
time to time, as the exasperated spider slowly shifts ground, the
wasp turns on her back and slides along with the aid of her wings,
trying to get under the tarantula for a shot at the vital spot. During
all this maneuvering, which can last for several minutes, the tarantula makes no move to save itself. Finally the wasp corners it
against some obstruction and grasps one of its legs in her powerful
jaws. Now at last the harassed spider tries a desperate but vain
defense. The two contestants roll over and over on the ground. It is
a terrifying sight and the outcome is always the same. The wasp
finally manages to thrust her sting into the soft spot and holds it
there for a few seconds while she pumps in the poison. Almost
immediately the tarantula falls paralyzed on its back. Its legs stop
twitching, its heart stops beating. Yet it is not dead, as is shown by
the fact that if taken from the wasp it can be restored to some sensitivity by being kept in a moist chamber for several months.

After paralyzing the tarantula, the wasp cleans herself by drag-   13
ging her body along the ground and rubbing her feet, sucks the
drop of blood oozing from the wound in the spider's abdomen,
then grabs a leg of the flabby, helpless animal in her jaws and drags
it down to the bottom of the grave. She stays there for many minutes, sometimes for several hours, and what she does all that time
in the dark we do not know. Eventually she lays her egg and
attaches it to the side of the spider's abdomen with a sticky secretion. Then she emerges, fills the grave with soil carried bit by bit in
her jaws, and finally tramples the ground all around to hide any
trace of the grave from prowlers. Then she flies away, leaving her
descendant safely started in life.

14   In all this the behavior of the wasp evidently is qualitatively different from that of the spider. The wasp acts like an intelligent animal. This is not to say that instinct plays no part or that she reasons as man does. But her actions are to the point; they are not automatic and can be modified to fit the situation. We do not know for certain how she identifies the tarantula—probably it is by some olfactory or chemo-tactile sense—but she does it purposefully and does not blindly tackle a wrong species.

15   On the other hand, the tarantula's behavior shows only confusion. Evidently the wasp's pawing gives it no pleasure, for it tries to move away. That the wasp is not simulating sexual stimulation is certain because male and female tarantulas react in the same way to its advances. That the spider is not anesthetized by some odorless secretion is easily shown by blowing lightly at the tarantula and making it jump suddenly. What, then, makes the tarantula behave as stupidly as it does?

16   No clear, simple answer is available. Possibly the stimulation by the wasp's antennae is masked by a heavier pressure on the spider's body, so that it reacts as when prodded by a pencil. But the explanation may be much more complex. Initiative in attack is not in the nature of tarantulas; most species fight only when cornered so that escape is impossible. Their inherited patterns of behavior apparently prompt them to avoid problems rather than attack them. For example, spiders always weave their webs in three dimensions, and when a spider finds that there is insufficient space to attach certain threads in the third dimension, it leaves the place and seeks another, instead of finishing the web in a single plane. This urge to escape seems to arise under all circumstances, in all phases of life, and to take the place of reasoning. For a spider to change the pattern of its web is as impossible as for an inexperienced man to build a bridge across a chasm obstructing his way.

17   In a way the instinctive urge to escape is not only easier but often more efficient than reasoning. The tarantula does exactly what is most efficient in all cases except in an encounter with a ruthless and determined attacker dependent for the existence of her own species on killing as many tarantulas as she can lay eggs. Perhaps in this case the spider follows its usual pattern of trying to escape, instead of seizing and killing the wasp, because it is not aware of its danger. In any case, the survival of the tarantula species as a whole is protected by the fact that the spider is much more fertile than the wasp.

Vocabulary

a. *paragraph 1:* progeny
b. *paragraph 2:* temperate
c. *paragraph 5:* riffling
d. *paragraph 8:* tactile
e. *paragraph 9:* pungent, chitinous

Questions

1. What kind of audience is Petrunkevitch writing for in this essay? What evidence in the essay reveals the audience he envisions?
2. "The Spider and the Wasp" is primarily a minutely observed factual account, but its power as an essay depends on the author's fascination with his subject. What evidence of this personal involvement can you point to? Are Petrunkevitch's feelings ever explicitly stated? If so, where?
3. Analyze paragraph 12 for ways in which Petrunkevitch links sentences to make time relationships clear and form a coherent sequence. Mark the kinds of transitional devices that you discover in the paragraph.
4. Throughout the essay, identify examples of inductive reasoning.
5. What kinds of transitions does Petrunkevitch use to move from paragraph to paragraph? Explain the transition from paragraph 15 to paragraph 16.
6. What central idea gives unity to the essay? Show how the essay is unified.

Writing Assignments

1. Consider the ritual of the spider and the wasp, as Petrunkevitch reports it. Then, as a detached but fascinated observer, write a short process essay (under 1,000 words) describing in detail some human ritual. Here are a few suggestions:
   a. commuting
   b. going to the laundromat
   c. celebrating a birthday
   d. eating a lobster or an artichoke
   e. high-school graduation
   f. college registration
   g. calling for a date
   h. shopping at the supermarket
2. Closely observe some typical behaviour of your pet or some other animal, such as eating, begging, or stalking, and write a short process essay describing the behaviour in great detail.

JEFF TAYLOR

Jeff Taylor is a writer and master carpenter who lives in Oregon with his wife and daughter. The following essay first appeared in *Harrowsmith* magazine as the "Toolbox" piece, a how-to column to which Taylor frequently contributes. Taylor's process analysis shows that instructions on as seemingly mundane a subject as drywalling and plastering can sparkle with wit and insight.

The Master of Plaster

JEFF TAYLOR

1   **O**ur daughter, Serenity, is 10, the age when parents hope their young will discover the concept of gratitude (hope is cheap, fellow parents, but a thank you is always dear). We, her loving father and mother, have spent the past week remodelling her bedroom. We began by moving all her furniture into the living room. Then we ripped out the ancient carpet, old and funky with finger-paint blotches and a cat memo from a stray tom she had adopted. But the walls were the worst. A previous owner had mixed cornmeal into flat paint for a *faux* texturing job, creating a surface only slightly less abrasive than sandpaper.

2   Tonight, we are slowly burying this gritty surface under a better one. Memorize the following: *Do not ever become proficient in a skill you will dislike.* If you learn to do an ugly, unpleasant job, acquire a little hands-on experience and get good at it, you will do it often.

3   Somewhere over the course of my life, I learned to plaster. I can; therefore, I am. The sun went down hours ago. Our daughter is asleep, and even the television has signed off. Only Joy and I are awake, plastering our daughter's bedroom walls and ceiling at the ungodly hour of 3 in the morning.

4   All my energy for the work evaporated hours ago. "Is there any more coffee?" I ask my wife, who has white goo caked on her face, hair, clothing and hands. Joy could pass for a survivor of a bakery explosion. "You've already had three cups," she reminds me. The first cup was fortified with brandy, which seemed like a good idea at the time. Irish coffee contains the four essential food groups: sugar, caffeine, alcohol and fat. It liberates the creative impulse and numbs the intellect. However, now I would like something to slap me awake for a few more hours. Sleep beckons, and I must refuse.

5   True plastering, in the original sense, is almost a lost art, requiring a scratch coat (sometimes called a brown coat) of gypsum plaster over metal or wooden lath, a second coat over that, and a lime-based hard finish coat. It requires a practised hand. For one terrible

month many years ago, I chopped the nailed lath and mixed up plaster for a gentle elderly man who remembered how to create a wall the old-fashioned way. He had the patience of a saint, and in that month, I learned the basics of an obsolete craft. The work was viciously hard. Later, I took a job as a drywaller for a reformed murderer named Burt, who bore scars and tattoos as thick as the graffiti on a New York subway. He had the patience of an itchy rhino, but we got along. Hanging and plastering drywall was soulless work; it was also a lot easier than the old method.

Mercifully, drywall construction has replaced lath-and-plaster, but we can still use the word *plastering* to mean applying a perfectly uniform and pond-smooth finish to the walls and ceiling of a drywalled room. If you don't know how, give thanks to the universe. 6

Putting up sheets of drywall is the easy part. You hang the boards, cutting out little squares for switches and outlets or little circles for the overhead lights. The result is fairly pleasing to the eye, but it is not seamless yet. Now you must tape the joints and fill all the nail dimples. Then you must sand out all the burrs and rough edges. Apply another coat of joint compound, and sand again. Go over every joint and dimple a third time, and, by Saint Jude, sand everything once more. 7

One asks—Why? What madness causes humans to sand an entire room three times, to snort fine white dust six inches up both nasal passages? I will tell you why: If little granules of dried compound remain on the walls between coats, they will break loose under the trowel and plough grooves in the next coat of plaster. 8

Like every other building enterprise, plastering requires the proper tools. The tool in my left hand is a plasterer's hawk, used to hold the drywall compound, which by now weighs seven subjective tons. In my right hand is a drywall knife, or trowel. I usually call it a trowel, although it was called a plastering knife in hardware stores for many years. Some people still call it a knife, but anyone can tell that it is not really a knife at all. I own several hunting knives and pocketknives and have become quite proficient at recognizing a knife on sight. True, the drywall knife has a blade, but so do an axe, a chisel and a framing square, three more tools that plainly are not knives. So let us call it a trowel instead. 9

The trowel requires a bit of breaking in. Using a grinder, remove the sharp corners, rounding them off a little, no more than an eighth of an inch. Then bend the blade ever so slightly so that one face of the blade is convex and the other is concave. Since the convex side usually goes against the wall when I plaster, the tips don't leave ridges. For taped joints, I flip it over, using the concave side to apply joint compound. The compound shrinks as it dries; leaving a minor, nearly invisible bulge at the joint helps produce a flat surface. 10

11   Plastering is the least fun of human endeavours, at least in the beginning, middle and just before the end. The most massive wave of fatigue will come at the halfway mark in time, which is also the seven-eighths mark of energy reserves. You can't quit now or even think about a long break from the work. If you do, you'll abandon the project for a day and probably another one. This can stretch out into years of procrastination.

12   The prospect of having to texture the wall can cause those years to multiply. A friend of mine once rented a machine and proceeded to discover that he knew nothing about blown-on texture. In desperation, he found a comb and began brushing the plaster into patterns resembling a bad mistake. But he kept working, trying for that random uniformity that marks a hired professional's work, and by the time he was done, it looked merely unacceptable.

13   There is an easier way to plaster and texture, and the result looks quite professional. It seems to work best on old walls with bad texturing jobs. But be advised: It is experimental, a method I have been using for only 10 years without any failures.

14   Glop 2 gallons of premixed joint compound into a large bucket. Dump in 10 cups of silica sand. (Warning: Wear a mask, and take care not to breathe the dust.) Add 2 cups of water and 1 cup of acrylic bonding adhesive. Using a large cage-type or bladed paddle on the end of a large drill, mix everything for about one minute for an even consistency. I use a monster $^1/_2$-inch drill, because it has enough torque to turn the paddle without burning out, as did every $^3/_8$-inch drill I have ever used.

15   Now, if you wish, you can plaster this directly over the first (dry) coat of joint compound, which you will have already primed. Using a wide, broken-in drywall trowel, float it all very smooth (practise on a closet wall). Let it dry, but do not sand afterward, or ever; just scrape off any ridges, and then prime and paint. The result feels like a plaster wall but without the expense or deep unpleasantness of lath construction.

16   Please understand, for perfect results, you should probably apply this over a special drywall board with a porous paper facing that adheres to plaster without separating from the gypsum core. Some drywall manufacturers offer complete veneer-plaster systems that hybridize drywall boards and plaster, and for new construction, that's the way to go. But my method *seems* to work well over old surfaces, and new ones if they are primed first. Time

17   will tell.

       A bright light appears in the east window. Dawn: time for a bath. And then bed, delicious bed. We'll be finished with Serenity's room this week. She'll probably thank us, once or twice. That's all right. The real gratitude will come when Serenity has children of her own.

Vocabulary

a. *paragraph 1:* abrasive
b. *paragraph 5:* gypsum, lath
c. *paragraph 8:* granules
d. *paragraph 10:* convex, concave
e. *paragraph 14:* silica, acrylic, torque
f. *paragraph 16:* porous, hybridize

Questions

1. How does Taylor lead into the statement of his main purpose? What other purposes does he have in mind?
2. Why does he refer to his daughter at the beginning and the end of the essay?
3. Could you put up drywall using Taylor's directions? Which paragraphs are detailed enough to enable you to do so?

Writing Assignments

1. At one point Taylor wryly observes, "Do not ever become proficient in a skill you will dislike." Write a process analysis describing such a skill.
2. Each of the following processes contains several main stages; one or more of these stages contain steps or procedures. Give an analysis of one of the processes, or do so for a comparable process you know well. Distinguish the main from the subordinate stages and procedures carefully.
   a. replacing or repairing a flat tire
   b. cutting down a dead tree
   c. painting the outside of a house
   d. parking on a hill
   e. refinishing a piece of furniture
   f. doing a lab procedure
   g. preparing a meal

Cause and Effect

In many essays and books, causal analysis, as in explanations of the nature and effects of nuclear energy, is the chief method used. Causal analysis may take various forms (examination of immediate and mediate or remote causes, or formal and material causes, for example). However, writers do not always give the technical names of causes. It is nevertheless important to distinguish several kinds of analysis when the essay uses more than one.

Whereas there is only one kind of process analysis, there are several kinds of causal analysis. The kind of explanation that satisfies the ordinary person—the reason for a cold, for example—will usually not satisfy a scientist. (Later in this book we shall consider this more demanding kind of causal explanation as it is used in argument.) Usually we look for an event prior to the one we are trying to explain; but often there are many—some close to the event, some remote in time. For example, failure to study for an important exam may lead to a student's eventual failure in a course, and a subsequent drop in grade point average. The course failure—the immediate cause of the drop in the average—will probably be of most concern to university officials considering a scholarship renewal; the remote cause, the failure to study, probably will be of more concern to the student in seeking to improve. In writing about such events, our selection of one of them to discuss as the "cause" depends on the purpose of our analysis.

Objects, too, have more than one cause. One useful kind of analysis here distinguishes four related ones. Consider a dictionary. Its material cause is the paper, ink, and other materials used in its manufacture. Its formal cause is its shape—the alphabetic arrangement of words, and the arrangement of definitions according to a plan. Its efficient cause is the dictionary writer, and its final cause is the use intended for the dictionary. The analysis of a chemical compound is more rigorous, demanding an account of substances that form the compound and the process by which the formation occurs. We often combine process analysis ("how") with causal analysis ("why") because we are interested in both the how and the why of objects and of events.

PICO IYER

Pico Iyer is a widely published writer and a shrewd commentator on contemporary mores. He is the author of a novel, *Cuba and the Night*, and his

most recent non-fiction work is *Falling Off the Map*. The following is a
speech he gave in 1994 at the Institute of World Culture, in Santa Barbara,
California. In it, he warns of the dangers occasioned by recent technological breakthroughs and by the unexamined assumptions about the world as
one large family that have accompanied them.

Strangers in a Small World

PICO IYER

The global village is one of those ideas to
which almost everyone can give assent: it rhymes with all the
notions with which we buoy and congratulate ourselves—the family of man, the brotherhood of souls, the replacement of walls with
bridges. The global village tells us, in powerful, palpable ways, that
we're all one race under the skin and that, beneath all the superficial differences of custom and fashion and tongue, the fears and
fantasies of that villager in, say, Mali are not so different from our
own: he, too, after all, is moved by Michael Jackson rhythms and
transfixed by *Dallas* archetypes. Small wonder companies try to
concoct slogans like United Colors of Benetton: one touch of nur-
ture makes the whole world kin.

We accept, of course, that with proximity come problems, and
problems for which the old world order scarcely prepared us; that,
in the absence of external divisions, we are obliged to create and
consolidate our own new and artificial ones; that more and more
countries, in this time of mass migration, may seem as fractional-
ized as Lebanon; and that now, when any country sneezes (to
extend the age-old axiom), the whole world catches a cold. Yet, at
bottom, we are still ready to applaud the virtues of this new multiculturalism and its resuscitation of all our *e pluribus unum* hopes.
We know that we are enriched and educated by having Thai children in the classroom and Salvadoran refugees down the street;
that choices—the great luxury of a diverse consumer society—can
now multiply. We know too that the globe is our oyster in ways that
before only the rich could enjoy; we can fly around the world, and
the world can fly around us.

Yet it is precisely the blessings of this order—evident and indis-
putable as they are—that can blind us to its dangers, and they are
dangers for which we are as unguarded as children in first love: we

have no precedents to stay us or to guide us. When a stranger comes knocking on our door, we have no sense of his needs and expectations. If he is a smiling and exotic stranger, we may be doubly disarmed. And the very charms that his foreignness confers may lead us into places where we are soon quite lost.

4   The dangers of the global village begin, not surprisingly, with the problems of mobility: to put it simply, our vices are now global. Italians go to Prague and Havana to get cheap dates, and Germans can hop on a plane to Sri Lanka to find underage sex partners. Nigerians regularly get caught in Bangkok Airport with balloons of heroin in their stomachs, and the "economic miracle" in Japan is often, in small ways, subverted by the tens of thousands of immigrants from Iran and Israel who set up their own stalls and deals on the streets of Tokyo. Prostitution, to take one specific example, now takes unprecedented forms: Ghanaian girls in Antwerp, Russians throughout the Middle East, Dominicans in Spain. The menace of these freely moving bodies has gained an almost concrete meaning in the age of AIDS; now we have an all too literal metaphor for the danger of getting too close to a stranger, as the deadly virus is passed, like a kiss almost, from Africa to Haiti to Manhattan's West Village.

5   Even capital is not immune to the novel challenges of the "borderless economy": the BCCI scandal was, in part, a reflection of what can happen when a charming stranger arrives at the door and we do not know what to make of him. The Bank of America, remember, acquired a 25 percent share of BCCI in 1972, and the Bank of England gave BCCI a license. Both, in their way, were simply unprepared to deal with an entity whose codes they could not read.

6   Technology has, to be sure, eliminated some of our old divisions and corruptions; but it has also given us new ways of refining and compounding them. Even as many countries are now proudly marching down the Information Highway, many others (think of North Korea, Iraq, Myanmar) are better able than ever to bind their people to the Disinformation Highway. And while Salman Rushdie, the apostle of a new internationalism, sings the possibilities of a fresh, cross-pollinating world, he is stalked by an old ancestral order that embodies an almost medieval sense of self-enclosedness—and that prosecutes its *fatwa* in Tokyo and Istanbul and Bradford, England. We may say that the age-old pattern of migration from countryside to city is now global—that the bright student from rural India can now set his sights not on Bombay but on Cambridge, Massachusetts. But we must also add that the divisions that haunt many a big city are now global, so that much of the world resembles one big city, with South-Central on one side and Bel-Air on the other.

Deeper than the problems of sudden connectedness, however, are   7
the fundamental disconnections that the new globalism obscures.
As Edward Said has pointed out, the exile's predicament is made
more agonized these days by the fact that he can see what he has
left behind. He is surrounded by reminders of his home and rein-
forcements of his seeming closeness to it. The Cambodian in California can see Phnom Penh on his TV, and see the streets where he
courted his wife, and watch his old neighbors setting up their shops
again, and the ones who murdered his father saying "cheese"
before the cameras; he can even—and this is the ultimate tease—get
on a plane and be back there tomorrow. But if he makes the trip, he
will likely find that Phnom Penh is no closer to Long Beach than it
ever was, and that he is as much a foreigner there as in the new
home he has gained.

That is one of the greatest shadows of the illusory smallness   8
our new world offers. We are often told—and it *is* heartening—
that on the West Bank, Palestinians and Israelis both watch *L.A.
Law* on Sunday nights, on screens that have subtitles in both
Arabic and Hebrew. We read that the Khmer Rouge are tuning in
to *Santa Barbara*, and we feel that this establishes their humanity,
or at least a common link between us. But what they are learning
about us from *Santa Barbara* is doubtless as limited as what we
learn about them from the (already Western-filtered) movie *The
Killing Fields*. And when a Cambodian comes to America eager to
deal with Robin Wright, he will be as lost as one of us who goes
to Phnom Penh with images of Dith Pran in our heads. Vietnam
was famously the "living-room war." But now every war is in
our living room, and in half the living rooms of the world. Rod-
ney King is being beaten up in Johannesburg, and Bosnia is in
Miami every night. But the knowledge we get from this is no
deeper than the image, and the fact that we believe we have seen
the "real Cambodia" on our screens may well put us behind our
grandfathers, who could scarcely countenance such illusions.

Thus a man in Louisiana says "Freeze!" and a Japanese boy,   9
looking for a Halloween party, doesn't get it—and a life is lost, and
trust undermined. The problem is not one of complete misunder-
standing but rather—and more dangerously—of a partial understanding, or the illusion of understanding. People may play contract bridge across several countries on the Internet, but they cannot
communicate bluffs or poker faces on their computer screens; faxes
transmit words instantaneously, but they are not so good with
nuances or pauses.

Homogeneity, in fact, is not the fear: every culture sings   10
Madonna with a different accent. It is disguised heterogeneity

that is the threat, a world of differences that is veiled by surface similarities. And a world of differences made more difficult when everyone's living down the block. It is not just that the Afghan down the street has different customs from ours; even when he watches *Rambo III*, he is getting something very different from the screen than we are — is seeing it as a political piece and not an entertainment. For him McDonald's may be a status symbol, as surely as that quaint Central Asian restaurant is for us. And the very diversity of costumes and colors that seems so beguiling in the Opening Ceremonies of the Olympic Games becomes more charged when it's to be found in the divisions and rivalries within Timmy's classroom.

11   None of this, of course, is an argument for hardening our differences, or for living alone, or for denying the richness and opportunities that polyculturalism makes available. A little knowledge may be a dangerous thing, but ignorance is ten times worse, and suspicion can fulfill its prophecies as easily as trust. But the mingling of cultures that is our new inheritance makes imaginative and moral demands on us much harder than just the business of trying to "get along" or to "see the world through others' eyes," and forces us to carry our assumptions more lightly than we have ever done before.

12   In Michael Ondaatje's beautiful novel *The English Patient*, he presents a lyrical, often radiant vision of a world beyond nationalities, in which people are simply individuals, of indistinguishable origins, with a hundred different cultures singing inside them. That is a lovely and a liberating notion, and it is one echoed by those executives who tell us that soon there will be "no Japan, only Japanese." But it underestimates, perhaps, a need, a basic human need, for affiliation with something larger and a sense of belonging to a higher order. For Ondaatje, the desert is the model of a place where all distinctions are dissolved and people live as people; but as the fourteenth-century Arab writer Ibn Khaldun wrote, "Only tribes held together by group feeling can live in a desert."

13   If there is a real virtue to all the blessings of the global village, it inheres mostly in our recognition of how much our sense of obligation must be expanded and diversified, and how much our family responsibilities, if you will, must be extended more than they have ever been before. Insofar as we aspire to be our brothers' keepers, we have to acknowledge that we have five — soon eight — billion brothers, and that they are in Borneo and Bolivia and Benin. Insofar as we try to love our neighbors as ourselves, we have to admit that our neighbors are people with whom we share no common language, or past, or value. And the

smaller the distance between people, Freud reminded us, the greater, often, the dispute.

Vocabulary

a. *paragraph 2: e pluribus unum*
b. *paragraph 6: fatwa*
c. *paragraph 10:* homogeneity, heterogeneity

Questions

1. What relation does Iyer propose between progress in international relations and technological advancements? Has he provided enough evidence to establish this point?
2. Where does he show that the same cause can have both a positive and a negative effect?
3. Do you agree with Iyer's response to the problem he outlines in his essay? On what evidence do you base your agreement or disagreement —facts, expert testimony, or assumptions that you regard as self-evident?
4. Can the effects that Iyer ascribes to technological advances be attributed to other causes?

Writing Assignments

1. Write an essay on one of the following topics, using causal analysis and examples to develop a thesis. The more limited your focus and discussion, the stronger your thesis will be:
   a. cheating on examinations
   b. driving habits of teenagers
   c. family arguments or rivalries
   d. choosing a university or college
2. Present a dilemma that you believe should concern North Americans today. Introduce facts or expert testimony to show that the dilemma is a real one, anticipate a refutation of your problem and answer it, and state your own views on what can or should be done.

DAVID WARREN

David Warren was the founder and editor of *The Idler*, a Canadian magazine of some distinction, sadly now defunct. Using the name Otiosus, he wrote a regular column in the magazine. The following is an excerpt from a longer essay in which the writer reflects on the ways in which the technology involved in keeping accurate time reveals the whole mindset of Western civilization in matters religious and philosophical.

Time's Priggish Foreman

DAVID WARREN

1   One of the interesting questions in the history of technology is why the clock was developed to its potential in the West. According to Joseph Needham, the magnificent encyclopaedist of *Science and Civilization in China* (Cambridge Univ., 1954 &c.), the Sung emperors built at least three elaborate astronomical water-clocks. The last of these was designed by Su Sung, diplomat, administrator, and man of science. It was installed in the imperial capital of K'aifeng about the year 1094. Housed in a tower forty feet high, it ran from a clepsydra, or water-wheel with pivoted buckets. Remittent power from this wheel was transmitted through vertical shafts, turning wheels bearing jacks that popped into windows at the hours and quarters. Placards sprang up at the night watches. At the top, the positions of the "three luminaries" — the sun, the moon, the bowl of stars—were indicated upon an armillary sphere (inclined metal bracelets moving around an anchored celestial globe). The machine tracked the Chinese lunar calendar, while assisting in astrological divination for a court at which even the Emperor's copulations were made to follow the heavenly round.

2   The tower clock of K'aifeng, while cumbersome, was in advance of any timepiece in the contemporary West. For decades it inspired delighted wonder. But when, eventually, it began to seize with rust and swelling, few efforts were made to repair or replace it. The Mongols came, and took away the pieces.

3   According to Dr. Needham, garbled reports of this clock could have inspired European craftsmen to improve their primitive timekeeping devices, but this view has been demolished, most recently in David Landes's learned and happy volume, *Revolution in Time* (Harvard Univ., 1983). Landes surveys the modern history of timekeeping, asking and partially answering the question, "Why us?" Why did European people make the first purely mechanical, and therefore potentially portable, clocks? Why did we grasp the possibilities of clocks when the Chinese competition was sleeping? And, why did we persist through centuries while every other culture looked upon clocks as toys?

4   It is a commonplace that we live in a technological society that sprang from an industrial revolution in England during the European

Enlightenment. By waves it has spread, like that ancient flood in the Sumerian tablets, engulfing all previous human life, and leaving the Old World far beneath us, like Atlantis on its ocean bed. It is a breach in history so great, one might nearly say that all pre-industrial cultures have more in common with each other than with any post-industrial culture, and vice versa.

The clock is a pregnant symbol of this venture, in which man   5 aspires to liberate himself by the conquest of nature, including human nature. By the minding of clocks, European ideas, habits, and assumptions have penetrated to the last tributary of the Amazon, the last prehistoric hamlet in Mindanao.

Professor Landes points to the role that time played in Christ-   6 ian imagery and life. He mentions the monastic tradition, e.g., the Cistercians, who identified work with prayer and thus took punctuality very seriously. In fact we may dig several strata deeper. From the first century Christians had taken the prayers seriously, and had formed the habit of being punctual about *them*. They inherited the Jewish daily cycle of three prayers (after sunrise, before sunset, after dark), adding and elaborating in conscious competition.

By the sixth century the Christians recognized at least eight   7 times of prayer each day, marked upon Roman hours, which they also inherited. The Romans, following the Greeks, divided days and nights into twelve hours each, the day hours running from sunrise to sunset, and thus varying in length with the seasons though remaining constant on the Roman sundial once it was adjusted for latitude. The sun would be directly overhead at noon—the Roman *sext*, or sixth hour—whereas at noon by our clocks the sun is usually not perpendicular. That is because we have reverted to the Egyptian scheme wherein, regardless of season, the day is divided into twenty-four hours of equal duration, counting from an arbitrary midnight.

Working upon the Roman dial, the Christians appointed specific   8 prayers for Lauds, towards sunrise; Prime, at break of day; Terce, mid-morning; Sext, at noon; None, mid-afternoon; Vespers, at sunset; Compline, in the evening; and the various nocturnes or night watches that might be consolidated and anticipated in Matins.

Now, each of these hours came to be associated with an event   9 in the life of Christ, as recorded in the New Testament. He was resurrected towards sunrise, therefore Lauds became the Church's resurrection prayer; He sent down the Holy Ghost on the apostles at the third hour, Terce; He was nailed to the cross at the sixth hour, Sext; He tasted death at the ninth hour, None; He was taken down from the cross at sunset, Vespers; and He said that He would come again in judgement on a day when we look not for Him and at an hour when we are not aware, hence the night watches.

10   The daily prayers of the Jews, and of other ancient peoples, were not set for precise hours, but for the convenience of the community at approximate times of day. But the Christians, working with numbered hours, paired to an exact temporal symbolism, and with a monastic movement as a constant goad, became mechanistic. Through the latter centuries of the first millennium, the monks devised ingenious water-driven alarm clocks to wake them for their prayer shifts in the night. By day their intricate work shifts were choreographed by hundreds of little bells, with big ones to gong the Hours of Prayer.

11   The theatre of bells extended through the growing towns even before the introduction of mechanical clocks. Bells opened and closed the markets, called council meetings, proclaimed curfew, directed the sweepers from street to street.

12   Somewhere, before the twelfth century, someone struck upon the two-ball balance and the verge escapement with its crown wheel, the basic mechanism of the medieval clock. We cannot know how long it remained a curiosity. Suddenly, towards the end of the twelfth century, Western literature is tingling with references to clock towers.

13   The operation of such clocks was perturbed by friction and excess oil. There was a wide margin of error. Two centuries passed until improvements in metallurgy and craftsmanship brought the minute hand, which went round in four-minute staggers. Those officials entrusted with public clocks kept an eye on the heavens and made adjustments, often moving the hands by more than an hour after noticing where the sun was. If anyone had to time something accurately, he used a sand-glass, or a water-jar (unplugging it for the duration of the event, then weighing the spillage).

14   Still, mechanization proceeded. Time, which had always been both linear and cyclical, became more linear. The first halting steps were taken towards modern techniques of time management: towards hourly wages, flow charts, deadlines, the billing of time in professional invoices, the emphasis on fixed accounting periods, standard provision for vacations and sick leave, the proliferation of arguably time-saving devices, the deconsecration of holy days, elimination of movable feasts, internationalization of public holidays, homogenization of leisure time.

15   The mainspring was introduced early in the fifteenth century, and was made sufficiently reliable by the end of it to allow miniaturization. Gentlemen began to carry pocket watches.

16   Major improvements came in the seventeenth century, thanks to the astronomers. The more closely they studied the sky through polished lenses, the more they felt the need for seconds and fractions of

seconds as a co-ordinate of location for celestial bodies. First they nattered to the clockmakers to make the clocks run on time. Then they took the clocks apart, counting the teeth on the turning wheels. Soon there were hands to show the seconds. Galileo discovered the isochronism of the pendulum, and drew plans for a pendulum clock. By the end of the century, well-made clocks were true within ten seconds a day.

There is no end to this kind of fussiness. We had the quartz revolution. By now physicists assign times to subatomic events, and think in picoseconds (seconds divided into a million million parts). The earth is not good enough for them: it does not rotate at an absolutely constant speed. The General Conference on Weights and Measures has defined the second as "9,192,631,770 periods of the radiation corresponding to the transition between the two hyperfine levels of the ground state of the cesium-133 atom." Now, this is cutting it close. [17]

It would be wrong to say that the idea of eternity has been discredited, or that any of the religious traditions which until recently governed our habitual lives has been proved unworthy. That these have been abandoned, especially in the West, goes without saying. While I am a believing Christian (raised as a liberal agnostic and converted from atheism), I speak for members of all the surviving religious traditions—Western and Eastern Christendom; Orthodox and Reform Jewry; Sunni and Shia Islam; Hindu, Sikh, and Jain; Theravada and Mahayana Buddhism; Baha'i; Animist—when I express our surprise at the thoroughgoing secularization of the world. [18]

True, some of the more primitive and isolated cults *have* proved unequal to stress, and some collapsed after one glance at the modern world. But this does not apply to the great religions, which, having been around a long time, had often adapted to new economic and social conditions. There is no convincing argument that our century can raise against religion, that could not have been raised in other centuries. The arguments I hear against Christianity, for instance, are old hat; the Church first dealt with them nearly two thousand years ago. Questions like "What was God doing before He created the universe?" are still asked by grown children who think they have found the fallacy that will bring Christendom to its knees. On its knees it may be, but not because of *that*. [19]

So far as it is intellectual, and little of it is, the modern opposition to religion is glib. Yet the world has always been full of glib assertions that will not survive a moment's test. The many who reject customary religious belief also avoid religious instruction, and would be embarrassed if they had to explain what they reject. [20]

They are wiser to stay on the attack: to say that modern man is just too sophisticated, well educated, and well informed, to fall for the ancestral bunkum.

21   In case any reader has such a view, let me quickly demolish it for him. Polls have repeatedly shown that a large majority of the inhabitants of both Western Europe and North America believe in one or more of the following: ghosts, astrology, clairvoyance, mind-reading, flying saucers, witches, action-at-a-distance, miracle cures. The same polls show that credulity in each of these categories is significantly lower among people with fixed religious beliefs, and higher among those without them.

22   Please note that I do not resent genuine atheism. In the middle of every religious system are assertions that you can take or leave, and one may rationally do either. The genuine atheist must come to terms with the same heavy questions as the genuine believer. He must make similarly tough decisions about how to live, in light of what he believes to be true. I consider genuine atheism to be a valid creed, and if it were better organized I should add it to my list of great religions. My annoyance is not with atheism but with the lazy, cowardly, self-serving agnosticism that is the creed of the ignorant masses today, and of their intellectual mentors and panderers.

23   If I am candid, I will not pretend that the masses were much better informed when religion had its power. The mass of humanity has always been ignorant, so far as we have historical evidence. But you cannot accuse church or temple of causing this ignorance. It is the background condition of the state of nature. It hardly needs encouragement. It would be fond to suggest that technology and mass education have made a difference, either. We have advanced on some fronts, retreated on others.

24 An essential purpose of a religion, for a society, is to provide a cred-ible source of authority for the common man, who does not do his own thinking, much though we might wish that he did. It is to pro-vide reasonably serviceable answers, based on centuries of accumu-lated experience, to the questions of everyday life—to tell not only the faithful but the community at large which way is up, and which way down; what is right, and wrong; what is beautiful, and ugly; what takes courage, and what does not; what is true, and what isn't. More often than not church and temple have been a source of light, have been patrons of music, learning, literature, art, architec-ture, philosophy, science.

25   This is a function that is so inevitable in human society that someone will be filling it, even if church and temple are banned. We will have either a religion, or some absurd parody of one. Even our own post-Christian society has its self-appointed moral and spiritual

guides. In North America, for example, we have a kind of secular clerisy of the politically correct, who instruct the common people in how to behave through electronic and other media of information. And they get very stroppy if you challenge *their* dogmas.

It should go without saying, but I had better say anyway that I am not an agent of the Inquisition. Inasmuch as we can distinguish Church and State in any high culture, it is crucial that the Church have only a moral and spiritual authority, to supply what the State can never have; and the State a legal and material authority, to supply what the Church must never get. [26]

We live in a time when there is a State, but no Church, only a variety of churches and temples and video worldviews competing within a deregulated free market. It is a little like the world Augustine described in his *Confessions* and *City of God*. If you wanted, you could lead a life today much like the one he did in early manhood, flitting between the modern equivalents to Manichaeanism, neo-Platonism, Academicism, Gnosticism, Catholic Christianity, and whatever else was offered in the market-stalls of Carthage, Rome, Milan. [27]

Religion, from *religio*, meaning "conscientiousness, scrupulousness, exactness"; formed, possibly, around the ancient root *lig*, to bind; hence *lictor*, an attendant; *lex*, a law; and *ligare*, to surround, fasten, harness. *Religens*, careful, as opposed to *negligens*. [28]

Religion does not perform its civilizing function by winning debates, or proclaiming dogmas, or even by spreading good news. These are important deeds, but the daily mission is accomplished through a liturgy and calendar. This is what first captures the imagination of little children, and holds the allegiance of old women and men. The rest is for the intellectuals. [29]

And even among intellectuals, not much that is very deep in us comes by conscious argument, or through the rational will, but rather through the formation of habit. In moments of megalomania we may think that we have created ourselves, and formed our own opinions. But we are really quite derivative. People do not become good or honest because they decide to be so, although sometimes they make a conscious choice, in an heroic moment. For the other moments, they have formed habits, or have had habits formed for them, from many invisible and unremembered sources. [30]

This is not a Christian sermon. Every human culture before the invention of the second hand had religious customs. I lived in a Muslim city during the most impressionable years of my boyhood. I became accustomed to the *muezzin* chanting the hours of prayer, five times a day from the minaret (first cry at daybreak—the Christian Lauds). Whether Muslim or Infidel, everyone was a party to the passing spectacle of feasts and fasts, leading to Ramadan, the holy month—and its last [31] and most holy night, the Night of Destiny, when a bridge is extended from heaven to earth, and the angels of the Spirit descend upon it.

32   The ambiguous season of Advent, before the twelve merry days of Christmas; the midwinter Epiphany; Candlemas; Septuagesima; Ash Wednesday, and the poverty of Lent; Maundy Thursday, Good Friday, the vigil, the Dawn; the Paschaltide of rejoicing; the rogation days and Ascensiontide leading to the Pentecost; the long season of Trinity; Saint Michael and all Angels; the spooky succession of All Saints and All Souls; the great wheel turning with saints' days and commemorations from the Life of Our Lord; the weekly repetition of the days of creation; the daily recitation of the hours of prayer—this is more than ticking clockwork. It is eternity speaking, in the dialect of time.

Vocabulary

   a. *paragraph 1:* remittent, divination, copulations
   b. *paragraph 6:* monastic, strata
   c. *paragraph 10:* mechanistic, millennium, choreographed
   d. *paragraph 12:* verge escapement
   e. *paragraph 13:* metallurgy
   f. *paragraph 14:* deconsecration, homogenization
   g. *paragraph 16:* nattered, isochronism
   h. *paragraph 17:* subatomic
   i. *paragraph 18:* agnostic, atheism, secularization
   j. *paragraph 20:* bunkum
   k. *paragraph 21:* clairvoyance, credulity
   l. *paragraph 22:* mentors, panderers
   m. *paragraph 23:* fond
   n. *paragraph 25:* parody, clerisy, stroppy
   o. *paragraph 26:* Inquisition
   p. *paragraph 28:* scrupulousness
   q. *paragraph 29:* dogmas, liturgy
   r. *paragraph 30:* megalomania
   s. *paragraph 31:* minaret
   t. *paragraph 32:* rogation

Questions

   1. Warren begins his essay with the assertion that clocks, having been invented in China, were developed to their full potential in the West. How does he account for this development?
   2. Warren's argument is structured by a principle of seemingly casual association. Plot the essay's development by tracing its various stages.
   3. Why does Warren introduce so many religious and philosophical considerations?

4. The essay concludes with a reference to "eternity speaking, in the dialect of time." Does this phrase provide an appropriate conclusion for the essay?

Writing Assignments

1. Present your own examples of ways in which time has influenced your beliefs.
2. Write a cause-and-effect essay like Warren's on one of the following:
   a. weaponry
   b. travel
   c. bathrooms
   d. clothing
   e. education
   f. entertainment

ANNE HOLLANDER

Anne Hollander was born in Cleveland, Ohio, and educated at Barnard College in New York City. An art historian interested in the influence of the human form on aesthetic theories, she contributes regularly to such publications as *The Times Literary Supplement, The New York Times Magazine, The New Republic,* and *Commentary.* The following essay on the relationship between ideas of female beauty and clothing fashions exemplifies the kind of criticism that Hollander describes in the preface to her book *Seeing Through Clothes,* where she asserts that "clothes must be seen and studied as paintings are seen and studied—as connected links in a creative tradition of image-making."

Fashion and the Female Body

ANNE HOLLANDER

The strong appeal of female slimness in the twentieth century is usually accounted for by social and economic changes rather than through a purely aesthetic development of style. Feminine emancipation from many physical and moral restraints, the increasing popularity of sport for women, together with new possibilities for gainful employment and political power, all eventually contributed to the new physical ideal. Good sense and good health, mental and physical, were seen to be properly served by freedom and activity, and feminine clothing evolved so as to allow for these and (more importantly) for the look of these. What is meant by "modern" looks developed after the First World War with the aid of clothing that expressed (although it did not always provide) an ideal of comfort and the possibility of action.

2   The most important expressive element in this new visual conception of female dress was not the uncorseted torso but the shortened skirt. After women's skirts had risen off the ground, any given clothed woman was perceptibly smaller in scale than formerly. Hair was shortened, as well as skirts, and worn close to the head. Hats shrank. During most of the nineteenth century a fashionable woman's dress, including coiffure, headgear, and a possible muff, handbag, and parasol, had consisted of an extensive, complicated system with many different sections (sleeves, bodice, skirt, collar, train). These were all separately conceived and embellished and all tended to enlarge the total volume of the clothed body, partly by being difficult to perceive all at once. After the First World War a woman's dress came more and more to present a compact and unified visual image. This is what men's clothes had already succeeded in doing a century before. The new simplified and reduced clothes for women, although they were designed and made absolutely different from men's clothes and out of different fabrics, nevertheless expressed the new sense of the equality of the sexes— an equality, that is, with respect to the new character of their important differences.

3   Female sexual submissiveness, either meek or wanton, was no longer modish and no longer avowed by elements of dress. Feminine sexuality had to abandon the suggestion of plump, hidden softness and find expression in exposed, lean hardness. Women strove for the erotic appeal inherent in the racehorse and the sports car, which might be summed up as a mettlesome challenge: a vibrant, somewhat unaccountable readiness for action but only under expert guidance. This was naturally best offered in a self-contained, sleekly composed physical format: a thin body, with few layers of covering. Immanent sexuality, best expressed in a condition of stasis, was no longer the foundation of female allure. The look of possible movement became a necessary element in fashionable female beauty, and all women's clothing, whatever other messages it offered, consistently incorporated visible legs and feet into the total female image. Women, once thought to glide, were seen to walk. Even vain or fruitless or nervous activity, authorized by fashionable morbid aestheticism, came to seem preferable to immobility, idleness, passivity. The various dance crazes of the first quarter of the century undoubtedly were an

expression of this restless spirit, but its most important vehicle was the movies.

The rapid advance of the movies as the chief popular art made the public increasingly aware of style in feminine physical movement. Movies taught everyone how ways of walking and dancing, of using the hands and moving the head and shoulders, could be incorporated into the conscious ways of wearing clothes. After about 1920 the fact that women's clothes showed such a reduction in overall volume was undoubtedly partly due to the visual need for the completely clothed body to be satisfactorily seen *in motion.* Perfect feminine beauty no longer formed a still image, ideally wrought by a Leonardo da Vinci or a Titian into an eternal icon. It had become transmuted into a photograph, a single instant that represented a sequence of instants—an ideally moving picture, even if it were momentarily still. For this kind of mobile beauty, thinness was a necessary condition.

The still body that is nevertheless perceived as ideally in motion seems to present a blurred image—a perpetual suggestion of all the other possible moments at which it might be seen. It seems to have a dynamic, expanding outline. The actual physical size of a human body is made apparently larger by its movements, and if its movements are what constitute its essential visual reality, they must be what gives it its visual substance. Even if a body is perceived at a motionless instant, the possibility of enlargement by movement is implicit in the image. Before consciousness had been so much affected by photography, a body perceived as ideally still could be visually enlarged by layers of fat or clothing with aesthetic success, but a body that is perceived to be about to move must apparently replace those layers with layers of possible space to move in. The camera eye seems to fatten the figure; human eyes, trained by camera vision, demand that it be thin to start with, to allow for the same effect in direct perception. The thin female body, once considered visually meager and unsatisfying without the suggestive expansions of elaborate clothing (or of flesh, which artists sometimes had to provide), has become substantial, freighted with potential action.

It came about that all the varieties for female desirability conceived by the twentieth century seemed ideally housed in a thin, resilient, and bony body. Healthy innocence, sexual restlessness, creative zest, practical competence, even morbid but poetic obsessiveness and intelligence—all seemed appropriate in size ten. During the six decades following the First World War, styles in gesture, posture, and erotic emphasis have undergone many changes, but the basically slim female ideal has been maintained. Throughout all the shifting levels of bust and waist and the fluctuating taste in gluteal and mammary thrust, the bodies of women have been conceived as ideally slender, and clearly supported by bones.

Vocabulary

a. *paragraph 1:* aesthetic
b. *paragraph 2:* uncorseted, bodice, embellished
c. *paragraph 3:* wanton, mettlesome, immanent, stasis, morbid
d. *paragraph 4:* icon, transmuted
e. *paragraph 5:* implicit
f. *paragraph 6:* resilient, gluteal

Questions

1. What is Hollander's thesis? Where does she state it? How does she prove it?
2. Hollander argues for women's activity as the primary cause of fashionable slimness. What other causes does she suggest?
3. What other causes of fashionable slimness can you think of? Do these add to or detract from the strength of Hollander's argument?
4. For what audience is this essay intended? Is class a consideration? Level of education?

Writing Assignment

In a couple of paragraphs compare Hollander's and Sontag's views of the cultural determinants of beauty.

DAVID SUZUKI

Geneticist and broadcaster on radio (*Quirks and Quarks*) and television (*The Nature of Things*), David Suzuki was educated at Amherst, and at the University of Chicago, where he obtained his PhD in 1961. He is an international speaker and lecturer, and the recipient of numerous awards and honorary degrees. What distinguishes David Suzuki from the majority of his colleagues is his social conscience and his skills as a media personality— his willingness to "go public" with, and to make the public care about, his worry over various kinds of scientific research. As the following essay shows, Suzuki's social conscience often prompts him to focus his keen scientific training and concerns for the future of the human race on matters not strictly scientific—in this instance, children's attitudes toward the natural world.

Living with Nature

DAVID SUZUKI

I n spite of the vast expanse of wilderness
in this country, most Canadian children grow up in urban settings.
In other words, they live in a world conceived, shaped and domi-
nated by people. Even the farms located around cities and towns
are carefully groomed and landscaped for human convenience.
There's nothing wrong with that, of course, but in such an environment, it's very easy to lose any sense of connection with nature.

In city apartments and dwellings, the presence of cockroaches,
fleas, ants, mosquitoes or houseflies is guaranteed to elicit the
spraying of insecticides. Mice and rats are poisoned or trapped,
while the gardener wages a never-ending struggle with ragweed,
dandelions, slugs and root-rot. We have a modern arsenal of chemical weapons to fight off these invaders and we use them lavishly.

We worry when kids roll in the mud or wade through a puddle
because they'll get "dirty." Children learn attitudes and values very
quickly and the lesson in cities is very clear—nature is an enemy,
it's dirty, dangerous or a nuisance. So youngsters learn to distance
themselves from nature and to try to control it. I am astonished at
the number of adults who loathe or are terrified by snakes, spiders,
butterflies, worms, birds—the list seems endless.

If you reflect on the history of humankind, you realize that
for 99 per cent of our species' existence on the planet, we were
deeply embedded in and dependent on nature. When plants and
animals were plentiful, we flourished. When famine and drought
struck, our numbers fell accordingly. We remain every bit as
dependent upon nature today—we need plants to fix photons of
energy into sugar molecules and to cleanse the air and replenish
the oxygen. It is folly to forget our dependence on an intact
ecosystem. But we do whenever we teach our offspring to fear or
detest the natural world. The urban message kids get runs completely counter to what they are born with, a natural interest in
other life forms. Just watch a child in a first encounter with a
flower or an ant—there is instant interest and fascination. We
condition them out of it.

The result is that when my 7-year-old daughter brings home
new friends, they invariably recoil in fear or disgust when she tries
to show them her favorite pets—three beautiful salamanders that

her grandfather got for her in Vancouver. And when my 3-year-old comes wandering in with her treasures—millipedes, spiders, slugs and sowbugs that she catches under rocks lining the front lawn— children and adults alike usually respond by saying "yuk."

6   I can't overemphasize the tragedy of that attitude. For, inherent in this view is the assumption that human beings are special and different and that we lie outside nature. Yet it is this belief that is creating many of our environmental problems today.

7   Does it matter whether we sense our place in nature so long as we have cities and technology? Yes, for many reasons, not the least of which is that virtually all scientists were fascinated with nature as children and retained that curiosity throughout their lives. But a far more important reason is that if we retain a spiritual sense of connection with all other life forms, it can't help but profoundly affect the way we act. Whenever my daughter sees a picture of an animal dead or dying, she asks me fearfully, "Daddy, are there any more?" At 7 years, she already knows about extinction and it frightens her.

8   The yodel of a loon at sunset, the vast flocks of migrating waterfowl in the fall, the indomitable salmon returning thousands of kilometres—these images of nature have inspired us to create music, poetry and art. And when we struggle to retain a handful of California condors or whooping cranes, it's clearly not from a fear of ecological collapse, it's because there is something obscene and frightening about the disappearance of another species at our hands.

9   If children grow up understanding that we are animals, they will look at other species with a sense of fellowship and community. If they understand their ecological place—the biosphere—then when children see the great virgin forests of the Queen Charlotte Islands being clearcut, they will feel physical pain, because they will understand that those trees are an extension of themselves.

10   When children who know their place in the ecosystem see factories spewing poison into the air, water and soil, they will feel ill because someone has violated their home. This is not mystical mumbo-jumbo. We have poisoned the life support systems that sustain all organisms because we have lost a sense of ecological place. Those of us who are parents have to realize the unspoken, negative lessons we are conveying to our children. Otherwise, they will continue to desecrate this planet as we have.

11   It's not easy to avoid giving these hidden lessons. I have struggled to cover my dismay and queasiness when Severn and Sarika come running in with a large wolf spider or when we've emerged from a ditch covered with leeches or when they have been stung

accidentally by yellowjackets feeding on our leftovers. But that's nature. I believe efforts to teach children to love and respect other life forms are priceless.

Vocabulary

a. *paragraph 4:* photons, ecosystem
b. *paragraph 6:* inherent
c. *paragraph 8:* indomitable, ecological
d. *paragraph 9:* biosphere
e. *paragraph 10:* spewing, desecrate

Questions

1. What does Suzuki show to be the immediate cause of children's alienation from the natural world?
2. Suzuki is concerned chiefly with the general effects of this alienation. How is this concern basic to his purpose in writing the essay?
3. How does Suzuki handle potential objections with the assertion "This is not mystical mumbo-jumbo"?
4. What is the tone of this essay: alarmist, detached, hortatory? How does the tone help Suzuki achieve the desired effect?

Writing Assignments

1. Write an essay about how your own prejudices have inadvertently led to your alienation from nature.
2. Discuss some ways in which you could protect and strengthen the relationship Suzuki sees as endangered.

rgument

How you choose to build an essay depends on your purpose and audience. The purpose of most of the essays you have read so far in this book has been to illustrate, entertain, or inform, using various techniques of expository writing. Often, however, a writer's purpose is to persuade or convince the audience of the validity of an idea or an action.

The demands of exposition and persuasion are not the same. Your major concern in exposition is to be clear; your major concern in a persuasive argument is not only to be clear, but also to present your ideas in the most convincing way. In describing how to conserve fuel by driving properly, for example, your concern is to make the process clear; if your purpose is also to persuade drivers to change their driving habits, you will have to choose the best means of doing so. These means depend on the nature of your audience. If the audience is hostile to the idea of conservation, you might discuss conservation and make various appeals — for example, to conscience, public spirit, practical concerns—before turning to the matter of driving. If the audience is friendly to your topic, you probably need only remind them of the importance of conservation.

Persuasive arguments present additional challenges. You must construct a sound argument, arouse the interest of the audience through a legitimate appeal to their emotions, and show that you are honest and well informed on the issue and therefore deserve a hearing. Although some writers seek to avoid all emotional appeals in the belief that the soundness of the argument guarantees its persuasiveness, few arguments are entirely free of emotion. The problem is not how to rid the argument of emotion but how to balance emotion and reason so that the aroused reader considers the argument fully, gives rational assent to it, and can agree with the argument in whole or in part.

Argumentative or persuasive essays have a traditional organization that is easy to learn and put to use. Derived from the oration of the law courts and legislatures of ancient Greece and Rome, this organization shaped the expository essay that we have been considering—in particular, the division of the essay into an introduction that states the purpose and gives pertinent background, the main discussion or body, and the conclusion. The argumentative essay today, like the oration of ancient times, contains these divisions but expands them to meet the needs of the argument:

- *introduction*, or what was called the exordium or exhortation to the audience, appealing to the interest and goodwill of the audience, and stating the subject of the oration or essay;

- *division of proofs*, stating the thesis partly or fully and summarizing the evidence and arguments to be presented;
- *narration* or background, stating the facts of the case;
- *confirmation* or proof, arguing the thesis;
- *refutation*, answering opponents; and
- *conclusion*, reinforcing and summarizing the main argument and reinforcing the original appeal to the audience.

These parts may be combined or arranged in a different order—the narration or background perhaps combined with the confirming arguments, or the refutation coming before the confirmation. Often the division or outline of the argument is omitted, and instead of coming early, the thesis may be delayed until the conclusion.

In explaining your ideas or beliefs, or in debating an issue, you draw on personal experience and observation for illustration and evidence. But often you must turn to other sources of information when you have no experience with the matter under discussion. Opinions need the support of facts.

You may find your evidence in primary sources—first-hand accounts by participants and observers—and in secondary sources —later reports and interpretations by those not present. An eyewitness account is a different kind of evidence from the reconstruction of the event by a historian in later years. Though primary evidence might seem the more reliable, it may be contradictory in itself or be contradicted by other eyewitness evidence. At the time of the Northwest Rebellion of 1885, eyewitnesses disagreed on what they saw and heard. Researchers continue to disagree on what evidence to consider and how to interpret the evidence they do accept.

Establishing the reliability of secondary sources is also difficult. The researcher must discern the reliability of the author by looking for special circumstances or biases that may colour the evidence. Evidence seldom speaks for itself, and no presentation of evidence can be totally neutral or objective, even when the writer seeks to present it fairly; all interpretations are shaped by personal and cultural attitudes. The researcher thus must consider the weight an author gives to various kinds of evidence, as well as its interpretation. Both primary and secondary sources are therefore necessary in the search for facts.

Inductive Reasoning

After the evidence has been assembled, one process by which we reason from experience and observation is called *induction*. It is a kind of reasoning we engage in daily, for example, in drawing the conclusion that a red and swollen finger is probably infected or that numerous car accidents will follow a heavy snowfall.

Inductive reasoning often makes generalizations or predictions about classes of things or people. An example is the generalization that drivers in a particular age group will probably have a higher number of car accidents, or the broader generalization that, as a class, another group of people are safe drivers. The prediction may be based on various kinds of evidence—for example, the knowledge of how many of these drivers were in car accidents in a ten-month period, or statistical knowledge of the accident history of this group province-wide or nation-wide. No prediction can be made about any single member of the group, however, nor can the prediction be made with absolute certainty.

The problem in inductive reasoning is to choose particular instances that truly represent the group or class about which we are generalizing or making predictions. But, as in the sample precincts that pollsters use to predict the outcome of elections, it is impossible to guarantee that the limited number of people sampled are actually typical or representative. We also may be unaware of special circumstances that, if known, would weaken the generalization. These are important reasons for not claiming certainty for the generalization.

A "hasty generalization" is a judgement made on the basis of insufficient evidence or on the basis of special cases. Thus someone might argue that all people over 70 will have numerous accidents in the future (and therefore should pay higher insurance premiums) because a large number were involved in traffic accidents in a particular three-month period. The argument might be worth considering if the behaviour of these people and driving conditions could be shown to be typical. It would matter, however, if some of the drivers in these accidents proved to have impaired vision (by no means a characteristic only of older people) or if the accidents occurred in the harsh winter months. The generalization in question would then have been based both on special cases and on special circumstances.

Earlier we discussed some ways of analyzing cause and effect. These include tracing an effect to its recent or proximate cause (death because of famine) and to its more distant or remote causes (drought, soil erosion, ignorance, indifference, neglect). We also discussed the "four causes" of an object—the materials of its manufacture (material cause), the shape given it (formal cause), its maker (efficient cause), and its use (final cause).

Cause may also be analyzed through the words *necessary* and *sufficient*, as when we say that getting an "A" on the final exam is necessary but not sufficient to achieve an "A" in the course: an "A" on the final would be sufficient only if the exam was the sole determinant of the course grade. Notice what the words *necessary* and *sufficient* imply; they refer to the conditions or circumstances in which this event *might* occur. When scientists say that a necessary condition of getting a cold is exposure to a virus, they mean that a virus of some kind must be present—not that the virus always produces a cold. Other conditions obviously need to be present, but scientists do not now claim to know what these are. If the cold always occurs when a single condition is present, this condition would be sufficient to produce the cold. But scientists still do not claim to know all the causes.

In reasoning about cause in this way, we implicitly recognize that events, like the reasons for our actions, are complex and not simple. Yet this is not what some of our statements show. Statements that generalize about *the* cause of a cold or some other physical or social or political ill, as if a single cause could be identified and dealt with, are hasty generalizations. Another hasty generalization arises from the idea that one event must be the cause of another because it precedes it: I caught the cold "because" I was soaked in a rainstorm. The sequence of events does not necessarily make one event the cause of the next. Clearly we might have caught the cold even if we had not been soaked, and we cannot know whether getting soaked will always give us a cold—even if it always has in the past. This kind of reasoning is given a Latin name —the *post hoc* fallacy, from the expression *post hoc, ergo propter hoc* (after this, therefore because of this).

Deductive Reasoning

Induction, then, is reasoning from particular instances to a general conclusion or truth:

> I studied the equations but didn't do the practice problems, and I failed algebra. I studied my French but skipped the language lab and did poorly in French. I studied the formulas and performed the experiments carefully and passed chemistry [*three particular instances*]. Therefore, learning seems to depend on practice as well as study [*probable truth*].

Deduction, by contrast, is the process of inference—of reasoning from a general truth to another general truth or a particular instance:

> Since learning depends on constant study and practice [*general truth*], I passed algebra because I studied the equations and did the practice problems [*particular instance*].

In ordinary conversation, we say informally, "I passed algebra because I studied and did the practice problems." This statement is a shortening of the following syllogism, or formal argument:

The act of learning is an act that depends on study and practice.
The mastery of algebra is an act of learning.
Therefore, the mastery of algebra is an act that depends on study and practice.

Notice that the first two statements—called the *major premise* and the *minor premise*, respectively—were left unstated in our shortened statement (called an *enthymeme*). Where the full argument is stated, the premises and conclusion may occur in a different order:

The child needs to acquire fundamental skills in communication—to learn to read, write, and express himself flexibly and clearly—in order to function as a social creature [*major premise*]. The television experience does not further his verbal development [*conclusion*] because it does not require any verbal participation on his part, merely passive intake [*minor premise*]. (Marie Winn, *The Plug-In Drug*)

Where inductive arguments depend on the weight of factual evidence beyond the premises, deductive arguments depend on the premises alone as evidence for the conclusion. No other evidence is required because the premises are considered to be true—as in Arthur Schafer's argument about public morality, in "Morals in the Rat Race":

There are new things under the sun, but political scandal and corruption are not among them. There are dishonest people in every society. No political epoch has been without its share of crooks and charlatans.

From truths such as these, or long-held beliefs, or generalizations well supported by long experience, we make inferences, as in our original example. Thus, if it is true that learning depends on study and practice, and true also that the mastery of algebra is an act of learning, it must be true that mastering algebra depends on study and practice. Though no other evidence but the premises *need* be provided, we may decide to illustrate or defend one or both. For a true statement is not always obvious to everyone.

Inductive and deductive reasoning often work together, depending on the particular argument and what we consider the point at issue. Proponents of nuclear power plants may, for example, insist that the issue in making the decision to build the plant in a particular region is economic—the increasing power needs of industry. Opponents may argue that the issue is the danger of an accident or the difficulty of disposing of nuclear waste. Much of the debate may be given to establishing the point at issue.

The arguments employed in such a debate can and possibly will be inductive: statistical information on productivity and nuclear fuel, eyewitness accounts of nuclear plant operations, scientific reports on waste disposal, and the like. And the argument will be deductive in the inferences drawn from certain assumptions, perhaps ones on which the participants in the debate agree: that a high standard of living is a desirable goal in the community; that risk must be taken into account in making a decision about nuclear power; that high productivity depends on a dependable source of electrical power.

Argument must satisfy two requirements: the propositions that form the premises must be true, and the process of reasoning must be correct, or to use the technical term, must be *valid*.

Note that *valid* does not mean "true": an argument may be false in its premises, but still be valid if the process of inference from these premises is correct. Here is a valid argument, both of whose premises are false:

All Canadians are taxpayers.
All property owners are Canadians.
Therefore, all property owners are taxpayers.

We ask of an argument that it be valid in its reasoning and true in its premises. A valid argument whose premises are true is called *sound*. The argument just cited would be sound if, in fact, all Canadians do pay taxes, and all property owners (everywhere) are Canadians. The argument is, of course, unsound. Logicians have complex techniques for testing the validity of the many kinds of syllogisms; we cannot review them here. But we need to keep in mind a few characteristics that invalidate deductive arguments.

Someone says to us: "My neighbours must all be property owners because they all pay taxes." Something strikes us as wrong here, but what is it? We can construct the whole argument as follows:

All property owners are taxpayers.
My neighbours are taxpayers.
Therefore, my neighbours are property owners.

The trouble is with the middle term, "taxpayers." The major term of a syllogism is the predicate term of its conclusion; the subject of the conclusion is the minor term. The term that appears in the premises but not in the conclusion is the middle term:

All	A (middle)	is	B (MAJOR)
All	C (MINOR)	is	A (middle)
All	C (MINOR)	is	B (MINOR)

(The argument may not have more than these three terms.) For the argument to be valid, this middle term must be "distributed" in at least one of the premises; that is, it must refer to—be distributed among—all members of the class named. In the argument above, the middle term, "taxpayers," is undistributed in both premises—referring in each to some members of the class taxpayers, but not to all:

> All property owners are taxpayers.
> My neighbours are taxpayers.

Though all property owners are taxpayers, not all taxpayers own property. And though all my neighbours are taxpayers, not all taxpayers are my neighbours. But that is exactly what the conclusion asserts. The argument is thus invalid because the conclusion says more than the premises do.

Other invalid arguments can be analyzed more easily. The middle term must not be ambiguous, as in the following argument:

> Whoever helps himself is helped by God.
> A thief helps himself.
> Therefore, a thief is helped by God.

And both premises must be affirmative if the conclusion is so: if one of the premises is negative, so must be the conclusion. And, if both premises are negative, no conclusion follows. The following argument is invalid for this reason:

> No dogs are welcome visitors.
> Children are not dogs.
> Therefore, children are welcome visitors.

In developing arguments of our own, it is important to remember that an argument may seem logical because the process of reasoning is correct, and yet be unsound because the premises are questionable or false. In reading arguments, we need to consider both the premises that form them and the way the writer reasons from those premises.

In all debate, fairness and sound argument ideally should prevail. It hardly needs to be said that they often do not. Here are a few important "logical fallacies" a good argument avoids:

- *Arguing in a circle* is closely related to begging the question, where we assume as true what we are trying to prove: "No person who cares about jobs would oppose the bill because it is one that those who care about jobs in Cape Breton can support." The speaker has not given a reason to support the bill, but has merely restated the opening assertion.
- *Non sequitur* ("it does not follow"): The assertion "I oppose nuclear power because my father does" contains a hidden assumption—that Father knows best. Since this assumption is hidden, the second part of the statement does not follow from the first part clearly. Assumptions of this sort may be hidden because, once stated, the assumption shows the statement to be questionable or absurd.
- *Irrelevant conclusion*: If the point at issue is whether nuclear plants present a risk, the argument that they are needed is an irrelevant argument. It may, of course, be relevant to another issue.
- *Ad hominem* ("to the person") *argument*: I may attack my opponents rather than the issue—for example, by arguing that proponents of nuclear power are selfish and greedy. Even if they were people of bad character, their proposals must be judged on their merits. In other circumstances, such as an election campaign, the character of a person may be the issue.
- *Ad populum* ("to the people") *argument*: I may also appeal to popular prejudice to gain support—suggesting that Sir John A. Macdonald or some other revered and usually long-dead person would have favoured (or opposed) nuclear power. Such appeals to authority often depend on fear.
- *Either/or hypothesis*: I may set up two alternatives—nuclear power or economic depression—without allowing for other solutions.

ARTHUR SCHAFER

Arthur Schafer is a professor at the University of Manitoba. In the following essay from *The Globe and Mail*, Schafer discusses the widespread belief that "the pursuit of individual self-interest in the marketplace will lead to the general good." Basing his conclusions on his observations of modern society, he warns us about the dangers of using self-interest as the only standard of ethical conduct.

Morals in the Rat Race

ARTHUR SCHAFER

1   There are new things under the sun, but political scandal and corruption are not among them. There are dishonest people in every society. No political epoch has been without its share of crooks and charlatans.

2   Canadians have a vague sense, however, that the recent spate of corrupt practices in our society, like those occurring in our neighbor to the south, is a sign of something other than ordinary human fallibility. There seems to be a growing public cynicism, a sense that both personal and public morality have declined drastically. The question irresistibly poses itself: has dishonest behavior become so widespread that it threatens the very fabric of our society?

3   Is ours a civilization in decline? The evidence is less than conclusive, but it points toward an affirmative answer.

4   The most profoundly important innovation of Western liberal society has been to put the marketplace at the centre of all social transactions. The gospel according to Adam Smith assumes that the pursuit of individual self-interest in the marketplace will lead to the general good. When every citizen rationally pursues his self-interest, all will flourish.

5   Or so the theory would have it. But social reality can be rather disappointing, and the philosophy of liberal individualism is looking distinctly threadbare these days. The very competitive individualism that has produced for us a superabundance of televisions, VCRs, microwave ovens, and vacations in Florida now threatens to so undermine civic virtue that our culture crumbles from within. We cannot help but recall that the collapse of earlier civilizations—the Roman Empire comes to mind—was precipitated more powerfully by internal corruption than by external force.

6   Neo-conservatives such as U.S. President Ronald Reagan and British Prime Minister Margaret Thatcher lament the collapse of traditional social values: family, work, patriotism, restraint. They are right, of course. There has been a deep erosion of traditional values, but the process began several hundred years ago. What we are witnessing today is, perhaps, the culmination of a long historical process, a process accelerated by the policies of Mr. Reagan and Mrs. Thatcher.

7   Ironically, it is the very marketplace morality at whose shrine the neo-conservatives worship that produces the social disintegration

they lament. The pursuit of individual self-aggrandizement, individual gratification, individual pleasure has led more and more of us into the scramble for wealth and power. Ambition and hedonism prevail. Can any society survive when its citizens are all engaged in a furious competition to carve up the spoils?

As long as only a minority is motivated by ruthless self-interest, social bonds can remain largely intact. But when businessmen dishonor their contracts, when ordinary folk cheat on their income tax, when welfare recipients chisel the government, when doctors and nurses and policemen strike for higher pay, when politicians use their power to enrich themselves and their cronies, this should be seen as a dramatic sign that social cohesion is deeply threatened. 8

Business civilization regards work solely as a means to profit, income, consumption. Creative work ceases to be viewed as an end in itself. The cash nexus replaces the spirit of work; the real value of work is lost. 9

A similar process of devaluation occurs within the family. Men have never been slow to abandon their wives and children in the pursuit of self-interest. But the bonds of family solidarity now have become so attenuated that women seek their own freedom as single-mindedly as men. This may be the ultimate "triumph" of individual liberty. "I love your majesty according to my bond; no more nor less," Cordelia says to her father. If King Lear had achieved any wisdom along with grey hairs, he would have been thrilled by this testimony. Instead he was outraged. We know better. 10

Perhaps the most striking paradox of our times is that liberal market society can survive only as long as most people live by the value system that pre-dated the marketplace—the pre-bourgeois values of public-spiritedness, civic virtue, honesty and honor, mutual co-operation, family bonds. Instead, wherever we turn—to government, to business, to work, to the family—we observe a radical loosening of social bonds. It is the rapid spread of marketplace morality throughout society which now threatens the very existence of this society. 11

As the political economist Seymour Hirsch has pointed out, the things for which we are now all competing so frantically can, by their very nature, be available only for a small elite. Only a few can be generals. The rest must be privates (except in the Canadian Armed Forces). Only a few can enjoy their vacations on an unspoiled beach. When everyone can afford a car capable of travelling at speeds in excess of 170 kilometres an hour, all are forced by traffic congestion to creep along at 20 kilometres. When everyone achieves a home with a view, the view is likely to be of each other's homes. When everyone gets his PhD, the competitive advantage of this estimable degree tends to diminish, and its holders find themselves driving taxis. 12

13   It is important to realize that the central delusion of the affluent society is not that money does not buy happiness (though it does not). No, the central delusion is the belief that the benefits of affluence can be preserved when nearly everyone becomes "middle class." When everyone has a car, a home in the suburbs and a PhD, none of these things can deliver what they promise.

14   We must now face squarely a nightmare vision of our future: endless traffic jams, endless grey, box-like houses in endless, grey Mississauga, unemployed PhDs, businessmen on the make, families split, doctors milking their patients and patients suing their doctors, politicians on the take. And everyone lamenting the decline of morality while heaping praise upon the very institution that has led to this impasse.

15   The metaphor of a "rat race," although a cliché, is appropriate because the system ensures that we must run ever faster just to maintain our relative position in the competition. And we must compete as ruthlessly as the most unscrupulous or lose the golden palm.

16   A civilization that encourages the motive of self-interested calculation to rule every sphere of social life is on a sure path to moral bankruptcy. The ultimate freedom—from the bonds of community, family, friendship, and neighborliness—becomes the ultimate slavery. This way lies social disintegration.

17   Canadians are right to be deeply concerned. We are far richer than our parents and incomparably richer than our great-grandparents. Does anyone believe that we are also happier? Or better people? The challenge that faces us will not be an easy one to meet, for it is nothing less than the creation of a new sense of freedom, a sense of personal liberation that is compatible with the deeper values of community and public-spiritedness.

Vocabulary

a. *paragraph 1:* charlatans
b. *paragraph 2:* spate, fallibility
c. *paragraph 7:* shrine, neo-conservatives
d. *paragraph 8:* chisel
e. *paragraph 9:* nexus
f. *paragraph 15:* unscrupulous

Questions

1. Schafer argues by means of a series of examples to a generalization supported by them. We call this method of organizing an argument—moving from the specific to the general, from particulars of experience

to conclusions based on them—*inductive*. Would the generalization be unclear or difficult to understand if Schafer had begun with it?

2. How various are the examples Schafer presents? How effective are these in helping him make his case?

3. Why does Schafer say that the changes he describes represent a significant decline?

4. What other conclusions about Canadian society do you think are supported by these facts, and how are they supported?

Writing Assignments

1. In opposition to Schafer, argue that consumerism has had no profound effect on morality. Be careful not to generalize more broadly than your evidence allows.

2. Discuss the extent to which your own experience and observation support the conclusion Schafer reaches. If you believe his conclusion needs qualification, explain why it does.

WENDELL BERRY

Wendell Berry was born and educated in Kentucky. He has written novels, short stories, poetry, and a handbook on farming, but he is best known as an essayist. His books of essays include *The Long-Legged House, The Hidden Wound, Continuous Harmony, Recollected Essays: 1965–1980, The Gift of Good Land,* and *Standing by Words.* In his work, he consistently speaks out against the ways in which our use of modern technology has cut us off from our natural environment, as in the following essay on computers and writing.

Why I Am Not Going to Buy a Computer

WENDELL BERRY

Like almost everybody else, I am hooked to the energy corporations, which I do not admire. I hope to become less hooked to them. In my work, I try to be as little hooked to them as possible. As a farmer, I do almost all of my work with horses. As a writer, I work with a pencil or a pen and a piece of paper.

My wife types my work on a Royal standard typewriter bought new in 1956 and as good now as it was then. As she types, she sees things that are wrong and marks them with small checks in the margins. She is my best critic because she is the one most familiar with my habitual errors and weaknesses. She also understands, sometimes better than I do, what *ought* to be said. We have, I think, a literary cottage industry that works well and pleasantly. I do not see anything wrong with it.

3   A number of people, by now, have told me that I could greatly improve things by buying a computer. My answer is that I am not going to do it. I have several reasons, and they are good ones.

4   The first is the one I mentioned at the beginning. I would hate to think that my work as a writer could not be done without a direct dependence on strip-mined coal. How could I write conscientiously against the rape of nature if I were, in the act of writing, implicated in the rape? For the same reason, it matters to me that my writing is done in the daytime, without electric light.

5   I do not admire the computer manufacturers a great deal more than I admire the energy industries. I have seen their advertisements, attempting to seduce struggling or failing farmers into the belief that they can solve their problems by buying yet another piece of expensive equipment. I am familiar with their propaganda campaigns that have put computers into public schools in need of books. That computers are expected to become as common as TV sets in "the future" does not impress me or matter to me. I do not own a TV set. I do not see that computers are bringing us one step nearer to anything that does matter to me: peace, economic justice, ecological health, political honesty, family and community stability, good work.

6   What would a computer cost me? More money, for one thing, than I can afford, and more than I wish to pay to people whom I do not admire. But the cost would not be just monetary. It is well understood that technological innovation always requires the discarding of the "old model"—the "old model" in this case being not just our old Royal standard, but my wife, my critic, my closest reader, my fellow worker. Thus (and I think this is typical of present-day technological innovation), what would be superseded would be not only something, but somebody. In order to be technologically up-to-date as a writer, I would have to sacrifice an association that I am dependent upon and that I treasure.

7   My final and perhaps my best reason for not owning a computer is that I do not wish to fool myself. I disbelieve, and therefore strongly resent, the assertion that I or anybody else could write better or more easily with a computer than with a pencil. I do not see why I should not be as scientific about this as the next fellow: when somebody has used a computer to write work that is demonstrably better than Dante's, and when this better is demonstrably attributable to

the use of a computer, then I will speak of computers with a more respectful tone of voice, though I still will not buy one.

To make myself as plain as I can, I should give my standards   8
for technological innovation in my own work. They are as follows:

1. The new tool should be cheaper than the one it replaces.
2. It should be at least as small in scale as the one it replaces.
3. It should work clearly and demonstrably better than the one it replaces.
4. It should use less energy than the one it replaces.
5. If possible, it should use some form of solar energy, such as that of the body.
6. It should be repairable by a person of ordinary intelligence, provided that he or she has the necessary tools.
7. It should be purchasable and repairable as near to home as possible.
8. It should come from a small, privately owned shop or store that will take it back for maintenance and repair.
9. It should not replace or disrupt anything good that already exists, and this includes family and community relationships.

Vocabulary

a. *paragraph 4:* conscientiously
b. *paragraph 5:* propaganda, ecological
c. *paragraph 6:* superseded

Questions

1. In his introductory paragraph, how does Berry seek to predispose the reader favourably to his argument?
2. Do you consider his use of personal experience fair or unfair argument?
3. What assumptions about technology, society, and human relations underlie Berry's argument?
4. How practical are Berry's recommendations at the end of the essay?

Writing Assignments

1. Using Berry's list of conditions at the end of the essay, evaluate in detail some other technological innovation.
2. Write an argument for or against one of the following; in an additional paragraph identify one or more assumptions that underlie your argument, and explain why you hold these assumptions:
   a. building more nuclear power plants
   b. a ban on smoking in shopping malls

   c. periodic examination of licensed drivers
   d. required attendance of university classes
   e. compulsory gun registration

ALICE MUNRO

Alice Munro was born in 1931 in Wingham, Ontario. She studied English for two years at the University of Western Ontario before moving first to Vancouver and then to Victoria, where she ran a bookstore with her husband. She currently lives with her second husband on a farm near Clinton, Ontario. Her first collection, *Dance of the Happy Shades* (1968), won the Governor General's Award. She has followed this with a book every few years, consisting mostly of stories first published in *The New Yorker: Something I've Been Meaning to Tell You; Who Do You Think You Are?*, which also won the Governor General's Award; *The Moons of Jupiter; The Progress of Love*, which was among a handful of best books of the year selected by *The New York Times; Friend of My Youth*; and, most recently, *Open Secrets*. The title of her one novel, *Lives of Girls and Women*, neatly captures the continuing subject of Munro's fiction. In the following essay, she makes a compelling argument for a more sensible ecological and conservative use of a technological infrastructure that has outlived its original purpose — the abandoned regional railway line.

A Walk on the Wild Side

ALICE MUNRO

1   **W**here I grew up, on the rural west side of the town of Wingham in southern Ontario, the Maitland River was at the foot of our property. The river flats and the bottomlands were generally too stony for crops, but made good pasture. There were scattered trees where the cattle could shelter from the sun, and the river provided drinking water. From the rough natural vegetation of the bottomlands and river flats, the grazing cattle produced a grassy parkland that reached to the foot of our property in a grove of elm trees within sight of the house.

2   Downstream to the west, and visible from our place, a wide curve of the river had broadened the flats, and to the north, it had undercut a high steep bank covered with trees—the whole being, in

effect, a great amphitheater half a mile or more in width, floored with elm and maple parkland. On the high, distant skyline back from the amphitheater was Roly Grain's farmstead — house, barn, and silo. To the south, where Roly Grain's sideroad joined Highway 86 just at the bridge where the river completes its curve, the village of Zetland once thrived — remembered by my father, but in my time utterly vanished. When I was young, the skyline with Roly Grain's farmstead seemed to me the end of the world, and the vanished village whose time had ended somehow filled out that idea.

This scene — an amphitheater floored with parkland and reaching to the end of the world and joined to us by the river — was my first access to the countryside of southern Ontario, which was and has remained magical. When I was very young, I dreamt I saw a pure white horse with a jeweled bridle come down to drink at the river — but I didn't think that was a dream. When I lived in British Columbia, I longed for the sight of Ontario landscape — the big solitary oaks and beeches and maples looming in a summer haze in the open fields, the carpet of leeks and trilliums and bloodroot in the sunny woods before the leaves come out, the unexpected little rough hills with their hawthorns and tough daisies, the creeks and bogs and the long smooth grassy slopes. On a motor trip home via the state of Washington, we came out of the splendid mountains and forest onto the great rolling country of the Palouse–Big Bend wheatlands, and I felt as if I had retrieved a lost part of myself, because it was something "like home." 3

Some 15 or so years ago, I returned to Ontario to live, not to the place where I grew up but to a small town nearby and to essentially the same landscape. But things have changed. The elm trees are gone — the last one on our flats, a seeming survivor of the Dutch elm disease, fell in a storm in 1977. The bottomlands are no longer pastured, for reasons I have not investigated, and have grown up in coarse vegetation — tall grasses, stinging nettle, joe-pye weed, wild parsnip, thistles, goldenrod, hawthorn, and scrub willow, to name only a part of it — and the walkable land is gone. The local rivers and streams are not poisonously polluted but are often choked with various kinds of algae and water plants overstimulated by fertilizer runoff from cultivated fields. Even if I were to hack my way through the jungle of vegetation, the river doesn't have the swimmable water I once knew. 4

The amphitheater in the curve of the river belonged to our neighbors, but I regarded it as mine, or ours, or not anyone's — accessible to everyone not afraid of cows. This was generally the rule — you could walk the countryside on private property without fear of being hauled up for trespass. Now, more and more rural land is posted against trespass, and when I walk in the country, I would seldom 5 think of cutting across a piece of private land, posted or unposted, unless I had the owner's permission. The countryside of Ontario was once an unofficial recreation area for local people. For a variety of reasons—too many people, larger cultivated fields, the unpastured bottomlands—that day is gone. There has been no adequate replacement.

6   Two years ago my husband and I discovered the walking and bicycling trails in Wisconsin that have been converted from abandoned railways. Near Blue Mounds, a little west of Madison, on a fine summer morning, we came upon the Military Road Trail. When we are traveling, we find that our staying power is improved if we get about an hour's walk a day, and the trail was exactly what we were looking for. We walked from Blue Mounds to Barneveld, had lunch there in a pub right beside the trail, and walked back to Blue Mounds. We were so elated by this walk that we decided to change the itinerary of our trip to visit the other Wisconsin trails, and we were not disappointed. We talked about the reasons for our exhilaration and came up with something like this: "One of life's great pleasures is to feel possessive of your homeland, and one way to get that feeling is to see the country as a landscape that belongs to you and to which you belong, and to see it close up and at not too great a speed."

7   But Wisconsin is not our homeland. It was good to know that there was a government there that had taken this trouble to provide for its people—to recognize that the need to walk is as important as the need to drive on a highway. But it wasn't our government. So we came home with the hope that this sort of program could be started in southern Ontario, where at this very time so many railways are being abandoned. Recently one Sunday, we toured along the abandoned sections of the CPR from Credit Forks to Wingham, which has a branch to Fergus. Near Credit Forks, where the line crosses a secondary highway, we found 12 cars parked. They belonged to people who were walking the line, having clambered over the ridge of earth the company has bulldozed up to block passage to vehicles. At another crossing, we saw cyclists throwing their bikes over the barrier. All along the line from Wingham to Credit Forks, we encountered people walking and cycling, including a farmer who owned adjoining land. He said he would like to see the abandoned line become a trail. When you see valiant cyclists pumping along the thin edge of paved highways with the traffic roaring by, you can appreciate the appeal a controlled trail has for them, and you can also appreciate that the Ontario government, despite its advocacy of outdoor exercise, is doing nothing to facilitate cycling as an activity that large numbers of people could enjoy.

8   If the line west out of Credit Forks follows the same history as other abandoned railway lines in Ontario, there will be a brief period during which people will walk and bike along it, and then

the adjoining landowners will close it down, whether by legal purchase or not. One fence across the line effectively closes the whole section between road crossings. All across the province, bits and pieces of abandoned lines can be found, fragmented by closure by adjoining landowners. These potential trails are being lost. And they are not just trails but existing corridors of vegetation. Along the Guelph to Goderich line, we saw banks of wild strawberries, thimbleberry and wild raspberry bushes, tame cherry trees and lilac bushes gone wild, and many, many young elm trees—enough, perhaps, to form a reservoir within which an immunity could be developed to the Dutch elm disease. Wouldn't it be worth preserving our vegetation, our nurseries of elm trees? (And trees growing up along the tracks would provide privacy for the landowners.)

I've turned my celebration of southern Ontario countryside   9
into a plea, because I really believe that access to the land is a right and a necessity, just as paved roads and schools and hospitals are. I believe that it's important to our well-being. I think that people who see the landscape in this way will give thought to protecting and preserving it. The railways have been heavily subsidized, so surely we all have some claim on the lines when they are abandoned. If the provincial government would just accept custody of these lines, it would make possible a period in which interested parties could lobby for various plans, and the corridors wouldn't be immediately fragmented and lost. I hope they won't be.

Vocabulary

a. *paragraph 2:* amphitheater
b. *paragraph 7:* facilitate

Questions

1. What assumptions does Munro make about the physical and emotional needs of people?
2. The first three paragraphs are autobiographical. What does this opening contribute to her argument?
3. Does Munro seek to refute those who argue for the privatization of abandoned railway lines, or does she present supporting arguments only?
4. What conclusion does she derive from her assumptions?

Writing Assignments

1. Evaluate the following statement on the basis of your own experience: "One of life's great pleasures is to feel possessive of your homeland,

and one way to get that feeling is to see the country as a landscape that belongs to you and to which you belong, and to see it close up and at not too great a speed."

2. Using Munro's blend of personal experience and logical inference, defend an unconventional position on the use of civic space, heritage buildings, or natural resources.

MARNI JACKSON

Marni Jackson has been published widely in such magazines as *Saturday Night, Toronto Life,* and *Rolling Stone.* Her 1992 book, *The Mother Zone: Love, Sex & Laundry in the Modern Family,* is a common-sense reflection on the discrepancies between theory and practice on the domestic and maternal front. The book achieved an immediate popular success. The essay that follows was first published in *This Magazine,* another of the periodicals to which Jackson frequently contributes. In it she displays the wit and wisdom that made her first book so appealing and have won her two National Magazine Awards for humour.

Gals and Dolls:
The Moral Value of
"Bad" Toys

MARNI JACKSON

1   In the days before I actually had a child, child-rearing was a clearcut proposition: simply Raise Them Right. Minimal TV, no hooker-type dolls or plastic Uzis, and a constant flow of high-fibre ideas from the morally evolved parent to the vulnerable, blank-slate child. I felt sorry for parents who didn't have the gumption to stick to this plan. Then I had a son, and the rest is —well, not so much history as culture.

2   Not since the days of Spock have we had so much parental advice in the air—how to raise kids, how to ruin them, how to "juggle work and family." This is why it's so refreshing to read someone like Alice Miller, the psychoanalyst-turned-writer whose books explore the childhood roots of violence and creativity. She doesn't have a theory about raising kids. In fact, she argues that *any* system of moral values imposed on children is potentially damaging,

because too often the rules are there to serve the emotional needs of the parents, not the children. In the name of morality, we try to keep the unruly passions of children—not to mention memories of our own childhood—safe, tidy, and under control. Most pedagogy, good or bad, sends a hidden message to the child: "Your desires and feelings are not good enough. Feel this, think that, instead." If children require so much correction, then deep down—so they reason—they must be bad. Sooner or later the child who only hears this message learns to assemble an other-pleasing, false self around a core of inexplicable shame.

This doesn't mean that Miller thinks children ought to finger-   3
paint with their food and otherwise disport themselves as gods. Post-Spockian permissiveness is just another form of pedagogy, really. But the experience of her own patients convinced her that it was the ones who were raised rigidly, with an overabundance of "good values," who were most likely to grow into benumbed adults, lost to themselves and predisposed to violence. The violence erupts in response to long-stifled childhood anger, which began as a perfectly human response to a voice that said "Don't be who you are, be good." The moral here—if we dare draw one—is that excessive handwringing about the values we are giving our kids may be as much about peer vanity as anything else. Values are not external; they are intrinsic to the sort of relationship we have with our children, arising out of the ordinary, humdrum way a family works and plays. The boy or girl who receives fair treatment, as opposed to "moral" correction, quickly develops an exquisite sense of justice —one that is more likely to shame the parent, rather than the other way round. (I'm moralizing here, of course.) Even young children bring a surprising amount of savvy and shit-detection to the moral bargaining table. To assume otherwise is to inflate our roles as parents into the architects and owners of our children's souls.

Now, Miller was talking about some fairly rigid, loveless house-   4
holds—Hitler's and Goebbels', for instance. She wasn't necessarily addressing the problem of whether or not to buy your son a Nintendo, or to give your niece a Wet 'n' Wild Barbie. Nevertheless, I detect a lot of dubious pedagogy in our much-cogitated attitudes towards "good" and "bad" toys.

I know what happened with toy guns in our household. I went   5
from a serene pre-child conviction that guns would never cross our threshold to the ridiculous but amiable compromise my seven-year-old son and I have reached. Childish logic is impeccable. If you give him an innocent green water pistol for the bathtub, then why not the hideous toy M-16 in the backyard? If he can brandish a popsicle stick, why not a space laser? So he now owns a bow and arrow and a noncombat rawhide whip (history? art?), but he knows I have a

"thing" about realistic guns, so he doesn't ask for them. He watches plenty of TV (all right, too much), but after flat-out indoctrination on my part—moral interference in the name of what I can or cannot stand to overhear—he now flips past the more violent kids' shows, of his own volition. Of course, our definitions of "violent" are continually being refined. But he's kind by nature, and always has been. I try not to improve on that too much.

6   There was a time, not so long ago, that Barbie dolls were considered the worst sort of sex-stereotype propaganda. Barbie, with her foot permanently arched in the shape of a high heel, her long, scissoring legs, her high, hard, de-nippled breasts. It's true she's unswervingly represented a career gadfly, a weak-chinned Caucasian princess and a fashion flibbertigibbet—$11\frac{1}{2}$ inches of beige plastic that has been accused of encouraging eating disorders, mindless consumerism and low self-esteem in little girls. Small wonder that to the Birkenstock generation, Barbie was bad.

7   But little girls are not pushovers. They know what they like and they like Barbie. Now 31 years old (but ever ageless and firm of chin), Barbie has triumphed over pedagogy, to the tune of over $500-million annually. Last year was the biggest year for Barbie sales in history. Some 98 percent of Canadian girls aged four to ten have a Barbie—or four—in their bedrooms. Like Coca-Cola, she has insinuated her hourglass, bottle-shaped self into 67 countries around the world. None of this will surprise parents with daughters, but it was news to me.

8   I went into several department stores to get a blast of Barbie, a feel for Barbie, and there she was—row upon row of her and her almost identical pals, including li'l sister Skipper, brown-skinned Christie, freckle-faced sporty Midge, Hispanic Nia, red-haired vixen Ashley. Her countless outfits run the gamut from the tiny tubes of her pantyhose to wild salsa dresses, purses that turn into skirts and skirts that turn into hair bows. Her eminently loseable accessories include teacups, toe paint, Ferraris, guitars and running shoes.

9   After twenty years of feminism, you may ask, why don't little boys play with Barbies? What *is* it about girls and dolls, anyway? Boys play with He-men and Ninja turtle figures but the marriage between girls and their Barbies seems more enduring. Girls' sense of pink and blueness also seems more acute, more precocious, although I base this only on the fact that I bought my son some plain but *purplish* boots last year. They didn't bother him until he came home from school one day and announced he couldn't wear them because they were "girls' boots." Who had decreed this? "The girls in my room."

10   Are girls more proprietorial about identifiable girl things because they've already detected an imbalance in the adult world,

between boy toys (tanks and guns) and female fun? Or is it something simpler—that at a certain age, children want some kind of sex identity. Just because adults have bequeathed them a culture that offers only testosterone-poisoned orange He-men and anorexic beige Barbies, must we insist on snuffing out any sign of gender?

An eight-year-old girl in the neighborhood lugged over her five Barbies, in two pink vehicles, for my inspection. While twirling and braiding the long blonde tresses on one of them, she explained that although she doesn't want to *be* Barbie, she really likes to play with her. "We make up stories that are like real life and then we make the Barbies act them out," she said with admirable succinctness. "Her body isn't very realistic," she admits, pointing the ballistic bosom of one towards me. "In fact, the only realistic thing about it is her ears." If she were designing them, she would go for more variation. "Like, it would be neat to have a tattooed Barbie, or one with a bigger head. Her head is too small for her body." And Ken's definitely in a rut. "I wouldn't mind a bald Ken, for example."

The sad truth is, Barbie has left the bland, rug-haired Ken behind in a spangled cloud of dust. Ken sales only amount to 35 percent of their combined total—and in fact, his shelf presence suggests more like a ratio of ten Barbies to one Ken. Ken is looking more and more like a rented gigolo, or the guy who takes Barbie's outfits to the cleaners and back. His accessories are laughable (a slice of pizza, a kite, a basketball) and his weekend outfits are a bore (blue pin-striped smock and navy pants). The only thing you can do with him, apart from suicidal dives off the couch, is change his hair color from a terrible fecal-mustard color to an obviously touched-up brown. While Barbie has a choice of five stylish wedding gowns, Ken's lone wedding tuxedo is deplorable, a nylon unitard with an ill-fitting white jacket and a shiny bow tie. His loafers are interchangeable little boats. No wonder Barbie seems to prefer the company of her on-the-go girlfriends.

When I saw Ken strapped stiffly into the passenger seat of Barbie's huge new pink RV trailer, with plates that say "Barbie," I felt a stab of compassion for him. As I was gazing at this harsh spectacle, a couple wandered down the aisle. "Oh there's Ken," said the woman. "We were always so mean to Ken with our Barbies, we used to do terrible things to him. I don't know why." Laughing, they moved down the aisle to inspect a Baby Uh-Oh ("Give her a drink and uh-oh! . . . time to change her diaper!").

However retrograde she appears to be, I sense Barbie is a survivor. Her maddeningly firm little bosom and fashion-victim personality, her fickle careers are all voodoo tricks to ward off parental approval. If we had given Barbie a social conscience and sensible shoes, she might have moldered away at the bottom of the toy bin.

As it is, girls play with their uneducational Barbies as they always have, playing out the "mean babysitter" scenario, madly acting away, with no parent-pleasing values to inhibit their stories. Therapists may envy the Barbie blankness—she too can create a private, privileged space where any and every feeling is permitted. May Barbie be "bad" as long as she reigns, for it is her lack of redeeming social value that helps keep her true to the child's sense of play, instead of the parents' worst fears.

> [blank box]

Vocabulary

a. *paragraph 2:* pedagogy
b. *paragraph 3:* disport
c. *paragraph 4:* cogitated
d. *paragraph 5:* impeccable, indoctrination, volition
e. *paragraph 6:* gadfly, flibbertigibbet
f. *paragraph 7:* insinuated
g. *paragraph 8:* vixen, gamut
h. *paragraph 9:* precocious
i. *paragraph 10:* proprietorial, testosterone
j. *paragraph 11:* ballistic
k. *paragraph 12:* gigolo, unitard
l. *paragraph 14:* retrograde

Questions

1. What does the essay tell us about Jackson and her attitude toward sexism?
2. How does her reference to her son in paragraph 5 contribute to our impression of her?
3. What purpose is served by the bemused tone and the other humorous elements of the essay?
4. Why in paragraphs 12 and 13 does Jackson underscore the contrast between the uses of Ken and Barbie?
5. In the concluding paragraph, what basic premises or assumptions about the needs of young girls emerge? How does Jackson use these premises to summarize her argument?

Writing Assignments

1. Think of ways in which Barbie may have had a more negative influence than Jackson allows. Write an essay from a stronger feminist perspective that attempts to refute Jackson's claims.
2. Write an essay like Jackson's on the influence of guns in the lives of young boys.

> [blank box]

T.C. (TOMMY) DOUGLAS

As premier of Saskatchewan from 1944 to 1961, T.C. (Tommy) Douglas (1904–1986) was the leader of the first socialist government elected in North America. As national leader of the New Democratic Party, he made democratic socialism an important part of Canadian political life, arguing successfully for such programs as Medicare and a comprehensive pension plan. He fervently believed in the power of political action to alleviate suffering, and throughout his political life he made the underprivileged and the exploited his constituency. In the following speech to the House of Commons during a debate on capital punishment, he eloquently makes the case for abolition of the death penalty.

Capital Punishment

T.C. (TOMMY) DOUGLAS

There are times, Mr. Speaker, when the 1 House of Commons rises to heights of grandeur and becomes deeply conscious of its great traditions. I think this debate has been one of those rare occasions. There has been a minimum of rancour and there has been no imputation of motives because I think that the abolitionists and retentionists alike have been sincerely searching their consciences to see if we can honestly resolve a moral problem. This problem is, how can we abolish a brutal punishment without endangering the safety of society?

I am in favour of the motion to abolish capital punishment and 2 I am also supporting the amendment to put it on a five-year trial basis. I doubt that there is much new that can be said in this debate. The entire field has been well covered but I should like to put very briefly four reasons for my opposition to capital punishment. The first is that capital punishment is contrary to the highest concepts of the Judaic–Christian ethic. I do not propose to go into theological arguments, but both in this debate and in the discussions which have taken place outside the House many people have been quoting Scripture in support of retaining the death penalty.

It is always a dangerous practice to quote isolated passages of 3 Scripture. The Bible has been quoted in times past to support slavery, child labour, polygamy, the burning of witches, and subservience to dictators. The Scriptures have to be viewed as a whole. The Bible is not one book; it is many books. It does not have a static concept. It represents man's emerging moral concepts as they have grown through the centuries.

4   It is true that the Mosaic law provided the death penalty for murder. It is equally true, if one looks particularly at the 20th chapter of the book of Leviticus, that the Mosaic law provided the death penalty for 33 crimes, including such things as adultery, bestiality, homosexuality, witchcraft and sacrificing to other gods than Jehovah. It seems to me that those who want to pick out isolated texts from the Bible in support of retaining the death penalty for murder have to be equally consistent and ask that the death penalty be retained for all the other crimes listed in the Mosaic law.

5   Of course, those who take this position overlook several facts. They overlook, first of all, the fact that the Mosaic law was an advanced law for the primitive times in which it was formulated. It was later succeeded by the Hebrew prophets who introduced the idea of justice superseded by mercy, the possible redemption and reestablishment of the individual. They overlook the fact that if any nation in the world ought to feel itself bound by Mosaic law it should be the state of Israel. The state of Israel abolished the death penalty many years ago except for Nazi war criminals and for treason committed in times of war. The religious hierarchy of the state of Israel enthusiastically supported the Knesset in abolishing the death penalty in that country.

6   But for those of us who belong to the Christian religion it seems to me we have to remember also that the Christian religion went far beyond the Mosaic law. In the days of the founder of Christianity the Mosaic law still obtained. This law decreed that a woman taken in adultery could be stoned to death. We should remember the statement of Jesus of Nazareth, when he came upon a group of people preparing to stone such a woman to death. He said, "Let him who is without sin among you cast the first stone."

7   When the crowd had dwindled away so that only the woman was left he said to the woman, "Go and sin no more." It seems to me that this is the ultimate culmination of the Christian concept of the application of mercy and the possible redemption of the individual.

8   My second reason for opposing capital punishment is that I believe capital punishment brutalizes the society that uses it without providing any effective deterrent that cannot be provided equally well by life imprisonment. I believe that any society that practises capital punishment brutalizes itself. It has an effect upon that society and I do not believe that society can rid itself of murderers by itself becoming a murderer. Surely if brutality would deter the committing of a crime Great Britain should have been a place of law-abiding citizens because a little over 150 years ago there were over 200 crimes for which an individual could be put to death. Instead of making Britain a nation of law-abiders it was a country where crime abounded, where human sensibilities were dulled by the public execution of

criminals. It is rather significant that in that day, as in this, it was often the juries who were more humane than the lawmakers. It was only because juries refused to convict, knowing the terrible punishment which would follow, that the lawmakers were forced 150 years ago to remove the death penalty from a great many of the crimes for which it had been prescribed.

All of the evidence which can be gathered seems to indicate that the death penalty is not a unique deterrent and that life imprisonment can be equally effective. . . .   9

I readily agree, Mr. Speaker, that quoting endless statistics is not going to prove either the case for abolition or the case for retention, but there certainly seems to be no convincing volume of evidence which would satisfy any unbiased individual that abolishing the death penalty has resulted in an upsurge of homicide or that those states which have retained the death penalty are any freer of capital crimes than those which have not.   10

After all, Mr. Speaker, who is it that the death penalty deters? It has certainly not deterred the man who commits murder. Will it deter him in the future? Surely he can be deterred in the future by being incarcerated for the remainder of his life. Who is deterred if this man is hanged? Is he to be hanged as an example to the rest of the community? I can conceive of nothing more immoral than to break a man's neck as an example to other people, but if that is the argument then surely, as the Leader of the Opposition [Mr. Diefenbaker] said yesterday, we ought to have public executions.   11

The hon. member for Winnipeg South Centre [Mr. Churchill] said that the fear of death will deter men. The fear of death will deter normal men but when a man commits murder, is he normal? Can we understand the motivation that causes a man to take a human life? When a man commits homicide, does he sit down and assess whether he is committing it in a state that has capital punishment or in a state that has abolished capital punishment? I think not. In the main the man who commits homicide is the man who is mentally ill; the man who kills does not make the common, rational judgments that are made by the average individual.   12

An individual who has become so mentally sick that he will take another life or ravage a child is certainly not a mentally healthy or normal individual.   13

The third reason I am opposed to capital punishment, Mr. Speaker, is that I believe there are better ways to ensure the safety of society. I completely disagree with the hon. member for Winnipeg South Centre, who argued that we must be concerned about the safety of the public. When he asks which is the more important, the life of an innocent who may be killed or the life of a murderer, there is no doubt that the life of the innocent person is the more impor-   14 tant. But is the fact that we break a man's neck any guarantee that innocent people will not be hurt?

15   We are not suggesting removing the penalty. We are saying that the penalty which ought to be retained is one that will do the two things which are important. First of all, it must be a penalty which will remove the convicted person from human society as long as that person is likely to be a menace to the safety and well-being of his fellow-men. Second, that person should be given an opportunity to receive whatever psychiatric treatment and rehabilitation is possible in the light of his own particular circumstances.

16   What we have to decide is what we are trying to do, Mr. Speaker. Are we thinking purely of punishing somebody because they have done wrong? Are we thinking purely in punitive terms? Are we thinking purely in terms of vengeance or retribution? Or are we thinking of the two things I have mentioned, first, the safety of society by incarcerating the convicted murderer for life and, second, the possible rehabilitation and redemption of that individual? There is additionally the third great advantage that if society has made a mistake it is possible to rectify the mistake because justice is a human institution and like all human institutions it is liable to error.

17   I maintain that society has no right to take from a man something which it cannot restore to him. If society makes a mistake and confines a man to prison, depriving him of his freedom, when that mistake is found out society can at least restore to him his freedom and provide him with some compensation for the years he has been incarcerated. But if we hang a man and then find that a mistake has been made there is nothing at all which can be done to make amends.

18   My quarrel with the death penalty is that it is purely a negative attempt to promote the safety of society. We need to adopt positive measures to promote the safety of society. For instance, we need better law enforcement. In both Canada and the United States every year a great many unsolved crimes are committed. One of the best deterrents is for the criminal to know that if he does commit a crime he will be found out, that he will be incarcerated and put in a place where he can no longer be a menace to the community. We need quicker crime detection methods. For some types of crimes, particularly for those involving psychotics, there ought to be indeterminate sentences.

19   We all recall a case a few years ago in which a man sexually assaulted a child. He was sentenced to five years in jail. To my mind this was ridiculous because it was based purely on the punitive concept and not out of regard for the safety of the community. It was assumed that at five years less one day, when he was in jail,

he was a menace but at five years plus one day he was no longer a menace. Such an individual ought to be sentenced to be kept out of circulation until such time as a panel of judges, psychiatrists and social workers are as certain as a human person can be that the individual is no longer a menace to the safety of the community. I think that in many cases indeterminate sentences to keep out of circulation psychotics who are likely to commit crimes would be of great advantage. In the case I referred to the man got out of jail after five years. Within six months he had not only assaulted another child but had killed the child in the process. Had that individual been sentenced to an indeterminate sentence in the first instance he would not have committed this second heinous crime.

If we want genuine deterrents in this country we need a program of penal reform for the segregation of prisoners and for their rehabilitation so that young first offenders do not got to jail to take what is virtually a postgraduate course in crime.   20

Let us face the fact that when we talk about retaining capital punishment as a deterrent we are really trying to take the easy way out from solving our problems. In the long run society often gets the criminals it deserves.   21

Why do we have criminals? What is wrong with the society that produces criminals? Some years ago when I was attending Chicago University I remember that every newspaper in the United States had a heading, "Where Is Crawley?" Crawley was a young gunman who was being hunted across the United States for a series of murders.   22

A very great columnist in the United States wrote a column which he headed, "Why Is Crawley?" He said that the people of the United States, instead of asking "Where Is Crawley?", ought to take a little time out to ask "Why Is Crawley?" The columnist went over his history. He came from a broken home which the father had deserted and where the mother was out working all day. The boy lived on the streets. He was part of a gang of hoodlums. He was sent to a reformatory and then was back on the streets. He was without proper education and without any counseling. He was sent to jail and associated with hardened criminals. He came out of jail twice as tough as when he went in. By 19 he was a hardened criminal. By the time he was 21 he was a killer. He was finally shot down by the police who were trying to capture him.   23

I suppose one of the most lamentable murders in our time has been the killing of President John F. Kennedy. Yet, when one reads the story of the man who is believed to have been responsible for his death, we find that when Lee Oswald was a boy in school he was recommended to undergo psychiatric treatment because of the dangerous psychotic tendencies he then displayed. But there were   24 not enough psychiatrists to look after all the children in that particular part of New York City and this boy was not treated. This boy grew up with his psychotic tendencies expanding, and he is believed to have been responsible for extinguishing one of the brightest lights of our generation.

25   If we really want to tackle the problem of eliminating crime, we must tackle the problem of the slums which breed crime and we must tackle the problem of the lack of psychiatric clinics to take care of psychotics and persons who may become criminally dangerous. We need the kind of penal reform that will make possible the rehabilitation of first offenders with proper probation and parole. We need to go the roots of the cause of crime and to ask ourselves what it is that produces the murderer in society. . . .

26   My final point is that I am opposed to capital punishment because I believe that the measure of a nation is the manner in which it treats its misfits and its offenders. Capital punishment has already been abolished in most of the advanced nations of the Western world. The abolition of capital punishment has come to be taken as the hallmark of a nation's conscience. I want to see Canada take this great forward step, and I want to make a special appeal to the members of the House to consider how important for Canada and for its future will be the vote we shall take tonight.

27   I should not want to be in the shoes of the Prime Minister and the members of his cabinet who have to face up to this very difficult problem. Nobody has been hanged in Canada since 1962. If the motion tonight is defeated the government is going to be in an awkward position. Either it will have to commute those sentenced to death to life imprisonment, knowing that the House of Commons has just rejected a motion suggesting the abolition of the death penalty, or it will have to take the defeat of the motion as an expression of opinion and allow the death sentences to be carried out.

28   I urge the members of the House to consider the predicament which faces the Prime Minister and the cabinet. I want to urge the House to give a five-year trial to the abolition of the death penalty. If the fears that have been expressed prove to be warranted, if there is an upsurge in the rate of homicide, if we are faced with an increase in crime rate, then in five years the members of the House of Commons who are here then can allow the death penalty to become effective again simply by taking no action. But I would urge that we give this a chance, that we step into line with the progressive countries of the world which have already abolished the death penalty.

29   What I plead for is that we pass this resolution tonight, with the amendment, which will declare in principle that the House is in favour of abolishing capital punishment and replacement with life

imprisonment. If we do that then I believe the House of Commons will have won a great victory, not a victory that will be accompanied by the blaring of trumpets or the rolling of drums but a victory in that we will have taken a forward, moral step and left behind one of the last relics of barbarianism. We will be moving forward to a more humane approach in dealing with crime.

Vocabulary

a. *paragraph 1:* rancour
b. *paragraph 2:* Judaic–Christian, theological
c. *paragraph 3:* polygamy
d. *paragraph 4:* Mosaic law, bestiality, Jehovah
e. *paragraph 5:* superseded
f. *paragraph 7:* culmination
g. *paragraph 16:* punitive, incarcerating
h. *paragraph 19:* indeterminate
i. *paragraph 29:* barbarianism

Questions

1. Through what means does Douglas develop his argument—data, historical example, analogy, statistics? Or is his procedure primarily deductive?
2. What do Douglas's ideas about capital punishment, and his style in presenting them, reveal about his general view of human society?
3. Discuss the tone of Douglas's speech. What words does he use to convey it? How does the fact that it is a speech affect us?
4. Are there counter-arguments to each of the points Douglas raises? What are they?

Writing Assignment

Discuss your own attitude toward capital punishment. Try to re-create Douglas's eloquence by maintaining a clear sense of purpose and by addressing yourself to the plight of the human race itself.

GEORGE ORWELL

George Orwell (1903–1950) was the pseudonym of English novelist and essayist Eric Hugh Blair. Orwell was born in India, where his father was a customs official for the British colonial government. At the age of eight, he was sent to a school in England, and he later attended Eton on a scholarship.

Instead of attending Cambridge University, for which he had prepared, Orwell took a job with the Indian Imperial Police and, from 1922 to 1927, served in Burma. When he left the service, he returned to Europe, where he began his career as a journalist and novelist. The rise of totalitarianism in Europe led Orwell to write increasingly about its causes in essays such as the classic study of political language reprinted here, and in his most famous novels, *Animal Farm* and *Nineteen Eighty-Four.*

Politics and the English Language

GEORGE ORWELL

1   **M**ost people who bother with the matter at all would admit that the English language is in a bad way, but it is generally assumed that we cannot by conscious action do anything about it. Our civilization is decadent and our language—so the argument runs—must inevitably share in the general collapse. It follows that any struggle against the abuse of language is a sentimental archaism, like preferring candles to electric light or hansom cabs to airplanes. Underneath this lies the half-conscious belief that language is a natural growth and not an instrument which we shape for our own purposes.

2   Now, it is clear that the decline of a language must ultimately have political and economic causes: it is not due simply to the bad influence of this or that individual writer. But an effect can become a cause, reinforcing the original cause and producing the same effect in an intensified form, and so on indefinitely. A man may take to drink because he feels himself to be a failure, and then fail all the more completely because he drinks. It is rather the same thing that is happening to the English language: It becomes ugly and inaccurate because our thoughts are foolish, but the slovenliness of our language makes it easier for us to have foolish thoughts. The point is that the process is reversible. Modern English, especially written English, is full of bad habits which spread by imitation and which can be avoided if one is willing to take the necessary trouble. If one gets rid of these habits one can think more clearly, and to think clearly is a necessary first step toward political regeneration: so that the fight against bad English is not frivolous and is not the exclusive concern of professional writers. I will come back to this presently, and I hope that by that time the meaning of what I have

said here will have become clearer. Meanwhile, here are five specimens of the English language as it is now habitually written.

These five passages have not been picked out because they are
especially bad—I could have quoted far worse if I had chosen—but
because they illustrate various of the mental vices from which we
now suffer. They are a little below the average, but are fairly representative samples. I number them so that I can refer back to them
when necessary:

3

> 1. I am not, indeed, sure whether it is not true to say that
> the Milton who once seemed not unlike a seventeenth-cen-
> tury Shelley had not become, out of an experience ever
> more bitter in each year, more alien [*sic*] to the founder of
> that Jesuit sect which nothing could induce him to tolerate.
> (Professor Harold Laski, essay in *Freedom of Expression*)

> 2. Above all, we cannot play ducks and drakes with a native
> battery of idioms which prescribes such egregious colloca-
> tions of vocables as the Basic *put up with* for *tolerate* or *put at a
> loss* for *bewilder*. (Professor Lancelot Hogben, *Interglossa*)

> 3. On the one side we have the free personality: by definition
> it is not neurotic, for it has neither conflict nor dream. Its
> desires, such as they are, are transparent, for they are just
> what institutional approval keeps in the forefront of con-
> sciousness; another institutional pattern would alter their
> number and intensity; there is little in them that is natural,
> irreducible, or culturally dangerous. But *on the other side*, the
> social bond itself is nothing but the mutual reflection of these
> self-secure integrities. Recall the definition of love. Is not this
> the very picture of a small academic? Where is there a place
> in this hall of mirrors for either personality or fraternity?
> (Essay on psychology in *Politics* [New York])

> 4. All the "best people" from the gentlemen's clubs, and all
> the frantic fascist captains, united in common hatred of Social-
> ism and bestial horror of the rising tide of the mass revolu-
> tionary movement, have turned to acts of provocation, to foul
> incendiarism, to medieval legends of poisoned wells, to legal-
> ize their own destruction of proletarian organizations, and
> rouse the agitated petty-bourgeoisie to chauvinistic fervor on
> behalf of the fight against the revolutionary way out of the cri-
> sis. (Communist pamphlet)

> 5. If the new spirit *is* to be infused into this old country,
> there is one thorny and contentious reform which must be
> tackled, and that is the humanization and galvanization of
> the B.B.C. Timidity here will bespeak canker and atrophy of

the soul. The heart of Britain may be sound and of strong beat, for instance, but the British lion's roar at present is like that of Bottom in Shakespeare's *Midsummer Night's Dream*—as gentle as any sucking dove. A virile new Britain cannot continue indefinitely to be traduced in the eyes, or rather ears, of the world by the effete languors of Langham Place, brazenly masquerading as "standard English." When the Voice of Britain is heard at nine o'clock, better far and infinitely less ludicrous to hear aitches honestly dropped than the present priggish, inflated, inhibited, school-ma'amish arch braying of blameless bashful mewing maidens! (Letter in *Tribune*)

4   Each of these passages has faults of its own, but, quite apart from avoidable ugliness, two qualities are common to all of them. The first is staleness in imagery; the other is lack of precision. The writer either has a meaning and cannot express it, or he inadvertently says something else, or he is almost indifferent as to whether his words mean anything or not. This mixture of vagueness and sheer incompetence is the most marked characteristic of modern English prose, and especially of any kind of political writing. As soon as certain topics are raised, the concrete melts into the abstract and no one seems able to think in turns of speech that are not hackneyed: prose consists less and less of *words* chosen for the sake of their meaning, and more and more of *phrases* tacked together like the sections of a prefabricated henhouse. I list below, with notes and examples, various of the tricks by means of which the work of prose-construction is habitually dodged:

5   *Dying metaphors.* A newly invented metaphor assists thought by evoking a visual image, while on the other hand a metaphor which is technically "dead" (e.g., *iron resolution*) has in effect reverted to being an ordinary word and can generally be used without loss of vividness. But in between these two classes there is a huge dump of worn-out metaphors which have lost all evocative power and are merely used because they save people the trouble of inventing phrases for themselves. Examples are: *Ring the changes on, take up the cudgels for, toe the line, ride rough-shod over, stand shoulder to shoulder with, play into the hands of, no axe to grind, grist to the mill, fishing in troubled waters, rift within the lute, on the order of the day, Achilles' heel, swan song, hotbed.* Many of these are used without knowledge of their meaning (what is a "rift," for instance?), and incompatible metaphors are frequently mixed, a sure sign that the writer is not interested in what he is saying. Some metaphors now current have been twisted out of their original meaning without those who use them even being aware of the fact. For example, *toe to line*

is sometimes written *toe the line*. Another example is *the hammer and the anvil*, now always used with the implication that the anvil gets the worst of it. In real life it is always the anvil that breaks the hammer, never the other way about: a writer who stopped to think what he was saying would be aware of this, and would avoid perverting the original phrase.

Operators or *verbal false limbs*. These save the trouble of picking out appropriate verbs and nouns, and at the same time pad each sentence with extra syllables which give it an appearance of symmetry. Characteristic phrases are *render inoperative, militate against, make contact with, be subjected to, give rise to, give grounds for, have the effect of, play a leading part (role) in, make itself felt, take effect, exhibit a tendency to, serve the purpose of, etc., etc.* The keynote is the elimination of simple verbs. Instead of being a single word, such as *break, stop, spoil, mend, kill*, a verb becomes a *phrase*, made up of a noun or adjective tacked on to some general-purpose verb such as *prove, serve, form, play, render*. In addition, the passive voice is wherever possible used in preference to the active, and noun constructions are used instead of gerunds (*by examination of* instead of *by examining*). The range of verbs is further cut down by means of the *-ize* and *de-* formations, and the banal statements are given an appearance of profundity by means of the *not un-* formation. Simple conjunctions and prepositions are replaced by such phrases as *with respect to, having regard to, the fact that, by dint of, in view of, in the interests of, on the hypothesis that;* and the ends of sentences are saved from anticlimax by such resounding commonplaces as *greatly to be desired, cannot be left out of account, a development to be expected in the near future, deserving of serious consideration, brought to a satisfying conclusion*, and so on and so forth.

Pretentious diction. Words like *phenomenon, element, individual* (as noun), *objective, categorical, effective, virtual, basic, primary, promote, constitute, exhibit, exploit, utilize, eliminate, liquidate*, are used to dress up simple statements and give an air of scientific impartiality to biased judgments. Adjectives like *epoch-making, epic, historic, unforgettable, triumphant, age-old, inevitable, inexorable, veritable*, are used to dignify the sordid processes of international politics, while writing that aims at glorifying war usually takes on an archaic color, its characteristic words being: *realm, throne, chariot, mailed fist, trident, sword, shield, buckler, banner, jackboot, clarion*. Foreign words and expressions such as *cul de sac, ancien régime, deus ex machina, mutatis mutandis, status quo, Gleichschaltung, Weltanschauung*, are used to give an air of culture and elegance. Except for the useful abbreviations *i.e., e.g.*, and *etc.*, there is no real need for any of the hundreds of foreign phrases now current in English. Bad writers, and especially scientific, political, and sociological writers, are nearly always haunted by the notion that Latin or Greek words are grander than Saxon ones, and unnecessary words like *expedite, ameliorate, predict, extraneous, deracinated, clandestine, subaqueous*, and hundreds of others constantly gain ground from their Anglo–Saxon opposite numbers.* The jargon peculiar to Marxist writing (*hyena, hangman, cannibal, petty bourgeois, these gentry, lackey, flunkey, mad dog, White Guard*, etc.) consists largely of words and phrases translated from Russian, German, or French; but the normal way of coining a new word is to use a Latin or Greek root with the appropriate affix and, where necessary, the -ize formation. It is often easier to make up words of this kind (*deregionalize, impermissible, extramarital, nonfragmentary*, and so forth) than to think up the English words that will cover one's meaning. The result, in general, is an increase in slovenliness and vagueness.

8   *Meaningless words.* In certain kinds of writing, particularly in art criticism and literary criticism, it is normal to come across long passages which are almost completely lacking in meaning.† Words like *romantic, plastic, values, human, dead, sentimental, natural, vitality*, as used in art criticism, are strictly meaningless, in the sense that they not only do not point to any discoverable object, but are hardly ever expected to do so by the reader. When one critic writes, "The outstanding feature of Mr. X's work is its living quality," while another writes, "The immediately striking thing about Mr. X's work is its peculiar deadness," the reader accepts this as a simple difference of opinion. If words like *black* and *white* were involved, instead of the jargon words *dead* and *living*, he would see at once that language was being used in an improper way. Many political words are similarly abused. The word *Fascism* has now no meaning except in so far as it signifies "something not desirable." The words *democracy, socialism, freedom, patriotic, realistic, justice*, have each of them several different meanings which cannot be reconciled with one another. In the case of a word like *democracy*, not only is there no agreed defini-

---

*An interesting illustration of this is the way in which the English flower names which were in use till very recently are being ousted by Greek ones, *snapdragon* becoming *antirrhinum, forget-me-not* becoming *myosotis*, etc. It is hard to see any practical reason for this change of fashion: it is probably due to an instinctive turning away from the more homely word and a vague feeling that the Greek word is scientific.

†Example: "Comfort's catholicity of perception and image, strangely Whitmanesque in range, almost the opposite in aesthetic compulsion, continues to evoke that trembling atmospheric accumulative hinting at a cruel, an inexorably serene timelessness. . . . Wrey Gardiner scores by aiming at simple bull's-eyes with precision. Only they are not so simple, and through this contented sadness runs more than the surface bittersweet of resignation." (*Poetry Quarterly*.)

tion, but the attempt to make one is resisted from all sides. It is almost universally felt that when we call a country democratic we are praising it: consequently the defenders of every kind of régime claim that it is a democracy, and fear that they might have to stop using the word if it were tied down to any one meaning. Words of this kind are often used in a consciously dishonest way. That is, the person who uses them has his own private definition, but allows his hearer to think he means something quite different. Statements like *Marshal Pétain was a true patriot, The Soviet press is the freest in the world, The Catholic Church is opposed to persecution,* are almost always made with intent to deceive. Other words used in variable meanings, in most cases more or less dishonestly, are: *class, totalitarian, science, progressive, reactionary, bourgeois, equality.*

Now that I have made this catalogue of swindles and perver- 9 sions, let me give another example of the kind of writing that they lead to. This time it must of its nature be an imaginary one. I am going to translate a passage of good English into modern English of the worst sort. Here is a well-known verse from Ecclesiastes:

> I returned and saw under the sun, that the race is not to the swift, nor the battle to the strong, neither yet bread to the wise, nor yet riches to men of understanding, nor yet favour to men of skill; but time and chance happeneth to them all.

Here it is in modern English:

> Objective consideration of contemporary phenomena compels the conclusion that success or failure in competitive activities exhibits no tendency to be commensurate with innate capacity, but that a considerable element of the unpredictable must invariably be taken into account.

This is a parody, but not a very gross one. Exhibit (3), above, for 10 instance, contains several patches of the same kind of English. It will be seen that I have not made a full translation. The beginning and ending of the sentence follow the original meaning fairly closely, but in the middle the concrete illustrations—race, battle, bread—dissolve into the vague phrase "success or failure in competitive activities." This had to be so, because no modern writer of the kind I am discussing—no one capable of using phrases like "objective consideration of contemporary phenomena"—would ever tabulate his thoughts in that precise and detailed way. The whole tendency of modern prose is away from concreteness. Now analyze these two sentences a little more closely. The first contains forty-nine words but only sixty syllables, and all its words are those of everyday life. The second contains thirty-eight words of ninety syllables: eighteen of its words are from Latin roots, and one from Greek. The first sentence contains six vivid images, and only one phrase ("time and chance") that could be called vague. The second contains not a single fresh, arresting phrase, and in spite of its ninety syllables it gives only a shortened version of the meaning contained in the first. Yet without a doubt it is the second kind of sentence that is gaining ground in modern English. I do not want to exaggerate. This kind of writing is not yet universal, and outcrops of simplicity will occur here and there in the worst-written page. Still, if you or I were told to write a few lines on the uncertainty of human fortunes, we should probably come much nearer to my imaginary sentence than to the one from Ecclesiastes.

11   As I have tried to show, modern writing at its worst does not consist of picking out words for the sake of their meaning and inventing images in order to make the meaning clearer. It consists in gumming together long strips of words which have already been set in order by someone else, and making the results presentable by sheer humbug. The attraction of this way of writing is that it is easy. It is easier—even quicker, once you have the habit—to say *In my opinion it is not an unjustifiable assumption that* than to say *I think*. If you use ready-made phrases, you not only don't have to hunt about for words; you also don't have to bother with the rhythms of your sentences, since these phrases are generally so arranged as to be more or less euphonious. When you are composing in a hurry—when you are dictating to a stenographer, for instance, or making a public speech—it is natural to fall into a pretentious, Latinized style. Tags like *a consideration which we should do well to bear in mind* or *a conclusion to which all of us would readily assent* will save many a sentence from coming down with a bump. By using stale metaphors, similes, and idioms, you save much mental effort, at the cost of leaving your meaning vague, not only for your reader but for yourself. This is the significance of mixed metaphors. The sole aim of a metaphor is to call up a visual image. When these images clash—as in *The Fascist octopus has sung its swan song, the jackboot is thrown into the melting pot*—it can be taken as certain that the writer is not seeing a mental image of the objects he is naming; in other words he is not really thinking. Look again at the examples I gave at the beginning of this essay. Professor Laski (1) uses five negatives in fifty-three words. One of these is superfluous, making nonsense of the whole passage, and in addition there is the slip—*alien* for akin—making further nonsense, and several avoidable pieces of clumsiness which increase the general vagueness. Professor Hogben (2) plays ducks and drakes with a battery which is able to write prescriptions,

and, while disapproving of the everyday phrase *put up with*, is unwilling to look *egregious* up in the dictionary and see what it means; (3), if one takes an uncharitable attitude towards it, is simply meaningless: probably one could work out its intended meaning by reading the whole of the article in which it occurs. In (4), the writer knows more or less what he wants to say, but an accumulation of stale phrases chokes him like tea leaves blocking a sink. In (5), words and meaning have almost parted company. People who write in this manner usually have a general emotional meaning— they dislike one thing and want to express solidarity with another —but they are not interested in the detail of what they are saying. A scrupulous writer, in every sentence that he writes, will ask himself at least four questions, thus: What am I trying to say? What words will express it? What image or idiom will make it clearer? Is this image fresh enough to have an effect? And he will probably ask himself two more: Could I put it more shortly? Have I said anything that is avoidably ugly? But you are not obliged to go to all this trouble. You can shirk it by simply throwing your mind open and letting the ready-made phrases come crowding in. They will construct your sentences for you—even think your thoughts for you, to a certain extent—and at need they will perform the important service of partially concealing your meaning even from yourself. It is at this point that the special connection between politics and the debasement of language becomes clear.

In our time it is broadly true that political writing is bad writing. Where it is not true, it will generally be found that the writer is some kind of rebel, expressing his private opinions and not a "party line." Orthodoxy, of whatever color, seems to demand a lifeless, imitative style. The political dialects to be found in pamphlets, leading articles, manifestoes, White Papers and the speeches of undersecretaries do, of course, vary from party to party, but they are all alike in that one almost never finds in them a fresh, vivid, homemade turn of speech. When one watches some tired hack on the platform mechanically repeating the familiar phrases—*bestial atrocities, iron heel, bloodstained tyranny, free peoples of the world, stand shoulder to shoulder*—one often has a curious feeling that one is not watching a live human being but some kind of dummy: a feeling which suddenly becomes stronger at moments when the light catches the speaker's spectacles and turns them into blank discs which seem to have no eyes behind them. And this is not altogether fanciful. A speaker who uses that kind of phraseology has gone some distance toward turning himself into a machine. The appropriate noises are coming out of his larynx, but his brain is not involved as it would be if he were choosing his words for himself. If the speech he is making is one that he is accustomed to make

12

over and over again, he may be almost unconscious of what he is saying, as one is when one utters the responses in church. And this reduced state of consciousness, if not indispensable, is at any rate favorable to political conformity.

13   In our time, political speech and writing are largely the defense of the indefensible. Things like the continuance of British rule in India, the Russian purges and deportations, the dropping of the atom bombs on Japan, can indeed be defended, but only by arguments which are too brutal for most people to face, and which do not square with the professed aims of political parties. Thus political language has to consist largely of euphemism, question-begging and sheer cloudy vagueness. Defenseless villages are bombarded from the air, the inhabitants driven out into the countryside, the cattle machine-gunned, the huts set on fire with incendiary bullets: this is called *pacification*. Millions of peasants are robbed of their farms and sent trudging along the roads with no more than they can carry: this is called *transfer of population* or *rectification of frontiers*. People are imprisoned for years without trial, or shot in the back of the neck or sent to die of scurvy in Arctic lumber camps: this is called *elimination of unreliable elements*. Such phraseology is needed if one wants to name things without calling up mental pictures of them. Consider for instance some comfortable English professor defending Russian totalitarianism. He cannot say outright, "I believe in killing off your opponents when you can get good results by doing so." Probably, therefore, he will say something like this: "While freely conceding that the Soviet régime exhibits certain features which the humanitarian may be inclined to deplore, we must, I think, agree that a certain curtailment of the right to political opposition is an unavoidable concomitant of transitional periods, and that the rigors which the Russian people have been called upon to undergo have been amply justified in the sphere of concrete achievement."

14   The inflated style is itself a kind of euphemism. A mass of Latin words fall upon the facts like soft snow, blurring the outlines and covering up all the details. The great enemy of clear language is insincerity. When there is a gap between one's real and one's declared aims, one turns as it were instinctively to long words and exhausted idioms, like a cuttlefish squirting out ink. In our age there is no such thing as "keeping out of politics." All issues are political issues, and politics itself is a mass of lies, evasions, folly, hatred, and schizophrenia. When the general atmosphere is bad, language must suffer. I should expect to find—this is a guess which I have not sufficient knowledge to verify—that the German, Russian and Italian languages have all deteriorated in the last ten or fifteen years, as a result of dictatorship.

But if thought corrupts language, language can also corrupt thought. A bad usage can spread by tradition and imitation, even among people who should and do know better. The debased language that I have been discussing is in some ways very convenient. Phrases like *a not unjustifiable assumption, leaves much to be desired, would serve no good purpose, a consideration which we should do well to bear in mind*, are a continuous temptation, a packet of aspirins at one's elbow. Look back through this essay, and for certain you will find that I have again and again committed the very faults I am protesting against. By this morning's post I have received a pamphlet dealing with conditions in Germany. The author tells me that he "felt impelled" to write it. I open it at random, and here is almost the first sentence that I see: "[The Allies] have an opportunity not only of achieving a radical transformation of Germany's social and political structure in such a way as to avoid a nationalistic reaction in Germany itself, but at the same time of laying the foundations of a co-operative and unified Europe." You see, he "feels impelled" to write—feels, presumably, that he has something new to say—and yet his words, like cavalry horses answering the bugle, group themselves automatically into the familiar dreary pattern. This invasion of one's mind by ready-made phrases (*lay the foundations, achieve a radical transformation*) can only be prevented if one is constantly on guard against them, and every such phrase anaesthetizes a portion of one's brain. 15

I said earlier that the decadence of our language is probably curable. Those who deny this would argue, if they produced an argument at all, that language merely reflects existing social conditions, and that we cannot influence its development by any direct tinkering with words and constructions. So far as the general tone or spirit of a language goes, this may be true, but it is not true in detail. Silly words and expressions have often disappeared, not through any evolutionary process but owing to the conscious action of a minority. Two recent examples were *explore every avenue* and *leave no stone unturned*, which were killed by the jeers of a few journalists. There is a long list of flyblown metaphors which could similarly be got rid of if enough people would interest themselves in the job; and it should also be possible to laugh the *not un-* formation out of existence,* to reduce the amount of Latin and Greek in the average sentence, to drive out foreign phrases and strayed scientific words, and, in general, to make pretentiousness unfashionable. But all these are minor points. The defense of the English language implies more than this, and perhaps it is best to start by saying what it does *not* imply. 16

---

*One can cure oneself of the *not un-* formation by memorizing this sentence: *A not unblack dog was chasing a not unsmall rabbit across a not ungreen field.*

17   To begin with it has nothing to do with archaism, with the salvaging of obsolete words and turns of speech, or with the setting up of a "standard English" which must never be departed from. On the contrary, it is especially concerned with the scrapping of every word or idiom which has outworn its usefulness. It has nothing to do with correct grammar and syntax, which are of no importance so long as one makes one's meaning clear, or with the avoidance of Americanisms, or with having what is called a "good prose style." On the other hand it is not concerned with fake simplicity and the attempt to make written English colloquial. Nor does it even imply in every case preferring the Saxon word to the Latin one, though it does imply using the fewest and shortest words that will cover one's meaning. What is above all needed is to let the meaning choose the word, and not the other way about. In prose, the worst thing one can do with words is to surrender to them. When you think of a concrete object, you think wordlessly, and then, if you want to describe the thing you have been visualizing you probably hunt about till you find the exact words that seem to fit it. When you think of something abstract you are more inclined to use words from the start, and unless you make a conscious effort to prevent it, the existing dialect will come rushing in and do the job for you, at the expense of blurring or even changing your meaning. Probably it is better to put off using words as long as possible and get one's meaning as clear as one can through pictures or sensations. Afterward one can choose — not simply *accept* — the phrases that will best cover the meaning, and then switch round and decide what impression one's words are likely to make on another person. This last effort of the mind cuts out all stale or mixed images, all prefabricated phrases, needless repetitions, and humbug and vagueness generally. But one can often be in doubt about the effect of a word or a phrase, and one needs rules that one can rely on when instinct fails. I think the following rules will cover most cases:

1. Never use a metaphor, simile, or other figure of speech which you are used to seeing in print.
2. Never use a long word where a short one will do.
3. If it is possible to cut a word out, always cut it out.
4. Never use the passive where you can use the active.
5. Never use a foreign phrase, a scientific word, or a jargon word if you can think of an everyday English equivalent.
6. Break any of these rules sooner than say anything outright barbarous.

These rules sound elementary, and so they are, but they demand a deep change of attitude in anyone who has grown used to writing in the style now fashionable. One could keep all of them and still write bad English, but one could not write the kind of stuff that I quoted in those five specimens at the beginning of this article.

I have not here been considering the literary use of language, 18 but merely language as an instrument for expressing and not for concealing or preventing thought. Stuart Chase and others have come near to claiming that all abstract words are meaningless, and have used this as a pretext for advocating a kind of political quietism. Since you don't know what Fascism is, how can you struggle against Fascism? One need not swallow such absurdities as this, but one ought to recognize that the present political chaos is connected with the decay of language, and that one can probably bring about some improvement by starting at the verbal end. If you simplify your English, you are freed from the worst follies of orthodoxy. You cannot speak any of the necessary dialects, and when you make a stupid remark its stupidity will be obvious, even to yourself. Political language—and with variations this is true of all political parties, from Conservatives to Anarchists—is designed to make lies sound truthful and murder respectable, and to give an appearance of solidity to pure wind. One cannot change this all in a moment, but one can at least change one's own habits, and from time to time one can even, if one jeers loudly enough, send some worn-out and useless phrase—some *jackboot, Achilles' heel, hotbed, melting pot, acid test, veritable inferno*, or other lump of verbal refuse —into the dustbin where it belongs.

Vocabulary

a. *paragraph 1:* decadent, archaism, hansom cabs
b. *paragraph 3:* ducks and drakes, idioms, egregious, collocations, vocables, integrities, humanization, galvanization, canker, atrophy, virile, effete, languors, brazenly, mewing
c. *paragraph 5:* evocative, perverting
d. *paragraph 6:* symmetry, keynote, banal
e. *paragraph 7:* categorical, virtual, inexorable, expedite, ameliorate, extraneous, deracinated, clandestine, subaqueous, Anglo–Saxon, jargon, slovenliness
f. *paragraph 8:* totalitarian, reactionary, bourgeois
g. *paragraph 9:* commensurate
h. *paragraph 10:* parody
i. *paragraph 11:* humbug, euphonious, superfluous, scrupulous, debasement
j. *paragraph 12:* orthodoxy, phraseology
k. *paragraph 13:* euphemism, pacification, rectification
l. *paragraph 14:* inflated, cuttlefish, schizophrenia

m. *paragraph 15:* anaesthetizes

n. *paragraph 17:* Americanisms, colloquial, dialect

o. *paragraph 18:* quietism

Questions

1. Do the examples Orwell cites constitute sufficient evidence to prove his contention of a link between language and politics?
2. Compare the passage from Ecclesiastes quoted in paragraph 9 (King James Version) with modern renderings of it. Do you think these modern renderings are superior to Orwell's parody or to the King James Version? Why?
3. "If you or I were to write a few lines on the uncertainty of human fortunes," why would the writing come nearer to Orwell's parody than to the sentence from Ecclesiastes?
4. Given the assumptions Orwell makes in the whole essay, why are all issues "political issues"?
5. Orwell says in paragraph 17 that his concern has not been to promote a "standard English" or "to make written English colloquial." Explain what he means here. Has he not recommended the use of plain English words? What exceptions would he allow?
6. Is Orwell guilty anywhere of the kind of lazy thinking that makes writers reach for the handy cliché?

Writing Assignment

Have recent political developments borne out Orwell's argument about the links between tyranny and debased language? Write an essay updating his evidence (some clichés, for instance, date quickly) and draw your own conclusions.

3

Matters of Style

Introduction

None of us speaks or writes in the same way on all occasions: the differences depend on how formal the occasion is. A letter of application for a job will be more formal than a letter to a friend; a graduation speech will sound different from a locker-room conversation.

Each of us has a formal and informal language and, whether we know it or not, standards for judging their effectiveness. These standards come from the different groups we belong to—each group with its special idioms and vocabulary. Teenagers share a common language, which sometimes they have to translate for their parents; teenagers of a particular racial or ethnic background share a special dialect or language. So do teenagers of a particular city or region of the country. Though teenagers in Vancouver share expressions and idioms with all other teenagers in the city, they may share a special dialect with their families and with their friends. At school they may share a language with their teachers that is different from the dialect they speak at home. Even a family may have its own private language—special words and expressions to describe acts and feelings.

Cutting across these differences is a standardized English we hear on television and read in newspapers—a language sometimes less colourful and personal than these other languages, but serving as a medium for communication among diverse groups of people, not only in Canada but in other English-speaking countries. This standard has developed over a long period of time, and it changes less than the informal language and slang of particular groups. This standard, represented in the readings in this book, falls between two extremes—one formal and abstract in its content and sentences, the other informal and concrete:

[*Formal*] Of the influences that shape men's actions, none is more powerful than the images we carry in our heads. Every subject is apt to invoke in our minds a specific image, made up of concrete information, misinformation, folklore, desire and prejudice. Thus, how people see themselves as a nation determines to a large extent how they will respond to any new challenge. The roles we play in our family life, particularly with respect to our children, depend greatly on what roles we assign ourselves in the society around us. (Gerald Holton, "The False Images of Science")

[*Informal*] As I stopped for a moment outside a love shop, where the red satin lips dangling in the window had a "Going Out of Business" sign pinned to them, the full horror of the situation dawned on me. The sensual thrill of erotica had been all but eclipsed by the new mangiamania.

Well, damn it all, I thought. The old libidinous order can't be allowed to just pass away. Not while there's breath in this oh-so-willing body. I squared my shoulders and, turning my back forever on lettuce driers, marched bravely into the love shop.

L'Amour français was the promising title of the video cassette I selected and carried home with me in the deepening dusk.

Ah, what a treat. Curled up in bed with a lushly smutty movie, devouring lustful images more eagerly than champagne truffles from Fauchon . . . (Erika Ritter, "Mangiamania")

The abstract ideas of Holton could be stated less formally. But usage is a matter of convention and occasion as well as of personal choice, and if we would not be surprised to find his ideas stated informally, we probably would be surprised to find the rental of a pornographic movie described in formal language.

As a rule, informal writing is closer to the patterns of everyday speech; formal writing seems impersonal if it departs widely from these patterns. Much standard writing today has both formal and informal features: we find colloquialisms (*grabs a half-pound of beef, slaps it onto*) in company with abstract or less familiar words (*envision*). We also find striking balance and antithesis—a feature of formal sentences—in company with looser, more familiar phrasing and expressions:

What I would like to know is: how should I feel about the earth, these days? Where has all the old nature gone? What became of the wild, writhing, unapproachable mass of the life of the world, and what happened to our old, panicky excitement about it? Just in fifty years, since I was a small boy in a suburban town, the world has become a structure of steel and plastic, intelligible and diminished. (Lewis Thomas, "A Trip Abroad")

Tone

By the tone of a piece of writing, we mean the reflection of the writer's attitude toward the subject or reader. The possibilities are many: a piece of writing may be sarcastic, bitter, angry, mocking, whimsical, facetious, joyful, admiring, or indifferent. And we can reveal this attitude in numerous ways—most commonly by stating it directly:

> There should be more sympathy for school children. The idea that they are happy is of a piece with the idea that the lobster in the pot is happy. (H.L. Mencken, "Travail")

Or we can express our attitude indirectly—perhaps by exaggerating, sometimes to the point of absurdity, for a humorous or satirical effect, as in this parody of a soul-searching journal entry:

> I am plagued by doubts. What if everything is an illusion and nothing exists? In that case, I definitely overpaid for my carpet. If only God would give me some clear sign! Like making a large deposit in my name at a Swiss bank. (Woody Allen, *The Allen Notebooks*)

Or we can write sarcastically with a militant irony that tells the reader more directly what we mean:

> Exam from 8:00 A.M. to 10:30. About 150 students— unwashed, unshaven young males and reasonably well-groomed young females. A general sense of tedium and disaster. Half-past eight. Little coughs, the clearing of nervous throats, coming in clusters of sound, rustling of pages. Some of the martyrs plunged in meditation, their arms locked behind their heads. I meet a dull gaze directed at me, seeing in me with hope and hate the source of forbidden knowledge. . . . The great fraternity of C-minus, backbone of the nation, steadily scribbling on. (Vladimir Nabokov, "The Exam Room")

Irony arises from an obvious discrepancy between what we show and what we say. A common form of irony is understatement:

> I was born at Swanmoor, Hants, England, on December 30, 1869. I am not aware that there was any particular conjunction of the planets at the time, but should think it extremely likely.

> My parents migrated to Canada in 1876, and I decided to go
> with them. (Stephen Leacock, *Sunshine Sketches of a Little Town*)

Paradoxical statements also can be ironic:

> The only way to get rid of temptation is to yield to it.
> (Oscar Wilde, *The Picture of Dorian Gray*)

And so can statements that prepare us for one ending and then turn
around and surprise us with another:

> A little sincerity is a dangerous thing, and a great deal of it
> is absolutely fatal. (Oscar Wilde, *The Critic as Artist*)

As these examples suggest, the tone of a sentence, a paragraph, or
an essay is conveyed by the *voice* we try to express in writing. Voice
depends on the rhythms and nuances of speech, carried into the
modulations and rhythms of the sentences and paragraphs. False
starts in writing are often failures to discover the right voice or
tone. Too formal a sentence or choice of words may create the
impressions of distance or unconcern; a highly informal style may
suggest lack of seriousness or flippancy. Not surprisingly, we often
find as we write that we need to adjust the tone. An essay need not
express a single dominant tone, however: the expression of our attitude often changes as we turn to new ideas and details.

ARTHUR BLACK

Arthur Black is the host of the CBC weekly radio program "Basic Black,"
and a columnist who is syndicated throughout Canada. His first two
books, *Back to Black* and *That Old Black Magic*, were both shortlisted for the
Stephen Leacock Medal for humour. In the following essay, from *Arthur!*
Arthur! (1991), he displays his humour to fine effect in defence of onion-
eating and its consequences.

Take Your Breath Away

ARTHUR BLACK

This piece is an abject apology to all the   1
fans who were with me—briefly—down at the local arena last
Tuesday evening.

2   I understand why you abandoned me, left me to occupy the entire east wall of bleachers by myself while all of you huddled and crowded yourselves into the stands on the opposite side of the ice.

3   I'm not upset with your decision to shun me. I don't blame you a bit. No hard feelings.

4   It was the onions, wasn't it.

5   I knew it—knew it even when I was scarfing them down at dinner before the hockey game. But I couldn't stop myself.

6   Usually, I am a man of reasonable self-control. You could walk me through a boxcar full of cocaine and I wouldn't be tempted to sniff. I don't do heroin or hashish, absinthe or anabolic steroids. As for the number of times I've woken up in opium dens surrounded by geisha girls—I can count them on the fingers of one mitten.

7   I am not a frequenter of booze cans, gambling dens or the drawing rooms of houses of ill repute, but by cracky, show me a chive or a shallot and my lower lip begins to tremble. Wave a leek in my face and I whimper like a baby. Show me a Rubenesque Spanish seductively shucking its onion skins in slow motion and *eee-yaw!*—I turn into a ravening beast.

8   Yes, I'm an onion-luster. A harmless-enough mania, as addictions go—aside from the friendship fallout. People just don't take kindly to the thought of *tête-à-tête*-ing with someone whose breath can set fire to eyelashes and melt mascara. That's why my fellow hockey fans so enthusiastically vacated the entire east side of the arena last week. Considering the provocation (I'd eaten a fistful of green onions plus an order of garlic toast), I thought they handled themselves with poise and discretion, although I found the catcalls of "Beat it, flamethrower!" and "Hit the highway, laserbreath!" a tad overwrought. But I have to admit, if the tables were turned I'm not sure I'd want to get very chummy with a man who can singe cotton clothing and ignite paper articles by the simple act of exhalation.

9   Mind you, with a couple of Certs and a dollop of mouthwash I think I could mount a fairly spirited defence of the practice of onion eating. And I'd have plenty of evidence to back me up. Common sense, for starters. For centuries folk medicine practitioners around the world—from Confucius to my mother—have sworn by the efficacy of onions in warding off sniffles and sneezes. (Cynics don't dispute the cold-combating properties of onions; they say it's because no self-respecting virus could withstand the reek.)

10   And more good news—a study recently published in the *Journal of the National Cancer Institute* indicates that my favourite veggie can keep more than a bad case of sniffles at bay. The study, which was conducted by a joint team of U.S. and Chinese scientists, concluded that regular consumption of onions (and/or its elder cousin, garlic) significantly reduces the risk of stomach cancer. Previous

studies have shown that onion eating lowers the risk of heart disease, but the cancer link is something new.

How does the lowly onion accomplish all this? No one knows for sure, but scientists think it may be the presence of allyl sulphide. That's a chemical found in all allium vegetables—which is to say garlic, chives, leeks, shallots, scallions and garden-variety onions. In laboratory experiments, allyl sulphide has been very effective in inhibiting the growth of cancer cells.   11

But I don't eat onions because I'm a health nut. To tell you the truth, I think I'd eat 'em if they were as hazardous to your health as smoking cigarettes or sitting through a Michael Wilson speech.   12

I eat onions for two reasons: first, they taste great; second, I like to think they keep vampires away.   13

Okay . . . three reasons.   14

They always get me the best seat at hockey games.   15

Vocabulary

a. *paragraph 1:* abject
b. *paragraph 7:* shallot
c. *paragraph 9:* efficacy
d. *paragraph 11:* sulphide

Questions

1. How would you describe Black's tone?
2. What does Black gain by addressing the reader as "you"?
3. How would you describe the level of language used in the essay—formal, informal, colloquial, slang? What does the idiom contribute to the essay?
4. Is Black interested in anything besides entertaining us?

Writing Assignment

Imagine you are trapped in an elevator with other people. Create a dialogue that characterizes the speakers by conveying their respective reactions.

HARRY BRUCE

Harry Bruce was born in Toronto and educated at Mount Allison University and the London School of Economics. He began his career as a reporter for *The Ottawa Journal* in 1955. Since then he has worked as an editor, author, and free-lance journalist, and has contributed to the major Canadian magazines and newspapers. His books and articles have won a number of awards, including the Brascan Award for Culture. The selection that follows is from the title piece of his book *Each Moment As It Flies*.

The Softball Was Always Hard

HARRY BRUCE

1   **W**hen I tell young softball players I played the game bare-handed, they regard me warily. Am I one of those geezers who's forever jawing about the fact that, in his day, you had to walk through six miles of snowdrifts just to get to school? Will I tediously lament the passing of the standing broad jump, and the glorious old days when the only football in the Maritimes was English rugger, and when hockey was an outdoor art rather than indoor mayhem, and, at decent yacht clubs, men were gentlemen and women were *personae non grata*? No, but I will tell today's softball players that—with their fancy uniforms, batters' helmets, dugouts, manicured diamonds, guys to announce who's at bat over public-address systems and, above all, gloves for every fielder—the game they play is more tarted-up and sissy than the one I knew.

2   Softball bloomed in the Dirty Thirties because it was a game the most impoverished deadbeat could afford to play. For schools, it had the edge that soccer still has over North American football: it required no expensive equipment. It was the people's game in the worst of times. Unlike baseball, which calls for a field the size of a town, softball could flourish in one corner of a city park, on a vacant lot, in any schoolyard. The only gear you needed was a ball, a bat, a catcher's glove and mask, and a first baseman's glove, a floppy affair which I knew as a "trapper." Two amiable teams might even use the same gloves—two gloves for eighteen players.

3   In the Toronto gradeschool leagues of the Forties, gloves for all other players were outlawed. This meant that early in the season the hands of a boy shortstop felt as though a 300-lb. vice-principal had given him the strap. Any team that lasted long enough to reach the city finals, however, boasted little infielders with palms like saddle-leather. They learned to catch a line drive with both hands, not by snaring it with a glove big enough to hold a medicine ball. They cushioned the ball by drawing back their cupped hands at the split-second of impact. They fielded sizzling grounders by turning

sideways, dropping one knee to the ground, getting their whole bodies in front of the ball, then scooping it up, again with both small, bare hands.

A word about balls. The *New Columbia Encyclopedia* says, "Despite the name, the ball used is not soft," which may be the understatement of the tome's 3,052 pages. There were three kinds of softballs, and each was about as soft as anthracite. The best was simply a big baseball, with seams that were pretty well flush with the horsehide cover. Then there was a solid rubber ball with fake seams. After a while, this ball did soften up, but on grounds it no longer hurt enough for competition, it was then retired for use only in practice. Then there was the "outseam" ball. Perhaps it was not a sadist who invented it. Perhaps it was merely someone who sought durability in lean times. But the outseam was a quarter-inch ridge of leather so hard that, when you fielded a rifling, spinning grounder, the ball felt as though its real function was to rip the skin off your palms. The outseam ball was a character-builder.

We had no uniforms, but if you reached the city finals team sweaters might magically emerge from some secret cache in the school basement. Certain coaches had the stern theory that even these were bad news, that boys would be so captivated by their own spiffy appearance they'd lose that vital concentration on the game itself, and commit errors. Some boys played in the only shoes they owned, scampers or black oxfords. Others had beaten-up sneakers and, on most teams, some wore short pants and some long. But these youngsters, gangs of ragamuffins by today's standards of sartorial elegance in softball, played furiously competitive, heads-up ball.

If you played outside the school system, for a team sponsored by a camera shop, dairy, hardware store or greasy spoon, then you did get a sweater. You swaggered in it. You'd earned it. Not every kid was good enough to make a team with sweaters. They were advertisements of ability. Nowadays, of course, any kid with money can buy an Expos' jacket or a Pirates' cap. They're merely advertisements of disposable income, much like the $25 million worth of gear that the chains of athletic-shoe stores expected to sell in Canada during recession-ridden 1982.

But as a celebrator of softball austerity, I am a pipsqueak beside an eighty-year-old tycoon I know. As a boy in a Nova Scotia coal-mining town, he played cricket and street baseball with home-made bats and balls. To make a ball, boys hoarded string and wrapped it around a rock, or if they were lucky a small rubber ball. "We made very good balls," he said, "and we had just as much fun as kids have today with all their expensive stuff." In line with Canada's hoariest hockey tradition, he added, "We used a piece of frozen manure for a puck. It worked just about as good." It wasn't as durable as rubber, but in those days there was no shortage of horse poop.

8   I once played with a home-made baseball myself. Indeed, I placed the order for its construction. In the summer of '46, when I turned twelve, my father exiled me from Toronto to spend two months at the Bruce homestead on a Nova Scotian shore. That shore, even now, is as sleepy a spot as you're ever likely to find. Not even most Nova Scotians know where it is. But in 1946, the community was not merely remote, it was an anachronism. It hadn't changed much since Victoria had been queen, and to a kid from what he fancied as a bustling, modern metropolis, its empty beauty was at first desolating. This was the ultimate sticks, the boondocks with a vengeance, and I worked off my loneliness by playing catch with myself. Hour after hour, I hurled a Toronto tennis ball against a bluenose barn, catching it on the rebound.

9   Then I discovered potential ballplayers.

10   They lived on the farm next door. They were a big, cheerful family, and my knowing them then started my life-long love affair with the neighborhood. As things are unfolding now, I'll end up there for good. Anyway, several of these farm kids—the oldest was a gentle man of fifteen who, with one paralyzing hand, pinned me to a hayfield while I endured the sweet, excruciating humiliation of having his giggling, thirteen-year-old sister plant saliva on my face—were old enough to play a form of softball. Amazingly, however, they'd never played it, nor seen it. They'd never even heard the word.

11   I told the fifteen-year-old a softball bat was *this* long, and *this* thick at one end, and *this* thin at the other. He made one in half an hour. It wasn't exactly a Louisville Slugger but it had heft to it, and at the same time was light enough to enable the smaller kids to take a good cut at the ball. What ball? My tennis ball had split. When I knowledgeably declared that the heart of a real baseball was cork, the fifteen-year-old took me down to the stony shore to negotiate with a character I've preserved in memory as "the Ball-maker." He was a hermit who had just given up commercial fishing on his own. He would never again sail the small schooner he'd built, and she'd begun to rot where she lay, a few feet closer to Chedabucto Bay than the ramshackle hut where he somehow survived the seasons.

12   He was a "beach person," as surely as the salt-stunted spruce were beach trees, and therefore disreputable. If he had known women they had not been church-going women. He was thin, stooped, gnarled, and smelled as though he'd been embalmed in brine, rum, tar, tobacco juice, his own sweat and sinister doings. There was something wrong with one of his eyes and some of his fingers, and though he may only have been as old as I am now

(forty-eight), I thought he was ancient enough, and certainly evil enough, to have slit throats for Blackbeard.

The Ball-maker conversed with grunts, snarls, illogical silences, 13 and an accent so thick that, to me, it was a foreign language. But we struck a deal. He gave me a dime. If I would walk inland, following a brookside path through a forest of spruce and fir, and on past a sawmill to a general store, and if I would use the dime to buy him a plug of chewing tobacco, and, further, if I would then take the tobacco to him . . . well, he would meanwhile sculpt a baseball-sized sphere of cork. And he did. He fashioned it from three pieces: a thick, round disc and two polar caps, all jammed together with a single spike. The ball was so flawless it was spooky. I can still see it and feel it in my hand, a brown globe so perfect I wondered if the Ball-maker was a warlock.

Back at my friend's farm, we encased the cork in scratchy 14 manila twine till we had something bigger than a hardball but smaller than a softball. For bases, we dropped sweaters among the cowflaps in a pasture, and the lesson began. We would play the kind of teamless ball that's been known in a million schoolyards: as each batter went out, the fielders would all change positions to guarantee that every player got a crack at batting. As the ace from Toronto, I naturally led off. Trouble was, I adored the afternoon's first pitcher. It was she who'd kissed me in the hayfield.

She had hair like a blond waterfall, eyes like dark chocolate, 15 and skin I ached to touch and smell. Whenever we wrestled, she won. I still dislike that adult sneer, "puppy love." A boy of twelve can love a girl of thirteen with agonizing power. To make matters worse, he hasn't a hope in hell of even understanding the emotion that's racking his skinny being, much less satisfying it. All he knows is that she obsesses him, he yearns for her, he must always appear fine in her eyes.

She had never pitched in her life so it surprised me when she 16 tossed her waterfall in the sunlight and floated the ball gently into the strike zone. Her first pitch. It crept towards me, letter-high. It could have been hanging there in front of me on a string from the sky, and I stepped into it with all the style I'd learned from a hundred Toronto afternoons. Thwack! A line drive so fast no one saw it, and down she went. She crumbled in a heap of blouse, skirt, hair, and bare, beloved arms and legs. I had smacked her with the cursed, hairy ball square on her right eye. Her big brother got her sitting up, and we all huddled around her, with me bleating horrified apologies. She never cried. She managed a smile, got to her feet, and shakily went home.

When she turned up for our second game, she had the ugliest 17 black eye I have ever seen on a child. To me, it was a beauty mark.

She never blamed me for it. It became a bond, proof of a famous incident we'd shared. She was a tough, forgiving farm girl, and she and her brothers and sisters taught me something I'd not forget about the rough grace of the country folk down home. We played ball for weeks. We played till we pounded the ball to bits, till her eye was once more perfect, and summer was gone.

18   The car that drove me to the train station passed their farm. Sheets on the clothesline billowed in the usual south-westerly. With her brothers and sister, she was horsing around with their wolfish mutt. They stopped to watch the car moving along the dirt road, and then they all waved goodbye. I was glad they were too far away to see my face. I still lacked her control.

19   I have my own cabin on that shore now, and though most of those farmyard ballplayers of thirty-seven summers ago have moved away I still see one of them occasionally. He's a mere forty-six, and I like him now as I liked him then. Sometimes I walk along the gravel beach to a patch of grass, from which a footpath once led to a general store. The Ball-maker's shack is gone, but gray planks and ribs and rusty boat nails still endure the lashing of the salt wind that ceaselessly sweeps the bay. They're all that's left of his schooner. Wrecked by time, like bare-handed softball.

> ```
> 
> ```

Vocabulary

a. *paragraph 1:* geezers, rugger, mayhem
b. *paragraph 4:* anthracite, sadist
c. *paragraph 5:* spiffy, scampers, oxfords
d. *paragraph 8:* boondocks, bluenose
e. *paragraph 11:* ramshackle
f. *paragraph 12:* embalmed
g. *paragraph 13:* warlock
h. *paragraph 14:* cowflaps

Questions

1. To what extent does Bruce depend on colloquial or everyday spoken expressions in writing about softball?
2. How does he vary sentence length for effect? Is his writing loose in sentence construction, or is he writing at a general or formal level?
3. Is Bruce merely describing a pastime from his youth, or is he making a judgement about this world and developing a thesis?
4. Why does Bruce begin with a short history of softball? How does he signal the shift to a different aspect of his subject?
5. What technique does Bruce use in his conclusion? Does he effectively summarize the essay's central concerns? Does he avoid sentimentality?

Writing Assignment

Describe a restaurant through its appearance, the food it serves, and the speech of its employees and possibly its owner. Let your details express a judgement or make a point about the restaurant.

JONATHAN SWIFT

Jonathan Swift (1667–1745), the son of English Protestant parents, was born and educated in Ireland. In 1688 he went to England to seek a career in literature. Swift wrote satirical poems, essays, pamphlets, and tracts on the major issues of the day and became involved in many of its political and religious controversies. In 1713 he became Dean of St. Patrick's Cathedral in Dublin, and in the succeeding years wrote widely on various questions bearing on Ireland and England. His most famous satirical work, *Gulliver's Travels,* was published in 1726. Swift was deeply concerned about the sufferings that he had observed in his country from boyhood. Ireland, under the control of the British government, was an impoverished country—restricted in selling its goods and incapable of producing enough food to feed the population. Most of the poor were Catholic, a point that Swift emphasizes in his "modest proposal"—written in 1729 to suggest a remedy for the widespread starvation and misery of the country. Swift writes as a distinguished observer, anxious to perform a service to both the English and the Irish with his proposal. The persuasive means that Swift uses deserves the closest study.

A Modest Proposal

For Preventing the Children of Poor People in Ireland from being a Burden to their Parents or Country, and for Making Them Beneficial to the Public

JONATHAN SWIFT

It is a melancholy object to those who walk through this great town, or travel in the country, when they see the streets, the roads, and cabin-doors crowded with beggars of the female sex, followed by three, four, or six children, all in rags, and importuning every passenger for an alms. These mothers, instead of being able to work for their honest livelihood, are forced to employ all their time in strolling to beg sustenance for their helpless infants: who, as they grow up, either turn thieves for want of work, or leave their dear native country to fight for the Pretender in Spain, or sell themselves to the Barbadoes.

2   I think it is agreed by all parties, that this prodigious number of children in the arms, or on the backs, or at the heels of their mothers, and frequently of their fathers, is in the present deplorable state of the kingdom, a very great additional grievance; and, therefore, whoever could find out a fair, cheap, and easy method of making these children sound and useful members of the commonwealth, would deserve so well of the public, as to have his statue set up for a preserver of the nation.

3   But my intention is far from being confined to provide only for the children of professed beggars; it is of a much greater extent, and shall take in the whole number of infants at a certain age, who are born of parents in effect as little able to support them as those who demand our charity in the streets.

4   As to my own part, having turned my thoughts for many years upon this important subject, and maturely weighed the several schemes of other projectors, I have always found them grossly mistaken in their computation. It is true, a child, just dropped from its dam, may be supported by her milk for a solar year with little other nourishment; at most, not above the value of two shillings, which the mother may certainly get, or the value in scraps, by her lawful occupation of begging; and it is exactly at one year old that I propose to provide for them in such a manner, as, instead of being a charge upon their parents or the parish, or wanting food and raiment for the rest of their lives, they shall, on the contrary, contribute to the feeding, and partly to the clothing, of many thousands.

5   There is likewise another great advantage in my scheme, that it will prevent those voluntary abortions, and that horrid practice of women murdering their bastard children, alas, too frequent among us, sacrificing the poor innocent babes, I doubt more to avoid the expense than the shame, which would move tears and pity in the most savage and inhuman breast.

6   The number of souls in this kingdom being usually reckoned one million and a half, of these I calculate there may be about two hundred thousand couple whose wives are breeders; from which number I subtract thirty thousand couple, who are able to maintain their own children (although I apprehend there cannot be so many, under the present distresses of the kingdom); but this being granted, there will remain an hundred and seventy thousand breeders. I again subtract fifty thousand for those women who miscarry, or whose children die by accident or disease within the year. There only remain a

hundred and twenty thousand children of poor parents annually born. The question therefore is how this number shall be reared and provided for? which, as I have already said, under the present situation of affairs, is utterly impossible by all the methods hitherto proposed. For we can neither employ them in handicraft or agriculture; we neither build houses (I mean in the country) nor cultivate land: they can very seldom pick up a livelihood by stealing until they arrive at six years old, except where they are of towardly parts; although I confess they learn the rudiments much earlier; during which time they can, however, be properly looked upon only as probationers; as I have been informed by a principal gentleman in the county of Cavan, who protested to me, that he never knew above one or two instances under the age of six, even in a part of the kingdom so renowned for the quickest proficiency in that art.

7   I am assured by our merchants that a boy or girl before twelve years old is no salable commodity; and even when they come to this age they will not yield above three pounds or three pounds and half-a-crown at most, on the exchange; which cannot turn to account either to the parents or kingdom, the charge of nutriment and rags having been at least four times that value.

8   I shall now, therefore, humbly propose my own thoughts, which I hope will not be liable to the least objection.

9   I have been assured by a very knowing American of my acquaintance in London, that a young healthy child, well nursed, is, at a year old, a most delicious, nourishing, and wholesome food, whether stewed, roasted, baked, or boiled; and I make no doubt that it will equally serve in a fricassee or a ragout.

10   I do therefore humbly offer it to public consideration, that of the hundred and twenty thousand children already computed, twenty thousand may be reserved for breed, whereof only one-fourth part to be males; which is more than we allow to sheep, black cattle, or swine; and my reason is, that these children are seldom the fruits of marriage, a circumstance not much regarded by our savages, therefore one male will be sufficient to serve four females. That the remaining hundred thousand may, at a year old, be offered in sale to the persons of quality and fortune through the kingdom; always advising the mother to let them suck plentifully in the last month, so as to render them plump and fat for a good table. A child will make two dishes at an entertainment for friends; and when the family dines alone, the fore or hind quarter will make a reasonable dish, and, seasoned with a little pepper or salt, will be very good boiled on the fourth day, especially in winter.

11   I have reckoned, upon a medium, that a child just born will weigh twelve pounds, and in a solar year, if tolerably nursed, increaseth to twenty-eight pounds.

12   I grant this food will be somewhat dear, and therefore very proper for landlords, who, as they have already devoured most of the parents, seem to have the best title to the children.

13   Infants' flesh will be in season throughout the year, but more plentiful in March, and a little before and after: for we are told by a grave author, an eminent French physician, that fish being a prolific diet, there are more children born in Roman Catholic countries about nine months after Lent than at any other season; therefore, reckoning a year after Lent, the markets will be more glutted than usual, because the number of popish infants is at least three to one in this kingdom; and therefore, it will have one other collateral advantage, by lessening the number of papists among us.

14   I have already computed the charge of nursing a beggar's child (in which list I reckon all cottagers, labourers, and four-fifths of the farmers) to be about two shillings per annum, rags included; and I believe no gentleman would repine to give ten shillings for the carcass of a good fat child, which, as I have said, will make four dishes of excellent nutritive meat, when he has only some particular friend, or his own family, to dine with him. Thus, the squire will learn to be a good landlord, and grow popular among his tenants; the mother will have eight shillings net profit, and be fit for work till she produces another child.

15   Those who are more thrifty (as I must confess the times require) may flay the carcass; the skin of which artificially dressed, will make admirable gloves for ladies, and summerboots for fine gentlemen.

16   As to our city of Dublin, shambles may be appointed for this purpose in the most convenient parts of it, and butchers we may be assured will not be wanting; although I rather recommend buying the children alive, and dressing them hot from the knife, as we do roasting pigs.

17   A very worthy person, a true lover of his country, and whose virtues I highly esteem, was lately pleased, in discoursing on this matter, to offer a refinement upon my scheme. He said, that many gentlemen of this kingdom, having of late destroyed their deer, he conceived that the want of venison might be well supplied by the bodies of young lads and maidens, not exceeding fourteen years of age, nor under twelve; so great a number of both sexes in every country now being ready to starve for want of work and service; and these to be disposed of by their parents, if alive, or otherwise by their nearest relations. But, with due deference to so excellent a friend, and so deserving a patriot, I cannot be altogether in his sentiments; for as to the males, my American acquaintance assured me from frequent experience, that their flesh was generally tough and lean, like that of our schoolboys, by continual exercise, and their taste disagreeable; and to fatten them would not answer the charge.

Then as to the females, it would, I think, with humble submission, be a loss to the public, because they soon would become breeders themselves: and besides, it is not improbable that some scrupulous people might be apt to censure such a practice (although indeed very unjustly) as a little bordering upon cruelty; which, I confess hath always been with me the strongest objection against any project, how well soever intended.

But in order to justify my friend, he confessed that this expedient was put into his head by the famous Psalmanazar, a native of the island Formosa, who came from thence to London above twenty years ago; and in conversation told my friend, that in his country, when any young person happened to be put to death, the executioner sold the carcass to persons of quality as a prime dainty; and that in his time the body of a plump girl of fifteen, who was crucified for an attempt to poison the emperor, was sold to his Imperial Majesty's prime minister of state, and other great mandarins of the court, in joints from the gibbet, at four hundred crowns. Neither indeed can I deny, that if the same use were made of several plump young girls in this town, who, without one single groat to their fortunes, cannot stir abroad without a chair, and appear at playhouse and assemblies in foreign fineries which they never will pay for, the kingdom would not be the worse. 18

Some persons of a desponding spirit are in great concern about the vast number of poor people who are aged, diseased, or maimed; and I have been desired to employ my thoughts what course may be taken to ease the nation of so grievous an encumbrance. But I am not in the least pain upon that matter, because it is well known, that they are every day dying, and rotting, by cold and famine, and filth and vermin, as fast as can be reasonably expected. And so to the younger labourers, they are now in almost as hopeful a condition; they cannot get work, and consequently pine away for want of nourishment, to a degree, that if at any time they are accidently hired to common labour, they have not the strength to perform it; and thus the country and themselves are happily delivered from the evils to come. 19

I have too long digressed, and therefore shall return to my subject. I think the advantages by the proposal which I have made are obvious and many, as well as of the highest importance. 20

For first, as I have already observed, it would greatly lessen the number of papists, with whom we are yearly overrun, being the principal breeders of the nation as well as our most dangerous enemies; and who stay at home on purpose with a design to deliver the kingdom to the Pretender, hoping to take their advantage by the absence of so many good Protestants, who have chosen rather to leave their country than stay at home and pay tithes against their conscience to an idolatrous Episcopal curate. 21

22   Secondly, the poorer tenants will have something valuable of their own, which by law may be made liable to distress, and help to pay their landlord's rent; their corn and cattle being already seized, and money a thing unknown.

23   Thirdly, whereas the maintenance of a hundred thousand children, from two years old and upwards, cannot be computed at less than ten shillings a piece per annum, the nation's stock will be thereby increased fifty thousand pounds per annum; besides the profit of a new dish introduced to the tables of all gentlemen of fortune in the kingdom who have any refinement in taste. And the money will circulate among ourselves, the goods being entirely of our own growth and manufacture.

24   Fourthly, the constant breeders, besides the gain of eight shillings per annum by the sale of their children, will be rid of the charge of maintaining them after the first year.

25   Fifthly, this food would otherwise bring great custom to taverns; where the vintners will certainly be so prudent as to procure the best receipts for dressing it to perfection, and, consequently, have their houses frequented by all the fine gentlemen, who justly value themselves upon their knowledge in good eating; and a skillful cook, who understands how to oblige his guests, will contrive to make it as expensive as they please.

26   Sixthly, this would be a great inducement to marriage, which all wise nations have either encouraged by rewards, or enforced by laws and penalties. It would increase the care and tenderness of mothers towards their children, when they were sure of a settlement for life to the poor babes, provided in some sort by the public to their annual profit instead of expense. We should soon see an honest emulation among the married women, which of them could bring the fattest child to the market. Men would become as fond of their wives during the time of their pregnancy, as they are now of their mares in foal, their cows in calf, or sows when they are ready to farrow; nor offer to beat or kick them (as is too frequent a practice) for fear of a miscarriage.

27   Many other advantages might be enumerated. For instance, the addition of some thousand carcasses in our exportation of barrelled beef; the propagation of swine's flesh, and improvement in the art of making good bacon, so much wanted among us by the great destruction of pigs, too frequent at our tables, which are no way comparable in taste or magnificence to a well-grown, fat yearling child, which, roasted whole, will make a considerable figure at a Lord Mayor's feast, or any other public entertainment. But this, and many others, I omit, being studious of brevity.

28   Supposing that one thousand families in this city would be constant customers for infants' flesh, besides others who might have it

at merry meetings, particularly weddings and christenings, I compute that Dublin would take off annually about twenty thousand carcasses; and the rest of the kingdom (where probably they will be sold somewhat cheaper) the remaining eighty thousand.

I can think of no one objection that will possibly be raised against this proposal, unless it should be urged, that the number of people will be thereby much lessened in the kingdom. This I freely own, and it was indeed one principal design in offering it to the world. I desire the reader will observe that I calculate my remedy for this one individual kingdom of Ireland, and for no other that ever was, is, or I think ever can be, upon earth. Therefore let no man talk to me of other expedients: of taxing our absentees at five shillings a pound: of using neither clothes nor household furniture except what is of our own growth and manufacture: of utterly rejecting the materials and instruments that promote foreign luxury: of curing the expensiveness of pride, vanity, idleness, and gaming in our women: of introducing a vein of parsimony, prudence, and temperance: of learning to love our country, wherein we differ even from Laplanders, and the inhabitants of Topinamboo: of quitting our animosities and factions, nor act any longer like the Jews, who were murdering one another at the very moment their city was taken: of being a little cautious not to sell our country and consciences for nothing: of teaching landlords to have at least one degree of mercy towards their tenants: lastly, of putting a spirit of honesty, industry, and skill into our shopkeepers; who, if a resolution could now be taken to buy only our native goods, would immediately unite to cheat and exact upon us in the price, the measure, and the goodness, nor could ever yet be brought to make one fair proposal of just dealing, though often and earnestly invited to it. 29

Therefore I repeat, let no man talk to me of these and the like expedients, till he hath at least some glimpse of hope that there will ever be some hearty and sincere attempt to put them in practice. 30

But, as to myself, having been wearied out for many years with offering vain, idle, visionary thoughts, and at length utterly despairing of success, I fortunately fell upon this proposal; which, as it is wholly new, so it hath something solid and real, of no expense and little trouble, full in our own power, and whereby we can incur no danger in disobliging England. For this kind of commodity will not bear exportation, the flesh being of too tender a consistence to admit a long continuance in salt, although perhaps I could name a country which would be glad to eat up our whole nation without it. 31

After all, I am not so violently bent upon my own opinion as to reject any offer proposed by wise men which shall be found equally innocent, cheap, easy, and effectual. But before something of that 32 kind shall be advanced in contradiction to my scheme, and offering a better, I desire the author, or authors, will be pleased maturely to consider two points. First, as things now stand, how they will be able to find food and raiment for a hundred thousand useless mouths and backs? And, secondly, there being a round million of creatures in human figure throughout this kingdom, whose whole subsistence put into a common stock would leave them in debt two millions of pounds sterling, adding those who are beggars by profession, to the bulk of farmers, cottagers, and labourers, with the wives and children who are beggars in effect; I desire those politicians who dislike my overture, and may perhaps be so bold as to attempt an answer, that they will first ask the parents of these mortals whether they would not at this day think it a great happiness to have been sold for food at a year old, in the manner I prescribe, and thereby have avoided such a perpetual scene of misfortunes as they have since gone through, by the oppression of landlords, the impossibility of paying rent without money or trade, the want of common sustenance, with neither house nor clothes to cover them from the inclemencies of weather, and the most inevitable prospect of entailing the like, or greater miseries, upon their breed for ever.

33   I profess, in the sincerity of my heart, that I have not the least personal interest in endeavouring to promote this necessary work, having no other motive than the public good of my country, by advancing our trade, providing for infants, relieving the poor, and giving some pleasure to the rich. I have no children by which I can propose to get a single penny; the youngest being nine years old, and my wife past child-bearing.

Vocabulary

a. *paragraph 1:* importuning
b. *paragraph 2:* prodigious
c. *paragraph 4:* schemes, projectors, raiment
d. *paragraph 5:* bastard
e. *paragraph 6:* apprehend, rudiments, probationers, renowned
f. *paragraph 9:* fricassee, ragout
g. *paragraph 13:* prolific, papists
h. *paragraph 14:* squire
i. *paragraph 15:* flay
j. *paragraph 17:* venison
k. *paragraph 18:* mandarins, gibbet
l. *paragraph 19:* encumbrance
m. *paragraph 20:* digressed
n. *paragraph 21:* tithes, idolatrous, Episcopal curate

o. *paragraph 25:* vintners
p. *paragraph 26:* emulation, foal, farrow
q. *paragraph 27:* yearling
r. *paragraph 29:* expedients, parsimony, animosities
s. *paragraph 31:* consistence
t. *paragraph 32:* effectual, entailing

Questions

1. How would you describe the tone of "A Modest Proposal"? Cite examples to account for your description.
2. How does Swift use tone to establish the basic character and motives of his proposer in the opening paragraphs?
3. How does Swift reveal his attitude toward the proposer? Is Swift in accord with the proposer's general views of English motives? Are those motives stated directly or instead implied?
4. How persuasive do you find the essay? Is it an essay of historical interest or literary interest only, or does it have something to say to people today?

Writing Assignments

1. Write your own "modest proposal" for dealing with a current social or political evil. You may wish to write as yourself or, like Swift, impersonate someone who wishes to make a modest proposal. Maintain a consistent tone throughout your essay, or at least make any shifts in tone consistent with the character of your speaker and his or her motives in writing.
2. Contrast the tone of Swift's attack on the English with Orwell's discussion of political language. Distinguish the various rhetorical devices that they employ.

Figurative Language

Figurative language can increase the vividness of expository and persuasive writing. In the following section, some common figures of speech are defined and illustrated.

A simile is an explicit comparison (using *like* or *as*) that usually develops or implies one or more simple points of resemblance:

> I felt like a *flower*: a little parched, of course, a little gone in the neck, and with no real life to come, perhaps, only sham life, bowl life, easing its petals and lifting its head to start feeding on the day. (Martin Amis, *Money*)

A metaphor is an implicit comparison in which an object is presented as if it were something else:

> Each life is a game of chess that went to hell on the seventh move, and now the flukey play is cramped and slow, a dream of constraint and cross-purpose, with each move forced, all pieces pinned and skewered and zugzwanged. . . . But here and there we see these figures who appear to run on the true lines, and they are terrible examples. They're rich, usually. (Amis, *Money*)

Personification is the attribution of human qualities to abstract ideas or objects. Simile, metaphor, and personification unite in the following passage:

> Then Sunday light raced over the farm as fast as the chickens were flying. Immediately the first straight shaft of heat, solid as a hickory stick, was laid on the ridge. (Eudora Welty, *The Corner Store*)

One purpose of figures of speech is to evoke the quality of experience and give shape or substance to an emotion or awareness that up to the moment of its expression may be indefinite. In exposition a writer will depend on metaphor because of its property of expressing an attitude as well as representing an idea:

> England is not the jewelled isle of Shakespeare's much-quoted passage, nor is it the inferno depicted by Dr. Goebbels. More than either it resembles a family, a rather stuffy Victorian family, with not many black sheep in it but

with all its cupboards bursting with skeletons. It has rich relations who have to be kowtowed to and poor relations who are horribly sat upon, and there is a deep conspiracy of silence about the source of the family income. It is a family in which the young are generally thwarted and most of the power is in the hands of irresponsible uncles and bedridden aunts. (George Orwell, "England, Your England")

Imagery

A writer uses imagery to make an observation or impression perceptible to the senses, as in the following description of how a small town in North Dakota has changed:

> Sounds have changed; I heard not once the clopping of a horse's hoof, nor the mourn of a coyote. I heard instead the shriek of brakes, the heavy throbbing of the once-a-day Braniff airliner into Minot, the shattering sirens born of war, the honk of a diesel locomotive which surely cannot call to faraway places the heart of a wakeful boy like the old steam whistle in the night. (Eric Sevareid, "Velva, North Dakota")

Images convey impressions of sight, hearing, smell, taste, or touch. The following passages from an essay by Harry Bruce and from a novel by Alice Munro illustrate some of these:

> Back at my friend's farm, we encased the cork in scratchy manila twine till we had something bigger than a hardball but smaller than a softball. For bases, we dropped sweaters among the cowflaps in a pasture, and the lesson began. (Harry Bruce, "The Softball Was Always Hard")

> He turned and swore at us to get off, but we hung on, bloated with cheerful defiance like criminals born with cauls; we hung on with the rim of the sleigh cutting into our stomachs and our feet spraying snow, until we reached the corner of Mason Street, and there we flung off into a snowbank. (Alice Munro, *Lives of Girls and Women*)

We think in images constantly. Neither Bruce nor Munro could have expressed a sense of these particular experiences in abstract language. The more evocative our imagery when the situation calls for vivid impressions, the more directly will our words express experience. A passage will seem overwritten if a vivid representation of experience is not needed; so-called fine writing tries to be too evocative of sense experience. In the passages quoted above, the authors select primarily those details that will give the reader an impression of the physical sensations experienced.

Figurative language is particularly important in descriptive writing such as the following, which conveys an unusual experience and sensation:

> There is something quite deceptive in the sense of acceleration that comes just before a rapid. The word "rapid" itself is, in a way, a misnomer. It refers only to the speed of the white river relative to the speed of the smooth water that leads into and away from the rapid. The white water is faster, but it is hardly "rapid." The Colorado, smooth, flows about seven miles per hour, and, white, it goes perhaps fifteen or, at its whitest and wildest, twenty miles per hour—not very rapid by the standards of the twentieth century. Force of suggestion creates a false expectation. The mere appearance of the river going over those boulders—the smoky spray, the scissoring waves—is enough to imply a rush to fatality, and this endorses the word used to describe it. You feel as if you were about to be sucked into some sort of invisible pneumatic tube and shot like a bullet into the dim beyond. But the white water, though faster than the rest of the river, is categorically slow. Running the rapids in the Colorado is a series of brief experiences, because the rapids themselves are short. In them, with the raft folding and bending—sudden hills of water filling the immediate skyline—things happen in slow motion. The projector of your own existence slows way down, and you dive as in a dream, and gradually rise, and fall again. The raft shudders across the ridge-line of water cordilleras to crash softly into the valleys beyond. Space and time in there are something other than they are out here. Tents of water form overhead, to break apart in rags. Elapsed stopwatch time has no meaning at all. (John McPhee, "Running the Rapids")

ALLAN FOTHERINGHAM

Allan Fotheringham is a political columnist who is well known for his humorous attacks on public figures. He has published a number of books, including *Malice in Blunderland*, in which he roasted the Trudeau Liberals; *Look Ma . . . No Hands*, a satiric look at Canada's Conservatives; and *Capitol Offences*, a witty analysis of political life in Washington. He writes a regular column for *Maclean's*, where the following was first published. In it, he focusses his satire on the yuppie generation, one of his favourite targets in recent years, and displays the provocative humour and impatience with pretention that have made him one of Canada's most widely read journalists.

Downhill All the Way

ALLAN FOTHERINGHAM

Several years back, the wife—not a native British Californian—of a friend expressed great relief when they decided to move back east of the Rockies. "All the time I lived in Vancouver," she explained, "I felt I was in the middle of a beer commercial." 1

The water, the mountains, the salubrious climate, the sybaritic lifestyle—all was too much for her Presbyterian soul and she blissfully fled elsewhere, to suffer real winters and rubber boots. 2

It is good that the dear girl had not to suffer further by enduring a Christmas visit to Whistler, the ski and sin resort that is 90 minutes north of Vancouver as the Ford Bronco flies. They don't even know how to spell recession there. This is not a beer commercial. This is a champagne cocktail, with designer sun goggles. 3

Whistler in 1995 is typified by the guy spotted on the lift headed to the longest ski run in North America if not the universe. The four-body high-speed chair lift has not only a foot rest but a stiff plastic cover that lowers and shields the poor darlings from the drifting snow flakes. The only things missing are windshield wipers. Next year. 4

The guy being lofted skyward is talking on his cellular phone. He comes for a relaxing holiday and he's phoning his broker to sell 10,000. No wonder she moved east. 5

The Chateau Whistler, with its copper roof, is sort of a Meccano-set imitation of what the great CPR railway hotels in Banff and Jasper and Saskatoon and Quebec City made famous. The lobby would accommodate the Taj Mahal. A heated pool outside the bar emits steam and nymphs in bikinis who rise out of the mist as skiers in space-age boots skid to a stop at poolside. 6

In the lobby, large dogs woof and bark, drowning out the piano music. Only the rich bring dogs to a ski holiday. 7

One of Pierre Trudeau's sons is spending the Whistler winter as a ski bum. The Great Man himself skis here most seasons. Jean Chrétien is so smart as never to be seen on these slopes, which would immediately destroy his carefully crafted image as a little boy from Shawinigan with modest beans-and-toast tastes. 8

9   The reason he got elected was that he was photographed water-skiing—on one ski. It does not cost a dime to water-ski. It costs almost $50 a day (thanks to GST) to buy a Whistler lift ticket. The guy is not dumb. He avoids like a plague this place where waiters who look like Warren Beatty have taken a vow never to return sunglasses.

10   Hugh Smythe is a handsome devil who as a New Westminster high-school student came here as a lift assistant and forgot to leave and now runs Blackcomb Mountain, the slope of choice beside its cheek-and-jowl companion, Whistler Mountain. The leading American ski magazine has just named the twin-mountain resort, for the third straight year, the best ski destination in North America. Clubs and pizzas are taken into account, not to mention the sushi bars.

11   Smythe explains that skiing is recession-proof, since it is an upper-middle-class sport. (That's why Chrétien stays away.) These days he spends half his time flying to Mont Tremblant north of Montreal. Intrawest Corp. of Vancouver, which owns Blackcomb, is now doing to the Quebec resort what it did for Whistler.

12   What that means is that in Christine's, high in the sky near the Blackcomb peak, along with white tablecloths and crystal and cutlery, there is a dish called garlic and roasted brie, followed with corn-breaded oysters. That would be after they come swooping down from a run on the glacier, which is open for skiing through July and August, thanks to Jean-Claude Killy and his helicopters.

13   On his way to Mont Tremblant, Smythe stopped off at Stratton Mountain in Vermont, which Intrawest now owns as well as Panorama in the Rockies near Alberta. The brie-and-garlic boys expect in 1995 to grab two more American resorts, probably in California and Colorado, and get a listing on a U.S. stock exchange. Stay away, Jean.

14   There is little snow in Switzerland and Austria this winter. World Cup events are being cancelled and moved. Steve Podborski is now a permanent big man at Whistler, which has been smothered by the best snow in 25 years.

15   The snow bunnies at the bottom of the lift wear $3,000 on their backs, even before they break their legs. You need a crowbar to get into Umberto's restaurant, or be a relative. *The New York Times* is there every morning in the Chateau Whistler, 10:30 sharp—about the time the dogs start to woof.

16   On the benchlands above, the condos march upward, year upon year, outdoor Jacuzzis steaming in the sun, BMWs parked like prams outside. The deal now is ski-in, ski-out—put on your boards on the front stoop and at day's end, the garlic having done its work, glide right to your door.

It is somewhat removed from the welfare office in St. John's,   17
the frozen pond in Saskatchewan that produced Gordie Howe, the
soulless towers in Toronto that produce paper and bankruptcies,
the desiccated swivel servants outside Chrétien's office who are at
the Xerox machine, duplicating surveys demonstrating that most
Canadians asked about Quebec independence say they would
rather go fishing.

I'm glad my dear old friend east of the Rockies has never seen   18
Whistler. She would absolutely hate it.

Vocabulary

  a. *paragraph 2:* sybaritic
  b. *paragraph 17:* desiccated

Questions

1. How does the language used in the first three paragraphs reveal
   Fotheringham's attitude toward his subject?
2. How does Fotheringham expand the meaning of "Whistler" to make it
   signify more than just a place?
3. Why does Fotheringham select the details included in paragraph 15?
   How do these examples mark a shift from the opening of the essay?

Writing Assignments

1. Describe some aspect of your own neighbourhood or environment
   that has disappeared over time. Use images that re-create the physical
   scene and that convey your attitude to what has happened.
2. Narrate an experience in which you learned something unexpected
   about the world of nature. Let your reader see that world and undergo
   the experience as you did. Choose images that appeal to several of the
   senses, not just to one.

RICHARD SELZER

A surgeon and member of the faculty of the Yale School of Medicine,
Richard Selzer has written on medicine and the art of surgery in *Confessions
of a Knife, Letter to a Young Doctor,* and *Mortal Lessons,* in which these final
sections of the essay "Lessons from the Art" appear. Selzer writes about
medicine and physiology with unusual exuberance and feeling. His
metaphorical style is used to powerful effect in these pages on what it
means to be a surgeon.

Lessons from the Art

RICHARD SELZER

1   **A** man of letters lies in the intensive care unit. A professor, used to words and students. He has corrected the sentences of many. He understands punctuation. One day in his classroom he was speaking of Emily Dickinson when suddenly he grew pale, and a wonder sprang upon his face, as though he had just, for the first time, *seen* something, understood something that had eluded him all his life. It was the look of the Wound, the struck blow that makes no noise, but happens in the depths somewhere, unseen. His students could not have known that at that moment his stomach had perforated, that even as he spoke, its contents were issuing forth into his peritoneal cavity like a horde of marauding goblins. From the blackboard to the desk he reeled, fell across the top of it, and turning his face to one side, he vomited up his blood, great gouts and gobbets of it, as though having given his class the last of his spirit, he now offered them his fluid and cells.

2   In time, he was carried to the operating room, this man whom I had known, who had taught me poetry. I took him up, in my hands, and laid him open, and found from where he bled. I stitched it up, and bandaged him, and said later, "Now you are whole."

3   But it was not so, for he had begun to die. And I could not keep him from it, not with all my earnestness, so sure was his course. From surgery he was taken to the intensive care unit. His family, his students were stopped at the electronic door. They could not pass, for he had entered a new state of being, a strange antechamber where they may not go.

4   For three weeks he has dwelt in that House of Intensive Care, punctured by needles, wearing tubes of many calibers in all of his orifices, irrigated, dialyzed, insufflated, pumped, and drained . . . and feeling every prick and pressure the way a lover feels desire spring acutely to his skin.

5   In the room a woman moves. She is dressed in white. Lovingly she measures his hourly flow of urine. With hands familiar, she delivers oxygen to his nostrils and counts his pulse as though she were telling beads. Each bit of his decline she records with her heart full of grief, shaking her head. At last, she turns from her machinery to the simple touch of the flesh. Sighing, she strips back the sheet, and bathes his limbs.

The man of letters did not know this woman before. Preoccu- 6
pied with dying, he is scarcely aware of her presence now. But this
nurse is his wife in his new life of dying. They are close, these two,
intimate, depending one upon the other, loving. It is a marriage, for
although they own no shared past, they possess this awful, intense
present, this matrimonial now, that binds them as strongly as any
promise.

A man does not know whose hands will stroke from him the 7
last bubbles of his life. That alone should make him kinder to
strangers.

I stand by the bed where a young woman lies, her face post-operative, 8
her mouth twisted, in palsy, clownish. A tiny twig of the facial
nerve, the one to the muscles of her mouth, has been severed. She
will be thus from now on. The surgeon had followed with religious
fervor the curve of her flesh; I promise you that. Nevertheless, to
remove the tumor in her cheek, I had cut the little nerve.

Her young husband is in the room. He stands on the opposite 9
side of the bed, and together they seem to dwell in the evening
lamplight, isolated from me, private. Who are they, I ask myself, he
and this wry-mouth I have made, who gaze at and touch each other
so generously, greedily? The young woman speaks.

"Will my mouth always be like this?" she asks. 10

"Yes," I say, "it will. It is because the nerve was cut." 11

She nods, and is silent. But the young man smiles. 12

"I like it," he says. "It is kind of cute." 13

All at once I *know* who he is. I understand, and I lower my 14
gaze. One is not bold in an encounter with a god. Unmindful, he
bends to kiss her crooked mouth, and I so close I can see how he
twists his own lips to accommodate to hers, to show her that their
kiss still works. I remember that the gods appeared in ancient
Greece as mortals, and I hold my breath and let the wonder in.

Far away from the operating room, the surgeon is taught that some 15
deaths are undeniable, that this does not deny their meaning. To
perceive tragedy is to wring from it beauty and truth. It is a thing
beyond mere competence and technique, or the handsomeness to
precisely cut and stitch. Further, he learns that love can bloom in
the stoniest desert, an intensive care unit, perhaps.

These are things of longest memory, and like memory, they cut. 16
When the patient becomes the surgeon, he goes straight for the soul.

I do not know when it was that I understood that it is precisely 17
this hell in which we wage our lives that offers us the energy, the possibility to care for each other. A surgeon does not slip from his mother's
womb with compassion smeared upon him like the drippings of his

birth. It is much later that it comes. No easy shaft of grace this, but the cumulative murmuring of the numberless wounds he has dressed, the incisions he has made, all the sores and ulcers and cavities he has touched in order to heal. In the beginning it is barely audible, a whisper, as from many mouths. Slowly it gathers, rises from the streaming flesh until, at last, it is a pure *calling* — an exclusive sound, like the cry of certain solitary birds—telling that out of the resonance between the sick man and the one who tends him there may spring that profound courtesy that the religious call Love.

```
┌─────────────────────┐
│                     │
└─────────────────────┘
```

Vocabulary

   a. *paragraph 1:* perforated, peritoneal cavity, marauding, gouts, gobbets
   b. *paragraph 4:* orifices, dialyzed, insufflated
   c. *paragraph 8:* palsy
   d. *paragraph 9:* wry-mouth
   e. *paragraph 17:* cumulative, resonance

Questions

   1. How does Selzer personify the wound in paragraph 1, and to what purpose?
   2. What is Selzer comparing in the simile of the goblins in paragraph 1? What is the effect of this comparison?
   3. What is metaphorical about the statement in paragraph 4 that the professor "has dwelt in that House of Intensive Care"? What does Selzer gain in connotative meaning through this metaphor?
   4. What metaphor organizes paragraph 6, and how does Selzer develop or extend it?
   5. Why does the husband remind Selzer of the gods of ancient Greece?
   6. What similes and metaphors do you find in paragraphs 15 through 17? What feelings or ideas do these make vivid?
   7. What central idea or thesis is Selzer developing through these lessons from the art of the surgery?

Writing Assignments

   1. Write your lessons from another art you know how to perform—for example, the art of giving advice or the art of making friends. Use similes, metaphors, and personification where appropriate to make your ideas vivid to the reader.
   2. In their selection of details, good writers often appeal to more than the visual sense. Concentrate on the other senses by writing a description of a playground or a busy city street as a blind person would perceive it.

```
┌─────────────────────┐
│                     │
└─────────────────────┘
```

MARTIN AMIS

Martin Amis was born in 1949 and educated at Oxford. He is one of the most talented novelists of his generation. His novels include *Other People: A Mystery, The Rachel Papers, Money, London Fields, Time's Arrow,* and *The Information.* He is also a prolific writer of book reviews that are themselves superb essays. In the following excerpt from his introduction to *Einstein's Monsters,* a collection of short stories, he writes of the continuing threat posed by the very existence of nuclear weapons.

Einstein's Monsters

MARTIN AMIS

They squat on our spiritual lives. There may be a nuclear "priesthood," but we are the supplicants, and we have no faith. The warheads are our godheads. Nuclear weapons could bring about the Book of Revelation in a matter of hours; they could do it today. Of course, no dead will rise; nothing will be revealed (*nothing* meaning two things, the absence of everything and a thing called *nothing*). Events that we call "acts of God" — floods, earthquakes, eruptions — are fleshwounds compared to the human act of nuclear war: a million Hiroshimas. Like God, nuclear weapons are free creations of the human mind. Unlike God, nuclear weapons are real. And they are here.

Revulsion at MAD [Mutually Assured Destruction] is understandable and necessary. I suggest, however, that MAD is not just a political creation but a creation of the weapons themselves. Always we keep coming back to the weapons as if they were actors rather than pieces of equipment; and they earn this status, by virtue of their cosmic power. They are actors and, considered on the human scale, insane actors. The weapons are insane, they are MAD: they can assume no other form. In one of those philosopher's throat-clearings Anthony Kenny says that "weapons considered merely as inert pieces of hardware are not, of course, objects of moral evaluation. It is the uses to which they are put. . . ." This isn't so. Recent evidence strongly suggests that nuclear weapons, in their inert state, are responsible for a variety of cancers and leukaemias. What toxicity, what power, what range. They cause death even before they go off.

The A-bomb is a Z-bomb, and the arms race is a race between nuclear weapons and ourselves. It is them or us. What do nukes do? What are they for? Since when did we all want to kill each other? Nuclear weapons deter a nuclear holocaust by threatening a nuclear holocaust, and if things go wrong then that is what you get: a nuclear holocaust. If things don't go wrong, and continue not going wrong for the next millennium of millennia (the boasted forty years being no more than forty winks in cosmic time), you get . . . What do you get? What are we getting?

4   At the multiracial children's teaparty the guests have, perhaps, behaved slightly better since the Keepers were introduced. Little Ivan has stopped pulling Fetnab's hair, though he is still kicking her leg under the table. Bobby has returned the slice of cake that rightfully belonged to tiny Conchita, though he has his eye on that sandwich and will probably make a lunge for it sooner or later. Out on the lawn the Keepers maintain a kind of order, but standards of behaviour are pretty well as troglodytic as they ever were. At best the children seem strangely subdued or off-colour. Although they are aware of the Keepers, they don't want to look at them, they don't want to catch their eye. They don't want to think about them. For the Keepers are a thousand feet tall, and covered in gelignite and razor-blades, toting flamethrowers and machineguns, cleavers and skewers, and fizzing with rabies, anthrax, plague. Curiously enough, they are not looking at the children at all. With bleeding hellhound eyes, mouthing foul threats and shaking their fists, they are looking at each other. They want to take on someone their own size . . .

5   If they only knew it—no, if they only *believed* it—the children could simply ask the Keepers to leave. But it doesn't seem possible, does it? It seems—it seems unthinkable. A silence starts to fall across the lawn. The party has not been going for very long and must last until the end of time. Already the children are weepy and feverish. They all feel sick and want to go home.

Vocabulary

a. *paragraph 1:* supplicants
b. *paragraph 2:* inert, toxicity
c. *paragraph 3:* millennium
d. *paragraph 4:* troglodytic, gelignite, skewers, anthrax, hellhound

Questions

1. In paragraph 2, Amis points out how important metaphor can be in our thinking about nuclear weapons. What metaphor does he use to inform the argument in the first paragraph? How effective is it?
2. The fourth paragraph develops the metaphor of the tea party at some length. How effective is it?

3. How do the rhetorical questions function in paragraph 3?

4. How is the figurative language generally used to create an effect? Is Amis's appeal to the reader primarily emotional?

5. Do you think that Amis's rapid-fire style might leave some readers behind? For instance, does his piling of image upon image and metaphor upon metaphor convince or befuddle the reader?

Writing Assignment

Discuss another contemporary issue using an extended metaphor like Amis's tea party. Work at including detail to give the image specificity and depth.

THOMAS LYNCH

Thomas Lynch is an undertaker in Milford, Michigan, and the author of *Grimalkin & Other Poems*. This essay is an excerpt from "The Undertaking," which first appeared in *The London Review of Books*. His quirky humour and deadpan style enable him to desentimentalize the whole business of disposing of the dead, and he manages to tell us some important things about ourselves and our pretentions in the process.

Burying the Ungrateful Dead

THOMAS LYNCH

 Every year I bury one hundred and fifty of   1
my townspeople. Another dozen or two I take to the crematory to be burned. I sell caskets, burial vaults, and urns for the ashes. I have a sideline in headstones and monuments. I do flowers on commission. I rent my building: eleven thousand square feet, furnished and fixtured with an abundance of pastel and chair rail and crown moldings. The whole mess is mortgaged and remortgaged well into the next century. My modes of transport include a hearse, a limo, two Fleetwoods, and a minivan with darkened windows, which our price list calls a service vehicle and which everyone in town calls the Dead Wagon.

They die around the clock here, without apparent preference   2
for a day of the week or month of the year; there is no clear favorite

among the seasons. Nor does the alignment of the stars, the fullness of the moon, or the liturgical calendar have very much to do with it. They go off upright or horizontally, in Chevrolets and nursing homes, in bathtubs, on the interstates, in ERs, ORs, BMWs. And while it may be that we assign more equipment and more importance to deaths that occur in places marked by initials—ICU being somehow better than Greenbriar Convalescent Home—it is also true that the dead don't care. In this way, the dead I bury and burn are like the dead before them, for whom time and space have become mortally unimportant. This loss of interest among the dying is one of the first sure signs that something serious is about to happen. The next thing is they quit breathing.

3   Nor does *who* matter much either. To say, "I'm okay, you're okay, but him, he's dead!" is, for the living, a kind of comfort. It is why we drag rivers and comb plane wrecks. It is why MIA is more painful than DOA. It is why we have open caskets and classified obits. Knowing is better than not knowing, and knowing it is you is terrifically better than knowing it is me. Once I'm the dead guy, whether you're okay or he's okay won't interest me, because the dead don't care.

4   Of course, the living, bound by their adverbs and their actuarials, still do. That's the reason I'm in business. The living are careful and often caring. The dead are careless, or maybe it's care-less. Either way, they don't care. These are unremarkable and verifiable truths.

5   My former mother-in-law, herself an unremarkable and verifiable truth, was always fond of holding forth with Cagneyesque bravado—to wit: "When I'm dead, just put me in a box and throw me in a hole." But whenever I reminded her that we did, in effect, do that with everyone, the woman grew sullen and a little cranky. Later, over meatloaf and green beans, she would invariably burst forth with: "When I'm dead, just cremate me and scatter the ashes."

6   My former mother-in-law was trying to make carelessness sound like fearlessness. My kids would stop eating and look at each other. The kids' mother would whine: "Oh, Mom, don't talk like that." I'd take out my lighter and begin to play with it.

7   In the same way, the priest that married me to this woman's daughter—a man who loved golf and gold chalices and vestments made of Irish linen; a man who drove a great black car with a wine-red interior—this same fellow, leaving the cemetery one day, felt called upon to instruct me thus: "No bronze coffin for me. No sir! No orchids or roses or limousines. The plain pine box is the one I want, a quiet Low Mass, and the pauper's grave. No pomp and circumstance."

8   He wanted to be an example of simplicity, of prudence, of piety and austerity. When I told him that he needn't wait, that he could

begin his ministry of good example even today, that he could quit the country club and trade his luxury sedan for a used Chevette, that free of his Florsheims and cashmeres and prime ribs he could become the very incarnation of Saint Francis himself or Anthony of Padua — when I told the priest who married me these things, he said nothing at all, but turned his wild eye on me in the way that the cleric must have looked on Sweeney years ago, before he cursed him, irreversibly, into a bird.

What I was trying to tell the fellow was, of course, that being a   9
dead saint is no more worthwhile than being a dead philodendron. Living is the rub, and always has been. Living saints still feel the flames and stigmata, the ache of chastity and the pangs of conscience. Once dead, they let their relics do the legwork, because, as I was trying to tell this priest, the dead don't care.

And that is the truth, abundantly self-evident, that seems, now   10
that I think of it, the one most elusive to my old in-laws, to the parish priest, and to perfect strangers who are forever accosting me in barbershops and in cocktail bars and at parent–teacher conferences, hell-bent or duty-bound on telling me what it is they want done with them when they are dead.

I say, Give it a rest. Once you are dead, call it a day, and let the   11
old man or the missus or the thankless kids decide whether you are to be buried or burned or blown out of a cannon or left to dry out in a ditch. It's not your day to watch.

Last Monday morning Milo Hornsby died. Mrs. Hornsby called at   12
2:00 A.M. to say that Milo had "expired" and would I take care of it, as if his condition were like any other that could be renewed or somehow improved upon. At 2:00 A.M., yanked from sleep, I am thinking: Put a quarter in Milo and call me in the morning. But Milo is dead. In a moment, in a twinkling, Milo has slipped irretrievably out of our reach, beyond Mrs. Hornsby and the children, beyond the women at the laundromat that he owned, beyond the mailman, zoning board, town council, and chamber of commerce: beyond us all, and any treachery or any kindness we had in mind for him.

Milo is dead.   13

Xs on his eyes, lights out, curtains.   14

I do not rush to my senses, coffee and quick shave, Homburg   15
and greatcoat, warm up the Dead Wagon, and make for the freeway in the wee hours for Milo's sake. I do it for her, for she who has become, in the same moment and the same twinkling, like water to ice, the Widow Hornsby. I go for her, because she still can cry and care and pray and pay my bill.

The language of death certificates — Milo's says "Cardiopul-   16
monary Failure" — is the language of weakness. We are forever

dying of failures, of anomalies, of insufficiencies, of dysfunctions, arrests, accidents. Likewise, Mrs. Hornsby, in her grief, will be said to be breaking down or falling apart or going to pieces, as if there were something structurally awry with her. It is as if death and grief were not part of the Order of Things, as if Milo's failure and his widow's weeping were, or ought to be, sources of embarrassment. "Doing well" for Mrs. Hornsby would mean that she is bearing up, braving the storm, or being strong for the children. We have willing pharmacists to help her with this. Of course, for Milo, doing well would mean he was back in his hospital room holding his own, keeping the meters and monitors bleeping. I sign for him and get him out of there. At some level, I am still thinking Milo gives a shit, which by now we all know he doesn't.

17   Back at my place of business, upstairs in the embalming room, behind a door marked PRIVATE, Milo Hornsby is floating on a porcelain table under fluorescent lights. Unwrapped, outstretched, Milo is beginning to look a little more like himself—eyes wide open, mouth agape, returning to our gravity. I shave him, close his eyes, his mouth. We call this "setting the features." These are the features—eyes and mouth—that in death will never look the way they would in life, when they are always opening, closing, focusing, signaling, telling us something. In death what they tell us is that they will not be doing anything anymore. The last detail to be managed is Milo's hands—one folded over the other, over the umbilicus, in an attitude of ease, of repose, of retirement. They will not be doing anything anymore either.

18   When my wife moved out some years ago, I kept the children and the dirty laundry. It was big news in a small town. Although there was plenty of talk, no one knew exactly what to say to me. So they brought casseroles and beef stews, took the kids out to the movies or canoeing, brought their younger sisters around to visit me. What Milo did was send his laundry van around twice a week for two months, until I found a housekeeper. Milo would pick up five loads in the morning and return them by lunchtime, fresh and folded. I never asked him to do this. I hardly knew him.

19   After my housekeeper was hired, I went to thank Milo and to pay my bill. The invoices detailed the number of loads, the washers and the driers, detergent, bleaches, fabric softeners. I think the total came to sixty dollars. When I asked Milo what the charges were for pickup and delivery, for stacking and folding, for saving my life and the lives of my children, for keeping us in clean clothes and towels and bed linen, Milo said, "Never mind that. One hand washes the other."

20   I place Milo's right hand over his left hand, then try the other way. Then back again. Then I decide that it makes no difference, that one hand washes the other either way.

Every Monday morning Ernest Fuller comes to my office. He was   21
damaged in some profound way in Korea. The details of his damage are unknown to the locals. Ernest Fuller has no limp or anything missing, so everyone thinks it was something he saw in Korea
that left him a little simple, occasionally perplexed, the type to
draw rein abruptly in his daylong walks, to consider the meaning
of litter, pausing over bottle caps and gum wrappers. Ernest Fuller
has a nervous smile and a dead-fish handshake. He wears a baseball cap and thick eyeglasses. Every Sunday night Ernest goes to
the supermarket and buys up tabloids with headlines that usually
involve Siamese twins or movie stars or UFOs. Every Monday
morning Ernest brings me clippings of stories with headlines like:
601 LB. MAN FALLS THRU COFFIN—A GRAVE SITUATION, or,
EMBALMER FOR THE STARS SAYS ELVIS IS FOREVER. The
Monday morning Milo died, Ernest's clipping had to do with an
urn full of ashes that made grunting and groaning noises, that
whistled sometimes, and that was expected to begin talking. Certain scientists in England could make no sense of it. They had run
several tests. The ashes' widow, however—left with nine children
and no estate—was convinced that her dearly beloved and greatly
reduced husband was trying to give her winning numbers for the
lottery. "Jacky would never leave us without good prospects," she
said. "He loved his family more than anything." There is a picture
of the two of them—the widow and the urn, the living and the
dead, flesh and bronze, the Victrola and the Victrola's dog. She has
her ear cocked, waiting.

We are always waiting. Waiting for some good word or for the   22
winning numbers. Waiting for a sign or wonder, some signal from
our dear dead that the dead still care. We are gladdened when they
do outstanding things, when they arise from their graves or appear
to us in dreams or fall from their caskets. It pleases us to no end; as
if the dead still cared, had agendas, were yet alive.

But the sad and well-known fact of the matter is that most of us   23
will stay in our caskets and be dead a long time, and our urns and
graves will never make a sound. Our reason and requiems, our
headstones and High Masses, will neither get us in nor keep us out
of heaven. The meaning of our lives, and the memories of them,
will belong only to the living, just as our funerals do.

We heat graves here for winter burials, as a kind of foreplay   24
before digging in, to loosen the frost's hold on the ground before
the sexton and his backhoe do the opening. We put Milo in the
ground last Wednesday. The mercy is that what we buried there, in
an oak casket, just under the frost line, had ceased to be Milo. It was
something else. Milo had become the idea of himself, a permanent
fixture of the third person and past tense, his widow's loss of

appetite and her trouble sleeping, his absence in places where we look for him, our broken habits of him, our phantom limb, our one hand washing the other.

```

```

Vocabulary

a. *paragraph 2:* liturgical
b. *paragraph 4:* actuarials
c. *paragraph 8:* austerity
d. *paragraph 9:* stigmata
e. *paragraph 16:* anomalies
f. *paragraph 21:* Victrola
g. *paragraph 22:* requiems

Questions

1. Through what means does Lynch develop his argument — personal experience, eyewitness accounts, statistics, analogy, causal analysis, or a statement of beliefs or truths and deduction from them?
2. How has Lynch solved the problem of writing about the subject of death? What in his tone and attitude enables him to do so?
3. Lynch includes anecdotes in paragraphs 5 to 9. How appropriate is this kind of humour?
4. Look closely at the language in paragraphs 21 to 24. Note the use of imagery, metaphor, repetition, dialogue, etc. What purpose is served by this verbal inventiveness?
5. What use does Lynch make of the Milo Hornsby anecdote?

Writing Assignments

1. Think of an equally unpleasant subject and write an essay that alleviates readers' anxieties about it.
2. Think of an incident in which someone's actions apparently contradict his or her stated beliefs, and explore the truths that these inconsistencies reveal.

Reading and Writing

We each write for different reasons and for different audiences, and we each find our inspiration, ideas, and details in various ways. Nor is the act of writing always the same even for individual writers, as Dany Laferrière's and Cynthia Ozick's essays on writing suggest. Laferrière gives a playful account of the relation between the writer and his audience. Ozick believes that writers transmute the pain of childhood experiences into literary art. In his essay on simplicity, William Zinsser describes what happens in the course of writing and afterward, as we rethink and revise initial drafts. He shows how to deal with the problem of ready-made words and ideas. "The secret of good writing is to strip every sentence to its cleanest components," he states, and he illustrates how to do so. In his discussion of how writers develop, John Barth dismisses the notion that they learn exclusively from life. Barth says all serious writers must study their material, their medium, their craft, and their art, and that this study can be pursued within a university. Margaret Atwood describes the political context that all writers must consider. John Leo shows the ways in which the language of journalism can be corrupted. Carol Shields reminds us that literature is communication and thus presupposes a reader who is herself conditioned by a cultural context.

For all their variety, these seven essays present writing and reading as subjects fit for serious study, and as practical matters that reward skill, patience, and hard work.

WILLIAM ZINSSER

William Zinsser has had a long and varied career as a journalist, critic, columnist, and teacher of writing. His numerous essays are collected in *The Lunacy Boom* and other books. In this essay from *On Writing Well,* Zinsser discusses the clutter that infects so much American writing today, and emphasizes the importance of revision and editing in the act of writing. In the sample extract that concludes the essay, Zinsser gives an example of his own revising and editing.

Simplicity

WILLIAM ZINSSER

Clutter is the disease of American writing. We are a society strangling in unnecessary words, circular constructions, pompous frills and meaningless jargon.

2   Who can understand the viscous language of everyday American commerce and enterprise: the business letter, the interoffice memo, the corporation report, the notice from the bank explaining its latest "simplified" statement? What member of an insurance or medical plan can decipher the brochure that describes what the costs and benefits are? What father or mother can put together a child's toy—on Christmas Eve or any other eve—from the instructions on the box? Our national tendency is to inflate and thereby sound important. The airline pilot who announces that he is presently anticipating experiencing considerable precipitation wouldn't dream of saying that it may rain. The sentence is too simple—there must be something wrong with it.

3   But the secret of good writing is to strip every sentence to its cleanest components. Every word that serves no function, every long word that could be a short word, every adverb that carries the same meaning that's already in the verb, every passive construction that leaves the reader unsure of who is doing what—these are the thousand and one adulterants that weaken the strength of a sentence. And they usually occur, ironically, in proportion to education and rank.

4   During the late 1960s the president of a major university wrote a letter to mollify the alumni after a spell of campus unrest. "You are probably aware," he began, "that we have been experiencing very considerable potentially explosive expressions of dissatisfaction on issues only partially related." He meant that the students had been hassling them about different things. I was far more upset by the president's English than by the students' potentially explosive expressions of dissatisfaction. I would have preferred the presidential approach taken by Franklin D. Roosevelt when he tried to convert into English his own government's memos, such as this blackout order of 1942:

> Such preparations shall be made as will completely obscure all Federal buildings and non-Federal buildings occupied by the Federal government during an air raid for any period of time from visibility by reason of internal or external illumination.

5   "Tell them," Roosevelt said, "that in buildings where they have to keep the work going to put something across the windows."

6   Simplify, simplify. Thoreau said it, as we are so often reminded, and no American writer more consistently practiced what he preached. Open *Walden* to any page and you will find a man saying in a plain or orderly way what is on his mind:

> I went to the woods because I wished to live deliberately, to front only the essential facts of life, and see if I could not

learn what it had to teach, and not, when I came to die, discover that I had not lived. I did not wish to live what was
not life, living is so dear; nor did I wish to practice resignation, unless it was quite necessary. I wanted to live deep and
suck out all the marrow of life, to live so sturdily and Spar-
tan-like as to put to rout all that was not life, to cut a broad
swath and shave close, to drive life into a corner, and reduce
it to its lowest terms, and, if it proved to be mean, why then
to get the whole and genuine meanness of it, and publish its
meanness to the world; or if it were sublime, to know it by
experience, and be able to give a true account of it.

How can the rest of us achieve such enviable freedom from   7
clutter? The answer is to clear our heads of clutter. Clear thinking
becomes clear writing; one can't exist without the other. It's impossible for a muddy thinker to write good English. You may get away
with it for a paragraph or two, but soon the reader will be lost, and
there's no sin so grave, for the reader will not easily be lured back.

Who is this elusive creature, the reader? The reader is someone   8
with an attention span of about sixty seconds—a person assailed by
forces competing for the minutes that might otherwise be spent on
a magazine or a book. At one time these forces weren't so numerous or so possessive: newspapers, radio, spouse, home, children.
Today they also include a "home entertainment center" (TV, VCR,
video camera, tapes and CDs), pets, a fitness program, a lawn and a
garden and all the gadgets that have been bought to keep them
spruce, and that most potent of competitors, sleep. The person
snoozing in a chair, holding a magazine or a book, is a person who
was being given too much unnecessary trouble by the writer.

It won't do to say that the reader is too dumb or too lazy to keep   9
pace with the train of thought. If the reader is lost, it's usually
because the writer hasn't been careful enough. The carelessness can
take any number of forms. Perhaps a sentence is so excessively cluttered that the reader, hacking through the verbiage, simply doesn't
know what it means. Perhaps a sentence has been so shoddily constructed that the reader could read it in any of several ways. Perhaps
the writer has switched pronouns in midsentence, or has switched
tenses, so the reader loses track of who is talking or when the action
took place. Perhaps Sentence B is not a logical sequel to Sentence A
—the writer, in whose head the connection is clear, hasn't bothered
to provide the missing link. Perhaps the writer has used an important word incorrectly by not taking the trouble to look it up. The
writer may think that "sanguine" and "sanguinary" mean the same
thing, but the difference is a bloody big one. The reader can only
infer (speaking of big differences) what the writer is trying to imply.

10   Faced with such obstacles, readers are at first remarkably tenacious. They blame themselves—they obviously missed something,
and they go back over the mystifying sentence, or over the whole
paragraph, piecing it out like an ancient rune, making guesses and
moving on. But they won't do this for long. The writer is making
them work too hard, and they will look for one who is better at the
craft.

11   Writers must therefore constantly ask: What am I trying to
say? Surprisingly often they don't know. Then they must look at
what they have written and ask: Have I said it? Is it clear to someone encountering the subject for the first time? If it's not, that's
because some fuzz has worked its way into the machinery. The
clear writer is someone clearheaded enough to see this stuff for
what it is: fuzz.

12   I don't mean that some people are born clearheaded and are
therefore natural writers, whereas others are naturally fuzzy and
will never write well. Thinking clearly is a conscious act that writers must force upon themselves, just as if they were embarking on
any other project that requires logic: adding up a laundry list or
doing an algebra problem. Good writing doesn't come naturally,
though most people obviously think it does. The professional
writer is constantly being bearded by strangers who say they'd like
to "try a little writing sometime"—meaning when they retire from
their real profession, like life insurance or real estate. Or they say, "I
could write a book about that." I doubt it.

13   Writing is hard work. A clear sentence is no accident. Very few
sentences come out right the first time, or even the third time.
Remember this as a consolation in moments of despair. If you find
that writing is hard, it's because it *is* hard. It's one of the hardest
things that people do.

is too dumb or too lazy to keep pace with the ~~writer's~~ train of

thought. My sympathies are ~~entirely~~ with him. ~~He's not so dumb.~~ If

the reader is lost, it is generally because the writer ~~of the article~~ has

not been careful enough to keep him on the ~~proper~~ path.

(This carelessness can take any number of ~~different~~ forms. Perhaps

a sentence is so excessively ~~long and~~ cluttered that the reader, hacking

                                                          it
his way through all the verbiage, simply doesn't know what ~~the writer~~

means. Perhaps a sentence has been so shoddily constructed that the

several
reader could read it in any of ~~two or three different~~ ways. ~~He thinks~~
~~he knows what the writer is trying to say, but he's not sure.~~ Perhaps
the writer has switched pronouns in mid-sentence, or ~~perhaps he~~ has
switched tenses, so the reader loses track of who is talking ~~to whom~~ or
~~exactly~~ when the action took place. Perhaps Sentence B is not a logical
sequel to Sentence A -- the writer, in whose head the connection is
bothered to provide
~~perfectly~~ clear, has not ~~given enough thought to providing~~ the missing
link. Perhaps the writer has used an important word incorrectly by not
taking the trouble to look it up ~~and make sure~~. He may think that "sanguine" and "sanguinary" mean the same thing, but ~~I can assure you that~~
the difference is a bloody big one ~~to the reader.~~ *The reader* ~~He~~ can only ~~try to~~
infer ~~when~~ (speaking of big differences) what the writer is trying to
imply.
these
Faced with ~~such a variety~~ of obstacles, the reader is at first a
remarkably tenacious bird. He ~~tends to~~ blame himself. ~~He~~ obviously
missed something, ~~he thinks~~, and he goes back over the mystifying
sentence, or over the whole paragraph, piecing it out like an ancient
rune, making guesses and moving on. But he won't do this for long. ~~He~~
~~will soon run out of patience.~~ The writer is making him work too hard,
one
~~-- harder than he should have to work~~ and the reader will look for ~~a~~
~~writer~~ who is better at his craft.

The writer must therefore constantly ask himself: What am I trying
to say ~~in this sentence?~~ (Surprisingly often, he doesn't know.) ~~And~~ Then
he must look at what he has ~~just~~ written and ask: Have I said it? Is it
encountering
clear to someone ~~who is coming upon~~ the subject for the first time? If

it's not, ~~clear,~~ it is because some fuzz has worked its way into the machinery. The clear writer is a person ~~who is~~ clear-headed enough to see this stuff for what it is: fuzz.

I don't mean ~~to suggest~~ that some people are born clear-headed and are therefore natural writers, whereas ~~other people~~ others are naturally fuzzy and will ~~therefore~~ never write well. Thinking clearly is ~~an~~ a ~~entirely~~ conscious act that the writer must ~~keep forcing~~ force upon himself, just as if he were ~~starting out~~ embarking on any other ~~kind of~~ project that ~~calls for~~ requires logic: adding up a laundry list or doing an algebra problem ~~or playing chess.~~ Good writing doesn't ~~just~~ come naturally, though most people obviously think ~~it's as easy as walking.~~ it does. The professional

Two pages of the final manuscript of this chapter from the First Edition of *On Writing Well*. Although they look like a first draft, they had already been rewritten and retyped—like almost every other page—four or five times. With each rewrite I try to make what I have written tighter, stronger, and more precise, eliminating every element that is not doing useful work. Then I go over it once more, reading it aloud, and am always amazed at how much clutter can still be cut, In this Fourth Edition I've eliminated the sexist pronoun "he" to denote "the writer" and "the reader."

JOHN LEO

Having worked as a reporter for *The New York Times* and as an editor for *Commonweal* and *Time*, John Leo writes about the language of the journalist from first-hand experience. Leo does more than describe this language; like George Orwell, he discusses its causes. Leo focusses, however, on the day-to-day problems that encourage euphemism and other practices of the journalist.

Journalese as a Second Language

JOHN LEO

As a cub reporter, columnist Richard Cohen of *The Washington Post* rushed out one day to interview a lawyer described in many newspaper reports as "ruddy-faced." The man was woozily abusive and lurched about with such abandon that young Cohen instantly realized that the real meaning of ruddy-faced is drunk. This was his introduction to journalese, the fascinating second tongue acquired by most reporters as effortlessly as an Iranian toddler learns Farsi or a Marin County child learns psychobabble.

Fluency in journalese means knowing all about "the right stuff," "gender gap," "life the fast lane" and the vexing dilemma of being caught "between a rock and a hard place," the current Scylla–Charybdis image. The Middle East is "strife-torn," except during those inexplicable moments when peace breaks out. Then it is always "much troubled." Kuwait is located just east of the adjective "oil-rich," and the Irish Republican Army always lurks right behind the word "outlawed." The hyphenated modifier is the meat and potatoes of journalese. Who can forget "the break-away province of Biafra," "the mop-top quartet" (the mandatory second reference to the Beatles), and the "ill-fated Korean jetliner," not to be confused with the "ill-fitting red wig" of Watergate fame. Murderers on death row are often saved by "eleventh-hour" reprieves, which would be somewhere between 10:00 and 11:00 P.M. in English but shortly before midnight in journalese.

Much of the difficulty in mastering journalese comes from its slight overlap with English. "Imposing," for instance, when used to describe a male, retains its customary English meaning, but when used in reference to a female, it always means battle-ax. "Feisty" refers to a person whom the journalist deems too short and too easily enraged, though many in the journalese-speaking fraternity believe it is simply the adjective of choice for any male under 5 ft. 6 in. who is not legally dead. This usage reflects the continual surprise among tall journalists that short people have any energy at all. Women are not often feisty, though they are usually short enough to qualify. No journalist in America has ever referred to a 6-ft. male as feisty. At that height, men are simple "outspoken" (*i.e.*, abusive).

4   In general, adjectives in journalese are as misleading as olive sizes. Most news consumers know enough to translate "developing nations" and "disadvantaged nations" back into English, but far smaller numbers know that "militant" means fanatic, and "steadfast" means pigheaded. "Controversial" introduces someone or something the writer finds appalling, as in "the controversial Miss Fonda," and "prestigious" heralds the imminent arrival of a noun nobody cares about, as in "the prestigious Jean Hersholt Humanitarian Award."

5   Television anchorpersons add interest to their monologues by accenting a few syllables chosen at random. Since print journalists cannot do this, except when reading aloud to spouse and children, they strive for a similar effect by using words like "crisis" and "revolution." "Crisis" means any kind of trouble at all, and "revolution" means any kind of change at all, as in "the revolution in meat packing." "Street value" lends excitement to any drug-bust story, without bearing any financial relationship to the actual value of drugs being busted. Many meaningless adjectives, preferably hyphenated for proper rhythm, are permanently welded to certain nouns: blue-ribbon panel, fact-finding mission, devout Catholic, and rock-ribbed Republican. In journalese there are no devout Protestants or Jews, and no Democrats with strong or stony ribs.

6   Historians of journalese will agree that the first flowering of the language occurred in the sexist descriptions of women by splashy tabloids during the '30s and '40s. In contrast to Pentagonese, which favours oxymorons (Peacekeeper missiles, builddown), the tabloids relied on synecdoche (leggy brunette, bosomy blonde, full-figured redhead). "Full-figured," of course, meant fat, and "well-endowed" did not refer to Ford Foundation funding. "Statuesque" (too large, mooselike) and "petite" (too small, mouselike) were adjectives of last resort, meaning that the woman under discussion had no bodily parts that interested the writer. A plain, short woman, was invariably "pert." For years, masters of this prose cast about for a nonlibelous euphemism for "mistress." The winning entry, "great and good friend," used to describe Marion Davies' relationship to William Randolph Hearst, was pioneered, as it happens, by a non-Hearst publication, *Time* magazine. "Constant companion" evolved later, and gave way to such clunking modernisms as "roommate" and "live-in lover." Nowadays, the only sexuality about which journalese is coy tends to be homosexuality, and that is adequately covered by "he has no close female friends" or "he is not about to settle down."

In political campaigns, underdogs fight uphill battles and hope for shifts of momentum and coattail effects, all leading to rising tides that will enable the favorite to snatch defeat from the jaws of victory. A politician who has no idea about what is going on can be described as one who prefers "to leave details to subordinates." A gangster who runs a foreign country will be referred to as a "strongman" until his death, and "dictator" thereafter. "Strongman," like many terms in journalese, has no true correlative. "Nicaraguan Strongman Somoza" is not balanced with "Cambodian Weakman Prince Sihanouk." 7

What to say about a public figure who is clearly bonkers? Since it is unsporting and possibly libelous to write: "Representative Forbush, the well-known raving psychopath," journalese has evolved the code words "difficult," "intense," and "driven." If an article says, "Like many of us, Forbush has his ups and downs," the writer is wigwagging a manic-depressive. 8

Political journalese, of course, requires a knowledge of sources. An "unnamed analyst" or "observer" can often by presumed to be the writer of the article. The popular plural "observers," or "analysts," refers to the writer and his cronies. Insiders, unlike observer–analysts, sometimes exist in the real world outside the newsroom. This, however, is never true of quotable chestnut vendors in Paris, Greenwich Village bartenders, and other colorful folk conjured up on deadline to lend dash to a story. 9

Almost all sources, like most trial balloonists, live in or around Washington. In order of ascending rectitude, they are: informants, usually reliable sources, informed sources, authoritative sources, sources in high places and unimpeachable sources. Informants are low-level operatives, whose beans are normally spilled to police rather than to reporters. Informed sources, because of their informed nature, are consulted more often by savvy journalists. An unimpeachable source is almost always the President, with the obvious exception of Richard Nixon, who was not unimpeachable. 10

Journalese is controversial but prestigious, and observers are steadfast in averring that it has the right stuff. 11

CAROL SHIELDS

Carol Shields was born in 1935 in Oak Park, Illinois, and moved to Canada in 1957 with her husband, Donald Hugh Shields, with whom she had five children. She received her BA from Hanover College and an MA from the University of Ottawa (where in 1995 she also received an honorary doctorate). She lives in Winnipeg and teaches at the University of Mani-toba. Best known as the author of such celebrated novels as *Small Cere-monies, The Box Garden, Happenstance, A Fairly Conventional Woman, Swann: A Mystery,* and *The Republic of Love,* Shields has also published books of short stories and poetry, and an award-winning play, *Women Waiting.* Her most recent novel, *The Stone Diaries,* has won more prizes than any other Canadian book: runner-up for Britain's Booker–McConnel Prize, and recipient of the Governor General's Award and America's Pulitzer Prize, to name but the most prestigious. In the following essay, Shields muses on the necessity of, and responsi-bility for assuming, imaginative licence — that is, on the mistaken assumptions underlying what has come to be known as "appropriation of voice."

The Same Ticking Clock

CAROL SHIELDS

1   My friend Sarah was worried about her five-year-old son, Simon. "I hear voices in my head," he told her, "and they're talking all the time."

2   It took her a few days to figure out that the buzzings in his brain were nothing more than his own thoughts, the beginning of that lifelong monologue that occupies and imprisons the self.

3   It's here in the private, talky cave of our minds that we spend the greater part of our lives—whether we like it or not. And mostly, it seems, we do like it—"The Soul selects her own Society"—but there are times when the interior tissues thin and when the endless conversation grows unbearably monotonous, when it seems to be going back and forth across the same grooves of experience, the same channels of persuasion, and we long for release. Long, in fact, to become someone else. Even the most fortunate of us lead lives that are sadly limited; we can inhabit only so many places, follow so many lines of work, and can love a finite number of people. We're enclosed not just by the margins of time and by the accident of geography, but by gender and perspective, and by the stubborn resistance of language to certain modes of meditation.

4   Our own stories, moreover, are not quite enough; why else are our newspapers filled with Dear Abby and Ann Landers, with prob-lem columns for golden-agers, for adolescents, mid-lifers, parents, consumers, patients, and professionals? It's not for the solutions that

we devour this often execrable journalese, but for a glimpse of human dilemma, the inaccessible stories of others. Even the smallest narrative fragments have the power to seduce. School children read in their arithmetic books about Mary Brown who buys three pounds of turnips at twenty cents a pound and a kilo and a half of cheese at five dollars a kilo. How much change will she get back from a twenty-dollar bill? The answer arrives easily, or not so easily, but leaves us hungering after the narrative thread—who is this Mary Brown, what will she do with all that cheese, and what of her wider life, her passions and disappointments? A phrase overheard on a bus or perhaps a single name scratched on a wall has the power to call up the world. We want, need, the stories of others. We need, too, to place our own stories beside theirs, to compare, weigh, judge, forgive, and to find, by becoming something other than ourselves, an angle of vision that renews our image of the world.

Writers draw on their own experiences, though only a few draw directly. We want to imbue our fictions with emotional truth; does this require that we stay imprisoned in the tight little outline of our official résumés, that we must write about the Prairies because that's where we live, that we cannot make forays into the swamps of Florida or Mars or Baloneyland, that we must concentrate our steady eyes on the socio-economic class we come from and know best, that we must play it safe—because this is what it amounts to—and write about people of our own generation? A lot of energy has been lost in the name of authenticity; we fear far too much that critical charge—"it doesn't ring true"—and worry too little that it may not ring at all.

"When I write, I am free," Cynthia Ozick argues in one of her essays, collected in her book *Art and Ardor*—and she means utterly free, free to be "a stone, or a raindrop, or a block of wood, or a Tibetan, or the spine of a cactus." Our circumscription is largely of our own making, and at least a portion of it flows from a peculiar reluctance—whether caused by a stance of political purity or a fear of trespassing or "getting it wrong"—to experiment with different points of view, and, in particular, with shifts of gender.

We all know that a fully furnished universe is made up of men and women, and that women writers are often called upon to write about men, and male writers about women. Writers go even further at times, not just writing about the other sex, but speaking through its consciousness, using its voice. The question can be asked, and often is, how successful is this gender-hopping? Does any truth at all seep through? Maybe more than we think. Oscar Wilde had the notion that we can hear more of the author's true voice in her or his fictional impersonations than we can hear in any autobiography. (Not that he bothered with the niceties of gender pronouns.) "Man is least himself," he said, "when he talks in his own person. Give him a mask, and he will tell you the truth." A mask, he said, but he might also have said, a skirt. Or a small pointy beard.

8   This is not to say that crossing gender lines consists of trickery or sleight of hand; nor is it a masquerade as Anne Robinson Taylor, in her book *Male Novelists and Their Female Voices*, would like us to think; and certainly not an impersonation as Oscar Wilde suggests. To believe this is to deny the writer the powers of observation and imagination and also to resist the true composition of the universe, real or created, in which men and women exist in more or less equal numbers.

9   Nevertheless it is still considered a rare achievement for a man to have created a believable and significant woman, and a woman a believable and significant man. We point to these gender trips as exceptions, as marvels. Isn't it amazing, we say, that Brian Moore could get inside the head of Judith Hearne and make us believe in her? And Flaubert—how remarkable that he was able to comprehend the temperament of a French housewife, her yearnings and passion! And there must be a couple of others out there—aren't there? Jane Austen gave us a few men who were worth waiting three or four hundred pages for, although there's a chilliness about even the best of them. Charlotte Brontë uses the male voice in her novel *The Professor*, but the tone is painfully awkward. In writing the male character, Brontë says, she was working under a disadvantage; when writing about women she was surer of her ground. Joyce Carol Oates once remarked that she did badly with male narrators because for her the angle of vision was restricted, and too much feeling and self-awareness had to be sacrificed.

10   A few years ago women could point to their own lack of experience in the world of men, but this situation has been extraordinarily altered by legislation and by a revolution in thinking. What has also been altered is the kind of experience that can legitimately be brought to art—birth, motherhood, the rhythms of the female body, a yearning for love and the domestic component of our lives—which serious literature had previously suppressed. But the news is out: we all, male and female alike, possess a domestic life. The texture of the quotidian is rich with meaning, and the old problem-solution trick is beginning to look like a set-up, a photo opportunity for artificial crisis and faked confrontation. Acknowledgement of that fact leads us to the hypothesis that we are all born with a full range of sympathy toward both men and women—yet something, somewhere, gets in our way and makes us strangers. This is puzzling since, despite the inequities of the power structure, men have always had mothers, sisters, wives, daughters, just as women have had access, albeit limited, to the lives of fathers and brothers, husbands and sons. We have been

living under the same roofs all these years and listening to the same ticking clock.

It seems baffling, then, that in this day there should be so few   11
men and women writing well about the other sex and even sadder that they are not writing *for* the other sex. The world we are being offered as readers is only half-realized, a world divided down its middle. As readers we are being misled; as writers we are cheated. I wonder sometimes if the loneliness writers complain about isn't a result of scraping a single personality, our own, down to its last nuance.

What is needed is permission to leave our own skins, worrying   12
less about verisimilitude and trusting the human core we all share. Of course our experiences are necessarily limited — this is part of the human conundrum — but observation and imagination may lead us to what we intuitively know, and have known all along.

MARGARET ATWOOD

The following essay on the necessity for writers to be engaged in the social and political issues of their time represents the Margaret Atwood who continues to be an active promoter of Canadian cultural nationalism and a compelling voice of PEN International.

The Writer's Responsibility

MARGARET ATWOOD

The subject we have come together to   1
address is one which increases in importance as the giants of this world move closer and closer to violent and fatal confrontation. Broadly put, it is: what is the writer's responsibility, if any, to the society in which he or she lives? The question is not a new one; it's been with us at least since the time of Plato; but more and more the answers of the world's governments have taken the form of amputation: of the tongue, of the soul, of the head.

We in Canada are ill-equipped to come to grips even with the   2
problem, let alone the solution. We live in a society in which the main consensus seems to be that the artist's duty is to entertain and divert, nothing more. Occasionally our critics get a little heavy and start

talking about the human condition, but on the whole the audience prefers art not to be a mirror held up to life but a Disneyland of the soul, containing Romanceland, Spyland, Pornoland, and all the other Escapelands which are so much more agreeable than the complex truth. When we take an author seriously, we prefer to believe that her vision derives from her individual and subjective and neurotic tortured soul—we like artists to have tortured souls—not from the world she is looking at. Sometimes our artists believe this version too, and the ego takes over. *I, me* and *mine* are our favourite pronouns; *we, us* and *ours* are low on the list. The artist is not seen as a lens for focusing the world but as a solipsism. We are good at measuring an author's production in terms of his craft. We are not good at analyzing it in terms of his politics, and by and large we do not do so.

3   By "politics" I do not mean how you voted in the last election, although that is included. I mean who is entitled to do what to whom, with impunity; who profits by it; and who therefore eats what. Such material enters a writer's work not because the writer is or is not consciously political but because a writer is an observer, a witness, and such observations are the air he breathes. They are the air all of us breathe; the only difference is that the author looks, and then writes down what he sees. What he sees will depend on how closely he looks and at what, but look he must.

4   In some countries, an author is censored not only for what he says but how he says it, and an unconventional style is therefore a declaration of artistic freedom. Here we are eclectic; we don't mind experimental styles, in fact we devote learned journals to their analysis; but our critics sneer somewhat at anything they consider "heavy social commentary" or—a worse word—"message." Stylistic heavy-guns are dandy, as long as they aren't pointed anywhere in particular. We like the human condition as long as it is seen as personal and individual. Placing politics and poetics in two watertight compartments is a luxury, just as specialization of any kind is a luxury, and it is possible only in a society where luxuries abound. Most countries in the world cannot afford such luxuries, and this North American way of thinking is alien to them. It was even alien in North America, not long ago. We've already forgotten that in the 1950s many artists, both in the United States and here, were persecuted solely on the grounds of their presumed politics. Which leads us to another mistaken Canadian belief: the belief that it can't happen here.

5   It has happened here, many times. Although our country is one of the most peaceful and prosperous on earth, although we do not shoot artists here, although we do not execute political opponents and although this is one of the few remaining countries in which we can have a gathering like this without expecting to be arrested or blown up, we should not overlook the fact that Canada's record on civil rights

issues is less than pristine. Our treatment of our native peoples has been shameful. This is the country in which citizens of Japanese origin were interned during the Second World War and had their property stolen (when a government steals property it is called "confiscation"); it is also the country in which thousands of citizens were arrested, jailed and held without warrant or explanation, during the time of the War Measures Act, a scant eleven years ago. There was no general outcry in either case. Worse things have not happened not because we are genetically exempt but because we lead pampered lives.

Our methods of controlling artists are not violent, but they do exist. We control through the marketplace and through critical opinion. We are also controlled by the economics of culture, which in Canada still happen to be those of a colonial branch-plant. In 1960 the number of Canadian books published here was minute, and the numbers sold pathetic. Things have changed very much in twenty years, but Canadian books still account for a mere 25 percent of the overall book trade and paperback books for under 5 percent. Talking about this situation is still considered nationalistic chauvinism. Nevertheless, looked at in the context of the wider picture, I suppose we are lucky to have any percent at all; they haven't yet sent in the Marines and if they do it won't be over books, but over oil. 6

We in this country should use our privileged position not as a shelter from the world's realities but as a platform from which to speak. Many are denied their voices; we are not. A voice is a gift; it should be cherished and used, to utter fully human speech if possible. Powerlessness and silence go together; one of the first efforts made in any totalitarian takeover is to suppress the writers, the singers, the journalists, those who are the collective voice. Get rid of the union leaders and pervert the legal system and what you are left with is a reign of terror. 7

As we read the newspapers, we learn we are existing right now in a state of war. The individual wars may not be large and they are being fought far from here, but there is really only one war, that between those who would like the future to be, in the words of George Orwell, a boot grinding forever into a human face, and those who would like it to be a state of something we still dream of as freedom. The battle shifts according to the ground occupied by the enemy. Greek myth tells of a man called Procrustes, who was a great equalizer. He had a system for making all human beings the same size: if they were too small he stretched them, if they were too tall he cut off their feet or their heads. The Procrustes today are international operators, not confined to any one ideology or religion. The world is full of perversions of the notion of equality, just as it is full of perversions of the notion of freedom. True freedom is not being able to do whatever you like to whomever you want to do it to. Freedom that exists as a result of the servitude of others is not true freedom. 8

9   The most lethal weapon in the world's arsenals is not the neutron bomb or chemical warfare, but the human mind that devises such things and puts them to use. But it is the human mind also that can summon up the power to resist, that can imagine a better world than the one before it, that can retain memory and courage in the face of unspeakable suffering. Oppression involves a failure of the imagination: the failure to imagine the full humanity of other human beings. If the imagination were a negligible thing and the act of writing a mere frill, as many in this society would like to believe, regimes all over the world would not be at such pains to exterminate them. The ultimate desire of Procrustes is a population of lobotomized zombies. The writer, unless he is a mere word processor, retains three attributes that power-mad regimes cannot tolerate: a human imagination, in the many forms it may take; the power to communicate; and hope. It may seem odd for me to speak of hope in the midst of what many of my fellow Canadians will call a bleak vision, but as the American writer Flannery O'Connor once said, people without hope do not write novels.

DANY LAFERRIÈRE

Dany Laferrière was born in Port-au-Prince, Haiti, and currently divides his time between Montreal and Florida. In 1985 he published his first novel, *How to Make Love to a Negro (Without Getting Tired)*. That book went on to become a bestseller, first in French and then in English, and eventually was made into a highly successful movie. His other books include *Eroshima, An Aroma of Coffee,* and *Dining with the Dictator.* The essay that follows is from *Why Must a Black Writer Write about Sex.* The self-regarding irony of that title tells us much about Laferrière, who complains of the mixed blessings of instant fame in a world where books are sometimes known only by the writing on their covers.

How to Be Famous without Getting Tired

DANY LAFERRIÈRE

1   The title of my first novel made me famous. People who never read the book, especially those who had no intention of reading it, can quote you the title. It took me five

minutes to come up with it. Three years to write the book. If only I'd known . . . Forget about those hundreds of scribbled pages; all I needed were ten little words: How to Make Love to a Negro without Getting Tired.

The different reactions to the title would make a case study in themselves.   2

1. A cocktail party in Outremont, a tiny Montreal suburb.   3

"Are you the one who wrote the novel with that title?"   4

"I'm afraid so."   5

"Why do you say that? It's wonderful! You're so gifted!"   6

"Thank you."   7

(Should I make my move or not?)   8

She looked at me with a silly smile on her lips. Her husband smiled, too. They were art collectors who owned a clothing-store chain.   9

"My husband hasn't read the book, but your title really made him laugh, I can tell you that." She laughed, too. "It's hilarious!"   10

"We sell lingerie in some of our stores in smaller cities." The man looked vaguely embarrassed. "I was telling my wife that your title would be great in our catalogue."   11

"Not at all," I said. "I think it's a good idea."   12

"Don't listen to him," his wife, a voluptuous redhead, interrupted. "All he thinks about is business."   13

She laughed noisily and clapped her hands, which seemed to be her nervous tic.   14

"You'd actually do it! That's great! And best of all, he's not pretentious! You know, I absolutely must see you again."   15

"Now, listen," the husband said, slipping into his hard-headed businessman's voice. "We'll try it out in the spring catalogue. If it works, we'll sign a contract. I'm not racist, you understand, but I have to wait and see how the clientele reacts. But don't worry, I'm almost sure it'll work."   16

"What are you talking about? Of course it'll work."   17

She smiled at me as if we were already accomplices.   18

"It'll be an honor for us to have your name in our catalogue."   19

The husband led his wife off to the bar.   20

"Don't forget, we absolutely have to see each other. I insist . . ."   21

And she blew me a kiss.   22

2. In Madrid, a young feminist challenged me.   23

"I changed a word in your title. Do you want to know what it is?"   24

"Of course."   25

"How to make love to a Negro without getting *him* tired."   26

27   3. At the Leeds Film Festival, in England, this is what I told a girl who wanted to know why I chose a title like that.

28   "Young lady, if it weren't for that title, you probably wouldn't be here tonight."

29   The hall broke up.

30   4. In New York City, at the première of the film that was made from the novel, a girl (another one!) came up to me.

31   "Are you the author of that book?"

32   "Yes."

33   "Aren't you ashamed of using a title like that?"

34   "No."

35   She threw her glass of wine in my face.

36   5. In London, England, a very tall, very thin man put a drink into my hand.

37   "I've just finished a novel. My publisher tells me it will be a terrible success, but he doesn't like my title."

38   "Publishers are like that."

39   "My book is the first one, I believe," he said, smiling, "that speaks of a white man's attraction for black men."

40   "I see . . . "

41   "According to my publisher, it's going to create a tremendous scandal. I have a favor to ask of you." His voice dropped. "It's very personal . . . Naturally, you're free to say no."

42   Good Lord! I thought to myself, he's going to ask me to fellate him, right here, in the pub. These Englishmen are something else!

43   "May I borrow your title?"

44   "What?"

45   He smiled broadly.

46   "What do you think? It's never been done before — at least, never with the author's permission. My publisher says that if you agree, it's legally feasible. Your title is the only one that fits my subject. I've racked my brains, believe me, but all I find is your title."

47   "If mine is the only one, then take it. But I'm warning you, it'll bring you misery. It's not the kind of title you can get rid of easily."

48   *"How to Make Love to a Negro without Getting Tired*, by John Ferguson. My publisher will be absolutely overjoyed. You know, my publisher is a personal friend of Salman Rushdie's."

49   6. In Paris, a young woman who saw the lighter side of life told me over a glass of wine at the Café de Flore, "I bought your book, you know, but not to read it. I put it on my bedside table; it scares off pretenders.

7. A young white man in Chicago found the title offensive. A young black man in Los Angeles found it racist. A young Montreal woman found it sexist. *Jackpot!*

8. In Toronto, a woman was reading the book in a bus when she noticed that everyone was looking at her strangely.
"I didn't realize that people could read the title on the cover."
"And?"
"I've never been so embarrassed in my life."

9. In Tokyo, the title was completely changed because, as the Japanese distributor told me, "We don't have words like that in Japanese."

10. In Rome, a thin woman, just skin and bones, heading towards sixty, the contessa type, whispered in my ear.
"You'll never guess where I tattooed your title . . . "
"I give up."
"That's what I thought," she said mysteriously, then slipped into the crowd of party-goers at the Duchessa Bocconcini's villa.
How the hell could she have put a title that long on such a small body?

11. In Port-au-Prince, a very demanding friend told me, "The title's the only good thing about your book."

12. In Brussels, an African writer practically screamed at me, "Mark my words, brother, in three weeks no one will even remember your book!"

13. In Antwerp, the translator improved on the title, which became, in Dutch, *How to Make Love to a Negro without Turning Black.*

14. In the United States, all the major daily papers censored the title. *The New York Times, The Washington Post, The Miami Herald, The Los Angeles Times, The Chicago Tribune, The Daily News, The Boston Globe, The New York Post.* Every last one.
I was asked to change the title. I told them it was up to America to change.

15. In San Francisco, everyone liked the title. But that's San Francisco.

16. In Sydney, Australia, a straightforward young woman challenged me to prove the veracity of my title.
There are days like that.

69   17. In Stockholm, a young blonde (what a coincidence!) introduced me to her black lover.

70   "Ask Seko," she laughed, "who gets tired first."

71   "Seko, no doubt," I said.

72   Seko laughed a giant Guinean laugh.

73   "How to make love to two Negroes without getting tired," she murmured with night in her eyes.

74   Seko stopped laughing.

75   18. In Amsterdam, a young white South African woman demanded an answer to this painful question.

76   "How *do* you make love to a Negro without getting tired?"

77   "Let him do all the work."

78   19. All around the world, everyone asks me the same question. Why did you choose that title? Well, why not? One thing's for sure: I never want to hear about it again. I've overdosed on it. Nowadays, it makes me sick.

79   I'm going to tell you how it got started, once and for all. Bouba thought it up. I remember, we were walking down the rue Saint-Denis, in Montreal. It was raining. A summer rain. And Bouba said, as if in a dream, very slowly, "How to make love to a Negro when it's raining and you have nothing better to do." His title was too long, but it was funnier.

80   My first novel. The gods could at least have waited for the third before hitting on me. The first shot. Bull's-eye. Not even the first novel. The first novel's *title*.

>

JOHN BARTH

John Barth was born in Cambridge, Maryland, and educated at Johns Hopkins, where he currently teaches English and creative writing. His novels include *The Floating Opera, The End of the Road, Giles Goat-Boy, The Tidewater Tales,* and *The Last Voyage of Somebody the Sailor,* and they have won him a reputation as one of contemporary literature's most innovative, gifted, and amusing storytellers. Some of his essays on fiction are collected in *The Friday Book.* The following discussion of the place of creative-writing courses in higher education originally appeared in *The New York Times Book Review.*

Writing: Can It Be Taught?

JOHN BARTH

Can it be learned? Sure. Not by everybody, but by more writers per annum than anyone has time to read. Whatever the demand for their product, the supply of able American poets, novelists, and short-story writers has not declined in the second half of this century. An annual national poetry competition, for the Walt Whitman Award, a few years back received 1,475 manuscript *volumes* of verse from which to select and publish one winner; a poetry magazine with 520 subscribers may receive 10,500 poems from 1,875 contributors in a single year. The fiction and poetry editors of the few American large-circulation periodicals that still publish fiction and poetry are comparably deluged, as are the directors of the nation's better-known graduate programs in creative writing. Lots of literature out there.

Is the stuff any good? My experience of winnowing fiction applications to the Johns Hopkins University Writing Seminars is that if not many of them knock our socks off (and we don't want to be desocked by more than ten or a dozen yearly), only a few are downright incompetent. Somehow, somewhere, these multitudes of authors have more or less learned their trade, even before they apply to us or others for fine tuning.

It has been argued that while the supply of reasonably competent American literary artists may exceed their interested readership (the number of over-the-counter sales of that aforementioned Walt Whitman Award poetry collection was smaller than the number of entries from which it was selected), we have presently no writer of international stature; that our Saul Bellow and John Updike, our James Merrill and John Ashbery, are not in the transcendent league of William Faulkner, Ernest Hemingway, T.S. Eliot, Robert Frost; that since the death of Vladimir Nabokov (a nonnative at that), the most commanding figures in contemporary Western literature happen not to be Americans: Samuel Beckett, Jorge Luis Borges, Gabriel García Márquez. In short, that production is up, but quality is down.

4   My own feeling is that a chapter of our literary history that includes the compatriots mentioned above, plus Donald Barthelme, Robert Coover, Stanley Elkin, William H. Gass, John Hawkes, Bernard Malamud, Thomas Pynchon, and Kurt Vonnegut Jr. — to mention middle-aged fictionists only, and only a few of those — is a bright and busy chapter. If it turns out to be, after all, an entr'acte, then the entr'acte, like some of Molière's, may prove livelier than the play. But no matter; the question is beside our point. Genius, like matter in the universe, is thinly distributed; first-magnitude stars are nowhere common. According to *The New York Times* Winter Survey of Education in 1984, there are presently more than 300 degree-granting creative writing programs in American colleges and universities; but not even in America can one major in Towering Literary Artistry.

5   The writing people have in mind when they put the question, "Can it be taught?" is not usually "The Waste Land" or *One Hundred Years of Solitude*; nor is it on the other hand greeting-card doggerel and bodice-rippers. It is your average pretty-damn-good literary artifact as published by *The New Yorker* or *Esquire* or *The Atlantic*, say, or *The Paris Review* or *Antaeus*, or one of the better New York trade-book publishing houses, to be read with more pleasure than not by those who still actually read literature for pleasure.

6   Most such artifacts are the work of men and women who consider themselves writers by trade—rather, by calling; as the critic Earl Rovit has observed, the novelist in America practices a vocation that is seldom quite a profession, economically speaking, and for the poet and short-story writer it is even less so. The rest are the work of able now-and-thenners. All have more or less mastered the art of imaginative writing, as did their predecessors one way or another over the 4,500-year history of written literature. Doubtless there are people whom no amount of patient observation, instruction or practice can teach to serve a shuttlecock or tie a bowline on a bight; such folk find other métiers than badminton and marlinespike seamanship. But "the artful rendition of human experience into written words" (my version of Cleanth Brooks and Robert Penn Warren's definition of literature) gets mastered by the quite talented and approached by the rather talented, generation after generation. Given the inclination and the opportunity, those with any aptitude for it at all surely hone what skills they have, in the art of writing as in any other art, craft, skill.

7   It gets learned.

Can It Be Studied?

8   Boyoboy, can it ever. Since long before the invention of universities, not to mention university programs in creative writing, authors have acquired their authority in four main ways—first, by paying a certain

sort of attention to the experience of life as well as merely undergoing it; second, by paying a certain sort of attention to the works of their great and less great predecessors in the medium of written language, as well as merely reading them; third, by practicing that medium themselves, usually a lot (Charles Newman, the writer and critic, declares that the first prerequisite for aspiring writers is sufficient motor control to keep their pens moving left to right, line after line, hour after hour, day after day, and I would add year after year, decade after decade); and fourth, by offering their apprentice work for discussion and criticism by one or several of their impassioned peers, or by some more experienced hand, or by both.

None of this, obviously, implies an organized practicum course 9 in creative writing, much less a degree-granting program in it. Many and many an eminent writer has spoken out against such courses and programs, but none that I know of against the Fourfold Path such programs at best may conveniently embody. In his excellent book *The Art of Fiction* the late John Gardner cites Ernest Hemingway's remark that the way for a writer to learn his craft is simply to go away and write. He then properly adds, "Hemingway, it may help to remember, went away for free 'tutorials' to two of the finest teachers then living, Sherwood Anderson and Gertrude Stein." The most reclusive of apprentices usually flashes his or her scribblings at *somebody* and tremulously or truculently hangs upon response, for unlike a diary, a poem or story seen by no eyes but its author's can scarcely be said to exist.

Those four obvious, all but universal ways of learning how to 10 write correspond roughly to what I take to be the proper objects of study for all serious writers — their material ("human life," says Aristotle, "its happiness and its misery"), their medium (the language in general, the written language in particular), their craft (the rudiments of, say, fiction, together with conventional and unconventional techniques of their deployment), and their art (the inspired and masterful application of their craft and medium to their material). Not only does the first of these—the material—not imply a creative writing course; it is beyond the proper province of one, though the study of great literature is one excellent handle on "human life, its happiness and its misery." And real mastery of the fourth—the art, as distinct from the craft—is more the hope than the curricular goal of a sound writing program; it comes from mastery of the other three plus a dash of genius.

But these four objects of authorial study, and those four ways to 11 authority, were as surely the Egyptian scribe Kakheperresenb's in circa 2000 B.C. as they are the freshman poet's in this year's class at Iowa or Stanford, Columbia or Johns Hopkins. (Kakheperresenb was a postmodernist of the Middle Kingdom in Egypt, anticipator of

Donald Barthelme and William H. Gass and author of one of the earliest extant literary documents, a papyrus I call "Kakheperresenb's Complaint": "Would I had phrases that are not known, utterances that are strange, in new language that has not been used, free from repetition, not an utterance which men of old have spoken." Compare Mr. Barthelme's "Snow White"—"Oh I wish there were some words in the world that were not the words I always hear"—and Mr. Gass's "Willie Masters' Lonesome Wife"—"Why aren't there any decent words?" Written literature appears virtually to have begun with the eloquent fret that it is perhaps already played out, writing about writing. Moreover, as one might have guessed, the complaint is not original with Kakheperresenb; he's working an established Egyptian literary genre with a considerable history already by 2000 B.C. See the discussion "Complaint Literature," in Miriam Lichtheim's anthology, *Ancient Egyptian Literature*, Vol. I: *The Old and Middle Kingdoms*, which includes Kakheperresenb's specimen, among others.)

12   Well, but what about those 300-plus creative writing operations I mentioned earlier, a phenomenon scarcely to be found outside our republic and scarcely to be found inside it before VJ Day, since when it has proliferated like herpes simplex or the gypsy moth? The sheer numbers involved in that quixotic enterprise are certainly dismaying, as is the immense and touching irony that as fewer and fewer of us incline to read fiction and verse, more and more of us aspire to write it. Not economic recession, not declining literacy, failing bookstores, the usurpation of the kingdom of narrative by movies and television—nothing quenches the American thirst for courses in creative writing. In day school, night school, high school, college, graduate school, correspondence school, summer school, prison school, in writers' colonies and conferences and camps and cruises it is scribble, scribble, scribble, scribble, scribble, scribble, scribble. A very few of these student scribblers will become part of the next crop of American writers; the rest of that next crop are presently scribbling away too, more or less on their own, without benefit of departments and professors and classmates and diplomas in creative writing.

13   Either way, the thing gets learned, all right; and it gets learned, where it does, because it got studied, practiced, and reacted to, in or out of school.

Then Should It Be Taught?

14   Absolutely not, if it can't be; else 'twere fraud. But why on earth not, if it can be, when so astonishingly many want to learn it?

15   Whether it should be offered as a university major leading to the baccalaureate or merely as an elective adjunct to a rigorous general education; whether in either case there should be autonomous

departments of creative writing; whether a master's degree, not to mention a doctorate, is the proper accolade for a typescript volume of poetry or fiction neither more nor less likely to see eventual print than any other graduate thesis; whether, if I aspire like Joyce's Stephen Dedalus "to forge in the smithy of my soul the uncreated conscience of my race," I should do my apprentice racial-conscience forging in Dublin's Trinity College or the Trieste Berlitz School (where the aspiring writer Italo Svevo found a pretty good teacher, James Joyce, to look over his stuff) or Palo Alto or Baltimore or none of the above—these are questions about which the reasonable and knowledgeable, not to mention the unreasonable and ignorant, may disagree. Kay Boyle, late of San Francisco State, opined in these pages not long ago that all creative writing programs ought to be abolished by law. John Gardner, on the other hand, in his preface to the work aforementioned, declares, "I assume from the outset that the would-be writer using this book [which Gardner worked up out of his writing courses] can become a successful writer if he wants to, since most of the people I've known who wanted to become writers, knowing what it meant, *did* become writers."

I am less sanguine in this matter than Gardner ("knowing what it meant" is a participial escape hatch, to be sure), but far less absolute than Miss Boyle. A majority of the advanced apprentice writers I've coached at Johns Hopkins over the past dozen years—not one of them untalented, or he wouldn't have been invited—have not in fact become "successful writers," at least not yet, if success means rather often publishing what one writes. On the other hand, a very fair minority of them have. Of the two thieves crucified along with Jesus, St. Augustine writes: "Do not despair; one thief was saved. Do not presume; one thief was damned." Though many more of our diplomates than not will publish the occasional poem or story here and there along their subsequent way, the odds that one of them will turn into Mary Robison or Frederick Barthelme or Louise Erdrich are less favorable than Augustine's 50–50. 16

I think it just as well that this is so. As a Chesapeake water-man said about the fact that only one in a million blue crab eggs gets to be an adult crab, "It's a damn good thing; otherwise we'd be arse-deep in crabs." How many important new writers must emerge from an annual seminar of ten or a dozen to justify that seminar? One every several years would be an impressive score, in my opinion—so long as (1) the odds are understood, so that there's no false advertising (and what apprentice in any art doesn't understand them?); (2) it is understood further that extraordinary talent tends to cut through these odds, especially when that developing talent receives sustained and intelligent 17 critical attention; and (3) all hands are learning something useful about the ancient medium and craft of literature by working in that seminar room.

18   Among undergraduate writing majors, as might be expected, the success rate is considerably lower if success is measured by subsequent careers as publishing poets and fictionists. But that is the wrong measure, I think. How many undergraduate majors in history, economics, philosophy or literature expect or even wish to become professional historians, economists, philosophers or literary scholars? Their undergraduate major is the focus of their liberal education. A few will proceed to preprofessional graduate training in those fields—or come to it from other fields, as is the case with graduate-student writers. Most will become business people, lawyers, civil servants, teachers, journalists or administrators of this and that. Typical students in Johns Hopkins's Peabody Conservatory of Music, it is true, may hope to become celebrated musicians, but what they reasonably *expect* is a professional career involving music. What most of them in fact become is full- or part-time orchestra players, vocal and instrumental teachers, band and choir directors, piano tuners or music-store operators. A certain number will remain gifted amateurs.

19   Imaginative writing as a major field of study for college undergraduates is somewhere between the traditional liberal arts and the visual and performing arts. Among my own undergraduate classmates and near-classmates in the Hopkins seminars back in the Truman era, only two or three turned out to be professional writers in the usual sense (of those, the best known is Russell Baker of *The New York Times*); most have become the other things that our current undergraduates will become. Rather a lot of them have published the odd item, maybe even a novel or a book of verse, somewhere along the line. Nearly all of them write, in some significant capacity or other, in connection with their work—speeches, reports. My guess is that they all write at least a little better for their season in the seminars, immersed in the study and practice of literary craftsmanship.

20   I'll bet they all *read* more knowledgeably and appreciatively, too, from having attempted literature themselves, just as those who have taken ballet lessons understand things about Baryshnikov and "Firebird" that we more innocent onlookers don't. If the chief product of all those hundreds of American creative writing courses is successful readers rather than successful writers, what a service they render.

21   Which is not at all to argue that it should be taught even if it can't be.

But . . .

Of course it can, though not to everybody, and not by just anybody, and not necessarily in an official course on any sort of campus (though quite possibly and conveniently and effectively there). Not necessarily by a hotshot writer, either, though not impossibly by one.   22

So how come we do it in the university only in America? Because we're Americans, we do everything in our universities. A Pennsylvania State colleague of mine in bygone years was a senior professor in the department of dairy science whose professional specialty was chocolate almond ice cream (I'm not exaggerating half so much as you wish I were). That chap was the emperor of ice cream; his lab was the cutting edge of chocolate almond research. One ate high-tech ice cream in those parts. Oxford and Cambridge, Tübingen and Heidelberg—they'll catch on by and by.   23

Yes, yes, yes: The thing can be taught, here and there. Can you be taught it? Who knows? We can't squeeze blood from a turnip, but chances are we can get the turnip juices flowing, or help to, if they're in there.   24

Do not despair; do not presume. It can be learned by the able; it can be studied, by everybody and his brother; it can even (you know what I mean) be taught, even in school.   25

CYNTHIA OZICK

Cynthia Ozick was born in New York City and graduated from New York University and Ohio State. Her novels include *Trust*, *The Cannibal Galaxy*, and *The Messiah of Stockholm*. She has also published poetry, reviews, translations, short fiction, and two books of critical essays, *Metaphor and Memory* and *Art and Ardor* (from which "A Drugstore in Winter" is taken). Out of what seems a chaos of memories and impressions, she fashions a carefully structured account of what it means to become a writer.

A Drugstore in Winter

CYNTHIA OZICK

This is about reading; a drugstore in winter; the gold leaf on the dome of the Boston State House; also loss, panic, and dread.   1

2   First, the gold leaf. (This part is a little like a turn-of-the-century
pulp tale, though only a little. The ending is a surprise, but there is
no plot.) Thirty years ago I burrowed in the Boston Public Library
one whole afternoon, to find out—not out of curiosity—how the
State House got its gold roof. The answer, like the answer to most
Bostonian questions, was Paul Revere. So I put Paul Revere's gold
dome into an "article," and took it (though I was just as scared by
recklessness then as I am now) to *The Boston Globe*, on Washington
Street. The Features Editor had a bare severe head, a closed paren-
thesis mouth, and silver Dickensian spectacles. He made me wait,
standing, at the side of his desk while he read; there was no bone in
me that did not rattle. Then he opened a drawer and handed me fifteen dollars. Ah, joy of Homer, joy of Milton! Grub Street bliss!

3   The very next Sunday, Paul Revere's gold dome saw print.
Appetite for more led me to a top-floor chamber in Filene's department store: Window Dressing. But no one was in the least bit
dressed—it was a dumbstruck nudist colony up there, a mob of
naked frozen enigmatic manikins, tall enameled skinny ladies with
bald breasts and skulls, and legs and wrists and necks that horribly
unscrewed. Paul Revere's dome paled beside this gold mine! A
sight—mute numb Walpurgisnacht—easily worth another fifteen
dollars. I had a Master's degree (thesis topic: "Parable in the Later
Novels of Henry James") and a job as an advertising copywriter
(9:00 A.M. to 6:00 P.M. six days a week, forty dollars per week; if you
were male and had no degree at all, sixty dollars). Filene's Sale
Days—Crib Bolsters! Lulla-Buys! Jonnie-Mops! Maternity Skirts
with Expanding Invisible Trick Waist! And a company show; gold
watches to mark the retirement of elderly Irish salesladies; for me
the chance to write song lyrics (to the tune of "On Top of Old
Smoky") honoring our Store. But "Mute Numb Walpurgisnacht in
Secret Downtown Chamber" never reached the *Globe*. Melancholy
and meaning business, the Advertising Director forbade it. Grub
Street was bad form, and I had to promise never again to sink to
another article. Thus ended my life in journalism.

4   Next: reading, and certain drugstore winter dusks. These come
together. It is an aeon before Filene's, years and years before the
Later Novels of Henry James. I am scrunched on my knees at a
round glass table near a plate glass door on which is inscribed, in
gold leaf Paul Revere never put there, letters that must be read
backward: ⎡ PARK VIEW PHARMACY ⎤ . There is an evening smell of late
coffee from the fountain, and all the librarians are lined up in a row
on the tall stools, sipping and chattering. They have just stepped in
from the cold of the Traveling Library, and so have I. The Traveling
Library is a big green truck that stops, once every two weeks, on the
corner of Continental Avenue, just a little way in from Westchester

Avenue, not far from a house that keeps a pig. Other houses fly pigeons from their roofs, other yards have chickens, and down on Mayflower there is even a goat. This is Pelham Bay, the Bronx, in the middle of the Depression, all cattails and weeds, such a lovely place and tender hour! Even though my mother takes me on the subway far, far downtown to buy my winter coat in the frenzy of Klein's on Fourteenth Street, and even though I can recognize the heavy power of a quarter, I don't know it's the Depression. On the trolley on the way to Westchester Square I see the children who live in the boxcar strangely set down in an empty lot some distance from Spy Oak (where a Revolutionary traitor was hanged—served him right for siding with redcoats); the lucky boxcar children dangle their stick-legs from their train-house maw and wave; how I envy them! I envy the orphans of the Gould Foundation, who have their own private swings and seesaws. Sometimes I imagine I am an orphan, and my father is an imposter pretending to be my father.

My father writes in his prescription book: *#59330 Dr. O'Flaherty*   5 *Pow .60 | #59331 Dr. Mulligan Gtt .65 | #59332 Dr. Thron Tab .90.* Ninety cents! A terrifically expensive medicine; someone is really sick. When I deliver a prescription around the corner or down the block, I am offered a nickel tip. I always refuse, out of conscience; I am, after all, the Park View Pharmacy's own daughter, and it wouldn't be seemly. My father grinds and mixes powders, weighs them out in tiny snowy heaps on an apothecary scale, folds them into delicate translucent papers or meticulously drops them into gelatin capsules.

In the big front window of Park View Pharmacy there is a star-   6 tling display—goldfish bowls, balanced one on the other in amazing pyramids. A German lady enters, one of my father's cronies— his cronies are both women and men. My quiet father's eyes are water-color blue, he wears his small skeptical quiet smile and receives the neighborhood's life-secrets. My father is discreet and inscrutable. The German lady pokes a punchboard with a pin, pushes up a bit of rolled paper, and cries out—she has just won a goldfish bowl, with two swimming goldfish in it! Mr. Jaffe, the salesman from McKesson & Robbins, arrives, trailing two mists: winter steaminess and the animal fog of his cigar,* which melts into the coffee smell, the tarpaper smell, the eerie honeyed tangled drugstore smell. Mr. Jaffe and my mother and father are intimates by now, but because it is the 1930s, so long ago, and the old manners still survive, they address one another gravely as Mr. Jaffe,

---

* Mr. Matthew Bruccoli, another Bronx drugstore child, has written to say that he remembers with certainty that Mr. Jaffe did not smoke. In my memory the cigar is somehow there, so I leave it.

Mrs. Ozick, Mr. Ozick. My mother calls my father Mr. O, even at home, as in a Victorian novel. In the street my father tips his hat to ladies. In the winter his hat is a regular fedora; in the summer it is a straw boater with a black ribbon and a jot of blue feather.

7   What am I doing at this round glass table, both listening and not listening to my mother and father tell Mr. Jaffe about their struggle with "Tessie," the lion-eyed landlady who has just raised, threefold, in the middle of that Depression I have never heard of, the Park View Pharmacy's devouring rent? My mother, not yet forty, wears bandages on her ankles covering oozing varicose veins; back and forth she strides, dashes, runs, climbing cellar stairs or ladders; she unpacks cartons, she toils behind drug counters and fountain counters. Like my father, she is on her feet until one in the morning, the Park View's closing hour. My mother and father are in trouble, and I don't know it. I am too happy. I feel the secret center of eternity, nothing will ever alter, no one will ever die. Through the window, past the lit goldfish, the gray oval sky deepens over our neighborhood wood, where all the dirt paths lead down to seagull-specked water. I am familiar with every frog-haunted monument: Pelham Bay Park is thronged with WPA art—statuary, fountains, immense rococo staircases cascading down a hillside, Bacchus-faced stelae—stone Roman glories afterward mysteriously razed by an avenging Robert Moses. One year—how distant it seems now, as if even the climate is past returning—the bay froze so hard that whole families, mine among them, crossed back and forth to City Island, strangers saluting and calling out in the ecstasy of the bright trudge over such a sudden wilderness of ice.

8   In the Park View Pharmacy, in the winter dusk, the heart in my body is revolving like the goldfish fleet-finned in their clear bowls. The librarians are still warming up over their coffee. They do not recognize me, though only half an hour ago I was scrabbling in the mud around the two heavy boxes from the Traveling Library—oafish crates tossed with a thump on the ground. One box contains magazines—Boy's Life, The American Girl, Popular Mechanix. But the other, the other! The other transforms me. It is tumbled with story-books, with clandestine intimations and transfigurations. In school I am a luckless goosegirl, friendless and forlorn. In P.S. 71 I carry, weighty as a cloak, the ineradicable knowledge of my scandal—I am cross-eyed, dumb, an imbecile at arithmetic; in P.S. 71 I am pub-licly shamed in Assembly because I am caught not singing Christ-mas carols; in P.S. 71 I am repeatedly accused of deicide. But in the Park View Pharmacy, in the winter dusk, branches blackening in the park across the road, I am driving in rapture through the Violet Fairy Book and the Yellow Fairy Book, insubstantial chariots snatched from the box in the mud. I have never been *inside* the

Traveling Library; only grownups are allowed. The boxes are for the children. No more than two books may be borrowed, so I have picked the fattest ones, to last. All the same, the Violet and the Yellow are melting away. Their pages dwindle. I sit at the round glass table, dreaming, dreaming. Mr. Jaffe is murmuring advice. He tells a joke about Wrong-Way Corrigan. The librarians are buttoning up their coats. A princess, captive of an ogre, receives a letter from her swain and hides it in her bosom. I can visualize her bosom exactly —she clutches it against her chest. It is a tall and shapely vase, with a hand-painted flower on it, like the vase on the secondhand piano at home.

I am incognito. No one knows who I truly am. The teachers in P.S. 71 don't know. Rabbi Meskin, my *cheder* teacher, doesn't know. Tessie the lion-eyed landlady doesn't know. Even Hymie the fountain clerk can't know—though he understands other things better than anyone: how to tighten roller skates with a skatekey, for instance, and how to ride a horse. On Friday afternoons, when the new issue is out, Hymie and my brother fight over who gets to see *Life* magazine first. My brother is older than I am, and doesn't like me; he builds radios in his bedroom, he is already W2LOM, and operates his transmitter (*da-di-da-dit, da-da-di-da*) so penetratingly on Sunday mornings that Mrs. Eva Brady, across the way, complains. Mrs. Eva Brady has a subscription to *The Writer*; I fill a closet with her old copies. How to Find a Plot. Narrative and Character, the Writer's Tools. Because my brother has his ham license, I say, "I have a license too." "What kind of license?" my brother asks, falling into the trap. "Poetic license," I reply; my brother hates me, but anyhow his birthday presents are transporting: one year *Alice in Wonderland*, *Pinocchio* the next, then *Tom Sawyer*. I go after Mark Twain, and find *Joan of Arc* and my first satire, *Christian Science*. My mother surprises me with *Pollyanna*, the admiration of her Lower East Side childhood, along with *The Lady of the Lake*. Mrs. Eva Brady's daughter Jeannie has outgrown her Nancy Drews and Judy Boltons, so on rainy afternoons I cross the street and borrow them, trying not to march away with too many—the child of immigrants, I worry that the Bradys, true and virtuous Americans, will judge me greedy or careless. I wrap the Nancy Drews in paper covers to protect them. Old Mrs. Brady, Jeannie's grandmother, invites me back for more. I am so timid I can hardly speak a word, but I love her dark parlor; I love its black bookcases. Old Mrs. Brady sees me off, embracing books under an umbrella; perhaps she divines who I truly am. My brother doesn't care. My father doesn't notice. I think my mother knows. My mother reads the *Saturday Evening Post* and the *Woman's Home Companion*; sometimes the *Ladies' Home Journal*, but never *Good Housekeeping*. I read all my mother's magazines. My

9

father reads *Drug Topics* and *Der Tog*, the Yiddish daily. In Louie Davidowitz's house (waiting our turn for the rabbi's lesson, he teaches me chess in *cheder*) there is a piece of furniture I am in awe of: a shining circular table that is also a revolving bookshelf holding a complete set of Charles Dickens. I borrow *Oliver Twist*. My cousins turn up with *Gulliver's Travels, Just So Stories, Don Quixote*, Oscar Wilde's *Fairy Tales*, uncannily different from the usual kind. Blindfolded, I reach into a Thanksgiving grabbag and pull out *Mrs. Leicester's School*, Mary Lamb's desolate stories of rejected children. Books spill out of rumor, exchange, miracle. In the Park View Pharmacy's lending library I discover, among the nurse romances, a browning, brittle miracle: *Jane Eyre*. Uncle Morris comes to visit (*his* drugstore is on the other side of the Bronx) and leaves behind, just like that, a three-volume Shakespeare. Peggy and Betty Provan, Scottish sisters around the corner, lend me their *Swiss Family Robinson*. Norma Foti, a whole year older, transmits a rumor about Louisa May Alcott; afterward I read *Little Women* a thousand times. Ten thousand! I am no longer incognito, not even to myself. I am Jo in her "vortex"; not Jo exactly, but some Jo-of-the-future. I am under an enchantment: who I truly am must be deferred, waited for and waited for. My father, silently filling capsules, is grieving over his mother in Moscow. I write letters in Yiddish to my Moscow grandmother, whom I will never know. I will never know my Russian aunts, uncles, cousins. In Moscow there is suffering, deprivation, poverty. My mother, threadbare, goes without a new winter coat so that packages can be sent to Moscow. Her fiery justice-eyes are semaphores I cannot decipher.

10   Some day when I am free of P.S. 71, I will write stories; meanwhile, in winter dusk, in the Park View, in the secret bliss of the Violet Fairy Book, I both see and do not see how these grains of life will stay forever, papa and mama will live forever, Hymie will always turn my skatekey.

11   Hymie, after Italy, after the Battle of the Bulge, comes back from the war with a present: *From Here to Eternity*. Then he dies, young. Mama reads *Pride and Prejudice* and every single word of Willa Cather. Papa reads, in Yiddish, all of Sholem Aleichem and Peretz. He reads Malamud's *The Assistant* when I ask him to.

12   Papa and mama, in Staten Island, are under the ground. Some other family sits transfixed in the sun parlor where I read *Jane Eyre* and *Little Women* and, long afterward, *Middlemarch*. The Park View Pharmacy is dismantled, turned into a Hallmark card shop. It doesn't matter! I close my eyes, or else only stare, and everything is in its place again, and everyone.

13   A writer is dreamed and transfigured into being by spells, wishes, goldfish, silhouettes of trees, boxes of fairy tales dropped in

the mud, uncles' and cousins' books, tablets and capsules and pow-ders, papa's Moscow ache, his drugstore jacket with his special fountain pen in the pocket, his beautiful Hebrew paragraphs, his Talmudist's rationalism, his Russian-Gymnasium Latin and Ger-man, mama's furnace-heart, her masses of memoirs, her paintings of autumn walks down to the sunny water, her braveries, her rever-ies, her old, old school hurts.

A writer is buffeted into being by school hurts — Orwell, For-ster, Mann! — but after a while other ambushes begin: sorrows, deaths, disappointments, subtle diseases, delays, guilts, the spite of the private haters of the poetry side of life, the snubs of the glam-orous, the bitterness of those for whom resentment is a daily gruel, and so on and so on; and then one day you find yourself leaning here, writing at that selfsame round glass table salvaged from the Park View Pharmacy—writing this, an impossibility, a summary of how you came to be where you are now, and where, God knows, is that? Your hair is whitening, you are a well of tears, what you meant to do (beauty and justice) you have not done, papa and mama are under the earth, you live in panic and dread, the future shrinks and darkens, stories are only vapor, your inmost craving is for nothing but an old scarred pen, and what, God knows, is that? 14

Writing Effective Sentences

This part of the section on style will show you how to make your sentences more effective as you draft and revise your paragraphs and essays. Unity and proper emphasis are just as important in sentences as they are in paragraphs. In fact, sentences can be loosely viewed as miniature paragraphs. For example, in the same way that the topic sentence of a paragraph states the core idea that the remainder of the paragraph develops, the main clause of a simple or complex sentence states the core idea that the rest of the sentence develops through its modifiers:

> *I heard* instead the shriek of brakes, the heavy throbbing of the once-a-day Braniff airliner into Minot, the shattering sirens born of war, the honk of a diesel locomotive which surely cannot call to faraway places the heart of a wakeful boy like the old steam whistle in the night. (Eric Sevareid, "Velva, North Dakota"; italics added)

The core subject and verb of this complex sentence (*I heard*) is completed by a series of modified objects—the final object further modified by a lengthy subordinate clause beginning with the word *which*.

Just as a series of main ideas combine in a single paragraph, so can simple and compound sentences join to form larger, single sentences:

> You can walk down the streets of my town now and hear from open windows the intimate voices of the Washington commentators in casual converse on the great affairs of state [*simple sentence: main clause with compound predicate*]; but you cannot hear on Sunday morning the singing in Norwegian of the Lutheran hymns [*simple sentence: main clause with simple predicate*]; the old country seems now part of a world left long behind and the old-country accents grow fainter in the speech of my Velva neighbors [*compound sentence: two main clauses with simple predicates*]. (Sevareid, "Velva, North Dakota"; italics added)

And so can main and subordinate ideas, expressed in main and subordinate clauses and their modifiers, combine to form larger sentences:

Attic and screen porch are slowly vanishing [*main clause*] and lovely shades of pastel are painted upon new homes [*main clause*], tints that once would have embarrassed farmer and merchant alike [*subordinate clause modifying the appositive "tints"*]. (Sevareid, "Velva, North Dakota"; italics added)

Though the parallel between paragraphs and sentences suggested here is not exact (main clauses do not always contain the most important idea of a sentence), sentences do, like paragraphs, build from cores to which subordinate ideas and details must relate. And sentences, like paragraphs, also can contain two or more core ideas.

We write as we speak—stressing the core idea of a simple sentence and joining several core ideas into compound ones. We also place modifying words, phrases, and clauses in different positions in writing, as in speech, to gain different kinds of emphasis. In addition, we frequently make special use of the beginning and ending of a simple sentence for emphasis. We can, however, achieve emphasis in other ways. The following discussion illustrates these possibilities.

Addition and Modification

As a paragraph usually begins with a topic sentence that states the subject or central idea, so a sentence may begin with a main clause that performs a similar job. Here is a sentence from Northrop Frye's account of how students learn:

> *I am certainly no expert on the teaching of children,*
> > *but it* seems obvious
> > > *that all* such teaching has to follow the child's own rhythm of thought and development,
> > > *and not* project on him some half-baked adult mystique,
> > > *whether that* mystique claims to derive from the anti-intellectual left or the anti-intellectual right. (Northrop Frye, "Elementary Teaching"; italics added)

The three subordinate clauses—beginning *that all, and not, whether that* — qualify the idea expressed in the first main clause: they tell us Frye's "nonexpert" views on elementary teaching. Notice that these clauses are each as long as the main clause. Notice, too, that the third clause modifies an element in the second. English sentences can be modified endlessly. They are not, however, because the reader would soon lose sight of the central idea. The length of a sentence often depends on how many ideas and details a reader can grasp.

Emphasis

In speaking, we vary our sentences without much, if any, thought, interrupting the flow of ideas to emphasize a word or phrase, or to repeat an idea. The speaker of the following sentence, a witness before a royal commission, repeats certain phrases and qualifies his ideas in a typical way:

> My experience is that we hold people sometimes in jail, young people in jail, for days at a time with a complete lack of concern for the parents, if they do live in homes where parents live together, a complete lack of concern in many instances on the part of the community or other agencies as to where these young people are or what they are doing.

Sentences as complex and disjointed as this one seems when transcribed are understood easily when spoken, because the speaker is able to vary the vocal inflection to stress key words and phrases. Written punctuation sometimes clarifies the points of emphasis, but in a limited way. Because we cannot depend directly on vocal inflection for clarity and emphasis in writing, we instead suggest these inflections by shaping the sentence in accord with ordinary speech patterns. Clearly written sentences stay close to these patterns.

The core of English sentences, we saw, can be expanded, and at length, if each modifier is clearly connected to what precedes it. To achieve special emphasis, the writer may vary the sentence even more, perhaps by making special use of the end of the sentence—the position that in English tends to be the most emphatic:

> The cold passed reluctantly from the earth, and the retiring fogs revealed an army stretched out on the hills, *resting.* (Stephen Crane, *The Red Badge of Courage*; italics added)

Or the writer may break up the sentence so that individual ideas and experiences receive separate emphasis:

> The youth stopped. He was transfixed by this terrific medley of all noises. It was as if worlds were being rended. There was the ripping sound of musketry and the breaking crash of the artillery. (Crane, *The Red Badge of Courage*)

The relation of the subordinate clauses to other elements in a sentence is controlled largely by the requirements of English word order. The position of subordinate clauses that serve as nouns or adjectives (sometimes called *noun clauses* and *adjective clauses*) is rather fixed; the position of subordinate clauses that serve as adverbs (sometimes called *adverb clauses*) is not. The position of the adverb clause depends on its importance as an idea and on its length:

> I majored in zoology *because I like working with animals.*
> *Because I like working with animals*, I majored in zoology.

The position of the subordinate clause determines what information is stressed. In the first sentence, the subordinate clause seems to express the more important idea because it follows the main clause. In the second sentence, the main clause receives the emphasis. But the end of the sentence will not take the thrust of meaning if ideas appearing toward the beginning are given special emphasis.

Our informal spoken sentences show the least variation and depend heavily on co-ordination. The *stringy sentence* in writing—a series of ideas joined loosely with *and* and other conjunctions—is a heavily co-ordinated sentence without the usual vocal markers. The sentence *fragment*—a detached phrase or clause, or a sentence missing either a subject or a verb—sometimes derives from the clipped sentences and phrases common in speech.

Loose and Periodic Sentences

Sentences are sometimes classified as loose or periodic to distinguish two important kinds of emphasis: the use made of the beginning or the end of the sentence. The loose sentence begins with the core idea, explanatory and qualifying phrases and clauses trailing behind:

> It was not a screeching noise, only an intermittent hump-hump as if the bird had to recall his grievance each time before he repeated it. (Flannery O'Connor, *The Violent Bear It Away*)

If the ideas that follow the core are afterthoughts, or inessential details, the sentence will seem "loose" — easy and relaxed in its movement, a leisurely accretion of detail:

> It mingled with the smell of chalk dust and eraser crumbs, of crude ink splashed into ink-wells by unsteady jug-bearers, of apples and pencil shavings and gum. (Fredelle Bruser Maynard, "The Windless World")

A subordinate element will not seem unemphatic or plodding, however, if it expresses a strong action or idea:

> The giggle rose to a laugh, then to a piercing *falsetto* peal. He began to dance about the lobby, skipping and cackling. (Cam Stirling, "The Fall, Rise, and Fall of Elevators")

Opening with subordinate elements or with a series of appositives, the periodic sentence ends with the core:

> If we had not felt that, after coming to this conclusion, we were bound to set aside our private opinions on matters of detail, if we had not felt ourselves bound to look at what was practicable, not obstinately rejecting the opinions of others nor adhering to our own; if we had not met, I say, in a spirit of conciliation, and with an anxious, overruling desire to form one people under one government, we never would have succeeded. (Sir John A. Macdonald, "Confederation")

The strongly periodic sentence is usually reserved for unusually strong emphasis:

> To believe your own thought, to believe that what is true for you in your private heart is true for all men — that is *genius*. (Ralph Waldo Emerson, "Self-Reliance")

Most contemporary English sentences fall between the extremely loose and the extremely periodic. Compound sentences seem loose when succeeding clauses serve as afterthoughts or qualifications rather than as ideas equal in importance to the opening idea:

> At that point, things got pretty hot and heavy — at least, I imagine they did. (Erika Ritter, "Mangiamania")

Periodic sentences are used sparingly, with a distribution of emphasis more often through the whole sentence, as in Macdonald's sentence above. Sometimes two moderately periodic sentences will be co-ordinated, with a corresponding distribution of emphasis:

> Though reliable narration is by no means the only way of conveying to the audience the facts on which dramatic irony is based, it is a useful way, and in some works, works in which no one but the author can conceivably know what

needs to be known, it may be indispensable. (Wayne C. Booth, *The Rhetoric of Fiction*)

Climax

Periodic sentences achieve climax by delaying the main idea or the completion of the main idea until the end of the sentence. Even in loose or co-ordinated sentences, modifying or qualifying phrases and clauses following the main idea can be arranged in the order of rising importance — as in *I came, I saw, I conquered.* Here are sentences of Annie Dillard's that do the same:

> But shadows spread, and deepened, and stayed.

> I close my eyes and I see stars, deep stars giving way to deeper stars, deeper stars bowing to deeper stars at the crown of an infinite cone. (Annie Dillard, "At Tinker Creek")

A sense of anticipation, promoted through the ideas themselves, is necessary to climax. Anticlimax will result if the culminating idea is less significant than what has gone before. The resulting letdown may be deliberately comic:

> If once a man indulges himself in murder, very soon he comes to think little of robbery; and from robbing he next comes to drinking and Sabbath-breaking, and from that to incivility and procrastination. (Thomas De Quincey, *Supplementary Papers*)

Parallelism

The italicized words in the following sentence are parallel in structure; that is, they perform the same grammatical function in the sentence and, as infinitives, are the same in form:

> So long as I remain alive and well I shall continue *to feel* strongly about prose style, *to love* the surface of the earth, and *to take* a pleasure in solid objects and scraps of useless information. (George Orwell, *Why I Write*; italics added)

In speaking and writing, we make elements such as these infinitives parallel naturally. No matter how many words separate them, we continue the pattern we start. Indeed, our "sentence sense" tells us when a pattern has been interrupted. We know something is wrong when we read:

> I shall continue to feel strongly about prose style, to love the surface of the earth, and taking pleasure in solid objects and scraps of useless information.

Parallelism is an important means to concision and focus in sentences. It also allows us to make additions to the sentence without loss of clarity. A special use of parallelism is the balancing of similar ideas in a sentence for special emphasis:

> The savage bows down to idols of wood and stone: the civilized man to idols of flesh and blood. (George Bernard Shaw, *Man and Superman*)

Notice that the parallel phrases here are of the same weight and length. Writers can balance clauses as Sir John A. Macdonald does in the following example from "Confederation":

> Ourselves already threatened, our trade interrupted, our intercourse, political and commercial, destroyed, if we do not take warning now when we have the opportunity, and while one avenue is threatened to be closed, open another by taking advantage of the present arrangement and the desire of the Lower Provinces to draw closer the alliance between us, we may suffer commercial and political disadvantages it may take long for us to overcome.

The marked rhythm of this sentence creates a highly formal effect by slowing the tempo. Such exact balance interrupts the natural flow of the sentence, giving emphasis to most or all of its parts. For this reason it is exceptional to find sentences as studied and formal as this in modern writing. But we do find a moderate balance used to give a greater emphasis to similar ideas than ordinary parallelism provides.

Antithesis

When contrasting ideas are balanced in sentences and paragraphs, they are said to be in antithesis:

> History proves that dictatorships do not grow out of strong and successful governments, but out of weak and helpless ones. (Franklin D. Roosevelt)

This moderate balancing to heighten the contrast of ideas is found often in modern writing, though usually in formal discussions. Like the exact balance of similar ideas, the balancing of sentences containing antithetical phrases is exceptional today. The following passage is the climax of a long book on the history of Roman society:

> Rome did not invent education, but she developed it on a scale unknown before, gave it state support, and formed the curriculum that persisted till our harassed youth. She did not invent the arch, the vault, or the dome, but she used them with such audacity and magnificence that in some fields her architecture has remained unequaled. (Will Durant, *Caesar and Christ*)

Sentence Length

There is nothing inherently effective or ineffective, superior or inferior about short or long sentences, just as there is nothing inherently effective or ineffective in a single note of the scale. How effective a sentence is depends on what it does in a paragraph or essay. The very short, disconnected sentences in this passage by Guy Vanderhaeghe express the resignation that a man in his mid-thirties feels, having reconciled himself to a permanent estrangement from his wife:

> I'm tired. Waiting is tiring. And then because I don't want to see things I have to keep my eyes open. The rain makes this hard. It can lull you. I wonder how long it will keep up. It's a fine thing this smell of drenched, yielding earth. If I could only close my eyes without seeing things I could sleep. And if I could sleep I know I'd soon be as right as rain. Right, right as rain. (Guy Vanderhaeghe, *My Present Age*)

A sentence, as we have seen, often starts with the main idea and develops it:

> The speech of a small child is full of chanting and singing, and it is clear that the child understands what many adults do not, that verse is a more direct and primitive way of conventionalizing speech than prose is. (Northrop Frye, "Elementary Teaching")

How much detail a writer can provide depends on how prominent the main ideas are—whether in a sentence consisting of a single core idea, followed by a series of modifiers, or in one consisting of a series of connected core ideas or main clauses, modified as in this sentence:

> At this moment, in consequence of the ill-feeling which has arisen between England and the United States—a feeling of which Canada was not the cause—in consequence of the irritation which now exists, owing to the unhappy state of affairs on this continent, the Reciprocity Treaty, it seems probable, is about to be brought to an end—our trade is hampered by the passport system, and at any moment we may be deprived of permission to carry our goods through United States channels—the bonded goods system may be done away with, and the winter trade through the United States put an end to. (Sir John A. Macdonald, "Confederation")

Faulty Diction

The word *diction* refers in general to choice of words in speaking and writing. The choice may simply be a matter of vocabulary—as in exposition, when you name a specific tool in performing a job, or in descriptive writing, when you choose concrete words or phrases and vivid images to create a mental picture. The choice may also be emotional—as in persuasive writing, when you choose words that are exact but that also move the reader to accept an idea or take action. In addition, diction concerns not only the nature and use of words but also their misuse. You must not only find words with appropriate connotations but also avoid words with misleading connotations.

We hear much today about the abuse of language—particularly about euphemism and equivocation, such as that cited by William Zinsser in his discussion of language included in "Reading and Writing":

> During the late 1960s the president of a major university wrote a letter to mollify the alumni after a spell of campus unrest. "You are probably aware," he began, "that we have been experiencing very considerable potentially explosive expressions of dissatisfaction on issues only partially related." He meant that the students had been hassling them about different things. (William Zinsser, "Simplicity")

We can guess what Zinsser would say about contemporary political language—about such phrases as "credibility gap" and "positive reference input" to describe the good and bad reputations of office-holders and candidates, and in non-political discourse, "learning resource centres" and "interfaces between student and teacher" to describe libraries and conferences. Such vague and pretentious language can be comical, as George Orwell shows in "Politics and the English Language," but abuses of language can lead to the kind of muddled thinking that ultimately threatens our freedom as individuals.

The following suggestions will help you to identify some faults in diction.

1. Using the same word more than once in a sentence can be confusing if the senses are different:

   We were present for the presentation of the award.

   However, we need not avoid repeating a word if the senses are the same. Indeed, substituting can also be confusing.

   The person who entered was not the individual I was expecting.

   Though *individual* is a popular synonym for *person*, it has other meanings. The substitution could confuse the reader.

2. Needless repetition can make sentences hard to understand.

   There are necessary skills that writers need to make their ideas easy to understand and comprehensible.

3. Words that overlap in meaning can have the same effect:

   The result of the survey should produce a change in policy.

   The words *result* and *produce* mean the same thing in the sentence. The following sentence is satisfactory:

   The survey should produce a change in policy.

4. Euphemism — providing a mild or pleasant substitute for a blunt term—can be a source of ambiguity. Euphemisms such as *Young Offender* to describe a juvenile criminal and the phrase *mentally challenged* to describe slow learners help us avoid giving pain. What words should we use in speaking about children who have trouble learning or have broken the law? No

easy answers exist: we know the price of speaking bluntly, but also the price of hiding facts.

5. Equivocal terms are also a source of ambiguity because they have double meanings. The word *exceptional* is widely used to describe bright children as well as mentally and physically challenged ones or children who have broken the law. We need to know which children we are talking about.

6. A cliché is a phrase or saying that has become trite through overuse: *sweet as sugar, conspicuous by his absence, more sinned against than sinning*. A bromide is a comforting platitude: *it's the effort that counts, not the winning*. Both rob prose of conviction and vigour.

7. Mixed metaphors cause confusion and can be unintentionally funny:

   Blows to one's pride stick in the craw.

8. Technical words or jargon can also have the same effect. The words *interface* (to describe the boundary between two independent machines) and *software* (to describe accessory equipment) are useful words in computer language. They become jargon in a different sense of the word—to quote H.W. Fowler, "talk that is considered both ugly-sounding and hard to understand"—when borrowed to describe other things. A conference is not an "interface," and referring to a book as "software" suggests something mechanical or perhaps dispensable.

9. Circumlocution means taking the long way around—in other words, saying something in inflated language: saying "he has difficulty distinguishing the real from the imagined" when we mean "he lies." Euphemisms often depend on inflation of this kind.

GLOSSARY

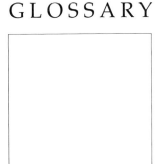

ALLUSION: An indirect reference to a presumably well-known literary work or a historical event or figure. The phrase "the Waterloo of his political career" is a reference to Napoleon's disastrous defeat at the Battle of Waterloo in 1815. The allusion implies that the career of the politician under discussion has come to a disastrous end.

ANALOGY: A point-by-point comparison between two unlike things or activities (for example, comparing writing an essay to building a house) for the purpose of illustration or argument. Unlike a comparison (or contrast), in which the things compared are of equal importance, analogy exists for the purpose of illustrating or arguing the nature of one of the compared things, not both.

ANTITHESIS: The arrangement of contrasting ideas in grammatically similar phrases and clauses (*The world will little note, nor long remember, what we say here, but it can never forget what they did here.*—Abraham Lincoln, *Gettysburg Address*). See *parallelism*.

ARGUMENT: Proving the truth or falseness of a statement. Arguments are traditionally classified as *inductive* or *deductive*. See *deductive argument* and *inductive argument*. Argument can be used for different purposes in writing. See *purpose*.

AUTOBIOGRAPHY: Writing about one's own experiences, often those of growing up and making one's way in the world. The autobiographical writings of Cynthia Ozick and Alice Munro describe their childhood experiences.

BALANCED SENTENCE: A sentence containing parallel phrases and clauses of approximately the same length and wording (*You can fool all the people some of the time, and some of the people all of the time, but you cannot fool all the people all of the time.*—Abraham Lincoln).

CAUSE AND EFFECT: Analysis of the conditions that must be present for an event to occur (*cause*) and of the results or consequences of the event (*effect*). An essay may deal with causes or with effects only.

CLASSIFICATION AND DIVISION: *Classification* arranges individual objects into groups or classes (GM cars, Chrysler cars, Ford cars). *Division* arranges a broad class into subclasses according to various principles (the broad class GM cars can be divided on the basis of their transmission or manufacturing unit).

CLICHÉ: A once-colourful expression made stale through overuse (*putting on the dog, mad as a wet hen*).

COHERENCE: The sense, as we read, that the details and ideas of a work connect clearly. A paragraph or essay that does not hold together seems incoherent. Transitions are a means of coherence.

COLLOQUIALISM: An everyday expression in speech and informal writing. Colloquialisms are not substandard or "illiterate" English. They are common in informal English and occur sometimes in formal English.

COMPARISON AND CONTRAST: The analysis of similarities and differences between two or more persons, objects, or events (A and B) for the purpose of a relative estimate. The word *comparison* sometimes refers to the analysis of similarities and differences in both A and B. *Block comparison* presents each thing being compared as a whole (that is, if the comparison is between A and B, then features a, b, c of A are discussed as a block of information, and then features a, b, c of B are compared to A in their own block of information). *Alternating comparison* presents the comparable features one by one (a, a, b, b, c, c).

COMPLEX SENTENCE: A sentence consisting of one main or independent clause, and one or more subordinate or dependent clauses (*The rain began when she stepped outside*).

COMPOUND SENTENCE: A sentence consisting of co-ordinated independent clauses (*She stepped outside and then the rain began*).

COMPOUND–COMPLEX SENTENCE: A sentence consisting of two or more main or independent clauses and at least one subordinate or dependent clause (*She stepped outside as the rain began, but she did not return to the house*).

CONCRETE AND ABSTRACT WORDS: Concrete words refer to particular objects, people, and events (Wayne Gretzky, the Olympics, the Rocky Mountains); abstract words refer to general shared qualities (cowardice, courage, beauty). Concrete writing makes abstract ideas perceptible to the senses through details and images.

CONCRETENESS: Making an idea exist through the senses. Writing can be concrete at all three levels—informal, general, and formal. See *concrete and abstract words*.

CONNOTATION: Feelings, images, and ideas associated with a word. Connotations change from reader to reader, though some words probably have the same associations for everybody.

CONTEXT: The surrounding words or sentences that suggest the meaning of a word or phrase. Writers may dispense with formal definition if the context clarifies the meaning of a word.

CO-ORDINATE SENTENCE: A sentence that joins clauses of the same weight and importance through the conjunctions *and, but, for, or, nor,* or *yet,* or through conjunctive adverbs and adverbial phrases (*however, therefore, nevertheless, in fact*).

DEDUCTIVE ARGUMENT: Reasoning from statements assumed to be true or well-established factually. These statements or assumptions are thought sufficient to guarantee the truth of the inferences or conclusions. In formal arguments they are called *premises*. A valid argument reasons correctly from the premises to the conclusion. A sound argument is true in its premises and valid in its reasoning. See *enthymeme, syllogism*.

DEFINITION: Explaining the current meaning of a word through its etymology or derivation, its denotation, or its connotations. Denotative or "real" definitions single out a word from all other words (or things) like it by giving *genus* and *specific difference*. Connotative definitions give the *associations* people make to the word. See *connotation*.

DENOTATION: The most generally accepted primary meaning of a word.

DESCRIPTION: A picture in words of people, objects, and events. Description often combines with narration and it may serve exposition and persuasion.

DIVISION: See *classification and division*.

ENTHYMEME: A deductive argument that does not state the conclusion or one of the premises directly. The following statement is an enthymeme: *Citizens in a democracy who refuse to register for the draft are not acting responsibly.* The implied premise is that the responsible citizen obeys all laws, even repugnant ones.

ESSAY: A carefully organized composition that develops a single idea or impression or several related ideas or impressions. The word sometimes describes a beginning or trial attempt that explores the central idea or impression instead of developing it completely.

EXAMPLE: A picture or illustration of an idea, or one of many instances or occurrences that is typical of the rest.

EXPOSITION: An explanation or unfolding or setting forth of an idea, usually for the purpose of giving information. Exposition is usually an important part of persuasive writing. Example, process analysis, causal analysis, definition, classification and division, and comparison and contrast are forms of exposition.

EXPRESSIVE WRITING: Essays, diaries, journals, letters, and other kinds of writing that present personal feelings and beliefs for their own sake. The expressive writer is not primarily concerned with informing or persuading readers.

FIGURE OF SPEECH: A word or phrase that departs from its usual meaning. Figures of speech make statements vivid and capture the attention of readers. The most common figures are based on similarity between things: see *metaphor, personification, simile*. Other figures are based on relationship: see *allusion. Metonymy* refers to a thing by one of its qualities (*the sceptre* for sovereignty). *Synecdoche* refers to a thing by one of its parts (*wheels* as a reference to racing cars). Other figures are based on contrast between statements and realities: see *irony*. Related to irony is *understatement*, or saying less than is appropriate (*Napoleon's career ended unhappily at Waterloo*). *Hyperbole* means deliberate exaggeration (*crazy about ice cream*). *Paradox* states an apparent contradiction (*All great truths begin as blasphemies*—G.B. Shaw). *Oxymoron*, a kind of paradox, joins opposite qualities into a single image (*lake of fire*).

FOCUS: The limitation of subject in an essay. The focus can be broad, as in a panoramic view of the mountains, or it may be narrow, as in a view of a particular peak. For example, a writer may focus broadly on the contribution to scientific thought of scientists from various fields, or focus narrowly on the achievements of astronomers or chemists or medical researchers, or focus even more narrowly on the achievements of Albert Einstein as representative of twentieth-century science.

FORMAL ENGLISH: Spoken and written English, often abstract in content, with sentences tighter than spoken ones, and an abstract and sometimes technical vocabulary.

GENERAL ENGLISH: A written standard that has features of informal and formal English.

IMAGE: A picture in words of an object, a scene, or a person. Though visual images are common in writing, they are not the only kind. Images can also be auditory, tactile, gustatory, and olfactory. Keats's line *With beaded bubbles winking at the brim* appeals to our hearing and taste as well as to our sight. His phrase *coming musk-rose* appeals to our sense of smell. Images help to make feelings concrete.

IMPLIED THESIS: The central idea of the essay, suggested by the details and discussion rather than stated directly. See *thesis*.

INDUCTIVE ARGUMENT: Inductive arguments reason from particulars of experience to general ideas—from observation, personal experience, and experimental testing to probable conclusions. Inductive arguments make predictions on the basis of past and present experience. An argumentative analogy is a form of inductive argument because it is based on limited observation and experience and therefore can claim probability only. Analysis of causes and effects is inductive when used in argument.

"INDUCTIVE LEAP": Making the decision that sufficient inductive evidence (personal experience, observation, experimental testing) exists to draw a conclusion. Sometimes the writer of the argument makes the leap too quickly and bases his conclusions on insufficient evidence.

INFORMAL ENGLISH: Written English, usually concrete in content, tighter than the loose sentences of spoken English, but looser in sentence construction than formal English. The word *informal* refers to the occasion of its use. A letter to a friend is usually informal; a letter of application is usually formal.

IRONY: A term generally descriptive of statements and events. An ironic statement says the opposite of what the speaker or writer means, or implies that something more is meant than is stated, or says the unexpected (*He has a great future behind him*). An ironic event is unexpected or is so coincidental that it seems highly improbable (*The fireboat burned and sank*).

JARGON: The technical words of a trade or profession (in computer jargon, the terms *input* and *word processor*). Unclear, clumsy, or repetitive words or phrasing, sometimes the result of misplaced technical words (*He gave his input into the decision process*).

LOOSE SENTENCE: A sentence that introduces the main idea close to the beginning and concludes with a series of modifiers (*The car left the expressway, slowing on the ramp and coming to a stop at the crossroad*). See *periodic sentence.*

METAPHOR: An implied comparison that attributes the qualities of one thing to another (the word *mainstream* to describe the opinions or activities of most people).

MIXED METAPHOR: The incongruous use of two metaphors in the same context (*The roar of protest was stopped in its tracks*).

NARRATION: The chronological presentation of events. Narration often combines with description and it may serve exposition or persuasion.

ORDER OF IDEAS: The presentation of ideas in a paragraph or an essay according to a plan. The order may be *spatial*, perhaps moving from background to foreground, or from top to bottom, or from side to side; or the order may be *temporal* or chronological (in the order of time). The presentation may be in the order of *importance*, or, if the details build intensively, in the order of *climax*. The paragraph or essay may move from *problem* to *solution* or from the *specific* to the *general*. Some of these orders occur together— for example, a chronological presentation of details that build to a climax.

PARALLELISM: Grammatically similar words, phrases, and clauses arranged to highlight similar ideas (*There are streets where, on January nights, fires burn on every floor of every house, sending fragrant smoke through the cold black trees. There are meadows and fields, long rows of old oaks, bridges that sparkle from afar, ships about to leave for Asia, lakes, horses, and islands in the marsh*— Mark Helprin). See *antithesis.*

PARAPHRASE: A rendering of a passage in different words that retain the sense, the tone, and the order of ideas.

PERIODIC SENTENCE: A sentence that builds to the main idea (*Building speed as it curved down the ramp, the car raced into the crowded expressway*). See *loose sentence.*

PERSONIFICATION: Giving animate or human qualities to something inanimate or inhuman (*The sun smiled at the earth*).

PERSUASION: The use of argument or satire or some other means to change thinking and feeling about an issue.

POINT OF VIEW: The place or vantage point from which an event is seen and described. The term sometimes refers to the mental attitude of the viewer in narration. W.O. Mitchell's *Who Has Seen the Wind* narrates the adventures of a boy on the Canadian prairies from the point of view of the boy, not of an adult.

PREMISE: See *syllogism*.

PROCESS: An activity or operation containing steps usually performed in the same order. The process may be mechanical (changing a tire), natural (the circulation of the blood), or historical (the rise and spread of a specific disease such as bubonic plague at various times in history).

PURPOSE: The aim of the essay as distinguished from the means used to develop it. The purposes or aims of writing are many; they include expressing personal feelings or ideas, giving information, persuading readers to change their thinking about an issue, inspiring readers to take action, giving pleasure. These purposes may be achieved through description, narration, exposition, or argument. These means can be used alone or in combination, and an essay may contain more than one purpose.

SATIRE: Ridicule of foolish or vicious behaviour or ideas for the purpose of correcting them. *Social satire* concerns foolish but not dangerous behaviour and ideas — for example, coarse table manners, pretentious talk, harmless gossip. Robertson Davies's *Tempest-Tost* is a social satire. *Ethical satire* attacks vicious or dangerous behaviour or ideas — religious or racial bigotry, greed, and political corruption. Stephen Leacock's *Arcadian Adventures with the Idle Rich* is an ethical satire.

SIMILE: A direct comparison between two things (*A growing child is like a young tree*). See *figure of speech, metaphor*.

SIMPLE SENTENCE: A sentence consisting of a single main or independent clause and no subordinate or dependent clauses (*The rain started at nightfall*).

SLANG: Colourful and sometimes short-lived expressions peculiar to a group of people, usually informal in usage and almost always unacceptable in formal usage (*nerd, goof off*).

STYLE: A distinctive manner of speaking and writing. A writing style may be plain in its lack of metaphor and other figures of speech. Another may be highly colourful or ornate.

SUBORDINATE CLAUSE: A clause that completes a main clause or attaches to it as a modifier (She saw *that the rain had begun. When it rains*, it pours).

SYLLOGISM: The formal arrangement of premises and conclusions of a deductive argument. The premises are the general assumptions or truths (*All reptiles are cold-blooded vertebrates. All snakes are reptiles*) from which particular conclusions are drawn (*All snakes are cold-blooded vertebrates*). This formal arrangement helps to test the validity or correctness of the reasoning from premises to conclusion. See *deductive argument*.

SYMBOL: An object that represents an abstract idea. The features of the symbol (the five joined rings of the Olympic flag) suggest characteristics of the object symbolized (the meeting of athletes from five continents for friendly competition). A *sign* need not have this representative quality: a green light signals "go" and a red light "stop" by conventional agreement.

THESIS: The central idea that organizes the many smaller ideas and details of the essay.

TONE: The phrasing or words that express the attitude or feeling of the speaker or writer. The tone of a statement ranges from the angry, exasperated, or sarcastic, to the wondering or approving. An ironic tone suggests that the meaning the speaker or writer intends to convey goes beyond what the words actually state.

TOPIC SENTENCE: Usually the main or central idea of the paragraph that organizes details and subordinate ideas. Though it often opens the paragraph, the topic sentence can appear later—in the middle or at the end of the paragraph.

TRANSITION: A word or phrase (*however, thus, in fact*) that connects clauses and sentences. Parallel structure is an important means of transition.

UNITY: The connection of ideas and details to a central controlling idea of the essay. A unified essay deals with one idea at a time.

CREDITS

The editors wish to thank the publishers and copyright holders for permission to reprint the selections in this book, which are listed below in order of their appearance:

Stephen J. Pyne, "Let It Burn," from *World Fire: The Culture of Fire on Earth.* Copyright © 1995 by Stephen J. Pyne. Reprinted by permission of Henry Holt and Co., Inc.

Joseph Epstein, "Outgrowing Envy," from "A Few Kind Words for Envy." Reprinted from *The American Scholar* 58, 4 (Autumn 1989). Copyright © 1989 by Joseph Epstein. Reprinted by permission of the publisher.

Barbara Ehrenreich, "The Cult of Busyness," from *The Worst Years of Our Lives.* Copyright © 1990 by Barbara Ehrenreich. Reprinted by permission of Pantheon Books, a division of Random House, Inc.

Joyce Maynard, "Four Generations," from *Domestic Affairs* (New York: Times Books, 1987). Reprinted by permission of the author.

Charles Gordon, "A Destructive Love Affair with Money." Reprinted from *Maclean's Magazine*, February 27, 1995, p. 13. Reprinted by permission of the author and *Maclean's Magazine*, Maclean Hunter Publishing, 1995.

Stephen Jay Gould, "Sex, Drugs, Disasters, and the Extinction of Dinosaurs," from *The Flamingo's Smile: Reflections in Natural History.* Copyright © 1984 by Stephen Jay Gould. Reprinted by permission of W.W. Norton & Company, Inc.

Susan Sontag, "A Woman's Beauty: Put-Down or Power Source?" Copyright © 1975 by Susan Sontag. Reprinted with the permission of Wylie, Aitken & Stone, Inc.

Katherine Govier, "Rethinking the Nature of Charity." Reprinted from *Chatelaine Magazine* (December 1989). Reprinted by permission of the author.

Ken Dryden, "Dryden's Backyard," from *The Game.* Copyright © 1983 by Ken Dryden. Reprinted by permission of Macmillan Canada.

Northrop Frye, "Elementary Teaching," from *The Stubborn Structure* (Methuen, 1970). Reprinted with permission from the Executors of the Estate of Northrop Frye.

David Macfarlane, "Love and Death," from *The Thinking Heart: Best Canadian Essays,* ed. George Galt (Kingston: Quarry Press, 1991), 181–87. Originally published in *Saturday Night*. Reprinted by permission of the author.

E.B. White, "Once More to the Lake," from *One Man's Meat.* Copyright © 1941 by E.B. White. Reprinted by permission of HarperCollins Publishers, Inc.

Meredith Chilton, "A Fugitive Pleasure: Perfume in the 18th Century," from *Best Canadian Essays, 1990*, ed. Douglas Fetherling (Saskatoon: Fifth House, 1990), 290–96. Originally published in *Rotunda* (Summer 1989). Reprinted by permission of the Royal Ontario Museum.

Bronwen Wallace, "An Auction at Mother's Childhood Home," from *Arguments with the World: Essays by Bronwen Wallace*, ed. Joanne Page (Kingston: Quarry Press, 1992), 149–52. Reprinted by permission of Quarry Press, Inc.

Walter Stewart, "Good Old Us," from *But Not in Canada.* Copyright © 1976 by Walter Stewart. Reprinted by permission of the author.

Robertson Davies, "A Few Kind Words for Superstition." Reprinted by permission of the author.

Wilfrid Sheed, "A Few of My Favorite Sins," from *Essays in Disguise*. Copyright © 1990 by Wilfrid Sheed. By permission of Alfred A. Knopf, Inc.

Sir James Jeans, "Why the Sky Looks Blue," from *The Stars in Their Courses*. Copyrighted by and reprinted with the permission of Cambridge University Press.

William J. Mitchell, "The Parable of the Pizza Parlor." Reprinted from *Scientific American* (May 1995), p. 112. Reprinted with permission. Copyright © 1995 by Scientific American, Inc. All rights reserved.

Ian McEwan, "The Plot Thickens for the Century's Final Chapter." Reprinted from *Financial Times Weekend*, December 24/25, 1995, Section II, p. 3. Copyright © 1994 by Ian McEwan. Reprinted by permission of the author c/o Rogers, Coleridge & White Ltd., 20 Powis Mews, London W11 1JN.

James Gorman, "Man, Bytes, Dog." Reprinted by permission. Copyright © 1984 by James Gorman. Originally in *The New Yorker*.

Richard M. Restak, "The Other Difference between Boys and Girls," from *The Brain*. Copyright © 1984 by Educational Broadcasting Corporation and Richard M. Restak, M.D. Used by permission of Bantam Books, a division of Bantam Doubleday Dell Publishing Group, Inc.

Hugh Rawson, "Wicked Words," from *Wicked Words: A Treasury*. Copyright © 1989 by Hugh Rawson. Reprinted by permission of Crown Publishers, Inc.

Joseph Brodsky, "Listening to Boredom," adapted from "In Praise of Boredom," from *On Grief and Reason*. First appeared in *Harper's Magazine* (March 1995). Copyright © 1995 by Joseph Brodsky. Reprinted by permission of Farrar, Straus & Giroux, Inc.

AUTHOR INDEX

READER REPLY CARD

We are interested in your reaction to *Prose Models*, Third Canadian Edition, by Gerald Levin, David Rampton, and Gerald Lynch. You can help us to improve this book in future editions by completing this questionnaire.

1. What was your reason for using this book?
   - ❏ university course
   - ❏ college course
   - ❏ continuing-education course
   - ❏ professional development
   - ❏ personal interest
   - ❏ other (please specify) _____

2. If you are a student, please identify your school and the course in which you used this book.
   _____

3. Which chapters or parts of this book did you use? Which did you omit?
   _____

4. What did you like best about this book? What did you like least?
   _____

5. Please identify any topics you think should be added to future editions.
   _____

6. Please add any comments or suggestions.
   _____

7. Please give your reaction to the readings listed by title and author in order of their appearance in the book, rating each essay from 1 (liked least) to 5 (liked best).

Title/Author	Rating	Didn't Read	Title/Author	Rating	Didn't Read
Part 1			The Plot Thickens ... (McEwan)	___	___
Let It Burn (Pyne)	___	___	Man, Bytes, Dog (Gorman)	___	___
Outgrowing Envy (Epstein)	___	___	The Other Difference ... (Restak)	___	___
The Cult of ... (Ehrenreich)	___	___	Wicked Words (Rawson)	___	___
Four Generations (Maynard)	___	___	In Praise of Boredom (Brodsky)	___	___
A Destructive Love ... (Gordon)	___	___	Idle Hands (Smiley)	___	___
Sex, Drugs, Disasters ... (Gould)	___	___	True North (Atwood)	___	___
A Woman's Beauty (Sontag)	___	___	Trading Commodities (Cohen)	___	___
Rethinking the Nature ... (Govier)	___	___	The Spider and ... (Petrunkevitch)	___	___
Dryden's Backyard (Dryden)	___	___	The Master of ... (Taylor)	___	___
Elementary Teaching (Frye)	___	___	The Stranger at ... (Iyer)	___	___
Darwin's Dangerous ... (Dennett)	___	___	Time's Priggish ... (Warren)	___	___
In Defense of Prejudice (Rauch)	___	___	Fashion and ... (Hollander)	___	___
Religion: Are We ... (Postgate)	___	___	Living with Nature (Suzuki)	___	___
Food Worship (Ehrenreich)	___	___	Morals in the Rat ... (Schafer)	___	___
The Haunting Powers ... (Grady)	___	___	Why I Am Not ... (Berry)	___	___
Deficits (Ignatieff)	___	___	A Walk on the ... (Munro)	___	___
Superwoman ... (Goodman)	___	___	Gals and Dolls (Jackson)	___	___
Part 2			Capital Punishment (Douglas)	___	___
The Exam Room (Nabokov)	___	___	Politics and ... (Orwell)	___	___
The Death of the Moth (Woolf)	___	___	*Part 3*		
The Halifax ... (MacLennan)	___	___	Take Your Breath ... (Black)	___	___
Life and Death ... (Graham)	___	___	The Softball ... (Bruce)	___	___
Main Street (Richler)	___	___	A Modest Proposal (Swift)	___	___
Parents Night (Nicol)	___	___	Downhill All ... (Fotheringham)	___	___
My Experience with ... (White)	___	___	Lessons from ... (Selzer)	___	___
Love and Death (Macfarlane)	___	___	Einstein's Monsters (Amis)	___	___
Once More to the Lake (White)	___	___	The Undertaking (Lynch)	___	___
A Fugitive Pleasure (Chilton)	___	___	Simplicity (Zinsser)	___	___
An Auction at ... (Wallace)	___	___	Journalese as a ... (Leo)	___	___
Good Old Us (Stewart)	___	___	The Same Ticking ... (Shields)	___	___
... Superstition (Davies)	___	___	How to be Famous ... (Laferrière)	___	___
A Few of My Favorite ... (Sheed)	___	___	Writing ... (Barth)	___	___
Why the Sky Looks Blue (Jeans)	___	___	A Drugstore in Winter (Ozick)	___	___
The Parable of ... (Mitchell)	___	___			

(fold here and tape shut)

MAIL ➤ POSTE

Canada Post Corporation / Société canadienne des postes

Postage paid
If mailed in Canada

Port payé
si posté au Canada

**Business
Reply**

**Réponse
d'affaires**

0116870399   01

0116870399-M8Z4X6-BR01

Heather McWhinney
Director of Product Development
HARCOURT BRACE & COMPANY, CANADA
55 HORNER AVENUE
TORONTO, ONTARIO
M8Z 9Z9

Getting straight "A"s doesn't have to be a mystery...

these practical, concise, and affordable study guides will tell you how!